GOVERNING PUBLIC HEALTH

This book contributes towards EU studies and the growing discourse on law and public health. It uses the EU's governance of public health as a lens through which to explore questions of legal competence and its development through policy and concrete techniques, processes and practices; risk and security; human rights and bioethics; accountability and legitimacy; democracy and citizenship; and the nature, essence and 'future trajectory' of the European integration project. These issues are explored first by situating the EU's public health strategy within the overarching architecture of governance and subsequently by examining its operationalisation in relation to the key public health problems of cancer, HIV/AIDS and pandemic planning.

The book argues that the centrality and valorisation of scientific and technical knowledge and expertise in the EU's risk-based governance means that citizen participation in decision-making is largely marginalised and underdeveloped—and that this must change if public health and the quality, accountability and legitimacy of EU governance and its regulation are to be improved. Subsequently the book goes on to argue that the legitimating discourses of ethics and human rights, and the developing notion of EU (supra-)stewardship responsibility, can help to highlight the normative dimensions of governance and its interventions in public health. These discourses and dimensions provide openings and possibilities for citizens to power 'technologies of participation' and contribute important supplementary knowledge to decision-making.

Governing Public Health stands on its own, as it masterfully blends together law, politics, sociology and numerous other disciplines to come up with a picture of the EU as an agent of biopolitics, which is as plausible as it is potentially disturbing. The book is an attack on the distortions and pitfalls of the dominant risk-based model of public health governance, representing the first—long overdue!—biopolitical analysis of EU law. Flear's crusade is to overturn our accepted vision of managing public health by arguing that the governed have the capacity to contribute important supplementary knowledge on the distortions and pitfalls in order to improve governance. This book deserves all respect and admiration.

Professor Dimitry Kochenov, University of Groningen

This book focusses on participation as a possible mediator of the relationship between law, one the one hand, and science and technology on the other. It argues that the tension between the democratic and technocratic aspects of regulation could, perhaps, be reduced by the use of participatory processes. That argument has a wider resonance than the public health field on which the book concentrates. EU scholars in the diverse fields where expertise and preferences circle each other nervously will want to study and apply the book's central ideas, and will find that they are clearly and attractively presented, and gain authority from the range of theory on which he relies.

Professor Gareth Davies, VU University Amsterdam

Flear … has written a very fine … book in *Governing Public Health* …. [It] is a thoroughly well-researched and interdisciplinary book that produces insightful and positive prescriptions for improving governance and the relationship between the state/supranational union and its citizens. Flear is clearly passionate about increasing the substantive involvement of 'the governed' in governing so that their needs, however so defined, are better met and respected … *Governing Public Health* merits reading and deep deliberation by all scholars interested in law and public health (including outside the EU) and the vital roles of the citizen in modern governance and democracy.

Dr Edward S Dove, Edinburgh Law School, *SCRIPTed*

There is much in this book which will be of significant interest to those who seek to develop an understanding of the engagement of EU law with public health …. [This] book is likely to serve as a stimulus for future research … on the relation between 'the governed' and the governance of public health by the EU. Understood in those terms, this is a scholarly and highly valuable analysis that provides much food for thought about the nature and limitations of governance in late modernity, and as such it is likely to find an appreciative readership both within EU studies and well beyond.

Professor Keith Syrett, Cardiff Law School, *Yearbook of European Law*

Governing Public Health

EU Law, Regulation and Biopolitics

Mark L Flear

•HART•
OXFORD • LONDON • NEW YORK • NEW DELHI • SYDNEY

HART PUBLISHING

Bloomsbury Publishing Plc

Kemp House, Chawley Park, Cumnor Hill, Oxford, OX2 9PH, UK

HART PUBLISHING, the Hart/Stag logo, BLOOMSBURY and the Diana logo are trademarks of Bloomsbury Publishing Plc

First published in hardback, 2015

Published in paperback, 2018

A catalogue record for this book is available from the British Library.

Library of Congress Cataloging-in-Publication data

ISBN: HB: 978-1-84946-220-4
PB: 978-1-50991-776-1

Typeset by Compuscript Ltd, Shannon

To find out more about our authors and books visit www.hartpublishing.co.uk. Here you will find extracts, author information, details of forthcoming events and the option to sign up for our newsletters.

Foreword

As the European Union finds itself at a crossroads following the economic crisis and, more precisely, its management by domestic and European Union elites, *Governing Public Health* highlights the importance of citizen participation in the design and implementation of public health regulatory interventions at the European Union level. Greater citizen participation might improve the quality of the latter and enhance the legitimacy of European Union governance. By deploying a normative lens, the author tackles successfully some crucial questions about the EU's public health strategy and its operationalisation in the domains of cancer, HIV/AIDS and other pandemics which have the potential to affect European Union performance if not addressed properly.

The author provides three main reasons for greater citizen involvement in public health decision-making. The first reason is that citizen participation is both a social good and a device for better governance. Citizens need to be pro-active in protecting their health and can enhance the input and output legitimacy of public policies. The second reason, which is linked to the first, is that, as neoliberalism infiltrates traditional non-market domains such as health, citizen engagement can act as a corrective to the emerging risk-based and market-oriented technologies and the increasing reliance of health actors on seemingly neutral technical and scientific knowledge. The third reason is the limited use of citizen participation in EU public health governance at present. According to the author, 'participation should be about sharing power and benefiting governance and the governed by improving the quality of the regulatory decisions made'. All those who take democracy seriously should welcome the proposed 'democratisation of public health'.

In defending the case for making public health policies more responsive and robust through citizen participation, the author charts the growing role of the EU as an actor in this domain and its formal legal competence. The discussion on the overarching EU health governance architecture and health strategy is accompanied by wonderfully written case studies on cancer, HIV/AIDS and other pandemics and serious cross-border threats to health. Risk, security, regulation, human rights and bioethics, all receive careful attention.

Governing Public Health defies disciplinary boundaries; it brings together insights from sociology, political science, law and critical legal studies in order to uncover the complex regulation of public health in the European Union. It is a timely book which will appeal to scholars of the European Union in many disciplines. It provides an indispensable roadmap to the links between law, (bio) politics and citizen engagement in the regulation of public health.

Professor Dora Kostakopoulou
School of Law, University of Warwick, 2015

Preface

Since the hardback version of this book appeared in 2015, there have been a number of important developments in European Union (EU) law relating to clinical trials that now warrant a brief mention. In relation to the law on clinical trials, as noted in places within the book (where there are references to this preface), Directive 2001/20/EC on the approximation of the laws, regulations and administrative provisions of the Member States relating to the implementation of good clinical practice in the conduct of clinical trials on medicinal products for human use [2001] OJ L121/34 will be replaced by Regulation (EU) 536/2014 on clinical trials on medicinal products for human use, and repealing Directive 2001/20/EC [2014] OJ L158/1. As noted in the main text, this new Regulation was not due to become applicable until at least 28 May 2016. The applicability of the Regulation was made subject to an independent audit that demonstrates the full functionality of the new EU portal for submitting applications and the database for storing and making them publicly available. The Regulation is now planned to apply from 2019.

The new EU portal, ie a single entry point for the submission of clinical trials information, will replace the current EU Clinical Trials Register. Information submitted through the portal is to be stored in the database. Under the new Regulation all information about clinical trials carried out within the EU and European Economic Area (EEA) must be placed in the registry and much of it must be publicly available. Subsequent applications for market authorisation of new pharmaceuticals must reference that data. In respect of applications for market authorisation of new pharmaceuticals that make use of data from clinical trials carried out in third countries, the trials in question must have been registered in a publicly accessible and free of charge database which is a primary or partner registry of, or a data provider to, the World Health Organisation's International Clinical Trials Registry Platform. On the face of the law, it appears that there might be less public availability and transparency in respect of data from third countries, ie given the reliance on third party registries. In light of this new legal regime there remains a strong case for citizen challenges to knowledge production and interventions in public health. The discursive strategy built and discussed in this book is, if anything, more relevant now than it was back in 2015.

Mark L Flear

Acknowledgements

The ideas in this book were developed in several different but nevertheless related articles published over the course of the last few years. Although the ideas are combined and usually rearticulated, some of the chapters draw on specific articles more than others. Chapters one and six draw on ideas first developed in 'The EU's Biopolitical Governance of Advanced Therapy Medicinal Products' (2009) 16 *Maastricht Journal of European and Comparative Law* 113 and the editorial to 'Symposium: New Technologies, European Law and Citizens' (2009) 16(1) *Maastricht Journal of European and Comparative Law* (a special issue I co-edited with Sara Ramshaw).

Key ideas discussed in depth in chapter six and applied throughout the rest of the second part of the book were first developed in '"Supra-stewardship": A Tool for Citizen Participation in European Union Pandemic Preparedness Planning' (2011) 62(5) *Northern Ireland Legal Quarterly* 677 and 'Regulatory or Regulating Publics? The European Union's Regulation of Emerging Health Technologies and Citizen Participation' (2013) 21(1) *Medical Law Review* 39 (which I co-wrote with Martyn Pickersgill). Chapter two owes some debt to the framework I first developed in 'The Open Method of Coordination on Health Care after the Lisbon Strategy II: Towards a Neoliberal Framing?' (2009) 13 *European Integration online Papers* (Article 12). A large part of chapter seven and a smaller part of chapter eight are also published in a slightly different version in 'Clinical Trials Abroad: The Marketable Ethics, Weak Protections and Vulnerable Subjects of EU Law' in A Albors-Llorens, K Armstrong and MW Gehring (eds), *Cambridge Yearbook of European Legal Studies,* Vol 16 2013–14 (Oxford, Hart Publishing, 2014).

This book benefited hugely from the support of ESRC Seminar Series RES-451-26-0764 (for which I was PI) and a British Academy Small Grant (SG-48186). I am very grateful to the funders for their support and interest in my research. These grants facilitated interaction with civil society actors in Brussels (including at events in the European Parliament and European Commission) and Amsterdam and a very interesting meeting with regulators at the European Medicines Agency in London. While those discussions provided rich insights into the governance of public health, the analysis in this book is my own and comes from viewing those discussions and wider documentation through the multi-disciplinary perspective outlined in chapter one, all of which in one way or another draw on Foucault and his (still insightful) way of looking at the world. The law, official documents, web-based materials and websites contained in this book are, to the best of my knowledge, accurate (and still available where they are web-based) as of 1 March 2015.

I am hugely thankful for the collaborations that led to several of the publications redeployed and to some extent repurposed in this book. Gratitude is also due to the School of Law, Queen's University Belfast for supporting my research, particularly in the final stages of this project. I am especially grateful to Sally Wheeler and John Morison for their encouragement, support and patience. Tammy Hervey and Thérèse Murphy have been unfailingly supportive in so many ways—I could not wish for better mentors. Anastasia Vakulenko has provided me with perhaps the greatest (re)education in thinking (prompting questions about why, how and to what ends), and I am hugely thankful for that, and for our friendship. Even the smallest conversation helps to stimulate one's imagination and interest. I have been gifted with valuable insights from many other people, and certainly too many to mention here without carelessly overlooking someone. Suffice to say I extend my thanks to all those with whom I have discussed the ideas set forth in this book.

Finally, I wish to extend my deepest affection and thanks for their unwavering support to my parents, Graeme and Jacqueline, and my brother David. This book is dedicated to the memory of my Uncle Edward, whose reassuring and motivational words continue to nourish me on this journey.

Table of Contents

Table of Cases

COURT OF JUSTICE OF THE EUROPEAN UNION

COMMISSION AND COURT OF HUMAN RIGHTS

UNITED KINGDOM

Table of Instruments and Legislation

EUROPEAN UNION INSTRUMENTS AND LEGISLATION

Primary Law

Regulations

Directives

Decisions

OTHER INSTRUMENTS

INTERNATIONAL INSTRUMENTS AND LEGISLATION

NATIONAL LEGISLATION

Belgium

Finland

Italy

Luxembourg

Netherlands

Portugal

United Kingdom

1

Context, Approach and Overview

I. INTRODUCTION

THIS BOOK IS about governing public health—and its core concern is with biopolitics and especially the role, scope and potential of citizen participation in legal and regulatory decision-making. The site of this study is the European Union's (EU's) public health governance and regulatory interventions. Citizen participation includes various techniques that seek to incorporate the perspectives of individuals and communities in regulating or governing.[1] From the outset of this project I was hopeful about the potential for citizen or public participation,[2] but I was also far more pessimistic about its actual incorporation and use in decision-making. This was despite the widespread view, which I share, that citizen participation is an important social good[3] and tool of governance, particularly in areas where the regulation of science and technology are very much at the fore.[4] This chapter explains the mix of pessimism and optimism that initially prompted the book, outlines its aims and arguments, and overviews what follows.

[1] The main reasons for the focus on 'governing' are mentioned below, but 'regulating' is used in places, for reasons that shall become apparent in the outline of the conceptual approach. Black's definition of regulation is 'the intentional use of authority to affect behaviour of a different party according to set standards, involving instruments of information-gathering and behaviour modification' (J Black, 'Critical Reflections on Regulation' (2002) 27 *Australian Journal of Legal Philosophy* 1). This understanding of regulation includes technologies with 'hard law', 'soft law', social norms and the market. See further: R Baldwin, M Cave and M Lodge, 'Regulation, the Field and the Developing Agenda' in R Baldwin, M Cave and M Lodge (eds), *The Oxford Handbook on Regulation* (Oxford, Oxford University Press, 2011).

[2] Unlike many of the actors and institutions that make use of participatory techniques, I do not use these terms interchangeably, but tend to prefer 'citizen participation'. My preference is informed by how I conceive of 'citizens', which is discussed later in the chapter in relation to biopolitics. For more detail on forms of participation and engagement, and its relation to scientific governance, see: A Irwin, 'The Politics of Talk: Coming to Terms with the "New" Scientific Governance' (2006) 36 *Social Studies of Science* 299. See further the discussion in ch 6.

[3] See: J Wilsdon and R Willis, *See-Through Science: Why Public Engagement Needs to Move Upstream* (London, Demos, 2004).

[4] See, eg Royal Society and the Royal Academy of Engineering, *Nanoscience and Nanotechnologies: Opportunities and Uncertainties* (London, Royal Society, 2004) ch 7 'Stakeholder and Public Dialogue'. For example a critique of participation offered by J Schummer, 'Identifying Ethical Issues in Nanotechnologies' in H ten Have (ed), *Nanotechnologies, Ethics and Politics* (Paris, UNESCO, 2007), 81, cited in R Brownsword, *Rights, Regulation and the Technological Revolution* (Oxford, Oxford University Press, 2008) 121, and with further discussion of definition and spheres of application, 120–22; J Tait, 'Upstream Engagement and the Governance of Science' (2009) 10 *EMBO Reports* S18–S22.

A. Starting Points

My initial prompt for this project came from the regular news reports on public health problems. Cancer and especially efforts to combat its causes, both at the national level and through global efforts to stem the consumption of tobacco products, is one example. Obesity is an increasingly important global concern related to patterns of consumption as well as the production and nature of what is consumed—and looking further back in time, food production methods were the cause for the vCJD crisis of the 1990s.[5] The terrible toll of the HIV/AIDS pandemic with deaths in the millions and many more affected principally in the global South has been a recurrent news item too and, like other pandemics, perhaps more so than non-communicative diseases. Those other pandemics include avian or bird flu and the strain known as H1N1, which although rarer and, as yet, not having anything like the impact of HIV/AIDS, have emerged in poorer countries. Those diseases tend to become recognised as a significant concern by the global North only when they threaten to spread quickly between distant locations across the globe and into the North. Ebola is just emerging as another prominent example of a disease chiefly affecting parts of the (poor) global South (in Africa) and threatening the (rich) global North. Reporting of those pandemics is often accompanied by reminders of past experience, especially Spanish influenza after World War I (which killed perhaps 20 million people). This background helps to ratchet up the sense of threat posed by public health problems and their potential to produce widespread and perhaps large scale death and social disruption. There are, of course, many other examples of public health problems that could be flagged. However a public health 'problem' is defined, it is necessarily to the exclusion of the many others that go largely unreported and unnoticed to widespread public and arguably regulatory perception. That said the reports related that public health *mattered*—and then in certain ways.

Indeed, the reports also have some features in common. They usually have significant transnational dimensions. More specifically, their cross-borderness is typically related to the movement of people and things, that is, markets. There is a sense, then, that these problems are a threat, danger or risk not just to people (who can suffer and die), but also to the normal functioning of the economy or marketplace, and that they emerge, at least in part, from its operation. Decisions are taken by actors in overlapping national, regional and international sites, spaces and fora. In the European context the EU is increasingly prominent and arguably eclipses the World Health Organisation (Europe) (WHO) as 'the' transnational actor in the field of public health.

In addition, a sense of emergency often accompanies transnational public health problems, especially those where the threat, danger or risk presented is high

[5] Variant Creutzfeldt-Jakob disease, which is said to develop from the transmission of bovine spongiform encephalopathy (BSE) from infected animal products to humans.

or even low but with potentially disastrous consequences; and that demands a response. Prominent if not always used responses in the EU and elsewhere include: increased monitoring and surveillance especially at national borders; adjustment of pandemic alert levels to the real or perceived threat level; border controls such as the refusal of entry and (even if not widely used, the potential for) quarantine; preparedness of public health infrastructures for pandemic influenza, with the latter including the stockpiling of vaccines; hospitalisation and other forms of social distancing; increased attention on anti-retrovirals or ARVs for HIV/AIDS; and, widespread and even ubiquitous hygiene advice. Unsurprisingly given the EU context of democratic societies, there is also a stress on justifying and legitimating interventions by reference to ethics and human rights, including those that involve voluntary take-up and compliance by the public, but especially those that might override individual consent and compel compliance.

A lot of effort goes into relating public health interventions to the EU's citizenry and other concerned parties (such as other regulatory authorities). Yet, legal and regulatory decision-making in relation to public health (at any level) seems dry and technical and, consequently, without at least a significant normative dimension. At the same time decision-making demonstrates the tightening links between formally accountable power and scientific and technical knowledge and expertise. These links are present not just in public health problems typified by high degrees of risk, but also rare pandemics, where there is usually scientific uncertainty or non-knowing about, inter alia, the type, scale and likelihood of risk.

B. Research Agenda and Aims

Whereas the scientific and technical nature of decision-making and a focus on security oriented and medical responses imply a narrowing of the potential for political–democratic contestation, the growing role of the EU (and wider transnationalisation) increases the distance between governance and the governed. In short, the democratic legitimacy and accountability of decision-making in public health clearly seems a lot more difficult, particularly in terms of citizen participation in governing. What makes this even more problematic is that it is happening at a time when scientific and technical knowledge and expertise in this context and others remain dominant even as uncertainty and non-knowing about the scale and nature of risk mean that they are increasingly undermined. Despite being key addressees of public health regulation, and being implicated in its implementation, the role of the EU's citizenry or indeed those who are not formally speaking citizens but are nevertheless affected by EU governance is rather opaque. It is unclear quite how citizens or publics are constructed, animated and mobilised by, in and through governance, and how they and their knowledge and expertise are implicated in decision-making (if at all) and in defining and shaping the boundaries of responsibility and accountability. All together, these are the main points underlying my pessimism about the current institutionalisation—role, use and configuration—of citizen participation in decision-making. More than that, this series of anecdotes and related features provides a central hunch: that a focus on public health, and its transnational dimension by reference to the EU, provides a window into governing at this time, what is often called late modernity, and in particular that it highlights key implications for democracy. A key context for this book, therefore, is the ongoing concern about a 'democratic deficit'[6] in EU governance, particularly as regards the regulation of risk.

The foregoing prompted the following cluster of related questions, which form the research agenda for this book, its aims and the arguments I seek to advance. How are public health problems constituted and understood—as a danger or threat to the circulation of people and things that is to markets? How are they regulated? What are the roles of risk and security in that regulation? And what are the roles of ethics and human rights in this relation? How do these relationships shape responsibilities and accountabilities in relation to the governance of public health? What is the significance of public health for the production and legitimation of the EU's identity, imagined socio-political order and project of rule? What are the attendant paradoxes, pitfalls and blind spots? In particular, how do the relationships determine or shape the (de)selection of certain responses and interventions? Further, how are citizens or publics configured in relation to legal and regulatory decision-making and how is that related to defining and shaping the boundaries of responsibility and accountability? Specifically, how do the relationships shape and constrain, but also open up, the possibilities for citizens (including those who are subject to governance) to demand and contest legal and regulatory decisions in the field of public health? How might citizens (again including those others) contribute towards legal and regulatory decision-making and why is their participation important?

The agenda for this book therefore picks up several 'big issues' of EU (legal) studies, and looks at them through the prism of public health as the particular case study. These 'big issues' include competence and its concretisation through policy; risk and security; human rights and bioethics; accountability and legitimacy; democracy and citizenship; and the nature, essence and 'future trajectory' of the European integration project. In bringing together these issues and considering

[6] The literature on the 'democratic deficit' is vast and some of the most salient examples include: C Harlow, *Accountability in the European Union* (Oxford, Oxford University Press, 2002); C Joerges and E Vos (eds), *EU Committees: Social Regulation, Law and Politics* (Oxford, Hart Publishing, 1999); PL Lindseth, 'Democratic Legitimacy and the Administrative Character of Supranationalism: The Example of the European Community' (1999) 99 *Columbia Law Review* 628; G Majone, 'Europe's "Democratic Deficit": The Question for Standards' (1998) 4(1) *European Law Journal* 5; G Majone, 'The Politics of Regulation and European Regulatory Institutions' in J Hayward and A Menon (eds), *Governing Europe* (Oxford, Oxford University Press, 2003); R Dehousse and C Joerges (eds), *Good Governance in an Integrated Market* (Oxford, Oxford University Press, 2002); C Joerges, 'Integration through De-legalisation' (2008) 33 *European Law Review* 291; F Scharpf, *Governing in Europe. Effective and Democratic?* (Oxford, Oxford University Press, 1999); A Arnull and D Wincott, *Accountability and Legitimacy in the European Union* (Oxford, Oxford University Press, 2002).

them in relation to an increasingly important substantive area of EU governance, the book aims to make a distinctive contribution to both EU studies and the burgeoning literature on 'law and public health'[7] in two related ways. The first contribution is to underline the role, responsibility and importance of the EU as a public health actor, the growing significance of its public health policy domain and beyond that the transnational dimension to public health (by reference to the EU). In that regard this book narrows its attention to reflect on citizen participation in *governing* at the EU level, a term that is selected in order to query the scope and role of citizen participation and advance the idea that it can and should amount to an active and substantive contribution to decision-making. The discussion in this book therefore advances a notion of citizen participation that is more akin to 'citizenship-as-participation' inspired by civic republican ideas of participants who genuinely share in power in order to shape and steer governance,[8] rather than 'citizenship-as-rights' often favoured in liberal accounts of formal citizenship, including in the EU context.[9]

In furthering that central aim the second contribution of this book is to adopt an analytic perspective that combines insights from critical theory, and in particular that inspired by Foucault and his notion of governmentality, with law and regulation studies, and key cognate disciplines, especially science and technology studies (STS), sociology, anthropology and bioethics.[10] Together the insights in this conceptual approach are used to highlight the framing and shape of public health governance, its significance to the EU's integration project in light of late modern configurations of power, and finally, to tease out the normative dimensions and implications for democratic rule. These issues have not been discussed together in law and regulation studies, especially not in EU studies. As such a related aim of this book is to encourage the growing discourse between law and regulation studies and those cognate disciplines seen in other areas.[11] In that regard this book also seeks to enrich those other disciplines with an indication of the resources that law and regulation can provide towards citizen participation as a way of revealing the normative in the scientific and technical.

[7] The most important field, but there are others too, such as 'law and health', 'law and science' and 'law and technology', to name the main ones.

[8] For discussion in the EU context see: A Wiener, *'European' Citizenship Practice: Building Institutions of a Non-State* (Oxford, Oxford University Press, 1998). More generally see: SR Arnstein, 'A Ladder of Citizen Participation' (1969) 35(4) *Journal of the American Institute of Planners* 216.

[9] R Bellamy, D Castiglione and J Shaw (eds), *Making European Citizens* (Basingstoke, Palgrave Macmillan, 2006); see further: D Kostakopoulou, *The Future Governance of Citizenship* (Cambridge, Cambridge University Press, 2008).

[10] These last three disciplines are salient to the discussion in the second part of the book.

[11] See: J Abraham and H Lawton-Smith (eds), *Regulation of the Pharmaceutical Industry* (Basingstoke, Palgrave Macmillan, 2003); J Aronson, *Genetic Witness: Science, Law, and Controversy in the Making of DNA Profiling* (Piscataway, Rutgers University Press, 2007); E Cloatre and M Pickersgill (eds), *Knowledge, Technology and Law* (Abingdon, Routledge, 2014); A Daemmrich, *Pharmacopolitics: Drug Regulation in the United States and Germany* (Chapel Hill, University of North Carolina Press, 2006); R Hindmarsh and B Prainsack (eds), *Genetic Subjects: Global Governance of Forensic DNA Profiling and Databasing* (Cambridge, Cambridge University Press, 2010); S Jasanoff (ed), *Reframing Rights: Bioconstitutionalism in the Genetic Age* (Cambridge MA, MIT Press, 2011).

The focus in this book is not only on the EU level of the multi-level system of governance,[12] but more particularly on the concrete techniques, processes and practices—the assemblages or technologies—deployed by the EU level in the area of public health, and teasing out how they are reflective of, embedded within and oriented towards the production and legitimation of the EU's identity, socio-political order and project of rule aimed at European integration. The study undertaken in this book is empirical in that it draws on extensive analysis of documentary sources assisted by interviews with key civil society actors that engage with the EU's public health governance.[13] The book is also normative in that it provides a critical account of the current institutionalisation of citizen participation in decision-making, a diagnosis of its limited scope and marginal status as a key concern based on an analysis of the techniques, processes and practices of the EU level of governance, and on the basis of the subsequent reflection a prescription for the enhancement of participation and through it wider governance and its regulatory interventions.[14]

C. Key Arguments and Next Steps

More than that citizen participation can and should amount to an active and substantive contribution to decision-making. The core or overall argument of this book is that engagement with citizen participation is vital not just as a value in itself, but also in order to enhance the quality of governance and its regulatory interventions. The diagnosis offered by this book (and outlined below) of the current institutionalisation of citizen participation in decision-making as a key concern helps to underscore why, while the prescription for the enhancement of participation and through it wider governance and its regulatory interventions, seeks to move the discussion forward and prompt further reflection. In relation to the diagnosis I make three related arguments, the first two of which are set out in the first part

[12] Put differently, this book is focused on the EU's regulatory order, which is one level of the multi-level system of governance. Within that system the EU level interacts with a range of other regulatory orders including those at the national level. See further: L Hooghe and G Marks, *Multilevel Governance and European Integration* (Oxford, Rowman & Littlefield Publishers, 2001).

[13] The project was funded by a British Academy Small Grant (SG-48186) with the ideas being developed further through support from an ESRC Seminar Series (RES-451-26-0764), for which I was PI, and which led to ML Flear and others (eds), *European Law and New Health Technologies* (Oxford, Oxford University Press, 2013). It was the former grant that provided the funding for visits to Brussels and Amsterdam, where I met with civil society actors involved in EU governance, and to London where I met with officials at the European Medicines Agency. The discussions with these actors informed the perspective taken in this book. Both sources of funding are gratefully acknowledged, as is the time of those who shared their insights.

[14] For reasons introduced in theory, concepts and methods below and that are deployed and elaborated in the second part of this book I do not reduce citizen participation to *civil society* or *stake holder* involvement in governance. Further, my concern is with reflection on the techniques, processes and practices as found in and constituted by discourse and their implications for citizen participation.

of the book. The first argument is that markets, risk and security, and ethics and human rights, provide the key contours for the EU's technology (that is, assemblage of components) governing public health and the policy domain, and that these contours are related in particular ways. Risk and more broadly security are geared towards regulating the dangers and threats attendant to the circulation of people and things within the internal market. In this relation ethics and human rights have limited roles and are principally deployed as legitimating devices. As a key consequence of this risk-based and market-oriented technology there is a distortion of public health attention, priorities and resources towards a focus on consequences and treatment using technological and magic bullet medical responses that optimise the circulation of people and things. At the same time prevention and related interventions in population that attend to the social, economic and political causes of public health problems might (and in some cases that are noted in the first part of the book actually seem to) receive less attention and resources.

The second argument is that this analysis points to the importance of neoliberalism through the underlying use, infiltration, perpetuation and extension of market-oriented ideas, values and rationalities into wider and formally non-market domains like public health. Importantly, the features of governance and their configuration by and through market reasoning are part of attempts to establish the boundaries of EU responsibility, that is, what the EU sees and projects as its responsibility, shaping its ability to take the credit for success, as well as the limits of its accountability and blame in the event of failure. In attempting to define the limits of its responsibility the EU is, in part, seeking to define failure—the trigger for determining the circumstances in which it can be held accountable. As well as the latter attempt at delimiting the boundaries of responsibility and accountability, the extension of market reasoning ensures knowledge is increasingly made to serve power, and the latter is itself extended materially (ie in terms of what it covers) and territorially, that is, in terms of the places where it applies and people enfolded into the regime and in relation to whom it has effects. These (re)configurations are central to neoliberalism and are also the structuring themes of the policy domain. The themes are embedded within, reflective of and central to efforts at producing and legitimating the EU, its identity, related imagined socio-political order of market actors and ultimately the project of European integration.

Reflecting on the latter in the opening chapter of the second part of the book (chapter six), I make a third argument, which is my diagnosis of the limited nature, shape and use of the current institutionalisation of citizen participation as a key concern. The centrality and valorisation of scientific and technical knowledge and expertise by and within the risk-based technology used to regulate public health implicitly devalues and limits the scope and potential for citizen participation in decision-making. In light of this I understand citizen participation itself as a technology or assemblage of components. Through this technology the EU's citizenry are rendered less as regulatory publics and are instead regulated into providing public legitimation and mediating the boundaries of responsibility and accountability.[15] The scientific and technical foundations of decision-making help to depoliticise and naturalise governance, which obscures its attendant paradoxes, pitfalls and blind spots, including the distortion of regulatory priorities and responses and the marginalisation of citizen participation. Revealing these normative dimensions of the technical and scientific is, given the stakes for the distribution of benefits and risks across society, and for health and life, perhaps 'the' core potential contribution of citizen participation, in that it can help to correct them.

In that regard, there remains the potential for citizens, including those that are subject to governance, to demand and contest decisions, in this context those that intervene in and relate directly to their lives, engendering what Foucault called biopolitics.[16] It is recognition of this potential that moves the discussion from diagnosis and towards a prescription that might bolster citizen participation in governing. The paradoxes, pitfalls and blind spots attendant to governance, and the effective limits on citizen participation, have common foundations in the contours and the underpinning structuring themes of governance and regulatory design. Reflecting on this there follows a fourth argument, which is that the foundations of governance and its paradoxes, pitfalls and blind spots open up space and create possibilities for citizen participation in decision-making, but going beyond the EU's citizenry to encompass those that are subject to governance, that is 'the governed'. In making that argument I suggest that these normative dimensions of governance can be revealed and underlined by using the discursive resources within governance itself, specifically, at this time, the legitimating discourses of human rights and bioethics, underscored by an emphasis on the EU's (supra-)stewardship responsibility.

These discourses are key resources for facilitating and powering discussion that generates supplementary knowledge on the paradoxes, pitfalls and blind spots attendant to governance, especially those that present under- or even unacknowledged regulatory failures and 'societal risks'. The risks and failures gain in importance and might be taken into account in decision-making through their articulation in terms of the legitimating discourses, with support from references to (supra-)stewardship responsibility. That is, through these discourses the failures and risk can be transformed into key 'institutional risks', that is risks to the EU's standing and reputation—and important knowledge that must be factored into decision-making. In short, the risk-based technology governing public health provides a 'way in' for participation impelled by the threat that if the

[15] ML Flear and MD Pickersgill, 'Regulatory or Regulating Publics? The European Union's Regulation of Emerging Health Technologies and Citizen Participation' (2013) 21(1) *Medical Law Review* 39.

[16] M Foucault, *The Birth of Biopolitics: Lectures at the Collège de France, 1978–79* (Basingstoke, Palgrave Macmillan, 2008). *Cf* T Lemke, '"The Birth of Biopolitics': Michel Foucault's Lecture at the Collège de France on Neo-Liberal Governmentality' (2001) 30(2) *Economy and Society* 190; W Brown, *Edgework* (Princeton NJ, Princeton University Press, 2005) 39–44. See further: M Dean, *The Signature of Power: Sovereignty, Governmentality and Biopolitics* (London, Sage Publications, 2013).

regulatory failures and 'societal risks' it identifies are left unaddressed, they could de-legitimate and undermine the EU's governance, identity as a security and public health actor and ultimately the project of European integration (since these are part of what public health governance is used to build). In this way participation might politicise and bring out the normative dimensions of the risk-based governing technology, and ensure the EU is held to account for its failures and more fully meets its responsibilities to its citizens.

Before I can make these related arguments over the course of the book, and move from the diagnosis of the current institutionalisation of citizen participation as an underdeveloped technology of governance as 'the' key concern, to a prescription for its enhancement and with it the quality of governance and its regulatory interventions, it is necessary to elaborate further on these introductory points. In the next section I seek to justify and explain the book's topic by, first, briefly outlining coverage of public health and the EU's role in it within legal scholarship and its sub- and most closely related disciplines, and second, introducing the limited consideration and marginal status of citizen participation in them. The third section provides an outline of the theory, concepts and methods—the conceptual approach—deployed in this book to meet its aims and advance its arguments. The final section provides an overview of the book. Over the course of which I further substantiate the initially pessimistic account about citizen participation in governing, but also attempt to provide a basis for optimism about the potential for participation that can propel continued engagement in this project by scholarship and citizens at large.

II. LAW, PUBLIC HEALTH AND PARTICIPATION

A. Law and Public Health: A Very Brief Overview

While the importance of public health seems axiomatic, at least in light of its prominence in media reports, it has hitherto been the subject of limited attention in legal scholarship, which provides the core context for this study and the field in relation to which it articulates most directly. To clarify, in this book I am not trying to determine whether there should be an EU dimension to public health law and governance. That is, I am not interested in determining whether there should be a single and to some extent harmonised 'EU public health law' or regime that is produced by the EU's institutions. Further, I am not trying to determine whether the EU should be engaged in public health. Instead, I examine and reflect critically upon the EU's public health policy domain as constituted by and through its published documentary record. As explained above in the agenda, this book uses public health as a way of exploring broader concerns related to governing in late modernity and the implications for democratic rule. As such what follows is a schematic overview of law and public health in light of the purpose and scope of the book. I provide only a very brief overview of scholarship on law and public health in order to clarify where it stands at present and to further justify this book on governing public health. That is followed by an introduction to consideration of citizen participation within key scholarships. Overall this section provides a jumping off point for what follows.

As an initial point, *health* has been described as a state of being 'that is subject to wide *individual, social and cultural interpretation*; it is produced by the interplay of individual perceptions and social influences' (emphasis added).[17] The idea of health is therefore highly subjective and intangible. In addition, a wide range of factors influence health, including geography, social and economic conditions and position. The classic medical definition provides that health is the 'absence of disease'[18]—an 'engineering or mechanical'[19] model of health. The emphasis of this model is on the adequate functioning of the human body, maintaining it and repairing it where necessary. The focus is on how disease impacts upon the human body conceived of as a machine.[20] Within this model medical professionals determine who is healthy, and who has access to treatment.[21]

The WHO's alternative definition is the first explicit and purposefully formulated, and the most widely used and recognised:[22] 'health' is a 'state of complete physical, mental and social well-being and not merely the absence of infirmity'.[23] This definition refers to the classic medical definition of health, but goes beyond it to encompass the pre-conditions of health: controls on the quality of food, environmental protection, the provision of public housing and welfare benefits. This is the so-called 'social model' of health.[24] The definition is clearly 'messianic in its intent',[25] idealistic and even utopian, in that it focuses on enhancing health rather than treating disease. Health is rendered as something to be worked towards and

[17] LJ Jones, *The Social Context of Health and Health Work* (London, Palgrave Macmillan, 1994) 3.

[18] There appears to be no specific source for this definition. It is however used in several publications without reference to other works. For example, Jones describes the definition as 'the most pervasive definition of health in the Western World'. Jones, ibid, 5.

[19] Jones, n 17 above, 5.

[20] T McKeown, *The Role of Medicine* (Oxford, Basil Blackwell, 1979); M Foucault, *The Birth of the Clinic* (London, Tavistock, 1976).

[21] C Helman, 'Introduction: The Scope of Medical Anthropology' in C Helman, *Culture, Health and Illness*, 4th edn (Oxford, Butterworth Heinemann, 2000) 5.

[22] RE Spector, *Cultural Diversity in Health and Illness*, 7th edn (London, Prentice Hall, 2008).

[23] World Health Organisation, *Constitution of the World Health Organisation* (Geneva, World Health Organisation, 1948) 14 UNTS 185.

[24] The medical model and the social model run parallel in this respect: disease and aging are viewed as processes of the loss of function (in the case of disease this occurs too early; in the case of aging this occurs in due time). Notions of chronic and acute, and progressivity or deterioration are key in both. The medical model and the social model are to be distinguished as follows: the doctor is interested in biological processes within the sick person whereas the sociologist is interested in the way the network of relations around the sick person develops. It has been said that it is not possible to decide what comes first and what is worse, 'bodily or social loss of function. Such questions of primacy and priority are issues to be fought out in the confrontation between adherents of a "medical model" and a "social model", in the competition between a well-established medical professional circle and the more recent professional circles of medical sociologists, social psychologists, social workers, and so on' (A de Swaan, *The Management of Normality: Critical Essays in Health and Welfare* (London, Routledge, 1990) 23–24).

[25] J Richman, *Medicine and Health* (London, Longman, 1987) 5.

is 'to be achieved by personal and social change as well as by medical advance'.[26] In this understanding health is a public or common concern and it must, therefore, encompass a focus on *public* health.[27] Crucially, although the WHO's definition is recent, it helps to highlight how the importance of balancing individual and societal or state interests means that public health has been a topic of enduring importance for law. This is apparent in Gostin's characteristics of public health law: 'Government's responsibility to advance the public's health; Coercion and limits on state power; Government's partners in the public health system; The population perspective; Communities and civic participation; The prevention orientation; Social justice'.[28] I return to participation as a characteristic below.[29]

More important for these introductory remarks is the wide breadth of what is encompassed in law's engagement with public health.[30] This is shared by the 2007 report of the Nuffield Council on Bioethics, *Public Health: Ethical Issues*[31] (Nuffield), which used the term 'stewardship' in order to frame state responsibility for public health and the role of law. The WHO has also used stewardship, going so far as to conflate it with governance. Its *World Health Report 2000* explains how stewardship essentially involves 'setting and enforcing the rules of the game and providing strategic direction for all the different actors involved',[32] and it is 'the very essence of good government', with the 'Ultimate'[33] responsibility falling on state governments, described elsewhere as the 'steward of stewards'.[34] Human rights and bioethics inform this version of stewardship: 'In addition to *improving overall levels of population health*, [its] objectives are likely to be framed in terms of equity, coverage, access, quality, and patients'[35] (emphasis added) rights. Moreover, stewardship 'is ultimately concerned with *oversight* of the entire system, avoiding myopia, tunnel vision and the turning of a blind eye to a system's failings' (emphasis added).[36] Broadly speaking national policies do not differ in the aim pursued, 'but rather in the *methods* [or means] adopted in pursuit of them' (emphasis added).[37] This responsibility is widely perceived as being fulfilled only by the provision of adequate health and social measures by the state. There is no obligation under the

[26] Jones, n 17 above, 6.

[27] See further: J Coggon, *What Makes Health Public?* (Cambridge, Cambridge University Press, 2012).

[28] LO Gostin, *Public Health Law*, 2nd edn (Berkeley, University of California Press, 2008) xxii.

[29] And discussed further in ch 6.

[30] Examination of the definition of 'law' in the context of 'health care law' has been provided by J Montgomery, *Health Care Law*, 2nd edn (Oxford, Oxford University Press, 2003) ch 1 'The Scope and Sources of Health Care Law'.

[31] Nuffield Council, *Public Health: Ethical Issues* (London, Nuffield Council on Bioethics, 2007).

[32] 'Message from the Director General, Gro Harlem Brundtland' in World Health Organisation, *World Health Report 2000* (Geneva, World Health Organisation, 2000) viii.

[33] 'Message' ibid. Also see: World Health Organisation, *World Health Day: International Health Security: Invest in Health, Build a Safer Future* (Geneva, World Health Organisation, 2007).

[34] P Travis and others, 'Towards Better Stewardship: Concepts and Critical Issues' in CJL Murray and DB Evans, *Health Systems Performance Assessment* (Geneva, World Health Organisation, 2003) 289.

[35] 'Governance': www.who.int/healthsystems/topics/stewardship/en/index.html.

[36] 'Message', n 32 above.

[37] TH Marshall, *Social Policy*, 5th edn (London, Hutchinson, 1985) 133.

right to health to provide a comprehensive health care system.[38] Nevertheless, the method chosen by many economically advanced countries has been such a system as well as comprehensive public health measures.

However, notwithstanding the WHO's definition of health, references to the international obligations of states in stewardship,[39] and growing academic commentary on 'global health law',[40] public health is arguably only recently becoming a field of specific attention in legal scholarship,[41] but is most often considered as part of wider national 'health law' or 'health care law'. Take Montgomery's definition of the latter: 'It embraces not only the practice of medicine, but also that of non-medical health care professions, the administration of health services *and the law's role in maintaining public health*' (emphasis added).[42] The focus in the consideration of public health tends to be on the professional–patient relationship in the context of the state's obligations for the protection of public health. Looking a little more widely, recent contributions to law and technology and the cognate discipline of regulation studies have increased attention on public health and transnational actors, but this tends to be in relation to the regulation of technology.[43] One notable exception is the work of Brownsword, one of Nuffield's authors, who has built on that report's identification of the transnational dimensions of state responsibility, and the roles of transnational actors, such as around pandemics, terming it 'super-stewardship' and 'a significant item of unfinished business'.[44]

There has also been growing consideration of public health per se rather than dealing with it as part of broader issues in human rights,[45] seen not just in relation

[38] European Social Charter (Revised) (3 May 1996, entered into force 1 July 1999) ETS 163 noted further in ch 2 at n 15 covers only the treatment of illness, not health promotion, and extends only to those unable to purchase care privately. As for the European Convention on Human Rights (4 November 1950, entered into force 3 September 1953) ETS 5, signature states are required to take reasonable steps to protect life under Art 2 on the right to life (*Osman v UK* [1999] 1 FLR 193).

[39] See further, ch 6.

[40] For an overview see: LO Gostin and AL Taylor O'Neill, 'Global Health Law: A Definition and Grand Challenges' (2008) 1(1) *Public Health Ethics* 53. LO Gostin and D Sridhar, 'Global Health and the Law' (2014) 370 *New England Journal of Medicine* 1732. See further: LO Gostin, *Global Health Law* (Boston MA, Harvard University Press, 2014).

[41] Seminally: Gostin, *Public Health Law*, n 28 above. This has been followed by further important works: Coggon, *What Makes Health Public?*, n 27 above.

[42] Montgomery, *Health Care Law*, n 30 above, 4.

[43] Brownsword, n 4 above; R Brownsword and M Goodwin, *Law and Technologies of the Twenty-First Century* (Cambridge, Cambridge University Press, 2012); R Brownsword and H Somsen, 'Law, Innovation and Technology: Before We Fast Forward–A Forum for Debate' (2009) 1 *Law, Innovation and Technology* 1; F Francioni (ed), *Biotechnologies and International Human Rights* (Oxford, Hart Publishing, 2007); T Murphy (ed), *New Technologies and Human Rights* (Oxford, Oxford University Press, 2009).

[44] R Brownsword, 'So What Does the World Need Now?' in R Brownsword and K Yeung (eds), *Regulating Technologies: Legal Futures, Regulatory Frames and Technological Fixes* (Oxford, Hart Publishing, 2008) 47 (this also provides an overview of the term as developed thus far). Developed in: ML Flear (ed), 'Papers from "A Symposium with Professor Roger Brownsword: Super-Stewardship in the Context of Public Health"' (2011) 62(5) *Northern Ireland Legal Quarterly* (Special Issue).

[45] J Harrington and M Stuttaford (eds), *Global Health and Human Rights* (Abingdon, Routledge, 2010); J Tobin, *The Right to Health in International Law* (Oxford, Oxford University Press, 2012); B Toebes and others (eds), *Health and Human Rights in Europe* (Cambridge, Intersentia, 2012).

to the right to health[46] or discussion of the implications of public health interventions for human rights, but also as a way to develop legal method.[47] Nevertheless, where the broader legal literature and regulation studies work considers public health the role of transnational actors receives little attention. And in each the EU receives scant attention[48]—including in discussion of 'global health law'. Within EU law public health has of course been implicated in different areas.[49] But the link between the EU and health was made only relatively recently[50] and it is still the 'new kid on the block'[51] of EU legal studies, albeit arguably one that is becoming increasingly coherent and displaying particular features.[52] But within that literature there is little on public health as a field in its own right. Instead public health tends to be seen more as a subset of the broader 'EU and health' field in formation or subsumed within the law of other European actors in 'European law' as it engages with new health technologies.[53] This seems to mirror the situation in medical law, where there is likewise little attention to public health per se except as part of the broader field,[54] although this is something that is gradually changing.[55]

[46] The evolution of health as a human right is traced in: B Toebes, '*The Right to Health*' in A Eide and others (eds), *Economic, Cultural and Social Rights* 2nd edn (Kluwer, The Hague, 2001). Initially drawing on Sigerist, Toebes traces the various attempts made to define health in the West, starting in antiquity and moving to the present day in: B Toebes, *The Right to Health as a Human Right in International Law* (Antwerp, Intersentia/Hart Publishing, 1999). See further: HE Sigerist, *Medicine and Human Welfare* (London, Oxford University Press, 1941). Also see: JM Zuniga, SP Marks, LO Gostin (eds), *Advancing the Human Right to Health* (Oxford, Oxford University Press, 2013)

[47] T Murphy, *Health and Human Rights* (Oxford, Hart Publishing, 2013).

[48] Within human rights this is surprisingly given the EU is increasingly a human rights organisation, and arguably 'the' human rights organisation in Europe, particularly after its Charter of Fundamental Rights gained equal status to the EU Treaties under the Lisbon Treaty 2009.

[49] Classically as a limitation on the 'four freedoms' and as a value to be taken into account in internal market legislation. See further, ch 2.

[50] Initially in the seminal TK Hervey and JV McHale, *Health Law and the European Union* (Cambridge, Cambridge University Press 2004) (followed-up by the revised and retitled work noted below). Subsequently there has been a lot more attention, see further: SL Greer, TK Hervey, JP MacKenbach and M McKee, 'Health Law and Policy in the European Union' (2013) 381(9872) *The Lancet* 1135; TK Hervey, A-M Farrell, S Devaney and T Murphy, 'The Impacts of European Union Law on the Health Care Sector: Institutional Overview' (2011) 16(4) *Eurohealth* 5; E Mossialos and others (eds), *Health Systems Governance in Europe: The Role of European Union Law and Policy* (Cambridge, Cambridge University Press, 2010); M Steffen (ed), *Health Governance in Europe: Issues, Challenges, and Theories* (London, Routledge, 2005). A notable but rare exception: SL Greer and P Kurzer, *European Union Public Health Policy: Regional and Global Trends* (London, Routledge, 2013).

[51] T Hervey, 'EU Health Law' in C Barnard and S Peers (eds), *European Union Law* (Oxford, Oxford University Press 2014) 621.

[52] TK Hervey and JV McHale, *European Union Health Law* (Cambridge, Cambridge University Press, 2015).

[53] Flear and others (eds), n 13 above.

[54] Montgomery, n 30 above, in which public health is considered in ch 2 'Public Health Law'; E Jackson, *Medical Law: Text, Cases, and Materials*, 3rd edn (Oxford, Oxford University Press, 2013), in which public health is given little if any specific prominence; JK Mason and GT Laurie, *Law and Medical Ethics*, 9th edn (Oxford, Oxford University Press, 2013) ch 2 'Public Health and the Patient-State Relationship'.

[55] Coggon, *What Makes Health Public?* n 27 above.

Overall, looking across law, its sub-disciplines and regulation studies, current discussion of public health still tends to treat it as part of other issues related to medicine and clinical decision-making, the organisation, delivery and financing of health care services, and questions of liability, and usually as part of wider 'health care law' or 'health law', that is, a subset of this broader field rather than a specific area for attention in and of itself. A key drawback of this organisation of scholarship is a diminution in the importance of 'public health' as an object of study at a time when public health problems seem to only gain in prominence. The general focus also remains on the national level at a time when law, governance and regulation are increasingly transnational or global.[56] Although this might be understandable given that transnational actors and processes usually operate with and through the national level,[57] keeping transnational dimensions largely latent reduces and even misses the importance of the circulation of people and things across borders in producing public health problems in the first place as well as the consequent importance of transnational actors in regulation.

There is, therefore, a space and need for a more concerted look at the roles of transnational actors and, given its prominence as a formally accountable actor the EU is a particularly important site in and of itself. In addition to the related limitations in the current scholarship, attention to the transnational sphere, and the EU as an example, is also justified since it is a sphere where the ideas, concepts and rationalities that underpin, orientate and direct law, governance and regulation are produced, (re)circulate from and between other sites, spaces, fora and levels of governance.[58] In that respect I realise that a more complete picture of EU governance of public health would involve a multi-level consideration of those dynamics and the related range of governance arrangements and regulatory instruments at Member State level, and lower still at the regional level where power is devolved.[59] Although such an analysis would of course be of much value in providing a fuller picture of the overlapping and interacting sites, spaces and fora that together govern public health, it is unfeasible within the confines of a single book.

Most extant analyses of public health in law and regulation studies also tend to focus on explaining, describing and evaluating current public health regimes and charting transitions between paradigms and eras.[60] Although these sorts of analysis draw attention to the design of governance and its regulatory interventions,[61]

[56] S Cassesse, 'The Globalisation of Law' (2005) 37 *New York University Journal of International Law and Politics* 973; A-M Slaughter, *A New World Order* (Princeton, Princeton University Press, 2004).

[57] S Sassen, *Territory, Authority, Rights: From Medieval to Global Assemblages* (Princeton NJ, Princeton University Press, 2008).

[58] See: SL Greer, *The Politics of European Union Health Policies* (Maidenhead, Open University Press, 2009). More generally see, eg: K Armstrong, *Governing Social Inclusion* (Cambridge, Cambridge University Press, 2010).

[59] See Hooghe and G Marks, *Multilevel Governance and European Integration*, n 12 above.

[60] Eg see: VK Yadavendu, *Shifting Paradigms in Public Health: From Holism to Individualism* (Springer, 2013).

[61] It is quite a recent development: E Jackson, *Law and the Regulation of Medicines* (Oxford, Hart Publishing, 2012), but with a focus on the UK.

consideration of public health regulation in light of the broader norms, values, rationalities and socio-political imaginaries it is reflective of and within which it is embedded remains largely unexamined—and their link to producing and legitimating socio-political order and projects of rule is even less apparent. Further, although the paradoxes, pitfalls and blind spots attendant to public health governance have been discussed at some length in law and regulation studies, the relation of those problems to and especially production by and through this larger design has received far more attention as key normative concerns in critical theory, bioethics, sociology, STS and anthropology.[62] Nevertheless, much of the attention in those disciplines, as well as in law and regulation studies looking beyond the national level of governance, has been on the United States (US) regime, global health and the way in which they overlap and relate. The EU and its relations with those other sites has received far less attention.[63]

B. Citizen Participation

Citizen participation is part of discussions about patient agency vis-à-vis medical decision-making and the shifting paradigms of public health.[64] Participation is also noted as a key characteristic of Gostin's influential notion of 'public health law':

> [M]any forward thinkers urge greater community involvement in public health decision-making so that policy formation becomes a genuinely civic endeavour. Under this view, citizens strive to safeguard their communities through civic participation, open forums, and capacity-building to solve local problems. Public involvement should result in stronger support for health policies and encourage citizens to take a more active role in protecting themselves and the health of their neighbours. Public health authorities, for example, might practice more deliberative forms of democracy, involving closer consultation with consumers and voluntary organisations that represent them (e.g. town meetings and consumer membership of government advisory committees). This kind of deliberative democracy in public health is increasingly evident in government-community partnerships ... (e.g. AIDS action and breast cancer awareness).[65]

Despite such acknowledgement, citizen participation in legal and regulatory decision-making is either a peripheral concern (as with the latter example

[62] See the literature cited in the discussion in chs 7 and 8 in particular.

[63] That is also the case in the growing attention on the EU's growing global role, which although welcome has tended to ignore (public) health as a field in itself. See: M Evans and P Koutrakos, *The International Responsibility of the European Union: European and International Perspectives* (Oxford, Hart Publishing, 2013).

[64] On the agency of patients in the context of the doctor–patient relationship, see, O O'Neill, *Autonomy and Trust in Bioethics* (Cambridge, Cambridge University Press, 2001) noting at 3: the 'widespread and energetic efforts to respect persons and their autonomy and to improve regulatory structures'. On shifting paradigms see, eg: M Schwab and S L Syme, 'On Paradigms, Community Participation, and the Future of Public Health' (1997) 87(12) *American Journal of Public Health* 2049.

[65] Gostin, *Public Health Law*, n 28 above, 18.

it is mentioned briefly as part of those wider discussions) or it remains largely untouched in mainstream law and regulation studies engagement with public health, including within human rights.[66] Indeed, consideration of participation is far more likely in environmental law and governance,[67] which is unsurprising given the legal innovation of the Aarhus Convention.[68] Relatedly, there are attempts to integrate citizen concerns in the design of policy, such as through impact assessment, in the context of the environment and other fields, including public health.[69] Yet even in the field of environmental law there is cause for concern about the nature and extent of the attention given to participation, with Lee observing that 'Some of the great hope [for participation] … seems to have waned since the turn of the century, or is certainly less visible in the official discourse around environmental decision-making'.[70] As I point out below and discuss further in chapter six, in the EU's official discourse around public health participation is even less visible and is instead underpinned and shaped by a more general approach to participation in science-based regulation.

Key rationales for citizen participation include the input of knowledge and perspectives, policy implementation and legitimation. Whatever the precise rationale, (early) engagement is commonly held to produce better regulation.[71] Indeed, there is a focus on, for example, earlier or 'upstream' participation, which is seen as preferable in efforts to reach agreement by, as Mandel explains, bringing '*together diverse stakeholders [in order] to produce a collaborative governance*

[66] An item for further research in relation to European law's engagement with new health technologies and in relation to human rights, see respectively: Flear and others (eds), n 13 above; Murphy, *Health and Human Rights*, n 47 above. It is worthwhile nothing that in human rights participation is mentioned in several instruments, eg: Committee on Economic, Social and Cultural Rights, 'General Comment No 12: The Right to Adequate Food (Art 11)' (12 May 1999) UN Doc E/C.12/1999/5; Art 28 Convention for the Protection of Human Rights and Dignity of the Human Being with regard to the Application of Biology and Medicine: Convention on Human Rights and Biomedicine (4 April 1997, entered into force 1 December 1999) ETS 164 (often referred to simply as the Oviedo Convention); Art 25 International Covenant on Civil and Political Rights (16 December 1966, entered into force 23 March 1976) 999 UNTS 171. For further discussion, see: H Potts, 'Participation and the Right to the Highest Attainable Standard of Health' (Colchester, University of Essex Human Rights Centre, 2009); AE Yamin, 'Suffering and Powerlessness: The Significance of Participation in Rights-Based Approaches to Health' (2009) 11(1) *Health and Human Rights: An International Journal* 5.

[67] See, generally: E Fisher, B Lange and E Scotford, *Environmental Law: Text, Cases, and Materials* (Oxford, Oxford University Press, 2013), especially chs 4, 5 and 13; M Lee, *EU Environmental Law, Governance and Decision-Making*, 2nd edn (Oxford, Hart Publishing, 2013) chs 7 and 8. See further: S Yearley, 'Bridging the Science-Policy Divide in Urban Air-Quality Management: Evaluating Ways to Make Models More Robust through Public Engagement' (2006) 24(5) *Environment and Planning C* 701.

[68] UN Economic Commission for Europe, Aarhus Convention on Access to Information, Public Participation in Decision-Making and Access to Justice in Environmental Matters (adopted 25 June 1998, entered into force 30 October 2001) 2161 UNTS 447. Mentioned again in ch 6.

[69] Impact assessment is discussed further in ch 2 and the implications for participation are taken up in ch 6.

[70] M Lee, n 67 above, 250.

[71] For discussion, see: R Baldwin, 'Is Better Regulation Smarter Regulation?' (2005) *Public Law* 485. Also see: R Baldwin, M Cave and M Lodge, *Understanding Regulation: Theory, Strategy, and Practice*, 2nd edn (Oxford, Oxford University Press, 2013).

system rather than a resource-draining adversarial battle' (emphasis added).[72] Consequently, there is concern for, as Brownsword puts it, the 'general features to be designed in[to]'[73] participation. Although the value of citizen participation is widely acknowledged and enhancing it is urged, much discussion within law and regulation studies including work centred on the EU,[74] has focused on the appropriate relationship between expert legal and regulatory reasoning and popular or lay understandings,[75] with particular attention given to the shape and design of procedures for participation. This is perhaps unsurprising in light of liberal accounts where democratic decision-making is delegated to trusted elites wielding scientific and technocratic knowledge and expertise. The focus on participatory procedures is especially apparent in situations where there is little possibility of substantive agreement and participation is essentially used to quell contestation, produce public legitimacy and maintain a functioning economy.[76]

STS has been enduringly critical of the ways in which participation tends to be institutionalised, especially where that has been for instrumental reasons.[77] Consequently, STS has been especially clear about the importance of reflecting on the use, role and configuration of citizen participation in relation to legal and regulatory decision-making. Indeed, in this discipline a popular view is that participation is a (potential) means of democratising science and technology and related decision-making and producing responsible and responsive innovation.[78] In that regard the EU's constitutional model has been a site of great hope.[79] Still, there has been much criticism of the use of citizen participation to merely enrol publics and induce trust in science-based issues and produce acquiescence, rather

[72] GN Mandel, 'Regulating Emerging Technologies' (2009) 1 *Law, Innovation and Technology* 75.

[73] Brownsword, n 4 above, 128. Further discussion at 120–28 includes: D Galligan, 'Citizens' Rights and Participation in the Regulation of Biotechnology' in Francioni (ed), *Biotechnologies and International Human Rights*, n 43 above.

[74] Notably, participatory rights have received growing attention: J Mendes, *Participation in EU Rule-making: A Rights-Based Approach* (Oxford, Oxford University Press, 2011).

[75] J Waldron, *Law and Disagreement* (New York NY, Oxford University Press, 1999).

[76] In this regard Brownsword notes how agreement is frustrated by the 'bioethical triangle' underpinning regulation of new medical and biotechnologies and comprising an empowering human rights perspective, a largely restrictive and disempowering dignitarian perspective and a pragmatic utilitarian perspective. See: R Brownsword, 'Human Dignity, Ethical Pluralism, and the Regulation of Modern Biotechnologies' in Murphy (ed), *New Technologies and Human Rights*, n 43 above.

[77] R Devon, 'Towards a Social Ethics of Technology: A Research Prospect' (2004) 8 *Techne* 99; S Jasanoff, 'Technologies of Humility: Citizen Participation in Governing Science' (2003) 41 *Minerva* 223; H Nowotny, 'How Many Policy Rooms Are There?' (2007) 32 *Science, Technology & Human Values* 479.

[78] K Bickerstaff and others, 'Locating Scientific Citizenship: The Institutional Contexts and Cultures of Public Engagement' (2010) 35(4) *Science, Technology & Human Values* 474; S Cunningham-Burley, 'Public Knowledge and Public Trust' (2006) 9 *Community Genetics* 204; R Evans and A Plows, 'Listening Without Prejudice? Re-discovering the Value of the Disinterested Citizen' (2007) 37(6) *Social Studies of Science* 827; MD Pickersgill, 'Research, Engagement and Public Bioethics: Promoting Socially Robust Science' (2011) 37 *Journal of Medical Ethics* 698; T Togers-Hayden, A Mohr and N Pidgeon, 'Introduction: Engaging with Nanotechnologies—Engaging Differently?' (2007) 1(2) *NanoEthics* 123.

[79] S Jasanoff, 'Biotechnology and Empire: The Global Power of Seeds and Science' (2006) 21 *OSIRIS* 273.

than to ensure a genuine contribution to decision-making.[80] This might occur, for example, through the use of promissory or anticipatory discourses which seek to talk the future into existence,[81] while at the same time constraining or even eliminating the conditions of possibility for other futures.[82] Of particular note is criticism of the 'deficit model' of citizens in need of education through their participation. A core contribution of STS has been to show how that model undermines participation and is replete with flaws. Among them a point that is taken up in the conceptual approach sketched in the next section, which is that individuals come to know things in different ways, possess different kinds of expertise, and are reflexively aware of limitations in their ability to understand, which they may actively seek to address.[83]

These insights have recently proven influential within regulation studies.[84] In particular, work on 'design-based regulation'[85] stresses how norms, values, virtues and behavioural options are 'designed-in' and 'designed-out' of technologies and thereby inhibit or prevent action and undermine human agency.[86] Of particular note in this regard is Yeung and Dixon-Woods' work on patient safety. They observe that 'when rules are embedded in the fabric of design, there is no legal or constitutional obligation on those who identify and design-in the rules to invite *participation from those likely to be affected*, let alone take into account other *stakeholder interests*' (emphasis added).[87]

[80] The role of STS in this regard has also been the subject of self-reflection by its scholars: P-B Joly and A Kaufman, 'Lost in Translation? The Need for "Upstream Engagement" with Nanotechnology on Trial' (2008) 17(3) *Science as Culture* 225; BE Wynne, 'Dazzled by the Mirage of Influence? STS-SSK in Multivalent Registers of Relevance' (2007) 32(4) *Science, Technology & Human Values* 491.

[81] M Fortun, *Promising Genomics: Iceland and deCODE Genetics in a World of Speculation* (Berkeley, University of California Press, 2008); A Hedgecoe and P Martin, 'The Drugs Don't Work: Expectations and the Shaping of Pharmacogenetics' (2003) 33 *Social Studies of Science* 327; MD Pickersgill, 'Connecting Neuroscience and Law: Anticipatory Discourse and the Role of Sociotechnical Imaginaries' (2011) 30(1) *New Genetics and Society* 27; N Brown, B Rappert and A Webster (eds), *Contested Futures: A Sociology of Prospective Technoscience* (Aldershot, Ashgate, 2000).

[82] For discussion of the use of bioethics in this way, see: Hedgecoe and Martin, ibid.

[83] A Irwin and M Michael, *Science, Social Theory and Public Knowledge* (Maidenhead, Open University Press, 2003); A Kerr, S Cunningham-Burley and A Amos, 'The New Genetics and Health: Mobilising Lay Expertise' (1998) 7(1) *Public Understanding of Science* 41; B Wynne, 'Knowledges in Context' (1991) 16 *Science, Technology & Human Values* 111; BE Wynne, 'Misunderstood Misunderstandings: Social Identities and Public Uptake of Science' (1992) 1 *Public Understanding of Science* 281.

[84] M Akrich, 'The De-scription of Technical Objects' in WE Bijker and J Law (eds), *Shaping Technology/Building Society: Studies in Sociotechnical Change* (Cambridge MA, MIT Press, 1992); N Oudshoorn and T Pinch (eds), *How Users Matter: The Co-Construction of Users and Technologies, New Edition* (Cambridge MA, MIT Press, 2005); S Woolgar, 'Configuring the User: The Case of Usability Trials' in J Law (ed), *A Sociology of Monsters: Essays on Power, Technology and Domination* (London, Routledge, 1991).

[85] L Lessig, *Code: And Other Laws of Cyberspace* (New York NY, Basic Books, 1999); R Brownsword, 'Code, Control and Choice: Why East is East and West is West' (2005) 25 *Legal Studies* 1.

[86] Brownsword, n 4 above; K Yeung, 'Towards an Understanding of Regulation by Design' in Brownsword and Yeung (eds), *Regulating Technologies*, n 44 above.

[87] K Yeung and M Dixon-Woods, 'Design-Based Regulation and Patient Safety: A Regulation Studies Perspective' (2010) 71(3) *Social Science & Medicine* 613, 617.

Importantly, this may '*reduce professional and public accountability* … and *transfer judgments on the tolerability of risk to unaccountable institutions for which there is little transparency or public accountability*' (emphasis added).[88]

At the same time STS has argued and shown that citizens have the potential to make a substantive contribution towards governing, especially by revealing and underlining the paradoxes, pitfalls and blind spots attendant to it.[89] The problems attendant to governance and regulation have also been recognised through the widespread use of the aforementioned risk-based governance tool of impact assessment and have of course been acknowledged in law and regulation studies. Still, the potential for participation to contribute knowledge on the problems is (as I have suggested) far less developed in those disciplines. Instead, within legal and regulation studies scholarship there is much attention given to demarcating the boundaries of responsibility and accountability in the event of failure and such matters as defining what 'failure' is and when and how it triggers blame. By contrast there is more attention given to the problems attendant to governance as key normative dimensions in cognate disciplines, especially bioethics, sociology, STS and anthropology. A key reason for this might be law/science disciplinary demarcations. These divisions obscure the normative content of scientific and technological knowledge and their material objects, and potentially shield them from engagement by law.[90]

C. Taking Citizen Participation Seriously

The critique provided by STS in particular raises serious doubts about whether, and if so the extent to which, citizen participation is taken seriously in law and regulation studies as an object of study and as more than a procedural means of legitimating decisions and governance more broadly. In making that observation and the related arguments advanced in this book I hope to assist democratisation. Moreover, I seek to identify and push back against the forces at work in late modernity—especially risk-based, medical and/or technical framings of public health problems—that variously shape, constrain and even limit democratic contestation and participation in governing, whether as a consequence of political purpose or through lack of reflection on the undemocratic implications of late modern configurations of power.

The citizen participation I have in mind ought to do more than assist in the mediation of responsibilities and accountabilities and the production of legitimacy. Participation should be about sharing power and benefiting governance and the governed by improving the quality of the regulatory decisions made. This is

[88] Ibid.

[89] Discussed in ch 6.

[90] For discussion, see: T Murphy and N Whitty, 'Risk and Human Rights in UK Prison Governance' (2007) 47 *British Journal of Criminology* 798.

particularly important given regulatory failures and the idea that risk, uncertainties and failure are endemic to risk society. In that light, further consideration of citizen participation is not just important as a value in itself or as a technique of legitimation—it could even prove vital in addressing and even forestalling the dangers and threats produced by or not fully tackled by governance and regulation. The conceptual approach adopted to take this study forward is outlined in the next section.

III. GOVERNING IN LATE MODERNITY: THEORY, CONCEPTS AND METHODS

A. Technologies of Governing: Risk, Freedom/Security and Governmentality

To recap, this book aims to bring out how the problems attendant to governance and the potential for citizen participation to reveal and underline them might be better related and developed in ways that are to their mutual gain. This core focus implies a methodological decision about how to view and think about 'EU law' and its relations with 'governance' and 'regulation' for that core purpose. As such the analysis in this book does not look at individual measures of EU (hard) law, judicial decisions interpreting these provisions, soft law, and opportunities for funding (all command, control or steering instruments). Instead, this book adopts a broad brush approach in order to consider the concrete techniques, processes and practices produced by the EU level, their related norms, values and rationalities, and it considers how they are reflective of and embedded within the EU's socio-political order and project of integration. This approach also brings out how the issues are undergirded by, related to one another, and configured within, the neoliberal conditions of late modernity. In the following I elaborate on these introductory points, trace how they are deployed throughout this book and track them to the subsequent discussion. In doing so I seek to explain how the theory, concepts and methods provide openings and possibilities for citizen participation that can be harnessed in order to enhance it and, in turn, governance and its regulatory interventions.

The analytic perspective used in this book to advance its agenda and related arguments combines insights from critical theory, law and regulation studies, sociology, STS, with anthropology and bioethics. Foucault's work is especially important to the first of these disciplines, but it has also informed the others. A foundational insight is that the key terms in the initial research questions—markets, risk and security, ethics and human rights—can be understood as discourses. For the purposes of this book they are to be found in the EU's own published documentary record. Attention to discourse is important in that it 'transmits and produces power; it reinforces it, but also undermines and exposes it, renders it fragile and makes it possible to thwart it' (emphasis added).[91] In this view power is relational,

[91] M Foucault, *The History of Sexuality: Volume One, The Will to Knowledge* (London, Penguin, 1998) 101.

mutable and double-edged in that it both constrains and creates openings or possibilities for (re)shaping. Further, power operates automatically, often without intention, and with hidden and unforeseen consequences.

Discourses both constitute and help to convey ideas, values and rationalities.[92] Consequently the way in which discourses articulate makes them central to framing issues,[93] and to producing, organising and utilising knowledge and experience, especially in legal and regulatory decision-making.[94] Discourses underpin and shape the design of the assemblage of knowledges, scientific and bureaucratic techniques, process and practices—in short, technologies—from a range of national, supranational and global actors and sources. I understand discourses as underpinning and comprising a technology of governing. As explained in the outline of the programmatic level of EU governance provided in the next chapter, this technology is made more specific and gains in importance through its deployment in efforts to produce and legitimate the EU's identity, socio-political order based on an innovative and competitive market economy in order to foster growth, jobs and prosperity, and ultimately the project of European integration.[95] As part of that the EU has a key role as a public health regulator in its own territory and globally. In short, focusing on the key discourses and their relationships is, therefore, a vital step towards mapping and understanding how public health problems are regulated, revealing the attendant distortions, failures, paradoxes, pitfalls and blind spots, and the limits and possibilities for citizen participation.

A key insight that explains the particular relation between markets, risk and security, and ethics and human rights, and thereby facilitates the first argument of this book, is how liberalism hinges security to markets in a particular way. Security is about regulating the dangers and threats attendant to a particular understanding of freedom as being about optimising the circulation of people and things. As Foucault put it, security provides the conditions of possibility for liberalism's central tenet of freedom, which is understood as 'the possibility of movement, change of place, and processes of circulation of both people and things'.[96] Freedom is 'one of the facets … of the deployment of apparatuses of security'.[97] Security is about

[92] VA Schmidt, 'Discursive Institutionalism: The Explanatory Power of Ideas and Discourse' (2008) 11 *American Review of Political Science* 303.

[93] M Hajer and D Laws, 'Ordering through Discourse' in M Moran, M Rein and RE Goodin (eds), *The Oxford Handbook of Public Policy* (Oxford, Oxford University Press, 2006).

[94] E Goffman, *Frame Analysis: An Essay on the Organisation of Experience* (Cambridge MA, Harvard University Press, 1974); M Rein and D Schön, 'Problem Setting in Policy Research' in C Weiss (ed), *Using Social Research in Public Policy Making* (Lexington MA, Lexington Books, 1977); DA Snow and others, 'Frame Alignment Processes, Micromobilisation and Movement Participation' (1986) 51 *American Sociological Review* 464.

[95] For discussion of these sorts of connections see: W Brown, *Regulating Aversion: Tolerance in the Age of Identity and Empire* (Princeton NJ, Princeton University Press, 2006); S Jasanoff, *Designs on Nature* (Princeton NJ, Princeton University Press, 2005).

[96] M Foucault, *Security, Territory, Population: Lectures at the Collège de France, 1977–78* (Basingstoke, Palgrave Macmillan, 2007) 48–49.

[97] Ibid, 49.

responding 'to a reality in such a way that … [it] cancels out the reality to which it responds … regulates it'.[98]

The discovery of population, the development of statistics to track its size and contours, including measurement of the incidence of disease through epidemiology, for example, valorised this knowledge and the experts producing and interpreting it, and provided the 'end and instrument of government' and made it 'possible to think, reflect, and calculate … outside the juridical framework of sovereignty'.[99] This not only made it possible to regulate dangers and threats to public health, but also gave rise to governmentality, which is not limited to law, but extends through its employment and infiltration of a range of imbricating discourses, techniques and elements that regulate everyday life and are constitutive of governance. Throughout this book I examine how the EU level of public health governance is a particular example of the transformation and integration of law and regulation within governmentality.

Especially important in that regard, and an essential link to what follows, is how security becomes understood less in terms of the protection of sovereignty and increasingly in terms of governmentality as being about the optimisation of the health and wealth of (non-state) *populations*. As de Larrinaga and Doucet explain, this is to be achieved through the 'assessment of threats … [and it] pays particular attention to the global and transboundary *circulation of threats* to [them]' (emphasis added).[100] The idea that security is geared towards regulating the *public health* dangers and threats attendant to the circulation of people and things is salient to the EU's internal market, which is discussed at the outset of chapter two, and referenced throughout the rest of the first part of the book. A final key point is that human rights and ethics are configured in relation to the central relationship between markets and security (and risk), but their central function seems to be the legitimation of governance and its regulatory interventions.

B. Regulating Risk

Thus far I have brought together insights that bring attention to the way in which the technology governing public health functions to optimise the circulation of people and things and tackles the attendant dangers and threats by framing them as risks to be regulated. As explained throughout the first part of the book the perceived risk of public health problems is central to the EU's governance and the nature and selection of its regulatory responses—and these include interventions within the EU and globally. Governance is in turn reflective of, embedded within and oriented towards the production and legitimation of the EU's identity,

[98] Ibid, 47.

[99] Ibid, 104–05. For application of these insights to the EU, see: W Walters and J Haahr, *Governing Europe: Discourse, Governmentality and European Integration* (Abingdon, Routledge, 2005).

[100] M de Larrinaga and MG Doucet, *Security and Global Governmentality* (Abingdon, Routledge, 2010) 17.

socio-political order and project of rule aimed at European integration. However, risk-based regulation has become more difficult given that risks, uncertainties and failures are increasingly recognised as being endemic to 'risk society'.[101] Nevertheless, as Balzacq points out: the '*social design* of a security problem *conditions and legitimates* the *kind of means* used to stop it' and as such it is a 'normative political act' (emphasis added).[102] As I point out as part of the first argument, interventions such as technological and magic bullet medical responses might be favoured by the EU's risk-based technology, in particular because it is reflective of and embedded within a regime that seeks to optimise the circulation of people and things. These sorts of interventions are more often the subject of discussion in sociology, anthropology and bioethics, for example, than law and regulation studies, but are important to the latter two as the key paradoxes, pitfalls and blind spots attendant to the EU's risk-based technology. Moreover, these normative dimensions provide the grounds for the core or overall argument and intervention of this book, which is that citizen participation is vital because it can help to reveal and underline them and enhance the quality of governance and its regulatory interventions.

That overall argument is all the more important for the EU, given how it has met with a crisis of public confidence, trust and legitimacy[103] in the wake of high profile regulatory failures such as the BSE[104] crisis of the 1990s (as well as ongoing concerns around the inequity of the legal and regulatory arrangements put in place to resolve the economic and financial crisis of the 2000s onwards). As a consequence of this there has been much debate about the shape and design of the regulation of scientific risk and uncertainty and its implementation,[105] which has included a turn to human rights and bioethics.[106] Law and regulation studies, with their focus on decision-making, are, as I have already pointed out, central to this debate, especially given renewed attention to the salience of the context of scientific uncertainty. The production of regulatory failures and risks, and the limited role of citizen participation, both follow (as I shall explain further in chapter six) from the design of governance and its regulatory interventions.

[101] U Beck, *Risk Society: Towards a New Modernity* (London, Sage Publications, 1986); U Beck, *World at Risk* (Cambridge, Polity Press, 2009); A Giddens, *The Consequences of Modernity* (Polity Press, Cambridge, 1990); A Giddens, 'Risk Society: The Context of British Politics' in J Franklin (ed), *The Politics of Risk Society* (Cambridge, Polity Press, 1998).

[102] T Balzacq, 'Preface' in *Securitisation Theory: How Security Problems Emerge and Dissolve* (London, Routledge, 2011) xiii. For Foucault influenced securitisation theory in the public health field, see: S Elbe, *Virus Alert: Security, Governmentality, and the AIDS Pandemic* (New York, Columbia University Press, 2009).

[103] For an overview, see: C Scott, 'Accountability in the Regulatory State' (2000) 27 *Journal of Law and Society* 38 and the references in n 6 above, especially: Scharpf, *Governing in Europe. Effective and Democratic?*; Arnull and Wincott, *Accountability and Legitimacy in the European Union.*

[104] That is, bovine spongiform encephalopathy.

[105] For discussion, see: M Everson and E Vos, 'The Scientification of Politics and the Politicisation of Science' in M Everson and E Vos (eds), *Uncertain Risks Regulated* (Abingdon, Routledge-Cavendish, 2009).

[106] O'Neill, n 64 above, 3, who in addition to noting the 'widespread and energetic efforts to respect persons and their autonomy and to improve regulatory structures', goes on to point out that, 'public trust in medicine, science and biotechnology has seemingly faltered'. See further, the discussion in ch 6.

In terms of design, Brownsword explains how regulators 'need to tailor their interventions to the perceived risk profile presented by a particular technology'[107]—or, indeed, other regulatory targets, such as public health problems (including new technologies as such problems). This involves determining such matters as when risk materialises; the degree of risk (whether it is low or high); the kind of harms or hazards to which risk to public health pertains and the potential for their ranking; and, finally, how risk relates to precaution (whether precaution occurs at risk assessment or somehow operates in risk management).[108] Rare public health problems, such as those emerging well beyond the EU but spreading (in)to it through the circulation of people and things, as well as those produced by new technologies, are especially problematic for the production of a risk profile in that so much is unknown and uncertain, and there is little agreement on a range of issues—including how the related risks 'should be framed, which methodologies should be adopted, [and] which values prioritised'.[109]

Knowledge—its creation, use and deployment—is central to these design-oriented discussions. As noted above, the study of disease through epidemiology has historically laid the basis for public health governance and its regulatory interventions. This is brought out by Foucault's idea of power/knowledge, which denotes the way in which changes in knowledge help to provide the basis for the production and exercise of governmental power and control. Knowledge is formulated as encompassing 'the vast assemblage of persons, theories, projects, experiments and techniques that has become such a central component of government'—it is 'the "know how" that makes government possible'.[110] A major contribution of STS that builds on power/knowledge is that of co-production. Knowledge, including scientific facts,[111] as well as its ideational and material products, are 'incorporated into practices of state-making, or of governance more broadly'.[112] This underlines the way in which the EU's risk-based technology for governing public health and its related regulatory interventions have a wider significance, that is, in terms of producing, reflecting and legitimating the EU's identity, socio-political order and European integration project.

[107] Brownsword, n 4 above, 118.

[108] Ibid, 118–19.

[109] Ibid, 119–20.

[110] N Rose and P Miller, 'Political Power Beyond the State: Problematics of Government' (1992) 43(2) *British Journal of Sociology* 172, 178.

[111] K Knorr Cetina, 'Laboratory Studies: The Cultural Approach to the Study of Science' in S Jasanoff and others (eds), *Handbook of Science and Technology Studies* (London, Sage Publications, 1995); B Latour, *Science in Action. How to Follow Scientists and Engineers through Society* (Cambridge MA, Harvard University Press, 1987); M Lynch and S Woolgar (eds), *Representation in Scientific Practice* (Cambridge MA, MIT Press, 1990); A Pickering (ed) *Science as Practice and Culture* (Chicago, University of Chicago Press, 1992).

[112] S Jasanoff, 'The Idiom of Co-Production' in S Jasanoff (ed), *States of Knowledge: The Co-Production of Science and the Social Order* (London, Routledge, 2004) 3. See, more generally: PK Feyerabend, *Against Method* (London, Verso, 1993); T Kuhn, *The Structure of Scientific Revolutions*, 2nd edn (Chicago, University of Chicago Press, 1970).

In that regard, accountability and legitimacy are, therefore, also key to risk regulation. Foucault's account of governmentality neglected the matter of legitimacy, which is perhaps understandable given the central objective of his work was to decentre the state and sovereignty in analyses of power. However, since the state remains important, even as its functions have been governmentalised and integrated in wider circuits of governing the global, it and state-like organisations like the EU remain the singularly accountable sites of power in late modernity. As such the legitimacy of such organisations and meeting their legitimation needs become vital concerns—as Black points out, the rhetoric of risk is a 'useful *legitimating* device' (emphasis added).[113] Public perceptions are an important part of legitimation efforts in that, as Power explains, they present a source of 'institutional risk', that is, a risk to the standing and reputation of the institution. Consequently managing that risk entails attempts at governing '*unruly perceptions*' and maintaining the '*production* of legitimacy in the face of these perceptions' (emphasis added).[114]

These matters become even more important in contexts of uncertainty or non-knowing about, inter alia, the type and scale of risk, such as in relation to the pandemics and other serious cross-border threats to health discussed in chapter five, and where the dominant modes and techniques of scientific and technical knowledge and expertise are undermined even as they remain central to decision-making. Brownsword points out that in these circumstances 'the legitimacy crisis becomes acute'[115]—and linking back to the discussion above, in this context citizen participation (with the focus on procedures for its facilitation) is seen as a key way of achieving accountability and legitimacy, if not through the contribution of knowledge.[116] As discussed in chapter six, citizen participation has become an increasingly important tool or technology for the EU's risk-based governance and regulatory interventions in general and is implicated in the fabrication of the boundaries of responsibility and the legitimation of the regulatory process[117] and its outcome that is, helping to foster trust and confidence in the safety of people and things in circulation within and into the internal market.[118] As I go on to explain, sensitivity to the 'institutional risk' posed by public perceptions and the wider importance of the legitimation of the EU's risk-based technology are key resources—providing a 'way in'—for enhancing citizen participation in decision-making and with it governance and its regulatory interventions.

[113] J Black, 'The Emergence of Risk-Based Regulation and the New Public Risk Management in the United Kingdom' (2005) *Public Law* 512, 519.

[114] M Power, *Organized Uncertainty* (Oxford, Oxford University Press, 2007) 21.

[115] Brownsword, n 4 above, 131.

[116] On the necessity of public engagement, see: DJ Fiorini, 'Citizen Participation and Environmental Risk: A Survey of Institutional Mechanisms' (1990) 15 *Science, Technology & Human Values* 226.

[117] Black, n 113 above; J Black, 'Tensions in the Regulatory State' (2007) *Public Law* 58.

[118] *Cf* G Bache, ML Flear and TK Hervey, 'The Defining Features of the European Union's Approach to Regulating New Health Technologies' in Flear and others (eds), n 13 above.

C. Neoliberalism

A supplementary and key resource for improving the shape and role of citizen participation is provided by an appreciation of the deployment, operation and implications of neoliberalism as that which undergirds EU governance and its regulatory interventions, and how that relates to the production and legitimation of the EU's identity, socio-political order and project of European integration. At the present time, in what is often called late modernity, governmentality and especially the central relationship between markets and security and the prominence of risk regulation, operates within, and is (re)organised by, neoliberal political rationality.[119] Recognition of the latter supports the second argument made in this book in particular, while providing the foundations for the subsequent arguments. Neoliberalism increasingly fuses governmentality with technical reason and means-end, or instrumental, market rationality. The latter is actively disseminated through the organisation of governance 'at a distance'[120] and related concepts of self-managing and sovereign subjects, in order to extend existing power relations and optimise life.[121] As a twist to the understanding of security within governmentality that will become salient to the discussion on preparedness planning in chapter five, and chiming with growing awareness of the importance of 'institutional risk', within neoliberalism there is an increasing focus on the protection of vulnerable *governance*—signalling reflexive governance as an approach—rather than vulnerable populations. Dean points out reflexive governance works by 'securing the mechanisms of *government*. Society itself can be changed, according to this view … through *transformation of the mechanisms* by which it had previously been governed' (emphasis added).[122]

More deeply, neoliberalism works to (re)configure several key relationships, such as those between governance and the governed, knowledge and power, sovereignty and territoriality, and power and responsibility. Through a focus on techniques, processes and practices I bring out how EU governance and its regulatory interventions are making use of, and being (re)organised by and within, neoliberalism. As that which undergirds the EU's risk-based technology governing public health, neoliberalism is central to attempts made at not just renegotiating but also more clearly delimiting the boundaries of responsibility and accountability. Further, within neoliberalism knowledge is increasingly made to serve power; and the latter is itself extended, even as governance itself is presented as limited. In effect, as mentioned above, governance is extended in terms of what

[119] Described as 'a way of doing things that … [is] oriented to specific objectives and that … [reflects] on itself in characteristic ways': N Rose, P O'Malley and M Valverde, 'Governmentality' (2006) 2 *Annual Review of Law Society and Science* 83, 84.

[120] M Dean, *Governmentality: Power and Rule in Modern Society*, 2nd edn (London, Sage Publications, 2009); H Kemshall, 'Social Policy and Risk' in G Mythen and S Walklate (eds), *Beyond the Risk Society* (Maidenhead, Open University Press, 2006).

[121] R Flynn, 'Health and Risk' in Mythen and Walklate, ibid.

[122] Dean, *Governmentality*, n 120 above, 226.

it covers (from knowledge creation to material interventions), the places where it applies and people enfolded in its operation and in relation to whom it has effects. Neoliberalism also implies the legitimacy needs of formally accountable sites of power, such as the EU, become ever more important as they also tighten their relations with science and technology,[123] and citizens engage with this reflexively as a 'knowledge society'.[124] Through the discussion in the first part of the book these (re)configurations will emerge as the structuring themes of the EU public health policy domain and are important to the subsequent discussion in the second part where they are suggested to open up spaces and possibilities for citizen participation.

A key implication of the operation of neoliberalism that is central to the project pursued in this book and the discursive strategy for enhancing citizen participation put forward in chapter six is the following. As Ong explains, in a move that seeks to efface the normative from governance, and depoliticise and naturalise, its objects 'are recast as non-political and non-ideological problems that need *technical solutions*' (emphasis added).[125] The effect of depoliticisation serves to, as Brown puts it, remove or mask those phenomena and subjects from comprehension of their '*historical* emergence and from a recognition of the *powers* that produce and contour [them]' (emphasis added).[126] In other words, the phenomena and subjects produced by the discourses appear to be naturally occurring. Normative matters, including the norms, values and socio-political imaginaries reflected in and underpinning governance, are obscured by the framing of public health problems as matters of risk necessitating technical solutions. This framing renders as natural and non-political both the techniques, processes and practices through which it is operationalised *and* their attendant paradoxes, pitfalls and blind spots, such as those related to the distribution of resources and other benefits and vulnerability. The framing, underpinned by neoliberalism, constrains the space for and frustrates biopolitics as well as citizen participation in decision-making.

Aiding this depoliticisation and naturalisation is the way in which risk individualises and responsibilises through notions of self-management. These work with the focus on the autonomous, rational, 'relentlessly self-interested subject of liberalism'[127] in law and especially human rights and bioethics, which discursively erases differences between citizens and their attendant disadvantages. Neoliberalism helps to support a number of broader trends in (public) health.

[123] Brown, *Regulating Aversion*, n 95 above, 15; Jasanoff, *Designs on Nature*, n 95 above, 5–6.

[124] D Bell, *The Coming of Post-Industrial Society: A Venture in Social Forecasting* (Harmondsworth, Basic Books, 1976); M Castells, *The Rise of the Network Society (= The Information Age, Vol I)* (Oxford, Blackwell, 1996); K Knorr Cetina, *Epistemic Cultures. How the Sciences Make Knowledge* (Cambridge MA, Harvard University Press, 1999); N Stehr, *Knowledge Societies* (London, Sage Publications, 1994).

[125] A Ong, *Neoliberalism as Exception: Mutations in Citizenship and Sovereignty* (London, Duke University Press, 2006) 3.

[126] Brown, *Regulating Aversion*, n 95 above, 15.

[127] W Brown, *States of Injury* (Oxford, Princeton University Press, 1995) 25, in the aptly titled 'Introduction: Freedom and the Plastic Cage'.

Over 10 years ago Montgomery noted there was a shift 'of emphasis *away* from collective and environmental work, *towards* a concentration on *individual responsibility* and *lifestyle issues*' (emphasis added).[128] The latter is seen in relation to, say, new diagnostic technologies, which make possible certain discourses on risk for those trying to determine their individual risk of cancer.[129] The shift towards reflexive governance might help to further obscure the normative content of legal and regulatory decisions, which remains concealed by and within the design of governance and its regulatory interventions. This effect might be abetted by the abovementioned tendency of legal and regulation studies scholarship to not delve deeper into the normative dimensions and consequences of the production, dissemination and wider use of the knowledge that underpins decision-making.

As that which undergirds the risk-based technology governing public health neoliberalism is also central to efforts at producing and legitimating the EU's socio-political order and project of European integration. This implies that the EU's prominence in news media 'status' updates such as those mentioned at the outset, and more detailed information provided online,[130] is not merely functional as an indispensable adjunct to the EU's core internal market project. Rather, the reports can also be understood as instances of the EU seizing hold of the opportunity to demonstrate its use and 'added value' in the face of 'public health threats'—and even 'emergency'. Indeed, the salience of public health—its centrality to how we live, the universally acknowledged desirability of health,[131] and its place as a core component and focus of formally accountable power and sovereignty—is also useful to the EU's integration project. When viewed from a governmentality perspective the EU's risk-based technology is of use as a support for producing and legitimating the EU's socio-political order and project of European integration, by ensuring it meets public needs and values, and tracks public opinion.[132]

D. Biopolitics and 'The Governed' as Citizens

The discussion in this book all relates, in one way or another, to the (re)configuration of relations between governance and the governed. Indeed, the sheathing of the normative and political within the technical, the alignment of scientific

[128] Montgomery, n 30 above, 23. This is part of a trend brought about by three key public health trends: changes in death rates or mortality; developments in the incidence of ill-health or morbidity; linked to that, changes in the understanding of what constitutes 'health' (averred to in discussion of definitions in the previous section and the influence of the WHO's definition).

[129] A Robertson, 'Biotechnology, Political Rationality and Discourses on Health Risk' (2001) 5 *Health* 293.

[130] Eg: 'Avian Influenza' ec.europa.eu/dgs/health_consumer/dyna/influenza/; 'Communicable Disease Threats Report (CDTR)' www.ecdc.europa.eu/en/publications/surveillance_reports/communicable-disease-threats-report/Pages/default.aspx.

[131] Richman, *Medicine and Health*, n 25 above.

[132] See, eg: 'Influenza H1N1' ec.europa.eu/health/communicable_diseases/diseases/influenza/h1n1/docs/eurobarometer_summary_20100224.pdf. For further discussion, see ch 6.

and technical knowledge and expertise to economic and political power, and the way in which that limits the potential for citizen participation (ie the third argument advanced in this book), when combined with the effects of depoliticisation and naturalisation, reduces and (re)structures the space between the economic and the social in liberalism, which in turn limits the space for biopolitics. As Ong explains, in terms of the relations between governance and the governed, neoliberalism 'reorganises connections among the governing, the self-governed, and political spaces, optimizing conditions for responding technically and ethically to *globalised uncertainty and threat*' (emphasis added).[133]

Nevertheless, as I have already noted, and as described in detail in chapter six and relating to the fourth argument advanced throughout the second part of the book, the governing technology's framing by risk (made out in the first argument), the (neoliberal) foundations of governance (outlined in making out the book's second argument) and its paradoxes, pitfalls and blind spots (implicated in making out the first argument), as well as the importance of legitimation and the shaping of public perceptions in that regard, open up space and create possibilities for citizen participation in decision-making in spite of the limits on its current shape and use (the third argument). These normative dimensions can be brought out by citizen participation that uses the discursive resources within governance itself in order to generate supplementary knowledge for decision-making (specifically, the legitimating discourses of human rights, bioethics and developing notions of (supra-)stewardship responsibility for public health). The extension of governance in terms of what it covers (from knowledge creation to material interventions), the places where it applies and the people enfolded in its operation and in relation to whom it has effects, is not without implications for those who come to comprise 'the governed'.[134] As I explain in chapter six, in relation to public health governance these include those with underlying medical conditions, limited access to education and economic resources, pregnant women, children and itinerants. Another notable group is non-EU citizens residing in Europe (including undocumented migrants), a group that often has difficulty accessing health services and health insurance and tends to experience more health problems than 'regular' EU citizens.

In this light the 'citizen' in citizen participation is unsettled and expanded to encompass more than those in possession of formal EU citizenship, that is those

[133] Ong, *Neoliberalism as Exception*, n 125 above, 14.

[134] Here I join with scholarship in citizenship studies: 'the claim that citizenship requires territorially bounded community is under challenge from theorists and activists who propound conceptions of "cosmopolitan citizenship", "global citizenship", "transnational citizenship", "postnational citizenship", "diasporic citizenship", and the like—and what we might call, collectively, the "citizenships of globalisation"'. MS Williams, 'Nonterritorial Boundaries of Citizenship' in S Benhabib, I Shapiro and D Petranović (eds), *Identities, Affiliations and Allegiances* (Cambridge, Cambridge University Press, 2007) 228.

who are also nationals of an EU Member State.[135] Importantly, resonating with the Foucauldian understanding of power that is foundational to this book, and recognised in STS (in its critique of the current institutionalisation of participation noted above), as well as in sociology and anthropology in particular, those citizens are endowed with agency. Those that are governed are increasingly (self-) reflexive,[136] purposive actors who engage in automatic monitoring of social reality. These subjects come to know themselves and relate to others through the prism of different knowledges and biomedical knowledge is foremost in the context of public health.[137] Through reflection on and application of this knowledge citizen participation might disrupt or destabilise the formal attempts to delineate and distribute responsibilities and accountabilities—and even renegotiate them so as to (re)responsibilise those who make (political) choices over the framing, nature, shape and direction of governance. The chief function of this book is to furnish discursive tools for participation that might (re)frame and (re)shape governance and sketch out some areas for attention by citizens in their attempts to demand and contest decision-making.

IV. OVERVIEW

The insights traced in the previous section are deployed in order to meet the book's aims and advance the related arguments over its two parts. The first part of the book proceeds in a broad brush fashion to trace how risk and security relate to markets, and how ethics and human rights relate to that central relationship, where they can be discerned at all. The next chapter sketches the EU's formal legal competence in the field of public health and situates it within the wider programmatic concerns of the overarching architecture of governance, especially the production and legitimation of the EU's identity, socio-political order based upon a competitive, innovative and optimised market-based economy and project of rule aimed at European integration. Subsequently I sketch the working out of competence through the more specific strategy aimed at consolidating,

[135] In the EU context see especially Art 9 TEU and Arts 20–24 TFEU (read with Art 18 TFEU on non-discrimination on the basis of nationality), which establish EU citizenship and its rights. Art 20(1) TFEU states 'Citizenship of the Union is hereby established. Every person holding the nationality of a Member State shall be a citizen of the Union. Citizenship of the Union shall be additional to and not replace national citizenship'. For further discussion, see: D Kostakopoulou, 'Ideas, Norms and European Citizenship: Explaining Institutional Change' (2005) 6(2) *Modern Law Review* 233.

[136] U Beck, *Risk Society: Towards a New Modernity* (London, Sage Publications, 1986); A Giddens, *Modernity and Self-Identity* (Cambridge, Polity Press, 1991). Foucault did not have a theory of reflexivity, but for such an addition to his thinking see: J Butler, *The Psychic Life of Power* (Stanford CA, Stanford University Press, 1997).

[137] Recognised in terms such as 'biological citizenship': A Petryna, *Life Exposed: Biological Citizens After Chernobyl* (Princeton NJ, Princeton University Press 2002); N Rose and C Novas, 'Biological Citizenship' in A Ong and S Collier (eds), *Global Assemblages: Technology, Politics, and Ethics as Anthropological Problems* (Oxford, Blackwell Publishing, 2005). See further, ch 6.

orchestrating and directing the technology governing public health and the policy domain as a whole.

The market-oriented rationale of that strategy is explained and elaborated by reference to its principles and objectives. Of those the principle of putting health in all policies is discussed more extensively for the ways in which it brings out the contours and underpinnings of the domain and its normative orientation and direction. Impact assessment as knowledge-based policy-making and then monitoring, measuring and evaluating as ways of governing through agency and performance are identified as being particularly important governing technologies. After which the growing importance of the EU's role as a security actor and its importance for the production of legitimacy are underlined. Finally, the importance of structured cooperation as the key approach for the EU's strategy is highlighted, and that is followed by discussion of funding through health programmes as a particular way of influencing and regulating national authorities, populations and individuals.

The discussion in chapter two is filled out across chapters three, four and five, which focus on the specific public health problems of, respectively, cancer, HIV/AIDS and finally other pandemics and serious cross-border threats to health. Overall these chapters explain how the various techniques, processes and practices governing the respective problems are aligned to and configured by and within the overarching architecture and its programmatic concerns via the more specific strategy for the public health policy domain. This selection of case studies for the chapters is justified by the research agenda for this book, which focuses on tracing the core contours and underpinnings that are constitutive of the technology governing public health and policy domain.

There are three further reasons for the selection. The first is that the EU's governance of public health is typically organised around specific problems. The second reason for the selection is that these three examples provide a combination of the EU's longstanding and more recent areas of engagement in public health, encompassing communicable and non-communicable diseases, and governing in the face of varying degrees of risk and more recently uncertainty and non-knowing. The selection is therefore quite comprehensive in terms of the types and range of public health risks regulated by EU governance. The final reason for this selection is that the individual case studies are likely to be models for the governance of other public health problems and the regulatory interventions adopted, and in that regard it includes the most important examples (as apparent from a reading of the EU's documentary record). The selection is therefore likely to be extensive enough to permit the breadth and depth of analysis required for the research agenda pursued in this project, which uses public health as a prism through which to examine a cluster of key issues in EU studies and contribute towards 'law and public health'.

Chapter three discusses the EU's approach to cancer, situates it within the wider governance of major and chronic diseases and conditions, and then links the specific EU partnership approach to governing cancer to the overarching architecture via the public health strategy. Through an analysis of the rationale and objectives of the cancer partnership, its areas and actions for a comprehensive policy response, and finally the stress on steering national responses, knowledge production and governing through the agency and performance of actors are noted as centrally important to the EU's approach. The thrust towards extending and deepening EU involvement at the national level is the final point. Chapters four and five highlight the growing importance of a stronger focus at the EU level on the securitisation of public health, that is, the regulation of the dangers or threats to the circulation of people and things. While the external dimension of EU governance is noted in relation to cancer, it is in relation to these other public health problems that it gains in prominence.

Chapter four examines the EU's governance of HIV/AIDS, touches on and explains its importance by reference to the wider governance of sexually transmitted illnesses and communicable diseases, and again emphasises the securitisation of public health, in particular through an emphasis on prevention and the internal and external dimensions of governance. The discussion again links the EU's approach to HIV/AIDS in its territory and neighbouring countries to the overarching architecture via the public health strategy. The significance of the focus on external governance understood as governing the EU's periphery and beyond is noted as particularly important to the EU's developing identity and security and public health actor. The main contours of the EU's governance are given prominence and noted as including a focus on distributed responsibilities. After which the centrality of prevention and attention to most at risk regions and societal groups and finally knowledge (again) are highlighted.

Chapter five looks at EU level preparedness planning for pandemics (like influenza) and an apparently open-ended cluster of other serious cross-border threats to health. The chapter begins by sketching the very recent genesis of this aspect of public health governance at the EU level. Security, and especially regulation of risk (through preparedness), is again emphasised as a key preoccupation of the internal and external dimensions of EU regulation. The chapter stresses how the focus is, as in relation to HIV/AIDS, on ensuring the operation of the market, that is, the free circulation of people and things within the internal market. Again ethics and human rights seem to be used more as legitimating devices for the security of the free movement market imperative.

The outline of the contours, underpinnings and techniques, processes and practices of the technology governing public health and the policy domain in these chapters comprises the main contribution of the first part of the book, and provides the platform for the second part, which diagnoses citizen participation itself as an underdeveloped technology and therefore 'the' key concern of this book and makes a prescription for enhancing and powering it as a way of improving governance and its regulatory interventions. The diagnosis is made in chapter six, which begins by summarising the findings in the first part of the book, in particular, highlighting the defining features and risk as the dominant framing for the governing technology, but one that is underpinned by and oriented towards market optimisation understood as being about the circulation of people and things. The chapter identifies the (re)configurations ongoing in governance—those between governance and the governed, knowledge and power, sovereignty and territoriality, and power and responsibility—as the structuring themes of the EU level of the multi-level system of public health governance.

The discussion then moves to make use of these findings by considering the implications of the EU's governance of the public health problems for biopolitics and the role, use and configuration—the institutionalisation—of citizen participation in decision-making. The discussion draws on the previous chapters to describe how the defining features, dominance of risk and the structuring themes undergirding governance open space and provide possibilities for citizen participation in governance. I nominate the legitimating discourses of human rights and bioethics, and the developing notion of (supra-)stewardship responsibility, as the discursive means and strategy for facilitating and powering discussion—for public querying—around framing, distribution and vulnerability that generates supplementary knowledge on the paradoxes, pitfalls and blind spots attendant to governance. I explain how these latter provide a 'way in' for participation impelled by the threat that, if unaddressed, regulatory failures and 'societal risks' could produce 'institutional risks' that undermine and delegitimate the EU's governance, identity as a security and public health actor, socio-political order and project of European integration.

The final two chapters deploy the discursive strategy by using a broad brush approach in order to underline the normative dimensions of the technical through a cluster of related examples. Chapter seven examines the normative dimensions of framing and explains how the focus on risk directed towards economic optimisation produces a distortion of governance priorities and a related preference for technological and medical regulatory interventions. Subsequently, the implications for knowledge production are discussed by reference to the examples of indicators and clinical trials. Throughout the focus is on the implications for distortions in the focus of governance, the distribution of attention and resources and vulnerability. The discussion on clinical trials focuses on their performance abroad for the simple reason that it helps to throw normative concerns into sharper relief.

Chapter eight builds on the discussion in the previous chapter to tease out some of the implications of regulatory interventions in the field of public health. The focus is on vulnerability and the consequences for that given the skewing of attention and resources towards magic bullet responses and technological fixes. Pharmaceuticals are the focus of the discussion since, for reasons summarised in chapter six and underlined in chapter eight, they are seemingly the intervention that receives increasing attention and resources within this governance, especially as it relates to the external sphere. Chapters seven and eight underline the importance of citizen participation in querying the techniques, processes and practices of governance itself, including knowledge creation and extending to regulatory interventions.

In chapter nine I overview the key findings, reconsider my initial concern about the current role, use and configuration of citizen participation in light of the foregoing discussion, and explain whether and if so how the mix of pessimism and optimism that prompted the book has changed. Overall, through this book I hope to prompt ongoing critical reflection on the roles and uses of citizen participation in governing and make a case for its continued relevance, both as a value in itself, and for the enhancement of the quality of governance and regulatory interventions.

Part I

Governing Public Health

2

EU Public Health Governance: From the Overarching Architecture to the Health Strategy

I. INTRODUCTION

IN THIS CHAPTER I sketch the overarching level of European Union (EU) governance and some of its central techniques, processes and practices. In the next section I provide a sketch of the EU's formal legal competence in the field of public health and situate it within the wider programmatic concerns of the overarching architecture of governance, especially the production and legitimation of the EU's identity, socio-political order and project of rule. Subsequently, I trace how the formal boundaries of EU responsibility and accountability provided in law are gradually filled out through governance. That proceeds in the third section where I outline the working out of competence through the more specific strategy aimed at consolidating, orchestrating and directing the public health policy domain as a whole through techniques, processes and practices of governing at a distance. The market-oriented rationale, principles and objectives of the strategy is explained. The principle of putting health in all policies is discussed more extensively for the ways in which it brings out the contours and underpinnings of the domain and its normative direction. Several sets of techniques, processes and practices, or governing technologies are identified as particularly important: first, impact assessment as knowledge-based policy-making and then monitoring, measuring and evaluating as ways of governing through agency and performance. After which the growing importance of the EU's role as a security actor and its importance for the production of legitimacy are underlined. The final section overviews the structured cooperation approach and focuses on the example of funding through health programmes as a particular way of influencing the behaviours of national authorities, populations and individuals in ways that are conducive to the aims of the policy domain.

This chapter provides the foundations for the platform assembled over the first part of this book, which is the basis for the discussion in the second part. This chapter advances the first two of the main arguments of this book. The first of the arguments is that the key contours for the technology governing public health and its policy domain are markets, risk and security, and ethics and human rights. However, it shall quickly become apparent that risk is the dominant framing. In addition, risk is directed towards achieving security understood as being about regulating the dangers or threats attendant to the circulation of people and things within the internal market. Ethics and human rights will emerge more as legitimating devices for this risk-based regime rather than as freestanding frames.

In this chapter I shall also seek to advance the second main argument, which is that neoliberalism undergirds, configures, orientates and directs the governing technology and policy domain. In that way neoliberalism is central to attempts at establishing the boundaries of EU responsibility. As well as the latter attempt at delimiting the boundaries of responsibility and accountability, the extension of market reasoning by and through neoliberalism also ensures knowledge is increasingly made to serve power. The latter will become especially clear in terms of what the EU's governing technology purports to cover and the places and people it seeks to govern and in relation to whom it has effects. These (re)configurations are central to neoliberalism and in this chapter they begin to emerge as the structuring themes of the policy domain. Finally, I point out how the themes are embedded within, reflective of and central to efforts at producing and legitimating the EU, its identity, related imagined socio-political order of market actors and ultimately the project of European integration. Overall, this analysis will provide starting points for the other main arguments of this book, which are advanced in the second part of the book. There I shall diagnose citizen participation as a key concern given how it is underdeveloped and undermined and make a prescription for enhancing it, and through it governance and its regulatory interventions.

II. THE EU AND PUBLIC HEALTH: LEGAL COMPETENCE, GOVERNANCE AND RESPONSIBILITY

A. Legal Competence

Perhaps most striking about the engagement of EU law with public health, as found in its written texts or sources, is the prominence of the market and the way in which public health relates to that in shaping the boundaries of responsibility. Indeed, within the EU free movement is privileged by the centrality of the internal market in its foundational Treaties (as amended).[1] Establishment of the internal market is required by Article 3(3) Treaty on European Union (TEU) and it is defined in Article 26(2) Treaty on the Functioning of the European Union (TFEU) as 'an area without internal frontiers in which the *free movement* of goods, persons, services and capital is ensured' (emphasis added). Moreover, free movement is linked to security as part of the EU's mission, for instance, in the Preamble to the TEU at Recital 12, where the Member States are 'resolved to facilitate the free movement of persons, while ensuring the safety and security of their peoples, by

[1] After the Treaty of Lisbon, which came into force on 1 December 2009, these comprise a skeletal (and amended) TEU which is fleshed out in the TFEU (replacing the EC Treaty).

establishing an area of *freedom, security and justice*' (emphasis added).[2] Article 3 TEU elaborates and states the EU shall:

> offer its citizens an area of freedom, security and justice without internal frontiers, in which free movement of persons is ensured in conjunction with appropriate measures with respect to external border controls, asylum, immigration and the prevention and combating of crime.

Elsewhere, in the TFEU provisions on free movement of goods,[3] persons[4] and services,[5] public health is recognised and protected through express derogations,[6] and supplemented by justifications created through the jurisprudence of the Court of Justice of the European Union (CJEU).[7] These provisions concern negative harmonisation (they are de-regulatory) and are supplemented by the possibility of positive harmonisation (re-regulation) through the adoption of legislation under (principally) Article 114 TFEU for the establishment and functioning of the internal market. The internal market is an area of shared competence under Article 4(2)(a) TFEU. Under Article 9 TFEU the 'the Union *shall take into account* requirements linked to ... *a high level of ... protection of human health*' (emphasis added) in the definition and implementation of its policies and activities. Consistent with the latter provision, Article 114(3) requires the European Commission (Commission) to take 'as a base a high level of protection' of, inter alia, health, 'taking account in particular of any new development based on scientific facts'. In short, public health articulates to the core focus of the internal market in which risk is instantiated as being about regulation of the dangers or threats attendant to the circulation of people and things. Public health is protected at either the Member State level (where measures restrictive of free movement are justified) or through EU level legislation. The regulation of public health is however underpinned by and directed towards the continued functioning of the market—and in this way the regulation of public health is governmentalised, in that it is about ensuring the optimal circulation of people and things.

[2] For a summary of legislation see: europa.eu/pol/justice/index_en.htm. For discussion: N Walker (ed), *Europe's Area of Freedom, Security and Justice* (Oxford, Oxford University Press, 2004). See further: D Kostakopoulou, 'The Area of Freedom, Security and Justice and the European Union's Constitutional Dialogue' in C Barnard (ed), *The Fundamentals of EU Law Revisited* (Oxford, Oxford University Press, 2007).

[3] Arts 28–36 TFEU.

[4] Arts 45–48 TFEU on workers and Arts 49–55 TFEU for establishment.

[5] Arts 56–62 TFEU for services.

[6] In relation to goods there is a public health derogation to Art 34 TFEU which prohibits quantitative restrictions on imports and measures having equivalent effect in Art 36 TFEU as 'the protection of health and life of humans, animals or plants' (this derogation is also available in respect of Art 35 TFEU, which mirrors Art 34 in relation to exports). Public health is also available as a derogation to the free movement of workers in Art 45 TFEU and to the freedom of establishment and freedom to provide services in Art 52 TFEU (made applicable to services by Art 62 TFEU).

[7] Eg: Case 120/78 *Rewe-Zentrale AG v Bundesmonopolverwaltung für Branntwein ('Cassis de Dijon')* [1979] ECR 649; Case 178/84 *Commission v Germany (Beer Purity)* [1987] ECR 1227; Case C-76/90 *Säger v Dennemeyer* [1991] ECR I-4221; Case C-55/94 *Gebhard v Consiglio dell'Ordine degli Avvocati e Procuratori di Milano* [1996] ECR I-4165; Case C-237/94 *O'Flynn v Adjudication Officer* [1996] ECR I-2617. See further: C Barnard, *The Substantive Law of the EU: The Four Freedoms*, 4th edn (Oxford, Oxford University Press, 2013).

Moreover, this implies internal and external dimensions to governance: regulation of the circulation of people and things *within* and *into* the internal market.

Building on these legal foundations more specific attention is given to public health in Article 168 TFEU, formerly Article 152 EC Treaty (EC),[8] for which the Commission's Directorate General for Health and Consumer Protection (DG Santé—before the new European Commission in 2014 it was known as DG SANCO) is responsible. Under Article 6 Treaty on the Functioning of the European Union (TFEU) health is an area of supporting and complementary competence where EU action can provide 'added value'. Article 168 underlines that the primary responsibility lies with the Member States, but, consistent with Article 6 TFEU, EU action is essentially limited to incentive measures. This underscores how public health has gradually become a more important area of EU responsibility even as it is still limited in scope and provides the basis for governing at a distance. Article 168(1) reflects Article 9 TFEU and even builds on it (given the requirement merely to take health protection 'into account' is found only in the latter) by stating a '*high level of human health protection* shall be ensured in the *definition and implementation of all Union policies and activities*' (emphasis added). However, such mandatory action is only complementary to Member State policies, and it must be of 'added value' in order to be compliant with the principles of subsidiarity[9] and proportionality[10] under Article 5 TEU.

More particularly Article 168(1) goes on to state the complementary and limited nature of EU action in mandatory terms:

> Union action, which *shall complement national policies*, shall be directed towards *improving public health, preventing* physical and mental illness and diseases, and *obviating sources of danger to physical and mental health.* (Emphasis added)

Actions to address these issues:

> shall cover the fight against the major health scourges, by promoting research into their causes, their transmission and their prevention, as well as health information and education, and monitoring, early warning of and *combating serious cross-border threats to health.* (Emphasis added)

Finally, the EU 'shall complement the Member States' action in reducing drugs-related health damage, including information and prevention'.

The limited nature of EU competence is underlined by Article 168(7) TFEU, which states the EU must also respect Member State responsibilities over 'the *definition* of their health policy and for the *organisation and delivery* of health services and medical care' (emphasis added).

The addition of the mention of combating serious cross-border threats to health to the text of the former Article 152 EC by Article 168(1) seems intended

[8] This was previously Art 129 European Community Treaty, which was introduced by the Treaty of Maastricht in 1992. The Treaty of Amsterdam renumbered Art 129 EC with Art 152 EC.

[9] Art 5(3) TEU.

[10] Art 5(4) TEU.

to reflect and codify the EU's growing and developing governance of pandemics and other serious cross-border threats to public health. Article 168(5) TFEU specifically precludes the adoption of harmonisation measures and underscores the complementary nature of EU competence.

However, Article 168(2) provides the legal base for the adoption of measures, including guidelines and indicators, exchange of best practice, and mechanisms for periodic monitoring and evaluation,[11] which include the Open Method of Coordination (OMC). This is itself an amendment of the original legal competence for action in public health found in Article 152 EC. In addition, Article 168(5) TFEU provides for the adoption of:

> incentive measures designed to protect and improve human health and in particular to *combat the major cross-border health scourges*, measures concerning monitoring, *early warning of and combating serious cross-border threats to health*. (Emphasis added)

Article 168(2)(1) TFEU provides that within the areas covered by the article the EU '*shall encourage cooperation*' and '*if necessary, lend support* to their action' (emphasis added). Moreover, reinforcing Article 4(3) TEU on the principle of sincere cooperation, the Member States are required to work in liaison with the Commission to coordinate among themselves their policies and programmes in the areas referred to Article 168(1) TFEU.

Further, of particular interest to transnational—indeed, international—communicable public health problems is the formal basis for the EU's external relations in the public health under Article 168(3) TFEU. This provides that both the EU and its Member States '*shall* foster cooperation with *third countries* and the *competent international organisations* in the sphere of public health' (emphasis added). Overall, Article 168 TFEU provides the scope for greater coordination between Member State law and policy and thus more intrusive engagement in public health, despite the emphasis on the EU providing 'added value'.[12] In sum, again the focus is on the regulation of circulation of people and things *within* and *into* the internal market, and as such cooperation and coordination are required, and a range of techniques, processes and practices are available to produce specific responses to public health problems.

Although public health is recognised and protected in the EU's constitutional legal order, and it might be thought to operate as a counterweight to free movement (perhaps seen most vividly in Article 3(3) TEU's reference to 'a highly competitive *social* market economy' (emphasis added), which seemingly prefigures the internal market), it is commonly thought that there is an inherent bias towards the economy in the EU's constitutional make-up, which ensures the subordination and

[11] *Cf* ML Flear, 'The Open Method of Coordination on Health Care After the Lisbon Strategy II: Towards a Neoliberal Framing?' (2009) 13(1) *European Integration online Papers*, available at: eiop.or.at/eiop/texte/2009-012a.htm.

[12] As required by the principle of subsidiarity in Art 5(1) and (3) amended Treaty on European Union (TEU).

devaluing of non-economic values, such as public health.[13] This is indeed apparent given the centrality of the internal market and the way in which public health relates to it. Moreover, although Article 168 TFEU augments EU responsibility for public health, the competence and therefore responsibility is supportive of and complementary to that of the Member States. The scope of permissible action is also clearly defined and limited as such. This should also be read within the context of the focus on the internal market. That is, Article 168 strengthens the scope for the regulation of threats or dangers to the cross-border circulation of people and things to be regulated, this in order to ensure their continued circulation and the functioning of the internal market.

In addition, and in common with the international level[14] and mentions in the laws of its Member States,[15] within the EU's constitutional legal order health is not

[13] See generally: M McKee, E Mossialos and R Baeten, 'The Implications of European Law for Health Care' in M McKee, E Mossialos and R Baeten (eds), *The Impact of EU Law on Health Care Systems* (Brussels, PIE-Pieter Lang, 2002) (although quite old, still a key piece); V Hatzopoulos, 'Health Law and Policy: The Impact of the EU' in G de Búrca (ed), *EU Law and the Welfare State: In Search of Solidarity* (Oxford, Oxford University Press, 2005).

[14] World Health Organisation (WHO), *Constitution of the World Health Organisation* (Geneva, World Health Organisation, 1948) 14 UNTS 185; Art 25 Universal Declaration of Human Rights (10 December 1948) UNGA Res 217A (III), UN Doc A/810, 'Everyone has the right to a standard of living adequate for the health and well-being of himself and his family, including food, clothing, housing and medical care and necessary social services'; Art 12 International Covenant on Economic, Social and Cultural Rights (16 December 1966, entered into force 3 January 1976) 993 UNTS 3, speaks of 'the highest attainable standard of physical and mental health'. At a regional level the Member States of the EU are parties to the European Social Charter (Revised) (3 May 1996, entered into force 1 July 1999) ETS 163. This declares the 'bare bones' of health to be as follows: 'everyone has the right to benefit from any measures enabling him to enjoy the highest standard of health attainable' (Article 11); 'anyone without adequate resources has the right to social and medical assistance' (Article 13). Part II adds the 'flesh' to these bones. Under Art 11 the signatory countries have undertaken: to remove so far as possible the causes of ill-health; to provide advisory and educational facilities for the promotion of health and the encouragement of individual responsibility in matters of health; and to prevent as far as possible epidemic, endemic and other diseases, as well as accidents. The European Convention on Human Rights (4 November 1950, entered into force 3 September 1953) ETS 5 (ECHR) lacks an explicit provision dealing with 'health care'. Yet, it is conceivable that the right to life in Art 2 includes a right to health and a resulting responsibility of the Member States of the EU (signature states must take reasonable steps to protect life (*Osman v UK* [1999] 1 FLR 193), though it is less clear whether this includes a right to health care and the requirement that states provide it (*X v Ireland* (1976) 7 DR 78; *Association X v United Kingdom* (1978) 14 D&R 31). Other references to health are contained in: Art 24 United Nations Convention on the Rights of the Child (20 November 1989, entered into force 2 September 1990) 1577 UNTS 3; Arts 11, 12 and 14 Convention on the Elimination of All Forms of Discrimination against Women (18 December 1979, entered into force 3 September 1981) 1249 UNTS 13; Art 3 Convention for the Protection of Human Rights and Dignity of the Human Being with regard to the Application of Biology and Medicine: Convention on Human Rights and Biomedicine (4 April 1997, entered into force 1 December 1999), ETS 164 (Oviedo Convention) and its additional Protocols. See Further: J McBride, 'Protecting Life: A Positive Obligation to Help' (1999) 23 *ELR Human Rights Survey* 43; T Murphy, *Health and Human Rights* (Oxford, Hart Publishing, 2013). As for the EU Charter (mentioned in the text) it 'places emphasis on the *institutional duties of states and international bodies* to respect and protect core rights and values as a matter of *obligation*' (J Kenner, 'Economic and Social Rights in the EU Legal Order: The Mirage of Indivisibility' in T Hervey and J Kenner (eds), *Economic and Social Rights Under the EU Charter of Fundamental Rights—A Legal Perspective* (Oxford, Hart Publishing, 2003, 4 (emphasis added)).

[15] Over 100 national constitutions now include provisions on the right to health, the right to health care, or health-related rights such as a right to a healthy environment—see: P Hunt, 'The Human

just an area of EU competence, it is also a right.[16] Albeit originating in the market integration project, where it proved central to achieving a great many legal victories by previously disempowered individuals and social movements,[17] and has helped to highlight social struggles and transform social attitudes,[18] human rights in the EU has long become an accepted and central discourse in its own right. Indeed, Article 2 TEU states that the EU is 'founded on the values of respect for human dignity, freedom, democracy, equality, the rule of law and respect for *human rights*' (emphasis added). Article 6(3) TEU makes 'fundamental freedoms', as guaranteed by the European Convention on Human Rights (ECHR) and 'constitutional traditions common to the Member States', general principles of EU law. Further, Article 6(1) TEU now gives the previously non-binding Charter of Fundamental Rights of the European Union (EU Charter) the same legal status as the Treaties. Within the EU Charter (and resonant with Article 9 TFEU and Article 168(1) TFEU) public health is implicated in

Right to the Highest Attainable Standard of Health: New Opportunities and Challenges' (2006) 100 *Transactions of the Royal Society of Tropical Medicine and Hygiene* 603. There are references to the right to health or health-related rights in the constitutions of several Member States of the EU, eg Belgium (Art 23(1) refers to 'economic, social and cultural rights' and 23(3)(2) states that these rights include the right to 'social security, to health care and to social, medical and legal aid'), the Netherlands (Art 22(1) states that the 'authorities shall take steps to promote the health of the population'), Luxembourg (Art 11(5) observes that the 'law organises social security, health protection'), Italy (Art 32 states that the 'Republic protects health as a fundamental right of the individual and as a concern of the collectivity and guarantees free care to the indigent'), Portugal (Art 64(1) states that 'all have the right to health protection and the duty to defend it and to promote it') and Finland (Ch 2, s 19(3) asserts that the 'public authorities shall guarantee for everyone … adequate social, health and medical services and promote the health of the population'). The United Kingdom, with its unwritten constitution, recognises the responsibility through various Acts of Parliament and subordinate norms (there is a plethora of legislation for the United Kingdom, eg the Health and Social Care Act 2012 (for reform of the English National Health Service—health is a devolved matter and the other components of the United Kingdom (Northern Ireland, Scotland and Wales) have their own legislation)).

[16] For a discussion of the right to health in particular see the references in ch 1, nn 45–47.

[17] Such as on the rights of transsexuals in Case C-13/94 *P v S & Cornwall City Council* [1998] ECR I-2143—an issue which was very far from the minds of the original drafters of the Treaties. On the issue of gay rights see: C Stychin, '"We Want to Join Europe, not Sodom": Sexuality and European Union Accession in Romania' in C Stychin, *Governing Sexuality: The Changing Politics of Citizenship and Law Reform* (Oxford, Hart Publishing, 2003); C Stychin, 'Same-Sex Sexualities and the Globalisation of Human Rights Discourse' (2004) 49 *McGill Law Journal* 951.

[18] Eg Case C-249/96 *Grant v South West Trains* [1998] ECR I-621, in which then European Court of Justice decided that the concept of 'sex' in Art 141 EC did not cover sexual orientation. The case was decided shortly after the adoption of the Treaty of Amsterdam, which introduced Art 13 EC, and provides the Council may adopt legislative measures to combat discrimination in the fields of race, religion, disability, age and sexual orientation in the sphere of employment and vocational training. This meant that a legal challenge by a lesbian employee of a company policy to provide travel concessions to heterosexual partners only was not successful. But the case succeeded in publicising the issue and it contributed to the push for legislation under Art 13 EC. Specifically, Directive 2000/78/EC establishing a general framework for equal treatment in employment and occupation [2000] OJ L303/16 was adopted, which prohibits discrimination on the grounds of religion or belief, disability, age and sexual orientation. The Racial Equality Directive (Directive 2000/43/EC implementing the principle of equal treatment between persons irrespective of racial or ethnic origin [2000] OJ L180/22) has a wider scope, prohibiting discrimination on the grounds of racial or ethnic origin in employment, vocational training, education, social protection, social advantages and access to goods and services (including housing).

the final portion of Article 35 on the right to health care in the mention of human health protection (discussed further in Chapter 6):

> Everyone has the right of access to preventive health care and the right to benefit from medical treatment under the conditions established by national laws and practices. *A high level of human health protection shall be ensured in the definition and implementation of all the Union's policies and activities.* (Emphasis added)

Nevertheless, it is market optimisation that remains the central concern. In that regard the regulation of the dangers or threats to the circulation of people and things is centrally important and as such risk emerges as the dominant framing of EU engagement in public health.

B. The Overarching Architecture and Programmatic Priorities of EU Governance

That becomes even clearer when EU law on public health is situated within the aims, objectives and programmatic priorities and orientation of the overarching level of governance. The delineation of the boundaries of responsibility and accountability is shaped at this broad overarching level and, as I go on to explain, worked out and further specified in policy and the related concrete techniques, processes and practices of the technology governing public health. The technology governing public health and constituting the policy domain is reflective of and embedded within the EU's overall concerns and priorities, which are themselves aimed at producing and legitimating its socio-political order and project of European integration. The key starting point for making out the programmatic priorities of the overarching level of European governance is the 2000 European Council Lisbon Strategy.[19] For instance, research, including into health, was presented as:

> the *driver* for the *production and exploitation of knowledge* [making it] above all a *linchpin* in the implementation of the Lisbon strategy to make Europe the *most* dynamic and competitive, *knowledge-based economy* in the world, capable of sustaining economic growth, employment and social cohesion [by 2010]'.[20] (Emphasis added)

EU funding of projects in the health sphere, especially in relation to research and development was, and continues to be, seen as integral to the creation of a European Research Area, which aims to 'reinvigorate research in Europe',[21] and is linked to the Lisbon Strategy as part of the so-called 'knowledge triangle' of research,

[19] Council of the European Union, *Presidency Conclusions—Lisbon European Council, 23rd and 24th March* (Brussels, 2000). K Armstrong, 'Governance and Constitutionalism after Lisbon' in *JCMS Symposium: EU Governance after Lisbon* (2008) 46 *Journal of Common Market Studies* 413.

[20] European Commission, *Building the ERA of Knowledge for Growth*, COM (2005) 118 final, 2.

[21] European Commission, *Towards a European Research Area*, COM (2000) 6 final, 5.

education and innovation.[22] Importantly, while EU funding is limited by the principle of 'European added value',[23] it is directed at enabling discourse between researchers in different Member States in order to foster economic competitiveness of European industry,[24] and integration.[25] In this way the EU's priorities valorise scientific and technical knowledge and expertise—(re)configuring governance and those who are governed by and through that knowledge and expertise. Another key aspect of the Lisbon Strategy is the role of steering mechanisms in attempting to ensure adherence to the programme, such as through the OMC (noted above).[26] Moreover, public health is implicated in another way: the management of health threats to the economy, through attempts to regulate any dangers attendant to the circulation of people and things that might undermine economic optimisation.

The Lisbon Strategy was subsequently refocused on growth and jobs,[27] linking research into health and the management of health threats even more closely to the central goal of economic optimisation. In 2010 this refocus was intensified in light of the recent global (and European) financial and economic crisis in the Commission 'Europe 2020' strategy for economic growth.[28] Further, references in Europe 2020 to public health bolster the link between it and the economy. For example, health is linked to smart and inclusive growth because, for instance, 'keeping people healthy and active for longer has a positive impact on productivity and competitiveness'. Moreover, linking to the drive for innovation, it is noted as helping to 'make the healthcare sector more sustainable and find new cures for health conditions'. In addition, improving work skills and creating employment are key factors as health 'employs 1 in 10 of the most qualified workers in the EU'. Finally, the increase in older people and its potential impact also provides a key reason with 'financing rising healthcare costs and access to a dignified and independent life for the aging population will be central to the political debate'.[29]

Moreover, of Europe 2020's seven flagship initiatives four are deemed 'most relevant to public health':[30] the Innovation Union; the digital agenda for Europe;

[22] European Commission, *Putting Knowledge into Practice: A Broad-based Innovation Strategy for the EU*, COM(2006) 502 final.

[23] Decision 1982/2006/EC concerning the Seventh Framework Programme of the European Community for research, technological development and demonstration activities (2007–13) [2006] OJ L412/1.

[24] TK Hervey and JV McHale, *Health Law and the European Union* (Cambridge, Cambridge University Press, 2004) 243–44.

[25] R Gusmão, 'Research Networks as a Means of European Integration' (2003) 23 *Technology in Science* 386.

[26] *Cf* Flear, n 11 above.

[27] W Kok, *Facing the Challenge: The Lisbon Strategy for Growth and Employment. Report from the High Level Group Chaired by Wim Kok* (Brussels, European Commission, 2004).

[28] See, generally: 'Europe 2020' ec.europa.eu/europe2020/index_en.htm. Also see: European Commission, *Smart Regulation in the European Union*, COM (2010) 543 final; European Commission, *Europe 2020 Flagship Initiative Innovation Union*, COM (2010) 546 final.

[29] 'Europe 2020—for a healthier EU' ec.europa.eu/health/europe_2020_en.htm.

[30] Ibid.

the agenda for new skills and jobs; and finally the European platform against poverty. To focus on the innovation union[31] it is particularly revealing in that it:

> 'aims to maximise the EU's capacity for innovation and research and channel it towards societal challenges. The European Commission's aim is to make Europe a world-leader in developing innovative ways to promote *active and healthy ageing*—a challenge common to all European countries'.[32] (Emphasis added)

Noteworthy here is how innovation is linked to research, and this is then directed at societal challenges, but these are used to promote the optimisation of ageing, ie an ageing population is to be an economically active one that contributes towards the wider economy.

The latter is made clearer in a pilot project, the so-called European Innovation Partnership on Active and Healthy Ageing,[33] which was launched in 2011. The partnership draws together a variety of actors towards a 'main objective ... to increase the average healthy lifespan in the EU by two years by 2020'. Older EU citizens are to be optimised through ways that seek to 'enable ... [them] to lead healthy, active and independent lives'. Improving the sustainability of social and healthcare systems is part of this. But all of these are then linked directly to economic optimisation, revealing that societal optimisation, including in relation to health, is aimed at that. The point is to 'boost and improve the competitiveness of the markets for innovative products and services that respond to the ageing challenge both at EU and global level, thus creating new opportunities for businesses'.[34]

Another useful example is the agenda for new skills and jobs, the third flagship initiative. The agenda is even more explicit in linking health to the economy in such a way as to instrumentalise the former for the latter:

> [It] will help to highlight the *economic role* of mental health and the health of the workforce. This should result in improved working conditions and workplaces that prioritise the health and well-being of their employees, thus reducing health inequalities, workforce shortages and absenteeism. The EU is also supporting research into the growing incidence of mental illnesses in the work place.[35] (Emphasis added)

The focus on optimising the economy by and through the exploitation of knowledge (such as that produced by research into health)[36] and the creation of patients as consumers of health products and services shapes the wider health policy domain, where it is linked to EU funding of innovation through its Framework Programmes (FP), and now under Horizon 2020, so-called governance by dominium.[37]

[31] 'Innovation union' ec.europa.eu/research/innovation-union/index_en.cfm.

[32] 'Europe 2020—for a healthier EU', n 29 above.

[33] 'European Innovation Partnership on Active and Healthy Ageing' ec.europa.eu/research/innovation-union/index_en.cfm?section=active-healthy-ageing.

[34] 'Europe 2020—for a healthier EU', n 29 above.

[35] Ibid.

[36] 'Commission launches consultation on EU 2020: a new strategy to make the EU a smarter, greener social market' europa.eu/rapid/pressReleasesAction.do?reference=IP/09/1807.

[37] T Daintith, 'The Techniques of Government' in J Jowell and D Oliver (eds), *The Changing Constitution* (Oxford, Oxford University Press, 1994).

For instance, in FP7,[38] even basic research—including on health[39]—is framed as a driver of growth and understood as signifying a forward march of progress,[40] rather than being regarded as a means of increasing knowledge and understanding as ends in themselves.[41] In short, knowledge is produced and commodified, and regulation and governance built on that foundation, in order to foster economic optimisation. Moreover, innovation is not without implications for public health, with risk, safety and responsible regulation being central to the EU's exploitation of new and emerging (health) technologies more broadly. This architecture has been further refined with research and innovation funding now being consolidated under 'Horizon 2020'.[42] What this makes clear is that the creation, use and dissemination of knowledge is increasingly tied to and determined by power; knowledge is not just a support for power, it is also shaped by power. In other words, knowledge and power are co-productive.[43] As discussed below, this relationship is mirrored in the specific concrete techniques, processes and practices of knowledge creation operationalising the priorities of the overarching level of governance in the EU's health strategy.

This overarching architecture was of course preceded by, and now encompasses, other core policy documents, such as *European Governance*,[44] which outlined and sought to further openness, participation, accountability, effectiveness and coherence as the five principles of good governance, and through that model to shape the gathering and use of knowledge for decision-making and the relations between expertise and governance. Importantly, this approach was stimulated by regulatory failures such as the BSE (Bovine Spongiform Encephalopathy) and (subsequent) vCJD (variant Creutzfeldt-Jakob Disease) crises of the 1990s. The crises of the 1990s produced a collapse in consumer confidence, and the responsibility was

[38] Decision 1982/2006/EC, n 23 above.

[39] Eg nanotechnologies are highlighted in the FP7 objectives, in such references as 'the development and validation of new therapies … diagnostic tools and medical technologies'. The activities to be funded include 'Innovative therapeutic approaches and intervention' ie 'To research, consolidate and ensure further developments in advanced therapies and technologies with potential application in many diseases and disorders such as new therapeutic tools for regenerative medicine'. Importantly, much of the focus of FP7 is on 'translational research', which attempts to translate basic research into usable (or marketable) technologies (see: Proposed Priorities for Innovative Health Research 2012, ec.europa.eu/research/health/pdf/fp7-health-2012-orientation-paper_en.pdf).

[40] *Cf* SHE Harmon, 'Motivating Values and Regulating Models for Emerging Technologies: Stem Cell Research Regulation in Argentina and the United Kingdom' in M Freeman (ed), *Law and Ethics* (Oxford, Oxford University Press, 2008).

[41] G Bache, ML Flear and TK Hervey, 'The Defining Features of the European Union's Approach to Regulating New Health Technologies' in ML Flear and others (eds), *European Law and New Health Technologies* (Oxford, Oxford University Press, 2013).

[42] 'Horizon 2020' ec.europa.eu/research/horizon2020/index_en.cfm?pg=home&video=none.

[43] On this term see: S Jasanoff, 'The Idiom of Co-production' in S Jasanoff (ed), *States of Knowledge* (London, Routledge, 2004). See the discussion on knowledge in ch 1.

[44] European Commission, *European Governance: A White Paper*, COM (2001) 428 final. For further discussion on the importance of this document for governance, see ch 5; and on the implications of the document for citizen participation, see ch 6.

seen to fall on failures in the use and institutionalisation of scientific knowledge[45] in Member State and EU structures. As a response, therefore, there was reinvigorated and reoriented risk regulation through the separation of risk analysis and management functions, including, as I have outlined, in the EU's approach to public health (which sees it becoming increasingly important in relation to coordination of responses to cross-border public health problems, but with most key management functions remaining at the Member State level).

Governing public health is increasingly central to producing and legitimating the EU's identity and socio-political order based on and oriented towards a more innovative, profitable and competitive health sector and wider economy in order to foster growth, jobs and prosperity through healthy citizens and freely circulating products and services. That becomes even more apparent through attention to the more specific priorities of the strategy and its operationalisation (at the strategic and overall public health policy level) through risk-based techniques, processes and practices. Importantly, the framing of the governing technology and policy domain by risk and its operationalisation helps to distract attention away from the extension and dissemination of market rationality into the formally non-market domain of public health, and with it the extension of EU governance into a domain that is formally the main responsibility of EU Member States.

III. OPERATIONALISING THE OVERARCHING STRATEGY IN THE FIELD OF PUBLIC HEALTH: *TOGETHER FOR HEALTH*

These broad overarching concerns, and especially the relationship between markets and the regulation of public health through risk, provide the general steer for, and help to constitute, both the EU's technology governing public health and its related policy domain. Central to the achievement of these programmatic concerns and priorities is 2007's *Together for Health: A Strategic Approach for the EU 2008–13*.[46] The framing of the governing technology and policy domain by and through risk becomes even more apparent in this strategy, which works to further delineate the EU's responsibility as a public health actor and its accountability in the event of failure. More than that, the strategy is directly linked to the EU's legal competence under Article 168 TFEU:

> The EC's important role in health policy has been reaffirmed in the Reform Treaty which was agreed by EU Heads of State and Government in Lisbon on 19 October 2007, and which proposes to reinforce the *political importance of health*.[47] (Emphasis added)

[45] M Everson and E Vos, 'The Scientification of Politics and the Politicisation of Science' in M Everson and E Vos (eds), *Uncertain Risks Regulated* (Abingdon, Routledge-Cavendish, 2009).

[46] European Commission, *White Paper, Together for Health: A Strategic Approach for the EU 2008–13*, COM (2007) 630 final; European Commission, *Commission Staff Working Document Accompanying White Paper, Together for Health: A Strategic Approach for the EU 2008–13*, SEC (2007) 1376. For an overview of initiatives, see: European Commission, *Commission Staff Working Document, Report on European Governance (2003–04)*, SEC (2004) 1153. Also see: ec.europa.eu/health/strategy/policy/index_en.htm.

[47] European Commission, *Together for Health*, ibid, 2.

The EU's strategy deals with health and not just public health, and as such it encompasses the fostering of coordination and cooperation between Member States across seemingly the full sweep of health law and policy, ranging from quality of health care, value for money of new health technologies and compensation for cases of medical malpractice incurred abroad. As such it purports to be 'a coherent framework—a first EC Health Strategy—to give direction to Community activities in health'.[48] These were supported by 'broad consultations … [which] show a consensus among stakeholders about how the Community should carry out its role in health' and highlight the importance of collaboration through the 'need for the EC, Member States and stakeholders to work together to *achieve real results*' (emphasis added).[49] Foremost among these results is the way in which the consequent strategy supports and defines, further orientates and directs the governing technology and policy domain, which are in turn reflective of and embedded within the overarching architecture and programmatic level of governance, and aimed at producing and legitimating the EU's identity, socio-political order and project of European integration.

A. The Market-Oriented Rationale

The starting point for making these linked points out is the rationale for EU action, which is based on Article 168 TFEU and is expressed in the following terms:

> Member States have the *main responsibility* for health policy and provision of healthcare to European citizens. The EC's role is not to mirror or duplicate their work. However, *there are areas where Member States cannot act alone effectively and where cooperative action at Community level is indispensable.* These include *major health threats* and *issues with a cross-border or international impact*, such as pandemics and bioterrorism, as well as *those relating to free movement of goods, services and people.*[50] (Emphasis added)

The EU's responsibility and accountability is clearly delimited by the role of the Member States; EU competence is supportive of and complementary to that of the Member States and focused on promoting cooperation in order to tackle specific kinds of public health problems. The EU's role—where it can provide 'added value' in accordance with the principle of subsidiarity—is centred very much on risk, specifically, by regulating the dangers or threats attendant to the circulation of people and things. That encompasses not just the internal market, but also includes a strong international dimension, ensuring that EU governance extends beyond its own territory. In this way the strategy seeks to ensure the EU's

[48] Ibid, 3.

[49] Ibid, 3. At fn 3: 'In 2004, the Commission held an open consultation asking what future health action the EU should take (Reflection process on EU health policy: ec.europa.eu/health/ph_overview/strategy/reflection_process_en.htm). A second consultation was conducted in 2007 on operational aspects and priorities of a future strategy (ec.europa.eu/health/ph_overview/strategy/results_consultation_en.htm)'.

[50] Ibid, 2.

technology—the techniques, processes and practices constitutive of the policy domain—governs at a distance and affects not only those (principally citizens) in the territory of the EU, but also those affected by public health problems that are deemed to constitute major international health threats and issues that threaten the EU. In these ways 'Work on health at Community level adds value to Member States' actions, particularly in the area of *prevention of illness*' (emphasis added).[51]

One of *Together for Health's* key strategic objectives (noted again below) builds on Article 168(1) TFEU to make major threats to health one of the main challenges to be addressed by *Together for Health*, including through the EU's global role and international cooperation with third countries consistent with Article 168(3) TFEU:

> [P]andemics, major physical and biological incidents and bioterrorism pose potential major threats to health. Climate change is causing new communicable disease patterns. It is a *core part* of the Community's role in health to *coordinate and respond rapidly to health threats globally* and to *enhance the EC's and third countries' capacities to do so*. This *relates to the Commission's overall strategic objective of Security*.[52] (Emphasis added)

Here risk is explicitly about producing security, but it is understood as being about the regulation of the dangers or threats to the circulation of people and things rather than the protection of the EU's territory. Moreover, this concern with risk and security is geared towards tackling emergencies involving the EU's territory, its periphery and beyond. As such governing public health emergencies becomes a central concern and constitutes the EU as a *global* public health actor.

But health—achieved through security as free circulation—is directly linked to, reflective of and embedded in the programmatic priorities of the overarching level of governance, especially economic optimisation: 'This Strategy reinforces the importance of health in policies such as the Lisbon Strategy for Growth and Jobs, emphasising the links between health and economic prosperity'.[53] This is augmented by the idea that *Together for Health* '*supports* the overall Europe 2020 strategy' (emphasis added).[54] The latter 'aims to turn the EU into a smart, sustainable and inclusive economy promoting growth for all—one prerequisite of which is a population in good health' (emphasis added).[55] Another example of the pursuit of economic optimisation found in Europe 2020 through the health strategy is the focus on 'investing in health'.[56] These sorts of examples configure and transform the use and function of (public) health for the achievement of the EU's programmatic priorities and ultimately the production and legitimation of the EU's identity, socio-political order and European integration project. Indeed, it is noted that

[51] Ibid.
[52] Ibid, 3.
[53] Ibid, 2.
[54] 'Health strategy' ec.europa.eu/health/strategy/policy/index_en.htm.
[55] Ibid.
[56] Ibid. Also see: European Commission, *Commission Staff Working Document, Investing in Health*, SWD (2013) 43 final; European Commission, *Towards Social Investment for Growth and Cohesion—Including Implementing the European Social Fund 2014–20*, COM (2013) 83 final.

'As well as being a value in itself, health is a precondition for economic prosperity. Efficient spending on health can promote growth'.[57] Moreover, 'Europe needs smart investments in health' and these are threefold: 'spending smarter but not necessarily more in sustainable health systems; investing in people's health, particularly through health—promotion programmes; investing in health coverage as a way of reducing inequalities and tackling social exclusion'.[58]

Several key figures help to support the link between health and the economy and the former's framing by the latter. The end of the list rounds off with mention of 'Differences in life expectancy at birth across the EU Member States: from 8 years for women to 12 years for men' and that 'Major and chronic diseases are responsible for 87% of deaths in the EU (2009)'.[59] A number of other figures begin the list and foreground the economy as being the reference point for attention to health, including that 'Health expenditure in the EU accounts for around 10% of GDP and almost 15% of public spending' and the 'health and social sector workforce accounts for 10% of all jobs in the EU'.[60]

The link between health and the economy therefore helps to provide the key rationale for *Together for Health* and through it the EU's responsibility and accountability for public health framed as a matter of risk regulation in order to generate market security (that is, ensuring the regulation of the circulation of people and things). Moreover, a mid-term review of the strategy found that it 'acts as a reference for actions taken at national and EU levels and confirmed that the principles and objectives identified in 2007 *will remain valid for the next decade in the context of Europe 2020*' (emphasis added).[61] So the link between health and the economy is to be maintained and even strengthened in light of the focus of Europe 2020 on economic optimisation. In short, and as I go on to elaborate in more detail, public health is not just a value and objective in itself. Instead public health is framed by risk, and is about security in that it regulates the market in order to optimise the free circulation of people and things, and it is therefore aimed at facilitating economic growth. The latter is not the ultimate end, but is rather the means chosen for meeting the wider programmatic priorities of producing and legitimating the EU's identity, socio-political order and project of European integration.

B. Overview of Principles and Objectives

The relationships between the overarching level of EU governance, its programmatic concerns, and the strategy shaping the technology governing public

[57] 'Health strategy', n 54 above.

[58] 'Investing in health' ec.europa.eu/health/strategy/policy/index_en.htm.

[59] 'Key figures' ec.europa.eu/health/strategy/policy/figures/index_en.htm.

[60] Ibid.

[61] 'Together for Health' ec.europa.eu/health/strategy/policy/index_en.htm. See further: 'Evaluation' ec.europa.eu/health/strategy/evaluation/index_en.htm. Also see: Public Health Evaluation and Impact Assessment Consortium (PHEIAC), *Mid-Term Evaluation of the EU Health Strategy 2008–13* (ec.europa.eu/health/strategy/docs/midtermevaluation_euhealthstrategy_2011_report_en.pdf).

health and constituting the policy domain, are also reflected in the four core principles—shared health values, 'health is the greatest wealth', health in all policies and 'strengthening the EU's voice in global health'—underpinning three strategic objectives—fostering good health in an ageing Europe, protecting citizens from health threats and supporting dynamic health systems and new technologies—which organise and direct the strategy even more closely. Indeed, as I go on to explain, like the rationale for the strategy, these principles and objectives are in turn tied to, underpinned by and directed at meeting broader aims and priorities found within the overarching architecture and programmatic level of EU governance. That is, the focus is on producing a socio-political order founded upon the improved competitiveness of EU industry, consequent economic growth, an optimised internal market through the circulation of healthy citizens and products and services (especially those related to health), and ultimately the EU's identity as a key global public health regulator and its project of European integration.

As for the first of the core principles, shared health values:

> *Health policy, both internal and external, should be founded on clear values.* The Commission has been working with Member States to define a value-based approach to healthcare systems. In June 2006 the Council adopted a statement on common values and principles in EU healthcare systems, listing the *overarching values of universality, access to good quality care, equity and solidarity.* A new statement on common values for health policy in the broader sense will build on this. The Council has also invited the Commission to take into account and integrate the *gender dimension which the Strategy will take forward.*[62] (Emphasis added)

Rights are mentioned in this context, and it is the EU's own main iteration that is given centrality: 'The Charter of Fundamental Rights recognises citizens' right of access to preventive healthcare and the right to benefit from medical treatment. Several international declarations recognise fundamental rights relating to health'.[63]

It is in relation to rights that participation is mentioned within another core value, citizens' empowerment. This is noted as 'becoming increasingly patient-centred and individualised, with the patient becoming an active subject rather than a mere object of healthcare'. Noting the Citizen's Agenda, which is essentially a forum for discussion among key stakeholders, it is pointed out that '*Community health policy must take citizens' and patients' rights as a key starting point. This includes participation in and influence on decision-making*' (emphasis added).[64] Health literacy is one means noted as key to facilitating empowerment. Participation is also mentioned in relation to a process for determining the consequences of policy, so-called impact assessment, which I discuss further below. However, these mentions of participation need to be read within the context of a series of other policy documents that elaborate on its shape, scope and configuration in relation

[62] European Commission, *Together for Health*, n 46 above, 3–4. For the Council's statement, see: *Council Conclusions on Common Values and Principles in European Union Health Systems* (2006/C 146/01).

[63] Ibid, 4. Citing: Universal Declaration of Human Rights, International Covenant on Economic, Social and Cultural Rights and the Convention on Human Rights in Biomedicine, n 14 above.

[64] Ibid, 4.

to expertise and decision-making, especially *European Governance*,[65] and I return to consider the latter in the second half of the book.[66]

To provide a limited introduction to that discussion, it is important here to note the valorisation of scientific and technical knowledge and expertise as a shared health value. Augmenting the importance of expert knowledge as the foundation for decision-making, 'health policy must be based on the best scientific evidence derived from sound data and information, and relevant research'. Of course, the Commission is central to decision-making, given its right of initiative and role as guardian of the Treaties.[67] But as an addition to this role the Commission—and as a corollary, the EU—are given a central role derived from the 'unique position to assemble comparable data from the Member States and regions and must answer calls for better information and more transparent policymaking, including through a system of indicators covering all levels (national and subnational)'.[68] This (re)configures governance and those who are governed by and through the scientific and technical knowledge and expertise.

The second core principle, 'health is the greatest wealth' reveals further the alignment of (public) health to economic optimisation. Indeed, health is not just a value in itself; as at the overarching level of governance it is actually linked to and framed by the economy as being about the latter's optimisation:

> Health is important for the wellbeing of individuals and society, but a healthy population is also a prerequisite for economic productivity and prosperity. In 2005, Healthy Life Years (HLY) was included as a Lisbon Structural Indicator, to underline that the population's life expectancy in *good health*—not just length of life—was a key factor for economic growth. (Emphasis added)

Linking forward to the importance of health across diverse policy areas, it is noted that 'policy in many sectors has a role in improving health for the benefit of the wider economy'.[69] Health policy is further justified as a contribution to the economy:

> Spending on health is *not just a cost, it is an investment*. Health expenditure can be seen as an economic burden currently amounts to an average of 3% of their Member States' total annual budgets for health compared to 97% spent on healthcare and treatment, but the real cost to society are the direct and indirect costs linked to ill-health as well as a lack of sufficient investment in relevant health areas. It has been estimated that the annual economic burden of coronary heart disease can amount to 1% of GDP, and the costs of mental disorders to 3–4% of GDP. Healthcare spending should be *accompanied by investment in prevention, protecting and improving the population's overall physical and mental health*.[70] (Emphasis added)

[65] European Commission, *European Governance*, n 44 above.

[66] See ch 6.

[67] P Craig and G de Búrca, *EU Law: Text, Cases and Materials*, 5th edn (Oxford, Oxford University Press, 2011) ch 2 'Institutions' and ch 5 'Legislation and Decision-making'.

[68] European Commission, *Together for Health*, n 46 above, 4.

[69] Ibid, 5.

[70] Ibid.

The final italicised portion highlights the reasoning for this investment in health: it is not about maximising health per se. Instead the investment is again about maximising population health in order to optimise the economy.

Finally, health is further instrumentalised as a growth sector in itself, in that it is 'a major provider of employment and training: the health and social care sector has been a key driver of the expansion of the services sector since 2000 (up to 2.3 million jobs)'. Health also functions as part of the wider economy, such as through the take-up of innovative technologies, and it 'supports regional policy and social and economic cohesion'. The centrality of health to economic optimisation is leveraged to justify a growing role for the EU, especially in the gathering and production of knowledge about health on a global scale and through interaction with other key actors:

> The understanding of economic factors relating to health and illness and the economic impact of health improvement both in the EU and globally must be enhanced including through developing information and analysis in the Commission as well as working closely with partners such as countries like the US or Japan as well as international bodies such as the OECD and the European Observatory on Health Systems and Policies.[71]

Overall, in the *Together for Health* strategy health is linked to and deemed key to 'economic prosperity'.[72] Health policy is instrumentalised for economic optimisation; public health is about regulating the dangers and threats attendant to the circulation of people and things. This framing of the EU's governing technology and related policy domain by risk, which is aimed at security in order to produce economic optimisation, is reflective of and embedded within broader programmatic concerns that seek to produce and legitimate governance and its regulatory interventions in public health, and in turn the EU's imagined socio-political order and project of European integration. Significantly, neoliberalism undergirds, orders and directs the EU's approach towards that ultimate end, and that is especially apparent in the rationale, core principles and strategic objectives of *Together for Health* through a series of major (re)configurations. They are between power and responsibility, governance and the governed, knowledge and power, and sovereignty and territoriality, in order to generate economic optimisation. These are part of the extension and dissemination of market rationality into the formally non-market domain of public health.

C. Health in All Policies (HIAP)

The specific orientation and direction of the EU's governance of public health, and its relationship and the significance of its achievement for broader programmatic priorities, is underscored by the strategy's third core principle of health in all policies. Founded upon Article 168(1) TFEU HIAP further highlights the

[71] Ibid.

[72] 'Healthy Life Years' ec.europa.eu/health/indicators/healthy_life_years/index_en.htm.

governmentalisation of security, which is marked by the shift from security as being about the protection of state sovereignty to being about the protection of the EU's population: it is the '*population's* health [which] is not an issue for health policy alone' (emphasis added). The other policy areas encompass:

> regional and environment policy, tobacco taxation, regulating pharmaceuticals and food products, animal health, health research and innovation, coordinating social security schemes, health in development policy, health and safety at work, ICT, and radiation protection, as well as coordination of agencies and services regulating imports.[73]

More specifically, HIAP encompasses attention to health in EU initiatives like the renewed social agenda,[74] the focus on 'health is wealth' found in the overarching economic strategy of Europe 2020, the sustainable development strategy,[75] cohesion policy and its provision of funding aimed at reducing regional economic/ social disparities in Europe,[76] and the implementation of policy through the health programmes (discussed below) and the work of EU agencies.[77]

In addition, coordination among policy areas is facilitated by a Council of the EU working party[78] as well as between Commission departments through a so-called 'inter-service group' aimed at coordinating health across their activities. Special attention is given to health care systems, global health, health and environment, and HIV/AIDS through the work of thematic sub-groups. Health is also a key area of the work of the Social Protection Committee and the Committee of the Regions. Research is the foundation for new technologies, and EU funding through the Framework Programmes and now Horizon 2020 facilitates a focus on eHealth as well as health technology assessment. The latter is 'way of assessing the ways science & technology are used in healthcare and disease prevention. It covers medical, social, economic, and ethical issues'.[79] Finally, a focus on health education among young people working in tandem with WHO Europe's own initiative[80] and health and the environment[81] rounds out HIAP.

[73] European Commission, *Together for Health*, n 46 above, 6.

[74] 'Renewed social agenda' ec.europa.eu/social/main.jsp?catId=547.

[75] European Commission, *Mainstreaming Sustainable Development into EU Policies: 2009 Review of the European Union Strategy for Sustainable Development*, COM (2009) 400 final, 13–15. Also: 'Sustainable Development' ec.europa.eu/environment/eussd/.

[76] Managed by the Member States, the structural funds are coordinated by the Commission, ie the Regional Development Fund is managed by Directorate General for Regional Development, while the European Social Fund is managed by Directorate General for Employment and Social Affairs.

[77] 'EU agencies' ec.europa.eu/health/health_policies/eu_agencies/index_en.htm.

[78] European Council, *Council Conclusions on the Implementation of the EU Health Strategy—Outcome of Proceedings*, Brussels, 20 November 2008, register.consilium.europa.eu/pdf/en/08/st16/st16139.en08.pdf.

[79] 'Health technology assessment' ec.europa.eu/health/technology_assessment/policy/index_en.htm.

[80] WHO Europe, *Children's Environment and Health Action Plan for Europe*, adopted by Fourth Ministerial Conference on Environment and Health, Budapest, Hungary, 25 June 2004.

[81] European Commission, *A European Environment and Health Strategy*, COM (2003) 338 final; European Commission, *The European Environment and Health Action Plan 2004–10*, SEC (2004) 729.

Importantly, HIAP helps to extend the web of relationships between the EU and a range of actors. One example is the partnerships developed by the Commission '*to promote goals of the Strategy*, including with NGOs, industry, academia and the media' (emphasis added).[82] HIAP also helps to establish, mediate and legitimate relationships between the EU and the wider world, since health in *all* policies necessarily concerns the EU's external relations. Indeed, 'This HIAP approach must also be used in *external policies* including development, external relations, and trade. Globalisation means that both *health problems and solutions reach across borders*, and these often have cross-sectoral causes and implications' (emphasis added).[83] In other words, the cross-borderness of public health problems is leveraged by the EU in order to extend and legitimate its role as a *global* actor, which is in turn of use to securing *its* role and wider project of integration amongst its *own* (domestic) population and their national governments and authorities.

The concern with ensuring the circulation of people and things across borders provides the basis for public health governance, that is because it is necessary to regulate the attendant dangers and threats. The latter problems provide the basis for cross-border institutions like the EU and its policies to intervene as (part of) the solution. Through HIAP the reach of the governing technology and policy domain extends far beyond (public) health per se to touch upon and govern other policy domains. The importance of 'Developing *synergies* with these and other sectors' is said to be 'crucial for a strong Community health policy'.[84] Yet, since the EU's governing technology and policy domain are oriented and directed towards the programmatic priorities found in the overarching level of governance, HIAP also facilitates the extension and dissemination of market rationality into wider policy domains, many of which will, like public health, be formally non-market areas. And the latter becomes even more apparent through the operationalisation of HIAP and with it the EU's health strategy—and beyond that the programmatic priorities of the overarching level of governance—through various risk-based techniques, processes and practices that comprise more specific governing technologies.

i. Technologies of Knowledge-based Policy-making: Impact Assessment

The broad contours of HIAP reflect the importance of the regulation of public health threats and dangers across seemingly all areas of EU activity in order to achieve economic optimisation, and how this is of use to the production and legitimation of the EU's identity, the socio-political order and project of European integration. A more specific governing technology or tool facilitating HIAP

[82] European Commission, *Together for Health*, n 46 above, 6.

[83] Ibid. See further: European Commission, *Combating HIV/AIDS within the European Union and in the Neighbouring Countries, 2006–09*, COM (2005) 654 (discussed in ch 4) and European Commission, *EU Strategy for Action on the Crisis in Human Resources for Health in Developing Countries*, COM (2005) 642.

[84] European Commission, *Together for Health*, n 46 above, 6.

is impact assessment (IA) of EU initiatives, which are produced by the lead service within the Commission.[85] This is essentially a technology of knowledge-based policy-making—and as such it highlights the centrality and valorisation of scientific and technical knowledge and expertise to decision-making and the tightening relations between knowledge and power. More specifically, as I go on to explain, the importance of knowledge also further attests to its growing *shaping* by power, in this instance, the needs of EU governance to provide a basis for its decision-making. Although the EU has made a limited attempt at carrying out a *health* impact assessment along the lines of the WHO's model,[86] the IA is far more important as a way of ensuring that health figures across policy domains, at least in principle. IA also (re)configures governance and those who are governed, that is by and through the scientific and technical knowledge and expertise it gathers and centralises as the foundation for decision-making.

IA is described as 'a process that *prepares evidence for political decision-makers* on the advantages and disadvantages of possible policy options by assessing their potential impact' (emphasis added).[87] The lead service prepares the IA and assembles its own and stakeholder expertise in order to define the problem to be addressed and the objectives of the policy response. The steps in formulating the IA help to ensure a case is made for action where the EU has competence (as of course it does in the field of public health), that EU action is justifiable (respecting the principle of subsidiarity in situations where competence is supporting and complementary, such as public health under Article 168 TFEU), and the policy response (legislation or non-binding soft law and more informal measures) is deemed necessary (respecting the principle of proportionality) and directed by clearly defined objectives that address the problem.

There then follows an assessment of the economic, social and environmental consequences of the available policy initiatives.[88] Rounding out the IA process is a comparison of the main options in terms of their effectiveness, efficiency and coherence in solving the problem and a consideration of future monitoring and evaluation to be organised. To focus here on the assessment of consequences, these are the so-called three pillars of sustainability, which mark at least an initial attempt at ensuring sustainable development as a cross-cutting idea founded in

[85] A Renda, *Impact Assessment in the EU: The State of the Art and the Art of the State* (Brussels, Centre for European Policy Studies, 2006); R Salay and P Lincoln, 'Health Impact Assessments in the European Union' (2008) 372 *Lancet* 860.

[86] WHO, 'Health Impact Assessment' www.who.int/hia/en/. For discussion see: M Hübel and A Hedin, 'Developing Health Impact Assessment in the European Union' (2003) 81(6) *Bulletin of the World Health Organization* 463. More generally, see: J Kemm, J Parry and S Palmer (eds), *Health Impact Assessment: Concepts, Theory, Techniques and Applications* (Oxford, Oxford University Press, 2004); J Kemm (ed), *Health Impact Assessment: Past Achievement, Current Understanding, and Future Progress* (Oxford, Oxford University Press, 2012); M O'Mullane (ed), *Integrating Health Impact Assessment with the Policy Process: Lessons and Experiences from Around the World* (Oxford, Oxford University Press, 2013).

[87] 'Impact assessment' ec.europa.eu/governance/impact/index_en.htm.

[88] European Commission, *Impact Assessment Guidelines*, SEC (2009) 92.

the Treaties[89] is factored into all policy domains. As such IA is a central element of the EU's Sustainable Development Strategy (SDS), which was launched at the 2001 Gothenburg European Council.[90] Although prominent in both social and environmental impacts, health is especially prominent in relation to the former.[91]

For example, there is attention to workers' health and their 'rights and obligations'.[92] More importantly, a range of questions are designed to elicit consideration of public health and safety. They include 'Does the option affect the health and safety of individuals/populations, including life expectancy, mortality and morbidity, through impacts on the socio-economic environment (working environment, income, education, occupation, nutrition)?', 'Does the option increase or decrease the likelihood of health risks due to substances harmful to the natural environment?', 'Does the option affect lifestyle-related determinants of health such as diet, physical activity or use of tobacco, alcohol, or drugs?' and 'Are there specific effects on particular risk groups (determined by age, gender, disability, social group, mobility, region, etc.)?'[93] Rights and to a lesser extent ethics (which are arguably inflected in other considerations) are implicated. For instance, rights are given more specific attention, such as in relation to 'Social inclusion and protection of particular groups', 'Gender equality, equal treatment and opportunities, non-discrimination', and 'individuals, private and family life, personal data'.[94]

To begin reflection on IA, the context provided by the power relations that undergird, striate and organise the EU's technology governing public health help to throw the neoliberal underpinnings orienting and directing IA into sharper relief. Indeed, IA is not just an important aspect of the SDS; it is also closely tied to the EU's 'Better Regulation' agenda.[95] IA 'focuses on examining whether the impact of major policy proposals is sustainable and conform to the principles of Better Regulation'.[96] The latter encompass simplification, reduction of administrative burdens, and the use of a knowledge-based approach to legal and regulatory decision-making.[97] The final principle is derived from the Lisbon Strategy's goal of making the EU the most competitive and dynamic knowledge-based

[89] Formulated as a fundamental long-term objective in Art 3(3) TEU and Art 11 TFEU.

[90] European Council, *Gothenburg European Council. 15 and 16 June 2001. Presidency Conclusions.*

[91] For discussion of the integration of health and environment through health impact assessment, see: M Negev and others, 'Integration of Health and Environment through Health Impact Assessment: Cases from Three Continents' (2012) 114 *Environmental Research* 60.

[92] European Commission, *Impact Assessment Guidelines*, n 88 above, 35.

[93] Ibid, 36.

[94] Ibid, 35.

[95] 'Impact assessment' ec.europa.eu/governance/impact/index_en.htm.

[96] European Commission, *Impact Assessment*, COM (2002) 276, 3.

[97] European Commission, *Inter-institutional Agreement on Better Law-making*, 2003/C 321/01bet; European Commission, *Better Regulation for Growth and Jobs in the European Union*, COM (2005) 97 final; European Commission, *A Strategic Review of Better Regulation in the European Union*, COM (2006) 689.

economy in the world.[98] In other words, just as economic optimisation is central to the Lisbon Strategy, it is also central to the rationale for the adoption of IA in policy-making.[99]

Importantly, sustainable development has been narrowed by the subsequent refocusing of the Lisbon Strategy on growth and jobs in 2005[100] and 2010's Europe 2020 strategy. For instance, the latter is: 'about delivering growth that is: *smart*, through more effective investments in education, research and innovation; *sustainable*, thanks to a decisive move towards a low-carbon economy; and *inclusive*, with a strong emphasis on job creation and poverty reduction' (emphasis added).[101] Implemented in part through the seven flagship initiatives noted above, this highlights how sustainable development is subsumed by and within subsequent strategies directed at economic optimisation. And this suggests that IA is a tool that aims to promote economic optimisation—the dominant concern directing the overarching level of EU governance and the achievement of the ultimate programmatic priorities of producing and legitimating the project of European integration.

This analysis is consistent with the findings of others,[102] and can be further exemplified by attention to a few key features of the IA process. These features underscore how not just IA's orientation within EU governance, but also its design is undergirded and shaped by neoliberalism. This is apparent in, say, the fact that IA is essentially an ex ante risk-based and therefore technical process and tool that seeks to identify areas for governance interventions, produces and gathers evidence (knowledge) including that which provides ex post assessments of policy effectiveness, such as indicators. The neoliberal foundations of IA are also apparent in its use of expert analyses in order to audit and justify options, thereby reducing and managing the risk of the option(s) selected, including the 'institutional risk' to the EU, such as in relation to its reputation and public confidence in its legal and regulatory options and eventual decisions. IA is therefore a more specific way of governing at a distance,[103] with various objectives, such as designing 'better policies

[98] European Commission, *Commission Staff Working Paper, Impact Assessment: Next Steps. In Support of Competitiveness and Sustainable Development*, SEC (2004) 1377; European Commission, *Inter-Institutional Common Approach to Impact Assessment*, 2005. ec.europa.eu/governance/impact/docs/key_docs/ii_common_approach_to_ia_en.pdf.

[99] See: European Commission, *Mainstreaming Sustainable Development into EU Policies: 2009 Review of the European Union Strategy for Sustainable Development*, COM (2009) 400 final, 13–15. Also: ec.europa.eu/environment/eussd/.

[100] Kok, *Facing the Challenge*, n 27 above. Also see: European Commission, *Integrated Guidelines for Growth and Jobs 2005–08*, COM (2005) 141; European Commission, *Working Together for Growth and Jobs a New Start for the Lisbon Strategy*, COM (2005) 24.

[101] 'Priorities' ec.europa.eu/europe2020/europe-2020-in-a-nutshell/priorities/index_en.htm.

[102] See further: B Ballantine and B Devonald, 'Modern Regulatory Impact Analysis: The Experience of the European Union' (2006) 44 *Regulatory Toxicology and Pharmacology* 57; A-K Bäcklund, 'Impact Assessment in the European Commission—A System with Multiple Objectives' (2009) 12 *Environmental Science & Policy* 1077; TF Ruddy and LM Hilty, 'Impact Assessment and Policy Learning in the European Commission' (2008) 28 *Environmental Impact Assessment Review* 90.

[103] For discussion, see: T Richardson and M Cashmere, 'Power, Knowledge and Environmental Assessment: The World Bank's Pursuit of "Good Governance"' (2011) 4(1) *Journal of Political Power* 105.

and laws', facilitating 'better-informed' decision-making, 'early coordination within the Commission',[104] and public communication of these.

To focus on problem definition, the initial step in the IA process, this involves explaining:

> [W]hy the existing or evolving situation is not sustainable, and why public intervention may be necessary. Public intervention is normally justified on the grounds of market/regulatory failures, or because of equity concerns or a discrepancy between the fundamental goals of the EU and the existing situation. In practice, the need for intervention often arises from a combination of these reasons.[105]

So a range of legal principles inform and shape IA and serve to provide the basis for decision-making on the basis of the option(s) selected. I have already noted the legal basis for EU action under Article 168 TFEU and how it provides scope for public health oriented reasons for intervention. This again demonstrates how the assessment of the risk of EU activities on policy is explicitly integrated in the process of problem definition, as well as how IA is also a risk-based technology in that it is partly an exercise in rendering the EU auditable and inspectable, a point I return to below in relation to indicators.

Objectives are formulated and set out in order to provide an 'understanding of what a future policy is supposed to achieve'. They underpin and provide a crucial support for governance, for without them:

> [I]t is difficult to identify possible courses of action, and even more difficult to compare policy options. Objectives provide the only effective criteria for assessing the success or failure of the proposed policy options. Without clear objectives it is also impossible to monitor implementation of the policy and to evaluate whether it has produced the desired effects. Finally, setting objectives is a key step in determining the level of ambition of any policy and in linking it to existing Community policies.[106]

Importantly, in shaping the objectives of the policy response there is a requirement to 'Ensure that the objectives are coherent with existing EU policies and strategies, such as the Lisbon and Sustainable Development Strategies, respect for Fundamental Rights as well as the Commission's main priorities and proposals'.[107] Since, as I have argued, economic optimisation is of central importance to the first two examples[108] this requirement actually seems to ensure that the framing that occurs through both the definition of the problem to be addressed and the objectives of the policy response is underpinned by and directed towards achieving that central purpose. In other words, the shape, design and use of IA as a governance

[104] European Commission, *Impact Assessment Guidelines*, n 88 above, 6.

[105] Ibid, 21.

[106] Ibid, 27.

[107] Ibid, 5.

[108] For discussion, see: ML Flear and T Pfister, 'Contingent Participation: Imaginaries of Sustainable Technoscientific Innovation in the EU' in E Cloatre and M Pickersgill (eds), *Knowledge, Technology and Law* (Abingdon, Routledge, 2014).

tool implicitly favours the EU's overarching and programmatic priorities, which narrows and potentially forecloses the range of possible (and permitted) policy responses (they are designed out) and creates an implicit bias towards others, that is those oriented towards markets (they are designed in).

In this way, IA as a specific technology of governance is reflective of and embedded within the concerns and priorities of the overarching level of EU governance and its programmatic concerns and priorities.[109] This is not only apparent at the level of framing, but also in the other concrete steps in the process. So, for example, in relation to consideration of the economic, social and environmental consequences of policy initiatives, there is no guarantee that health per se, or indeed rights and ethics, will trump wider objectives of IA, and foremost among them, economic optimisation as the EU's central concern. Indeed, the consideration of health and other matters as impacts after problem (and issue) definition limits the potential for it to be considered as a value in itself, rather than as a value that is instrumentalised for economic optimisation. Consideration of economic, social and environmental impacts seems something of an afterthought. They appear to be at least partly 'tick box' exercises aimed at minimising risks to the EU's standing and reputation ie key 'institutional risks'. Of course consideration of these kinds of risk arguably raises institutional awareness of the different impacts of the policy options selected. Yet, even as it might be shown that the option with the 'best' or least adverse impacts is chosen, the process works to legitimate the choice(s) already made within the neoliberal frame.

As another specific example of a concrete step in the IA process, the second to last step—a comparison of the main options in terms of their effectiveness, efficiency and coherence in solving the problem identified at the start—notably involves cost-benefit analysis. Cost-benefit analysis, with its weighing of costs and benefits is explicitly about reducing costs to the economy and increasing benefits in order to optimise under the guise of regulatory simplicity and effectiveness. This sort of calculation might determine that non-market values such as health are costs, since they are not always readily reducible to market optimisation as a clear benefit. Together these tools of analysis not only further demonstrate the infiltration and deployment of market rationality in policy-making; they also highlight how the circuit is completed and the framing of IA as being about promoting economic optimisation seeks to instrumentalise non-market values such as health and makes ethics and human rights concerns more like legitimating devices. The final step in the IA process—a consideration of future monitoring and evaluation to be organised—raises additional points, and links to indicators, and so I consider its salience below.

More deeply, IA as a whole reflects the (neoliberal) (re)configuration between knowledge and power. Specifically, IA is an instance of the widespread turn

[109] For discussion see: L Kolakowski, *Positivist Philosophy* (Harmondsworth, Penguin, 1972).

towards evidence based policy-making,[110] including within medicine[111] and public health,[112] which is in turn reflective of wider reorientations of legal and regulatory decision-making towards 'what works'[113] and reflexive governance, including at the EU level.[114] This ensures a focus on empirical evidence of effectiveness rather than an ideological tussle over the ends of law and policy, including social purposes, and the means adopted to achieve them. In other words, IA has 'quasi-scientific ambitions'.[115] IA builds on a technical—rational model of policy-making; even as it is underpinned and shaped in order to service the EU's particular priorities, IA purports to provide an objective body of knowledge shorn of values and therefore without political content or meaning.

The power effects of this are obvious. IA provides those seeking to make legal and regulatory decisions (in this case the EU) with an important because apparently authoritative, sound, objective and depoliticised basis—a powerful means of convincing those involved in producing decisions and the subjects of them of the appropriateness and justifiability of the option(s) (de)selected. These effects are enhanced through the integration of evidence within a few well-defined and sequential steps, which together constitute IA. These steps augment the apparently rational basis of decision-making, giving the impression that the decision reached is the best and/or only one that could—and should—logically be reached. Resort to IA recognises the constraints of 'bounded rationality'[116] (limits in information available and the time to make a decision) for the quality of decisions, while also seeking to leverage it as the central reason for IA in order to provide a firmer evidential basis for decision-making. The integration of expert analyses within the IA process is not only an attempt to demonstrate they have been taken into account, but also makes the point that in order to become usable and influential in policy expert and scientific and technical knowledge must be presented at the right time and in the right way.[117]

[110] N Cartwright and J Hardie, *Evidence-Based Policy: A Practical Guide to Doing it Better* (Oxford, Oxford University Press, 2012); SM Nutley, I Walter and HTO Davies, *Using Evidence: How Research Can Inform Public Services* (Bristol, Policy Press, 2007); S Owens, J Petts and H Bulkeley, 'Boundary Work: Knowledge, Policy, and the Urban Environment' (2006) 24 *Environment and Planning C* 633.

[111] R McSherry and J Haddock, 'Evidence-Based Health Care: Its Place within Clinical Governance' (1999) 8(2) *British Journal of Nursing* 113; DL Sackett and others, 'Evidence Based Medicine: What It Is and What It Isn't' (1996) 312(7023) *British Medical Journal* 71.

[112] RC Brownson, JE Fielding and CM Maylahn, 'Evidence-Based Public Health: A Fundamental Concept for Public Health Practice' (2009) 30 *Annual Review of Public Health* 175; VG Cesar, J-P Habicht, and J Bryce, 'Evidence-Based Public Health: Moving Beyond Randomised Trials' (2004) 94(3) *American Journal of Public Health* 400; RC Brownson and others, *Evidence-Based Public Health* (Oxford, Oxford University Press, 2010).

[113] HTO Davies, SM Nutley and PC Smith (eds), *What Works? Evidence-Based Policy and Practice in Public Services* (Bristol, Policy Press, 2001).

[114] K Bohme, 'Much Ado About Evidence: Reflections from Policy Making in the European Union' (2002) 3(1) *Planning Theory & Practice* 98.

[115] J Hertin and others, 'The Production and Use of Knowledge in Regulatory Impact Assessment—An Empirical Analysis' (2009) 11 *Forest Policy and Economics* 413, 413.

[116] H Simon, 'Bounded Rationality and Organizational Learning' (1991) 2(1) *Organization Science* 125.

[117] PM Haas, 'When Does Power Listen to Truth? A Constructivist Approach to the Policy Process' (2004) 11(4) *Journal of European Policy* 569.

However, one implication of the tightening relations between knowledge and power seen in IA is that the framing of this governance tool and its design demonstrates the instrumentalisation and shaping of knowledge, from its gathering, to its production and use. This again underscores the centrality and valorisation of scientific and technical knowledge and expertise to decision-making. Indeed, that knowledge and expertise both supports, stabilises and legitimates risk as the central framing of the EU's technology governing public health and the policy domain. And by narrowing and even foreclosing the range of possible (and permitted) policy options within that frame, IA also helps to justify and legitimate what *is* eventually selected. In supporting risk as the dominant framing IA also helps to extend EU governance and power across its territory and beyond (where the policy relates to third countries), and delimit the EU's responsibility and accountability.

In this way the relations between governance and governed are also drawn more clearly. Important for the time being is the way in which IA helps to shape public perceptions, manage, reduce and even forestall contestation, especially around the goals or ultimate end of governance, which are effectively sealed off from public questioning through the process of framing. Hence while IA aims to make the Commission's system accountable and transparent it is on the basis of a constrained range of possible (or permitted) options. This also makes 'political decisionmakers' alone competent to assess supposed value-neutral technical evidence, frame and select the appropriate policy response, while also reducing the scope for ex ante participation as well as ex post contestation. I consider participation further in the second part of the book.

In summary, IA is embedded within and reflective of the choices made at the overarching architecture of EU governance and operationalised in the EU's technology governing public health and constituting the policy domain.[118] IA obscures and depoliticises broader issues of framing and the normative orientation and direction of EU public health governance. IA is not just important for that governance, but its design and use is also shaped by and abets the production and legitimation of the EU's identity as a public health actor, its socio-political order based on a thriving, competitive and optimised market economy, and ultimately its integration project.

ii. *Technologies of Agency and Performance: Monitoring, Measuring and Evaluating*

Developing technologies to survey, measure and report progress with regard to health and not just public health policy continue in a similar vein. In a sense these are also knowledge-based technologies, but more clearly than IA, for example, these can be broadly understood as technologies of agency (that help or can be used to responsibilise actors) and performance (actors are ranked in relation to

[118] P Lascoumes and P Le Gales, 'Introduction: Understanding Public Policy through its Instruments—From the Nature of Instruments to the Sociology of Public Policy Instrumentation' (2007) 20 *Governance* 1.

other responsibilised actors and their performance relative to those others is used to steer or even impel adjustments in their own behaviour (should they fall below the standard or benchmark of best practice) or indeed that of others (where they are either at or above the standard, etc)).[119] Indicators facilitate monitoring and evaluation and are central to the formulation and implementation of policy as the final part of the IA process[120] and therefore of facilitating the third core principle of HIAP. Indicators are an important further concrete technique that supports and facilitates that core principle, as well as being a key component of the strategy put forward in *Together for Health*, and beyond that the wider technology governing public health. According to the Commission:

> *An indicator is a quantitative or qualitative measure of how close we are to achieving a set goal (policy outcome)*. They help us analyse and compare performance across population groups or geographic areas, and can be useful for determining policy priorities. *Health indicators based on reliable, comparable data are essential for designing strategies and policies to improve the health of Europeans, and monitoring their implementation.*[121] (Emphasis added)

More will be said about this important specific technique in the second part of this book[122]—here I introduce indicators and situate them within the EU's strategy for public health policy and the overarching architecture of EU governance. Indicators are one of several ways of auditing and measuring performance originating in the corporate world. Merry notes how these comprise 'technologies that were developed in the sphere of business regulation [but which] have jumped domains to human rights and corporate social responsibility'.[123] As for human rights, indicators are becoming a key way of monitoring human rights compliance,[124] in relation to which they provide 'numerical measures [that] make visible forms of violation and inequality that are otherwise obscured. Statistics on income, health, education, and torture, for example, are useful to assess compliance with human rights norms and progress in improving human rights conditions'.[125]

In other domains there are indicators on global governance, the rule of law, and gross domestic product. Indicators on (public) health are therefore just another example—but, like those others, they are essentially 'an instance of the dissemination of the corporate form of thinking and governance into broader social spheres. They are fundamental to modern forms of governmentality whether in the service of corporate, state, or reform modes of governance'.[126] This observation supports

[119] See further: M Dean, *Governmentality: Power and Rule in Modern Society*, 2nd edn (London, Sage Publications, 2009).

[120] European Commission, *Impact Assessment Guidelines*, n 88 above, 49–50.

[121] 'Indicators' ec.europa.eu/health/indicators/policy/index_en.htm.

[122] Specifically, ch 7.

[123] SE Merry, 'Measuring the World: Indicators, Human Rights, and Global Governance' (2011) 52(3) *Current Anthropology* S83.

[124] Murphy, n 14 above, ch 4 'A Measured Response'.

[125] Merry, n 123 above, S84.

[126] Ibid, S83.

the argument advanced throughout the first part of this book, which is that market rationality and neoliberal (re)configurations are not only integral to the EU's technology governing public health and the policy domain—they are also central to the production and legitimation of the EU's identity, socio-political order based on market optimisation, and the European integration project.

Indicators to evaluate and track the implementation of EU policy in *Together for Health* are in development and are identified[127] as much needed in that there is 'currently little access to systematic "bottom-up" information about how non-legislative EU-level initiatives are translated into concrete action in the member countries'.[128] These indicators will join the current range, the main examples of which are European Core Health Indicators (ECHI), HLY, and several other indicators that provide 'data on a wide range of factors affecting health, such as social, economic and administrative environment'.[129] Examples of the latter type of indicators include those on quality of life,[130] health and environment[131] and drug addiction indicators.[132]

ECHI and HLY are most important for public health governance. ECHI comprise a total of 88 indicators and around 50 of those are based on readily available data and are, therefore, fairly comparable, which is clearly important to creating a single EU policy domain in which Member States are ranked and their performance assessed. There are several main groups of indicators, such as those relating to the following: demographic and social situation and providing data on population, birthrate and unemployment; health status and providing data on, for example, infant mortality and HIV/AIDS; health determinants and providing data on the number of smokers and consumption of fruit and vegetables; and health interventions such as health care services and health promotion. ECHI are useful for policy evaluation *and* the formulation of policy.[133]

There are plans to develop and strengthen ECHI, especially through individual indicators relating to specific public health problems like cancer,[134] as well as their overall governance. For instance:

> As far as governance aspects are concerned *there is a widespread consensus about the need to move away from a project-based approach and pursue the embedding of ECHI into a permanent, institutional mechanism at EU level although not necessarily embodied by*

[127] In: Public Health Evaluation and Impact Assessment Consortium (PHEIAC), *Study to Measure the Implementation of EU Health Policies at National, Regional and Local Levels, Assessing the Utility of Existing Indicators for this Task and Developing New Indicators as Necessary* (2012).

[128] 'Evaluation' ec.europa.eu/health/strategy/evaluation/index_en.htm.

[129] 'Other indicators' ec.europa.eu/health/indicators/other_indicators/index_en.htm.

[130] 'Quality of Life (QOL)' epp.eurostat.ec.europa.eu/portal/page/portal/gdp_and_beyond/quality_of_life/context.

[131] 'Environment and health indicators system' ec.europa.eu/health/indicators/other_indicators/environment/index_en.htm.

[132] 'Key Indicators on Drug addiction' ec.europa.eu/health/indicators/other_indicators/drug_addiction/index_en.htm.

[133] 'Health in all policies' ec.europa.eu/health/health_policies/indicators/index_en.htm#.

[134] See ch 3.

> *means of EU legislation*. The abovementioned mechanism should preferably involve all the relevant public authorities ... since this would give ECHI a more formal recognition. The *ECHI shortlist should also be given a clearer legal status, as this has represented a barrier to its uptake in a number of countries*. It is widely recognised that the *European Commission should play a leading role in this mechanism as the primary coordinator of activities*. This could mean a stronger involvement of DG SANCO or Eurostat although the various options should not be seen as mutually exclusive, since a strong coordination between these two services is deemed at any rate necessary.[135] (Emphasis added)

The HLY indicator is discussed further in the second part of this book;[136] by way of introduction, it provides data on the number of years of disability-free life expectancy or the number of years a person can be expected to live without disability. The indicator is used to monitor health as an economic factor, focus on quality of life, measure the employability of older people and 'monitor progress made by people in access, quality and sustainability of healthcare'.[137] Unlike ECHI the HLY indicator is, therefore, explicitly linked to economic optimisation—and that is underscored by its place as one of the European Structural Indicators prompted by and underpinning the Lisbon Strategy and its successors. An initial proposal to create European Structural Indicators followed the Lisbon European Council[138] and HLY was eventually included in 2005,[139] but 'as a contribution to growth and sustainable development'.[140] This is of course consistent with what I argued above, which is that the architecture and priorities at the overarching level are very much geared towards generating economic optimisation as the means to achieving European integration and instrumentalise public health towards that end, which is seen here in the design, orientation and use of indicators.

Indicators establish the EU as a producer of data that renders national public health care outcomes and policies legible, and open for discussion at the EU level as their performance is ranked and evaluated. Indicators thus provide the basis for the development of a field for EU governance and interventions. Indicators permit what Rouse terms a 'more extensive and finer-grained knowledge', and like other examples this 'enables a more continuous and pervasive control of what people do, which in turn offers further possibilities for more intrusive inquiry and disclosure'.[141] The construction of EU governance suggests that even where indicators are not explicitly linked to economic optimisation, they are nevertheless underpinned by market rationality and function to consolidate governance of the flows

[135] European Commission, *Evaluation of the Use and Impact of the European Community Health Indicators ECHI by Member States* (Brussels, European Union, 2013) 7.

[136] See ch 7.

[137] 'Healthy Life Years' ec.europa.eu/health/indicators/healthy_life_years/index_en.htm.

[138] European Commission, *Structural Indicators*, COM (2003) 585 final.

[139] European Commission, *Report from the Commission to the Spring European Council, Delivering Lisbon, Reforms for the Enlarged Union*, COM (2004) 29/2.

[140] 'Healthy Life Years (HLY)' ec.europa.eu/health/indicators/healthy_life_years/hly_en.htm#fragment4.

[141] J Rouse, 'Power/Knowledge' in G Gutting (ed), *The Cambridge Companion to Foucault* (Cambridge, Cambridge University Press, 2003) 99.

of people and things within and into the territory of the EU, as well as in relation to those who are governed by and through knowledge.[142] As part of this consolidation indicators abet the (re)configuration of knowledge and power through their closer alignment and co-production, as well as the relationship between power and responsibility and accountability.[143]

That is apparent in, for instance, the way in which the Commission is made central to public health governance, and harnesses Member States, their governments and authorities, and makes them complicit in the establishment of the foundation for the EU's technology governing public health and the policy domain.[144] As Foucault observes 'power and knowledge directly imply one another … there is no power relation without the correlative constitution of a field of knowledge, nor any knowledge that does not presuppose and constitute at the same time power relations'.[145] By and through indicators actors' agency is leveraged. Indeed, indicators figure those who are monitored as possessing the capacity to make decisions, account for themselves, and take responsibility as such. Further, the function of indicators as part of monitoring, measuring and evaluating the Member States and prompting a change in their behaviour, demonstrates the role of performance in abetting the responsibilisation of actors.[146] The latter in turn helps to ensure compliance with EU level goals, objectives and ultimately the programmatic priorities in the overarching architecture of governance. Indicators and wider forms of knowledge gathered and produced at the EU level, such as that integrated into IA, open up knowledge domains while at the same time permitting the penetration of the national frame of reference of Member State authorities and a (re)framing in accordance with the EU level.[147]

The effect of depoliticisation attendant to the valorisation of scientific and technical knowledge and expertise by and through the risk-based techniques, processes and practices of governance such as indicators, helps to naturalise the extension of EU involvement in public health and with it neoliberalism. In short, knowledge is reduced to being about promoting the EU's version of market optimisation. The production of knowledge is linked to and reoriented by its place as a key part of the risk-based governing technology and policy domain. But the focus on risk as

[142] E Clarence, 'Technocracy Reinvented: The New Evidence Based Policy Movement' (2002) 17(3) *Public Policy and Administration* 1.

[143] See: HK Hansen and T Porter, 'What Do Numbers Do in Transnational Governance?' (2012) 6(4) *International Political Sociology* 409. For further discussion on numbers and their use in the construction of indicators, see ch 7.

[144] N Rose and P Miller, 'Political Power Beyond the State: Problematics of Government' (1992) 43(2) *British Journal of Sociology* 172; K Mitchell, 'Transnationalism, Neoliberalism, and the Rise of the Shadow State' (2002) 30(2) *Economy and Society* 165. In a different vein see: AM Peña, 'Governing Differentiation: On Standardisation as Political Steering' (2014) *European Journal of International Relations* 10.1177/1354066114523657.

[145] M Foucault, *The History of Sexuality: Volume One, The Will to Knowledge* (London, Penguin, 1998) 27.

[146] On technologies and agency and responsibility see: Dean, n 119 above.

[147] I do not explore reframing further, since the focus is on the current framing.

the dominant framing, and its use for regulating the dangers or threats to the circulation of people and things, effectively shields the field of knowledge creation (the basis for risk-based governance) and the alignment of regulatory processes with market rationality from public accountability.

Viewing indicators and wider technologies of knowledge within the context of the overarching architecture underlines the way in which they are embedded within, reflective of and function as part of the wider project of rule undergirded by neoliberalism. Public health is not just conflated with, but is subordinated to and framed by the economy with the consequence that the visibility and autonomy of EU and national non-market policy domains like public health is undermined. Indicators—as well as IA and other technologies that gather and produce knowledge—help to extend the power relations apparent at the overarching level of EU governance. Indicators also help to constitute the EU's identity as a public health actor, and support the production and legitimation of the ultimate objective of European integration as a central, if not always explicitly acknowledged, reason for the EU's various forays into public health governance.

D. The EU as a Security Actor and the Production of Legitimacy

The discussion has already made clear how the EU health strategy's design—the alignment of its objectives and principles to market-oriented objectives, and their configuration within the overarching architecture of EU governance—is undergirded, shaped and directed towards the EU's efforts at producing and legitimating its imagined socio-political order and project of rule by and through the (hoped for) consequent economic optimisation. The second of the three strategic objectives is also revealing in this regard. As a reminder the first objective of *Together for Health* is fostering good health in an ageing Europe and the third is supporting dynamic health systems and new technologies. The second objective of protecting citizens from health threats is particularly important in that it augments the link between public health and security—with the former being enfolded and underpinned by the latter, which is in turn related to regulating and optimising the circulation of people and things.

This protection is noted as an obligation under Article 168 TFEU and is extended under Article 168(3) to include EU '*responsibility* regarding the health of citizens in *third countries*'. External relations fits within the EU's work on 'scientific risk assessment, preparedness and response to epidemics and bioterrorism, *strategies to tackle risks from specific diseases and conditions*, action on accidents and injuries, improving workers' safety, and actions on food safety and consumer protection'. This is the starting point for proactive action by the:

> Commission … [which] will also focus on challenges that have not yet been fully addressed. *Globally, increased trade and travel have brought new risks by facilitating the spread of communicable diseases.* Combating pandemics or biological incidents and addressing the threat of bioterrorism requires Community-level cooperation and

> coordination between Member States and international actors. *Action is also needed on emerging health threats such as those linked to climate change*, to address its potential impact on public health and healthcare systems ... *A new focus is needed to tackle health threats within and outside the EU.*[148] (Emphasis added)

Perhaps more explicitly than elsewhere this highlights risk as the central frame for EU governance and public health interventions within its territory and *beyond*. This role resonates with the final of the strategy's four core principles (strengthening the EU's voice in global health), which I mention here and detail further later in this part of the book.[149] The EU's growing global role also underscores the extension of its governance and power not just across its own territory but also abroad through the fostering of the specific understanding of security. Moreover, the focus on security, and approaches to risk regulation such as preparedness[150] (rather than precaution)[151] in respect of serious cross-border threats to health, not only points to the securitisation of the EU's technology governing public health and the policy domain, but also to the governmentalisation of security. That is, security is increasingly understood in terms of the optimisation of the health and wealth of non-state *populations* at the EU level (the *EU's* population), and the focus of risk-based governance and interventions is on managing the global and transboundary *circulation of threats* to them.[152]

This notion of security reflects and is underpinned by the (re)configurations between power and responsibility, and sovereignty and territory, and helps to further define and consolidate the EU's responsibility in relation to public health and by implication those who are governed, that is those to whom the EU is responsible and accountable. The EU is not just a public health regulator, it is also a security actor. Indeed, a core concern of the strategy is with constituting the public health policy domain at the EU level through its governing technology—and security helps to make that possible. More clearly, the strategy 'also sets out implementation mechanisms for cooperation between partners, reinforcing Health in All Policies, and *increasing visibility and understanding about health at Community level*' (emphasis added).[153] While law is the foundation for EU responsibility, the latter is drawn more clearly as it is linked with and directed towards the broader framing by risk in order to address security as free circulation and produce economic optimisation.

[148] European Commission, *Together for Health*, n 46 above, 8–9.

[149] The role is important to each of the subsequent three chapters.

[150] Discussed more fully in ch 5 and in summary in ch 6.

[151] It is noteworthy that the precautionary principle does not appear in the EU's strategy, although it is of course salient to specific areas encompassed by public health governance, such as the regulation of food and the environment. See further: European Commission, *Communication on the Precautionary Principle*, COM (2000) 1 and Art 191 TFEU on the environment. For discussion see: M Lee, *EU Regulation of GMOs: Law and Decision-Making for a New Technology* (Cheltenham, Edward Elgar, 2008).

[152] *Cf* M de Larrinaga and MG Doucet, *Security and Global Governmentality* (Abingdon, Routledge, 2010) 17.

[153] European Commission, *Together for Health*, n 46 above, 3.

In other words, security is the central and necessary flip-side to free circulation. The focus on regulating free circulation structures and directs the technology governing public health and shapes the policy domain at the EU level, which is operationalised through a series of concrete techniques, processes and practices (more specific technologies). Moreover, knowledge about population (such as that constituted through indicators) facilitates the governmentalisation of security and the securitisation of public health; a relationship that also underlines the tightening relations between knowledge and power. Those who are governed comprise not only EU citizens in a formal sense, but those residing or moving within the EU's territory, and those in relation to whom the EU governs abroad, now as part of its attempts to foster security. In these ways security is, like the other components of the EU's approach to public health discussed above, integral to the extension of EU power into public health, and beyond that to the production and legitimation of the project of European integration.

IV. STRUCTURED COOPERATION: PUBLIC HEALTH POLICY IMPLEMENTATION AND THE HEALTH PROGRAMMES

A. Structured Cooperation

As an introductory point, the implementation of *Together for Health* builds on the distribution of responsibilities between the EU and its Member States found in Article 168 TFEU, in that the Member States 'must be closely involved in the implementation of the Strategy' and this is to be facilitated through a '*new EC-level structured cooperation mechanism*', with the purposes of advising the Commission and promoting coordination between the Member States. The mechanism has multiple uses in that it should 'assist the Commission in identifying priorities, defining indicators, producing guidelines and recommendations, fostering exchange of good practice, and measuring progress. It will also provide opportunities for local and regional involvement'.[154]

The mechanism supports and enhances the Commission's central position in public health governance. In particular, it bolsters the other techniques, process and practices aimed at governing public health, such as IA and indicators. Indeed, the mechanism assists in the gathering and production of knowledge through them, and their use in monitoring, measuring and evaluating Member State performance. As such the mechanism also enhances governing at a distance, with Member States and sub-national authorities being responsibilised into self-management and then (self-) governed through their performance. Further, cooperation with stakeholders is deemed to assist in that through it 'Value can be added to Member States' action'.[155] Here subsidiarity[156] is used to justify the extension of the Commission's web of relations with civil society actors, who are integrated

[154] Ibid, 10.

[155] Ibid.

[156] As a reminder, that is under Art 5(3) TEU.

through forums such as the Health Forum, the European Alcohol and Health Forum, and the Platform on Diet, Physical Activity and Health. The involvement of civil society actors through 'partnerships' helps to assist in the creation, functioning and legitimation of public health governance.

Together for Health is 'chiefly implemented' and the overarching steer for governance further operationalised through the EU Health Programme,[157] which I discuss below. The health programme is one of several other methods of implementing policy,[158] encompassing legislation, financial instruments, and EU-wide cooperation. Key examples of these are touched on to varying extents in the next three chapters. The health programmes are particularly important and as such warrant an introduction here.[159] The Commission is assisted by the Executive Agency for Health and Consumers. The second programme, for example, was established by legislation[160] and ran from 2008–13 and its three overarching objectives were to improve citizen's health security, promote health and reduce health inequalities, and the generation and dissemination of health information and knowledge. These all in their different ways reflected the further operationalisation of the overarching steer for governance through concrete techniques, processes and practices.[161] For instance, the second objective sought to increase healthy life years and promote healthy ageing, and therefore implemented aims and priorities of the overarching level of EU governance, and in doing so mirrored and extended the concern with economic optimisation found there.

The third objective again highlighted the importance of the gathering and production of knowledge as the basis for governance. Indeed, as noted above, this objective reinforced the EU's capacity to augment and expand its intervention in public health. The importance of governance through knowledge is underlined in the reference to 'exchanging knowledge and best practice on health issues'.[162] This in turn prepares the ground for the dissemination of neoliberalism throughout the public health policy domain and for its circulation both throughout the EU as well as beyond.

To focus on health security, this reflects and implements the second objective of protecting citizens from health threats in *Together for Health*. Indeed it highlights

[157] 'Health programme' ec.europa.eu/health/programme/policy/index_en.htm.

[158] 'Implementation and financing' ec.europa.eu/health/strategy/implementation/index_en.htm.

[159] 'Programme 2008–13' ec.europa.eu/health/programme/policy/2008-2013/index_en.htm.

[160] Decision 1350/2007/EC establishing a second programme of Community action in the field of health (2008–13) [2007] OJ L301/3.

[161] I Bruno, S Jacquot and L Mandin, 'Europeanisation through its Instrumentation: Benchmarking, Mainstreaming and the Open Method of Co-ordination … Toolbox or Pandora's Box?' (2006) 13(4) *Journal of European Public Policy* 519; P Lascoumes, and P Le Gales, 'Introduction: Understanding Public Policy through Its Instruments. From the Nature of Instruments to the Sociology of Public Policy Instrumentation' (2007) 20 *Governance* 1.

[162] 'Programme 2008–13' ec.europa.eu/health/programme/policy/2008-2013/index_en.htm. See further: Decision 1350/2007/EC, n 160 above.

the ongoing securitisation of public health through the implementation of governance. The objective encompasses:

> [D]eveloping the capacity of the EU community to *respond to communicable and non communicable diseases and health threats from physical, chemical and biological sources, including bio-terrorism;* for example with *emergency planning and preparedness measures* [and also] promoting actions related to patient safety through high quality and safe healthcare, scientific advice and risk assessment, safety and quality of organs, substances of human origin and blood.[163] (Emphasis added)

This reveals the scope and nature of securitisation. Covering a huge range of activities, many of which are elaborated across the course of the next three chapters, securitisation is again not just about the protection of the EU or its Member States (ie state sovereignty). Rather securitisation is also and increasingly about ensuring the regulation of the dangers and threats attendant to the circulation of people and things, and this is central to the EU's internal market. Moreover, although the scope of this objective is wide, there seems to be an emphasis put on public health emergencies and ensuring the EU has the capacity to respond, such as through preparedness planning.

B. EU Health Programmes: Steering Through Funding

The operationalisation of the overarching steer for EU governance through the technology governing public health is reinforced by EU funding as a central component. Funding is essentially regulation through 'steering'[164] rather than 'command and control' in that it is used to stimulate and support the development of EU public health policy. At the overarching level of governance there is funding by the Framework Programmes, now part of Horizon 2020. As I mentioned above these essentially instrumentalise public health for the EU's programmatic priority of generating economic optimisation, and through it the production and legitimation of the EU's socio-political order as a competitive economy and the project of European integration. Regional policy is another key example and it is aimed at ensuring social cohesion across the EU through structural funds. Those funds include the European Regional Development Fund that allocated €5bn to health infrastructure investment in 2007–13, and the European Social Fund, which funds health activities linked to ageing, e-health, health promotion and training.[165] Other examples include: funding to support information and communications technology, including in the area of health, although it is explicitly linked to competitiveness and innovation;[166] and the PROGRESS programme[167] supporting

[163] Ibid.

[164] This 'steering' is what Daintith calls 'government by dominium'. See: Daintith, n 37 above.

[165] 'EU Cohesion Policy and Health' ec.europa.eu/health/health_structural_funds/policy/index_en.htm.

[166] 'ICT Policy Support Programme as Part of the Competitiveness and Innovation Framework Programme (CIP)' ec.europa.eu/information_society/activities/ict_psp/index_en.htm.

[167] 'PROGRESS programme (2007–13)' ec.europa.eu/social/main.jsp?catId=327.

the implementation of the EU's objectives in employment, social affairs and equal opportunities. The latter is now integrated into the EU Programme for Employment and Social Innovation (EaSI) aimed at promoting 'a high level of quality and sustainable employment, guaranteeing adequate and decent social protection, combating social exclusion and poverty and improving working conditions'.[168]

The health programmes provide the most important source of funding in the public health policy domain. The first such programme (2003–08) financed 352 projects within other actions,[169] and was followed by the Second Programme of Community Action in the Field of Health (2008–13) noted above,[170] and the (current) Third Programme for the Union's Action in the Field of Health (2014–20).[171] To focus on the latter, funding under this programme is directly linked to supporting Article 168 TFEU, and perhaps more significantly, the priorities of Europe 2020, for which it is noted that the 'promotion of good health at Union level is also an integral part'.[172] EU funding under the programme is reflective of and embedded within and aimed at supporting and meeting the aims and programmatic priorities of the overarching level of governance. That is made apparent in the stress that the programme 'should promote synergies'[173] with the other sources of funding (and doubtless their aims and priorities) and the multiple rationales for EU funding:

> Keeping people healthy and active longer and empowering them to take an active role in managing their health, will have positive overall effects on health, including a reduction of health inequalities, *and a positive impact on quality of life, on productivity and competitiveness, while reducing pressures on national budgets. Support for, and recognition of, innovation*, which has an impact on health, *helps to take up the challenge of sustainability* in the health sector in the context of demographic change; and *action to reduce inequalities in health is important for the purposes of achieving 'inclusive growth'*.[174] (Emphasis added)

The focus on economic optimisation apparent here is underlined subsequently. For instance:

> *[i]n line with the objectives of the Europe 2020 Strategy*, the Programme should focus on a set of well-defined objectives and actions with clear, *proven Union added value*, and concentrate support on a smaller number of activities in *priority areas*.[175] (Emphasis added)

Those priority areas are found in the four overarching objectives: promoting health, preventing diseases and fostering supportive environments, and in doing

[168] 'EU Programme for Employment and Social Innovation (EaSI)' ec.europa.eu/social/main.jsp?catId=1081.

[169] Decision 1786/2002/EC adopting a programme of Community action in the field of public health (2003–08) [2002] OJ L271/1. See further: ec.europa.eu/health/programme/policy/2003-2008/index_en.htm.

[170] Decision 1350/2007/EC, n 160 above.

[171] Regulation (EU) 282/2014 on the establishment of a third Programme for the Union's action in the field of health (2014–20) and repealing Decision 1350/2007/EC [2014] OJ L86/1.

[172] Ibid, Recital 2.

[173] Ibid, Recital 21.

[174] Ibid, Recital 2.

[175] Ibid, Recital 5.

so bearing in mind health in all policies; protecting EU citizens from cross-border threats to their health; contributing to the development of health systems that are innovative, efficient and sustainable; and finally, facilitating improvements to the safety of and access to health care.[176]

In other words, the programme operates within the boundaries of EU responsibility and accountability, and acknowledges Member State responsibilities under Article 168,[177] but it seeks to steer Member State behaviour and extend EU power beyond those formal limits. In that respect, the Member States:

> are *encouraged* to identify health improvement as a priority in their national programmes and *to benefit from better awareness of the possibilities of Union funding for health*. Therefore, *the Programme should facilitate the uptake of its results into national health policies*.[178] (Emphasis added)

Consistent with the principle of subsidiarity funding under the programme is described as the 'means of promoting actions in areas where there is a Union added value' and that includes:

> *[E]xchanging good practices* between Member States; *supporting networks for knowledge sharing* or mutual learning; *addressing cross-border threats to reduce their risks and mitigate their consequences*; addressing certain issues relating to *the internal market* where the Union has substantial legitimacy to ensure high-quality solutions across Member States; *unlocking the potential of innovation in health*; actions that could lead to a *system for benchmarking* to allow informed decision-making at Union level; *improving efficiency by avoiding a waste of resources* due to duplication and optimising the use of financial resources.[179] (Emphasis added)

In short, EU funding seeks to support the full range of actions described elsewhere in this chapter—and more besides. Funding helps to support and it reflects the (re)configurations—the emerging structuring themes—underpinning the EU's public health policy domain. That support is underlined in a number of ways. For example, there is the growing alignment and co-production of knowledge and power, with knowledge being created and developed at the EU level in order to make possible and legitimate evidence-based (and depoliticised) decision-making. In addition, this knowledge is useful for the consolidation and perpetuation of the public policy domain—and the extension of EU power despite the formal and apparently limited boundaries of its responsibility and accountability under Article 168. The constitution of those who are governed by funding as part of the assemblage of components that together constitute the EU's technology governing public health is another structuring theme that is extended and supported by funding.

[176] Summarised in: European Commission, *The Third Health Programme 2014–20 Funding Health Initiatives*, ec.europa.eu/health/programme/docs/factsheet_healthprogramme2014_2020_en.pdf.

[177] Regulation (EU) 282/2014, n 171 above, Recital 7.

[178] Ibid, Recital 8.

[179] Ibid, Recital 6.

Looking at a couple of the areas that receive financial support under the health programme helps to highlight further how EU funding aims and priorities are configured within and directed at meeting the aims of Europe 2020 and the programmatic priorities found at the overarching level of EU governance. Innovation in (public) health is the first example, and it is a key aim, but it is more wide-ranging than focusing on advances in technology, and instead encompasses 'Fostering innovation in the field of public health interventions, prevention strategies, health system management and in the organisation and provision of health services and medical care, including health promotion and disease prevention interventions'.[180] Further, these are noted as having 'the potential to improve public health outcomes', and are ultimately linked back to Europe 2020 in that they are deemed to '*foster the competitiveness* of stakeholders and to *improve the cost-efficiency and sustainability* of health services and medical care' (emphasis added).[181]

The focus on economic optimisation is also underlined by the second example, that is the many references to the importance of using funding in order to bolster the internal market. In that regard it is noteworthy that: '*emphasis should be placed*, in accordance with the principle of subsidiarity, *on areas where there are clear cross-border or internal market issues at stake*, or where there are significant advantages and efficiency gains from collaboration at Union level' (emphasis added).[182] The programme is therefore aimed at supporting such key concerns of *Together for Health* (which of course builds on Article 168 TFEU). Significantly although the legal basis for the health programme is provided by Article 168(5) TFEU,[183] Article 114(3) TFEU (also noted above) is mentioned and used to align EU funding with its goal of ensuring a high level of health protection. That goal is to be achieved through:

> *special efforts to support actions required by, and contributing to, the aims of Union legislation in the fields of communicable diseases and other health threats*, human tissues and cells, blood, human organs, medical devices, medicinal products, patients' rights in cross-border healthcare, and tobacco products and tobacco advertising.[184] (Emphasis added)

In other words, risk is the dominant frame for actions under the health programme and, consistent with the wider framing of the technology governing public health of which funding is a key component, this instantiation of risk is about maintaining security or regulating the dangers or threats attendant to the circulation of people and things. The importance of regulating cross-border flows—and making them visible and governable through funding—is also apparent in the stress on making funds available to third countries and competent international organisations, consistent with Article 168(3) TFEU.[185] As I have argued throughout this

[180] Ibid, Recital 9.

[181] Ibid, Recital 9.

[182] Ibid, Recital 5.

[183] As mentioned above this provides for the adoption of incentive measures designed to protect and improve human health and especially in order to combat the major cross-border public health problems, and measures concerning monitoring, early warning of and combating serious cross-border threats to health.

[184] Regulation (EU) 282/2014, n 171 above, Recital 17.

[185] Ibid, Recital 22.

chapter, while risk frames the governing technology in order to generate economic optimisation through security, it is directed at producing and legitimating the EU's identity, its socio-political order and ultimately European integration.

V. CONCLUSION

This chapter began by outlining the formal boundaries of EU responsibility and accountability before turning to explain their shaping and configuration by, through and within the overarching level of EU governance and subsequently the more specific strategy aimed at consolidating, orchestrating and directing the public health policy domain as a whole. The discussion of the *Together for Health* strategy expanded to provide a fuller picture of specific regulatory technologies or assemblages of techniques, processes and practices. Together these latter comprise the EU's technology governing public health and constitute the policy domain. The discussion in this chapter provides the foundations for the platform assembled over the first part of this book and the starting point for the discussion in the second part of the book.

In providing the basis for that discussion, in this chapter I argued, first, that the key contours for the technology governing public health and its policy domain are markets, risk and security, and ethics and human rights. However, the latter two appear to function more as legitimating devices for risk as the dominant framing. Moreover, risk is attuned towards achieving security understood as being about regulating the dangers and threats attendant to the circulation of people and things within the internal market, and that further configures the EU's responsibility for public health. Despite the limited role of ethics and human rights they should not be dismissed as unimportant for the central project of this book. That is, as I go on to argue in the second part of the book, ethics and human rights can instead be considered as crucial resources for powering discussion and technologies of participation that reveal and underline the distortions, paradoxes and pitfalls attendant to the EU's risk-based governance and its regulatory interventions.

In setting up the subsequent discussion, this chapter also pointed to the importance of neoliberalism as that which undergirds, shapes and directs the EU's governing technology and policy domain. In that regard the discussion underlined the centrality and valorisation of scientific and technical knowledge and expertise to decision-making, and the way in which that (re)configures governance and the governed. More specifically, in addition to the latter a number of other key (re)configurations—between knowledge and power, sovereignty and territoriality, and power and responsibility—have started to emerge as structuring themes that, in addition to risk and security directed at economic optimisation, are important to mapping the full range of openings and possibilities for citizen participation, including the places where it applies and people enfolded in its operation and in relation to whom it has effects. Indeed, the EU seeks to govern public health within its own territory and beyond as part of its growing global role. In these main ways, neoliberalism is central to the EU's efforts at producing and legitimating its identity, related imagined socio-political order based on the internal market, innovative and competitive industries, economic optimisation, and ultimately the project of European integration.

Over the next three chapters I elaborate on the operationalisation of the overarching level of EU governance in order to fill out the first part of this book and round out the sketch of EU public health governance. The latter provides the basis for the discussion in the second part of the book. And it is there that the discussion turns towards the book's ultimate concern: diagnosis of the configuration of and the space for citizen participation in relation to decision-making as a key concern, and a prescription for enhancing its potential contribution of supplementary knowledge.

3

Cancer

I. INTRODUCTION

THE EUROPEAN UNION (EU) has been directly involved in the governance of cancer since the 1980s with the Europe Against Cancer programme.[1] That programme provided political support, funding and cooperation efforts through a partnership approach that, as I go on to explain, has continued to provide the basic model for governance in this area. Cancer was the first public health problem to receive attention after the introduction of what is now Article 168 Treaty on the Functioning of the European Union (TFEU) as the legal basis for health by the Treaty of Maastricht in 1992.[2] Prominent in the web-based overview of EU cancer governance is the introductory statement that the Europe Against Cancer programme was subsequently found to contribute towards a 'reduction of 9% in expected cancer deaths and a 10.5% reduction in risk of cancer death between 1985 and 2000' and being 'associated with the avoidance of 92,573 cancer deaths in the year 2000 in Europe'.[3]

More recently, in 2008 the European Parliament and Council of the European Union (Council) 'have also shown their *political commitment* and given *strategic direction* to future European cancer activities',[4] with the former adopting a resolution on combating cancer in the enlarged EU[5] and the Council producing conclusions on the importance of reducing the burden of cancer.[6] In the next section I introduce the current instantiation of the EU's main intervention in cancer and explain how it is situated within the wider overarching architecture of EU

[1] For discussion of the inception and development of EU cancer governance see: P Boyle and others, 'Measuring Progress against Cancer in Europe: How Has the 15% Decline Targeted for 2000 Come About?' (2003) 14 *Annals of Oncology* 1312. See further: TK Hervey, L Trubek and M Nance, 'The Construction of a Healthier Europe: Lessons from the Fight against Cancer' (2008) 26 *Wisconsin International Law Journal* 804.

[2] Art 129 European Community Treaty was introduced by the Treaty of Maastricht in 1992 and renumbered Art 152 EC by the Treaty of Amsterdam. For discussion, see: R Watson, 'Cancer becomes Public Health Priority for Europe' (1994)(308) 937 *British Medical Journal* 1.

[3] 'Cancer' ec.europa.eu/health/major_chronic_diseases/diseases/cancer/index_en.htm#fragment0. Citing OM Jensen and others, 'Cancer in the European Community and its Member States' (1990) 26(11–12) *European Journal of Cancer* 1167.

[4] European Commission, *Action Against Cancer: European Partnership*, COM (2009) 291 final, 2.

[5] European Parliament Resolution of 10 April 2008 on Combating Cancer in the Enlarged European Union, P6-TA(2008) 0121.

[6] Council of the European Union, *Council Conclusions on Reducing the Burden of Cancer, 2876th Employment, Social Policy, Health and Consumers Affairs Council Meeting*, Luxembourg, 10 June 2008.

governance and the public health strategy outlined in the previous chapter. This is followed by a closer look at the main components of the central EU intervention in cancer, which is through the aforementioned partnership approach. As I go on to explain, this latter way of governing seeks to bring the various techniques, processes and practices by and through which the EU engages with cancer into a more structured and cohesive whole. In this way EU cancer governance is aligned to, reflective of and embedded within the broader technology governing public health and the policy domain, and it—and its life changing and saving successes matter—for producing and legitimating the EU's project of integration.

This chapter therefore continues the mapping exercise begun in the previous one, and in doing so it extends the platform and basis for the diagnosis of the current institutionalisation of citizen participation in governing public health, which is set out in the second part of the book as 'the' key concern. In that regard the chapter advances further the first two core arguments of this book, the first of which is that the EU's governance of cancer demonstrates that risk is the dominant frame for public health problems and central to their (re)framing as matters of EU governance. Moreover, risk is attuned towards achieving security understood as being about regulating the dangers and threats attendant to the circulation of people and things within the internal market. Ethics and human rights shall again emerge more as legitimating devices for that ordering. Treatment of cancer through innovative technologies shall arise as a key priority—but one that is underpinned more by a concern for promoting industrial development and corporate profitability instead of health per se.

The chapter also advances the second core argument of the book, which is that neoliberalism operates in the governance of cancer, particularly in delineating the boundaries of EU responsibility and accountability through attempts at governing at a distance seen in the partnership approach involving responsibilised actors, and in terms of the alignment and co-production of knowledge, governance and power. The use and extension of neoliberalism is in turn part of the EU's broader programmatic priorities and efforts at producing and legitimating its identity, related imagined socio-political order of market actors and ultimately the project of European integration. The key contours and underpinnings of the EU's involvement in cancer will add to the openings and possibilities for citizen participation in governing public health, and provide the basis for the prescription for enhancing and powering technologies of citizen participation as a way of improving governance and its regulatory interventions put forward in the second part of the book.

II. FROM THE OVERARCHING ARCHITECTURE OF GOVERNANCE TO *ACTION AGAINST CANCER: EUROPEAN PARTNERSHIP* VIA *TOGETHER FOR HEALTH*

As discussed in the previous chapter, the strategy set forth in *Together for Health*[7] operationalises the programmatic concerns found in the overarching architecture

[7] European Commission, *White Paper, Together for Health: A Strategic Approach for the EU 2008–13*, COM (2007) 630 final.

of EU governance and thereby constitutes the technology governing public health and the policy domain. The EU approach to the regulation of cancer is part of the governance of major and chronic diseases and conditions—and these are reflective of, embedded and situated within the EU's public health strategy and the broader overarching governance architecture. Cancer is given special prominence, however, probably due to its aforementioned importance to EU public health governance from the 1980s onwards. Chronic diseases 'are diseases of long duration and generally slow progression'.[8] In addition to cancer they include cardiovascular diseases, respiratory diseases, diabetes and mental illness. Overall chronic diseases are among the leading causes of mortality, and within Europe they account for 86 per cent of the deaths.[9] HIV/AIDS is considered a chronic disease 'since the introduction of highly active retroviral therapy'[10]—but as I discuss in the next chapter, it is also communicable and as such it fits more neatly within the EU's governance of such diseases.

Health conditions can also damage the health status of individuals, and the EU provides some guidance via information sheets on a few conditions such as oral health, but overall they receive far less attention. EU action in relation to major and chronic diseases and health conditions is part of a wider international response,[11] which contextualises, supports and legitimates the EU's involvement and approach. The EU's approach involves attempts to deal with risk factors or behaviours such as smoking, alcohol abuse, unhealthy diet and sedentary lifestyle, which if reduced or eliminated can be crucial in prevention. In an effort to make those efforts effective they are '*based on targeted health promotion, prevention and early detection*' (original emphasis).[12] In addition, there is attention to the social and environmental determinants of disease. Tackling inequality becomes important given both the unequal distribution in those with chronic diseases as well as in relation to accessing prevention and control.

Major and chronic diseases and conditions are therefore generally non-communicable, and the EU's approach is to 'efficiently address the challenge of chronic diseases, [using] an *integrated, horizontal approach* … involving all the relevant levels, from communities to policy makers' (emphasis added)[13] in a reflection process instigated by the Council[14] which is itself a way of governing cancer at

[8] 'Chronic Diseases' www.who.int/topics/chronic_diseases/en/.

[9] 'Noncommunicable Diseases' www.euro.who.int/en/what-we-do/health-topics/noncommunicable-diseases. Also see: 'Major and Chronic Diseases' ec.europa.eu/health/major_chronic_diseases/policy/index_en.htm.

[10] 'Major and Chronic Diseases', ibid.

[11] Eg: 'United Nations High-level Meeting on Noncommunicable Disease Prevention and Control' www.who.int/nmh/events/un_ncd_summit2011/en/.

[12] 'Major and Chronic Diseases', n 9 above.

[13] Ibid.

[14] Council of the European Union, *Council Conclusions Innovative Approaches for Chronic Diseases in Public Health and Healthcare Systems*, 7 December 2010.

a distance. The Council's invitation to Member State governments begins by building on *Together for Health's* first core principle of shared health values:

> [T]he principles and overarching values of universality, access to good quality care, equity and solidarity, as endorsed in the Council conclusions on common values and principles in EU health systems of 2 July 2006, are of paramount importance for patients with chronic diseases.[15]

However, this reference to common values[16] is followed by the Council 'recalling' and articulating those shared values in relation to the broader overarching architecture for EU governance as a whole. In this way the governance of chronic diseases and conditions—including cancer—is positioned within and directed at achieving the EU's strategic and broader programmatic priorities.

Similarly, other salient aspects of *Together for Health* are noted, such as those relating to 'fostering good health in an ageing Europe and supporting dynamic health systems and new technologies', while Europe 2020 and its flagship initiatives on poverty and the Innovation Union (also discussed in the previous chapter) are stressed as 'providing for a pilot European innovation partnership in the field of active and healthy ageing'.[17] In light of the discussion on the overarching architecture in the previous chapter, these references point to the broader market-oriented rationale and (re)orientation for EU engagement in relation to chronic diseases and conditions. More specifically, the approach in this area mirrors the EU's way of governing public health sketched in the previous chapter, in that the EU is preoccupied with regulating the dangers or threats to the circulation of people and things. This framing of EU governance of chronic diseases and conditions by risk is therefore aimed at achieving security, which is understood as regulating such public health problems as dangers or threats to free circulation. That regulation is aimed at generating economic optimisation and, as shall become especially apparent throughout the discussion on cancer, delimiting the EU's responsibility and accountability, and meeting the broader programmatic priorities of producing and legitimating governance and its regulatory interventions, and, in turn, the EU's identity as a public health actor, socio-political order and project of European integration.

The EU's initiatives in relation to chronic diseases and conditions include efforts to deal with risk behaviours, integrate policy and action in order to tackle inequalities, address mental health, and improve the health and quality of life of older people and the efficiency of health care systems in line with Europe 2020's European Innovation Partnership on Active and Healthy Ageing. The gathering and production of knowledge is especially important as a condition and support for EU power and governance, such as through the focus on bolstering the European Core Health Indicators (ECHI) by 'making national statistics as reliable

[15] Ibid, 1.

[16] For the Council's statement, see: *Council Conclusions on Common values and principles in European Union Health Systems*, 2006/C 146/01.

[17] Council of the European Union, n 14 above, 1.

and comparable as possible, so they can serve as a good guide to policy effectiveness'. Building on the general discussion of ECHI in the previous chapter, in relation to chronic diseases and conditions this knowledge provides the basis for the EU's risk-based approach, such as by supporting 'public-awareness-raising and disease–prevention campaigns that *actively target high-risk* groups and individuals' (emphasis added).[18]

The EU's cancer governance is a specific instantiation of this integrated and horizontal approach for major and chronic diseases. The European Partnership for Action Against Cancer (EPAAC), which initially ran 2009–13 and is now in its next phase for 2014 onwards with the creation of national action plans which are discussed below, provided the main means of action and is illustrative of the concrete techniques, processes and practices deployed by the EU in this area.[19] Described as 'a sustainable action, following a *partnership approach*, involving a wide range of stakeholders working together in the fight against cancer' (emphasis added),[20] and supported by a joint action for funding under the EU Health Programme, EPAAC was set out in *Action Against Cancer: European Partnership*[21] (*Action Against Cancer*). The latter establishes the target of EPAAC as 'a 15% reduction by 2020 (510,000 new cases)'.[22] Prominent on the webpage is the fact that in 2008 cancer caused 29 per cent of deaths for men and 23 per cent for women[23]—making it the second most common cause of death. This figure is expected to increase in light of demographic changes such as ageing and helps to generate the grounds for EU intervention. Another key ground is inequality, which is apparent in, say, that in relation to lung cancer. The mortality rate in men in the worst performing Member State is over three times higher than in the best performing Member State. In relation to cervical cancer the mortality rate (obviously in women) is almost four times higher in the worst performing Member State than in the best performing Member State. Other inequalities are observed between the sexes, especially in relation to the same cancers. These inequalities, which are discerned from comparisons made on the basis of statistics, highlight how knowledge provides the means for determining the performance of Member States in comparison to others, against which they are, and as I go on to discuss below, can increasingly be ranked.

In light of cancer's risk profile, namely its prominent role in causing mortality, the '[European] *Commission* is therefore continuing its efforts to *support* Member States in their efforts to *protect the health of European citizens* by taking *concrete action*' (emphasis added)[24] through EPAAC. This reflects the idea of protecting

[18] 'Major and Chronic Diseases' n 9 above.
[19] 'Cancer', n 3 above.
[20] European Commission, *Action Against Cancer*, n 4 above, 10.
[21] Ibid.
[22] Ibid, 3.
[23] See further: Eurostat 2008, available at: epp.eurostat.ec.europa.eu/portal/page/portal/health/public_health/data_public_health/main_tables.
[24] 'Cancer', n 3 above.

the population; like wider major and chronic diseases cancer is constituted and regulated as a danger or threat to EU citizens. Given the preoccupation with ensuring the free circulation of people and things within the internal market, this again indicates both the governmentalisation of security and the securitisation of cancer governance. Moreover, neoliberalism undergirds, orders and directs the EU's approach towards that end through the (re)configurations between key relationships or structuring themes of the public health policy domain—power and responsibility, governance and the governed, knowledge and power, and sovereignty and territoriality, in order to optimise life—which were introduced in the previous chapter and are beginning to (re)appear in relation to cancer.

For example, the EU's population is referred to and constituted as being composed of European citizens—configured in relation to governance as 'the governed'—and they are those for whom the EU is responsible. Recognition of the primary role of the Member States and the supportive nature of EU responsibility is also, therefore, an attempt to build on Article 168 TFEU in order to further specify and delimit EU responsibility and accountability in the event of failure. Bringing together and responsibilising a range of actors through the partnership approach to governing cancer permits the extension of EU governance and power. At the same time, like the more general horizontal approach to governing major and chronic diseases and conditions, the partnership approach to cancer further delimits the EU's role and responsibility (and especially the European Commission (Commission's)), which makes it easier for the EU to evade blame in the event of a failure to meet the clearly defined targets for reducing the incidence of cancer. However, in the event of success both the EU and its Member States are able to claim credit, which is especially useful to the former's attempts at legitimating its intervention in cancer governance. In what follows I discuss EPAAC in greater depth, and in doing so I elaborate on the importance of neoliberalism in providing its underpinnings and normative orientation, and the way in which cancer governance is important to the EU's programmatic concerns, in particular the production and legitimation of its identity, socio-political order and the European integration project.

III. EUROPEAN PARTNERSHIP FOR ACTION AGAINST CANCER

A. Overview of Rationale and Objectives

The relationships between the overarching level of EU governance, its programmatic concerns, and the strategy shaping the technology governing public health and constituting the policy domain, are also reflected and elaborated in EPAAC's rationale and objectives. The rationale for EPAAC builds on the differences and inequalities between Member States as follows:

> [T]o support the Member States in their efforts to tackle cancer by *providing a framework for identifying and sharing information, capacity and expertise in cancer prevention and*

> *control, and by engaging relevant stakeholders across the European Union in a collective effort.* As demonstrated by the existing *stark differences and inequalities* in cancer incidence and mortality throughout the Community, there is considerable added value in working together on a European level to *prevent and control cancer* more effectively.[25] (Emphasis added)

Risk is the dominant frame for EPAAC. Consistent with the wider framing of the technology governing public health, as well as major and chronic diseases and conditions, this instantiation of risk through EPAAC is about producing security through the regulation—that is, prevention and control—of cancer as a danger or threat to the circulation of people (and things) within the internal market. Ethics and human rights are arguably inflected in concerns about dealing with differences and inequalities in the burden of cancer across the EU. Apart from that ethics and human rights are largely of marginal importance: as shall become more apparent in the ensuing they are leveraged as part of the starting point for governance, the pursuit of economic optimisation and the EU's programmatic concerns. More specifically, the focus of EPAAC, consistent with the principles of subsidiarity and proportionality that determine the justification and type of EU action,[26] is on producing 'added value' through a partnership encompassing those who are deemed 'relevant stakeholders' in order to gather and produce specific forms of knowledge (information) as well as expertise for the purpose of making cancer prevention and control more effective.

The rationale for EPAAC also makes apparent how the gathering and production of scientific and technical knowledge and expertise is central to it and occurs through various techniques, processes and practices or technologies of governing at a distance. These technologies are foundational to and make EU cancer governance possible. Indeed, the rationale for EPAAC provides the conditions and facilitates (through a framework) the identification and sharing of knowledge and expertise, and following the delimitation and distribution of responsibilities under Article 168 TFEU, ensures (most) implementation is left to the Member States. The EU is able to make a case for the 'added value' and legitimacy of its activities here, by apparently avoiding duplication of Member State activities, while also offering an important support for them. The centrality of scientific and technical knowledge and expertise to governance via the focus on evidence also (re)configures those who are governed, in this case those living with or who are otherwise affected by cancer.

Action Against Cancer has three main objectives: cancer as 'a model for application of the principles of the Health Strategy';[27] maximising years of life in good health; and EPAAC as a collective response to cancer. The first of these objectives places the governance of cancer (and EPAAC) squarely within the wider context of the *Together for Health* strategy noted above and discussed in detail in the previous

[25] European Commission, *Action Against Cancer*, n 4 above, 2.
[26] Art 5(3) and (4) TEU respectively.
[27] European Commission, *Action Against Cancer*, n 4 above, 2.

chapter. This objective therefore makes cancer a central public health problem for the operationalisation of the strategy. However, the burden of cancer noted above is transformed into purely economic terms. Indeed, as 'one of the major causes of ill health in the European Union, *associated with a considerable cost to society*, it is essential to invest in Europe's future health by taking longterm and sustainable actions to tackle cancer'. This is followed by reference to the over '17 million *disability-adjusted life-years* lost'[28] in 2005 due to cancer in the WHO Europe region.

Yet, as mentioned in the second objective, this data drawn from the Healthy Life Years indicator. This measure was stressed in *Together for Health* and introduced in the previous chapter, and shall be discussed later in this book.[29] This indicator is 'used by the Commission to assess the number of remaining years that a person of a certain age is expected to live disability-free, and is *used to monitor health as a factor in productivity and economic prosperity* to support health promotion policies' (emphasis added).[30] In other words, extending the more general approach for the public health domain and elaborating on EPAAC's rationale, reducing the incidence of cancer is made important less (if at all) because health is a value in itself, and more because it is a way of optimising the economy through the regulation of cancer as a danger or threat to a healthy and productive citizenry that can consume products and services. The second objective of *Action Against Cancer* itself links even more clearly to economic optimisation, with the ageing population and the context of the ongoing economic and financial crisis providing additional reasons for EU engagement:

> [C]onsidering the *socio-economic implications* of the expected rise of cancer as the European population ages, it is vital to tackle this disease more effectively in the EU … In these times of *financial instability, it is all the more important* to maintain investments in health, in particular through such preventive actions.[31] (Emphasis added)

The third objective adds to the rationale for EPAAC as well as fleshing out some of its core dimensions. Echoing the mainstreaming of health required by Article 168(1) TFEU seen in *Together for Health's* stress on health in all policies, EPAAC is noted as being needed so as to 'more effectively *coordinate activities and actions that are taken within different policy areas* by Member States and other stakeholders, with *the aim of reducing the increasing and unequal European burden of cancer*' (emphasis added).[32] In other words, although Member State competence (the primary responsibility) for cancer is respected, reference to the burden of cancer and ethics and human rights related concerns about its distribution is used to justify and develop a wide-ranging array of techniques, processes and practices. These allow the EU to build on Article 168 TFEU in order to elaborate, delineate

[28] Ibid, 2–3.
[29] See ch 7.
[30] European Commission, *Action Against Cancer*, n 4 above, 3.
[31] Ibid.
[32] Ibid.

and specify its role, responsibility and accountability, and identity as an actor in cancer governance.

More specifically, the national and regional differences in cancer incidence and mortality are deemed to provide:

> [C]onsiderable scope for reducing the European burden of cancer through a *joint response, guided by evidence-based strategies* for disease prevention and control. This *partnership approach* will help to *avoid scattered actions and the duplication of efforts*. It will also contribute to the *better use of the limited resources available*.[33] (Emphasis added)

Again, the burden of cancer is stressed, but it is instantiated here as 'European', a description that is used to further constitute the EU's role and identity as a public health actor and set out part of the rationale for its governance. The regulation of cancer through strategies of prevention and control requires evidence and prepares the ground for an EU role in the gathering and production of knowledge. 'Added value' is to be achieved through an efficient use of resources, and this is bolstered by mention of limited resources, which echoes and makes use of the context of the economic and financial crisis as a justification for EU action. The target of a 15 per cent reduction in the incidence of cancer by 2020 is important here in that in order to achieve this result the Member States should have in place so-called integrated cancer plans or national cancer plans (NCPs). The Commission considers that these 'should make a sustainable contribution to reducing the burden of cancer in the EU'[34] in line with the target.

Through these ways of governing cancer at a distance, principally by and through knowledge, the EU builds on the steps taken in the 1980s in order to extend and augment its governance—and power—into this sensitive and important policy area. The territory of the EU (and through international efforts, beyond the EU) provides both the focus and space for its intervention and protection efforts. This demonstrates the (re)configuration between sovereignty and territoriality through the EU's increasingly important role in the governance of cancer. The framing of EPAAC by risk, the leveraging of ethics and human rights related concerns of inequality and suffering, and the stress on apparently value neutral technical means of developing and implementing policy, also help to mask the extension and dissemination of market rationality into the formally non-market domain of cancer (and that of wider public health). This underlines how Article 168 TFEU is, as discussed in the previous chapter and shall become apparent in the rest of this part of the book, only a starting point for discerning and understanding the shape, nature and extent of EU competence in public health.

In these ways the creation, use and dissemination of knowledge is increasingly aligned to, supportive of, but also shaped by power; knowledge and power are co-productive. As I go on to explain, this is reflected in the more specific concrete techniques, processes and practices of knowledge gathering and production

[33] Ibid.
[34] Ibid.

that are so central to EPAAC. The continuing focus on evidence-based policy also underlines how EPAAC's risk-based framing and approach valorises and centralises scientific and technical knowledge and expertise as the basis for its activities. The importance of that knowledge also configures those who are governed in relation to governance. Like the EU's wider technology governing public health and the policy domain, EPAAC's rationale and objectives are linked to, underpinned by and directed at meeting the broader programmatic aims and priorities found within the overarching architecture of EU governance. The most important of which are the production and legitimation of the EU's identity, its socio-political order founded upon the improved competitiveness of its population and industry, consequent economic growth and market optimisation, and through them the European integration project. In the following I turn first to elaborate on these points by reference to the key areas of work and actions for EPAAC suggested by the Commission in *Action Against Cancer*, after which I outline and reflect further on their implementation.

B. Areas and Actions for a 'Comprehensive Policy Response'[35]

i. The Most Cost-effective Response

Since EPAAC focuses on the gathering and production of knowledge and expertise for prevention and control of cancer, it makes sense that prevention and health promotion is a key area of activity. Reflecting the wider approach to major and chronic diseases and conditions seen in EPAAC's rationale and objectives there is, therefore, a stress on a 'horizontal approach on the basis of tackling major health determinants' which 'is essential to curb the increasing burden of cancer throughout the European Union'. The burden—the threat or danger—of cancer is again presented as an EU matter. This paves the way for EU action such that:

> [Cancer's] prevention shall address on equal footing the lifestyle, occupational and environmental causes. It has been estimated that around one third of all cancers could be prevented by modifying or avoiding key risk factors such as smoking, being overweight, low fruit and vegetable intake, physical inactivity and alcohol consumption.[36]

Importantly, although existing health promotion mechanisms, such as the EU Platform for Action on Diet, Physical Activity and Health and the Alcohol and Health Forum, remain central, EPAAC 'will *act in complementary areas to ensure a comprehensive and coherent approach to cancer at EU level*' (emphasis added).[37]

In terms of lifestyle, health promotion 'on the basis of major health determinants has been a longstanding priority' for the Commission and includes

[35] Ibid.
[36] Ibid.
[37] Ibid, 8.

'strategies for nutrition, overweight and obesity-related health issues, and support for alcohol-related harm'. Tobacco control is highlighted as being of central importance, and it encompasses legislation aimed at harmonising the conditions for trade in the internal market,[38] facilitating international agreements[39] as part of the EU's global public health role,[40] and relations with third countries consistent with Article 168(3) TFEU and other efforts 'aimed at discouraging children and young people from taking up smoking, supporting smoking cessation and protecting all citizens against exposure to second-hand smoke, taking into account the need to tailor health promotion to specific population and target groups'.[41] The EU's governance of cancer is also implicated in, for example, the European Neighbourhood Policy (ENP):[42]

> In addition, *non-communicable diseases* (cardio-vascular, *cancer*, etc.) *pose a major disease burden in the ENP region*, as is the case in the EU. The ENP seeks to promote action in the field of public health in order to improve the general health status of the population and tackle specific issues such as communicable diseases.[43] (Emphasis added)

Occupational and environmental factors are likewise other important health determinants that create and widen the space for EU action. Here the basis for EU action is bolstered by reference to the World Cancer Report 2008 produced by the (World Health Organisation's (WHO's)) International Agency for Research on Cancer (IARC), which highlights that attention to environmental and workplace exposure are central to prevention. The EU has already taken this opportunity to introduce Registration, Evaluation, Authorisation and Restriction of Chemicals (often referred to simply as REACH) legislation that deals with general chemical exposure.[44] In relation to the workplace there exists legislation aimed at eliminating and minimising exposures to carcinogens and mutagens, which is updated

[38] Eg: 'Tobacco' ec.europa.eu/health/tobacco/policy/index_en.htm. See: Directive 2014/40/EU on the approximation of the laws, regulations and administrative provisions of the Member States concerning the manufacture, presentation and sale of tobacco and related products and repealing Directive 2001/37/EC [2014] OJ L127/1.

[39] Framework Convention on Tobacco Control, WHO, 21 May 2003. For discussion see, eg: R Hammond and M Assunta, 'The Framework Convention on Tobacco Control: Promising Start, Uncertain Future' (2003) 12 *Tobacco Control* 241; E Martin and E de Leeuw, 'Exploring the Implementation of the Framework Convention on Tobacco Control in Four Small Island Developing States of the Pacific: A Qualitative Study' (2013) 3 *British Medical Journal Open* e003982. 10.1136/bmjopen-2013-003982.

[40] Eg: European Commission, *The EU Role in Global Health*, COM (2010) 128 final. Discussed further in chs 4 and 5 (in terms of ensuring global preparedness for pandemics and other serious cross-border threats to health).

[41] European Commission, *Action Against Cancer*, n 4 above, 4.

[42] Discussed further in ch 4.

[43] 'European Neighbourhood Policy' ec.europa.eu/health/eu_world/policy/enp/index_en.htm.

[44] Regulation (EC) 1907/2006 of the European Parliament and of the Council of 18 December 2006 concerning the registration, evaluation, authorisation and restriction of chemicals (REACH), establishing a European Chemicals Agency, amending Directive 1999/45/EC and repealing Council Regulation (EEC) 793/93 and Commission Regulation (EC) 1488/94 as well as Council Directive 76/769/EEC and Commission Directives 91/155/EEC, 93/67/EEC, 93/105/EC and 2000/21/EC [2006] OJ L396/1.

on the basis of current scientific evidence.[45] A further example of EU prevention activities is the European Code Against Cancer (ECAC), which I discuss below.

Another key area of EU activity in the control of cancer is through engagement in detection, which in turn prepares the way for medical intervention through treatment and (hopefully) cure. Echoing the importance of evidence as the basis for EU intervention, the focus is on reduction and control:

> [B]y implementing *evidence-based strategies* for early detection and management of patients with cancer. This includes appropriate information to ensure awareness about the benefits of screening for those who should benefit from it. This is *an area where Community added value has already proven to be efficient in supporting Member States'* development of screening programmes for breast, cervical and colorectal cancer.[46] (Emphais added)

Reference to evidence (including of successful interventions) again demonstrates how knowledge is not just supportive of, but is itself a form of governance operating in several related ways. For example, the European Centre for Disease Prevention and Control (ECDC) provides guidance[47] that constitutes the scientific basis for the introduction of vaccines in EU countries for human papillomavirus (often referred to simply as HPV). The ECDC also funds the Vaccine European New Integrated Collaboration Effort (VENICE) platform on HPV and has established an expert group that seeks to facilitate HPV vaccination throughout the EU as a way of protecting against cervical cancer.[48] EU level market authorisation (noted again below) for HPV vaccines, such as Gardasil and Cervarix (produced by Sanofi Pasteur and GlaxoSmithKline respectively) is an essential complement to the achievement of the EU's prevention and control of cervical cancer strategies and the operationalisation of knowledge on HPV. EU 'added value' is also generated through the quality assurance guidelines produced by the Commission for the Member States on screening and which are referred to and used as a support in other areas of EU engagement, such as the aforementioned ECAC.

Moreover, reference to the 'added value' of EU knowledge-based action in relation to specific cancers feeds back into providing part of the justification for continued and further EU action, especially its 'added value'. The latter also helps to underscore the distribution of responsibilities between the EU and its Member States in line with the broader governance of cancer sketched above. In particular the centrality of Member State responsibility for detection helps to delimit and justify the EU's own role and accountability in the event of the failure to develop

[45] Directive 2004/37/EC of the European Parliament and of the Council of 29 April 2004 on the protection of workers from the risks related to exposure to carcinogenic or mutagens at work [2004] OJ L229/23.

[46] European Commission, *Action Against Cancer*, n 4 above, 4.

[47] European Centre for Disease Prevention and Control, *Guidance for the Introduction of HPV Vaccines in EU Countries* (Stockholm, ECDC, 2008).

[48] See further: www.ecdc.europa.eu/en/publications/Publications/0801_GUI_Introduction_of_HPV_Vaccines_in_EU.pdf.

detection efforts. For instance, the failure on the part of the Member States to ensure the availability of screening tests to the specified age group is a key objective and it is defined in, and identified by, reference to an EU legislative instrument (via a non-binding (soft law) Recommendation):

> [T]he volume of screening examinations in the EU *is less than half of the minimum annual number of examinations* that would be expected *if the screening tests specified in the Council Recommendation on cancer screening were available to all EU citizens* of appropriate age (approximately 125 million examinations per year).[49] (Emphasis added)

Other actions for EPAAC are *suggested*—and as shall become apparent, these also help to set the agenda for its work. The actions include overviewing the rollout of HPV vaccine and reviewing the Council Recommendation on cancer screening in light of scientific evidence and (underlining the EU's support and the failure of its Member States) the obstacles faced by the Member States in implementing their breast, cervical and colorectal cancer screening programmes. Assessing the effectiveness of EU policy in the area of tobacco control, extending the partnership approach to cancer across mechanisms such as the stakeholder forums on alcohol and nutrition, and reviewing ECAC and its implementation are some of the key further areas of activity for EPAAC.[50] In their different ways these examples build on previous EU actions and successes to provide a rationale for their continuation and expansion, and with them the EU's role, identity and responsibility in cancer governance. Beyond that the examples also facilitate the achievement of the EU's broader programmatic priorities.

ii. Bolstering Technologies of Knowledge-based Policy: Identification and Dissemination of Good Practice

A related area and action is the strengthening of the EU's responsibility for the identification and dissemination of good practice as a specific form of knowledge and expertise across the EU. Central here is a focus on a 'comprehensive cancer approach and multidisciplinary teams [which] can ensure more effective care for patients with cancer … Integrated cancer care, giving due consideration to psychosocial wellbeing and support, is a vital part of care that also should be encouraged'.[51] Such best practice is codified in the European guidelines for quality assurance in breast cancer screening and diagnosis, detailed further below. Other foci for attention are attention to quality of life for those whose cancer cannot be care, palliative care, which 'varies in quality between Member States and can benefit from exchange of good practices',[52] and cooperation on European Reference

[49] European Commission, *Action Against Cancer*, n 4 above, 4–5. Citing Recommendation 2003/878/EC on cancer screening [2003] OJ L327/34 and European Commission, *Report on the Implementation of the Council Recommendation of 2 December 2003 on Cancer Screening 2003/878/EC*, COM(2008) 882.

[50] European Commission, *Action Against Cancer*, n 4 above, 5.

[51] Ibid.

[52] Ibid, 6.

Networks (ERNs), especially in the area of rare diseases including cancers, and which are provided for in the Patient's Rights Directive.[53] It is noted ERNs:

> [S]hould provide healthcare to all patients who have conditions requiring a particular concentration of resources or expertise in order to provide affordable, high-quality and cost-effective care, and can also be focal points for medical training and research, information dissemination and evaluation.[54]

Again these are all stressed as area of 'EU added-value'.[55]

As with the previous area and action, a number of objectives are set out. These include concern for ethics and human rights by tackling inequalities in cancer mortality that can be dealt with through interventions and help to narrow the gap between best and worst performing Member States. This of course necessitates the monitoring, measuring and ranking of Member States—and it provides an additional motivation or spur for action provided by the Commission, which 'considers that a 70% reduction by 2020 is a feasible target, taking account of scientific developments and the different circumstances of different countries and cancers'. Importantly, this is concretised into an 'aim [that] *will be supported by the development of guidelines for models of best practice* in cancer-related care, taking into account national, regional and local contexts' (emphasis added).[56] In other words, the target of reducing the incidence of cancer requires the gathering and production of knowledge through monitoring, measuring and ranking—technologies of agency and performance—which in turn provides the basis for the production of best practice guidelines. These guidelines then require further rounds of monitoring, measuring and ranking in order to ensure and assess their implementation and track progress towards achievement of the target.

Finally, other agenda-setting areas and actions for EPAAC are suggested—including 'Sharing knowledge and expertise on different models for comprehensive and integrated cancer care, and in particular the organisation of care, with the aim of developing consensus around definitions and models of care, including chronic and palliative care'[57]—and through them knowledge again emerges as to the condition and means for their realisation and the extension of EU involvement, responsibility and power in cancer governance. The latter also underscores the tightening and co-productive relations between knowledge and power, the continuing valorisation of scientific and technical knowledge and expertise in decision-making, and the consequent configuration of those who are governed (including patients and medical professionals) in relation to governance.

[53] Art 12 Directive 2011/24/EU on the application of patients' rights in cross-border healthcare [2011] OJ L88/45.

[54] European Commission, *Action Against Cancer*, n 4 above, 6.

[55] Ibid.

[56] Ibid.

[57] Ibid.

iii. Cooperation and Coordination in Cancer Research as a Technology of Knowledge Production

These structuring themes and implications of the EU's risk-based governance are also apparent in relation to research into cancer, which adds an important dimension to the EU's role in the production, use and dissemination of knowledge about cancer. EU governance of cancer research also demonstrates more clearly the infiltration of market rationality and with it corporate interests into the formally non-market domain of public health. It is noted that a 'comprehensive cancer approach should include all aspects of cancer research, ranging from prevention to translational and clinical research. Health research is of central importance to the EU's research commitments',[58] for example, with funding of €750 million being allocated to cancer research over the course of the Sixth and Seventh Framework Programmes. Since most cancer research takes place at Member State level 'it is considerably fragmented and diverse across the EU' and as such 'the Community aims to step up its efforts to improve EU-wide coordination within this field *in line* with the European Research Area's objectives'.[59] That is, in addition to steering research carried out by academia, small and medium enterprises and larger industrial 'partners'[60] through funding there is an additional effort at coordination within and in order to reinforce the EU's wider governance of research. And that of course reflects the aims and priorities in the overarching architecture of the Lisbon Strategy, in particular the focus on producing economic optimisation through the instrumentalisation of knowledge.

Clinical trials and biomedical research are particularly important in that regard. In relation to the former the Clinical Trials Directive (CTD), and soon to be replaced by the Clinical Trials Regulation (CTR),[61] is particularly relevant in that it seeks to ensure good practice in the conduct of clinical trials for medicinal products for human use and compliance with it is required for market authorisation.[62] The EU law applicable to clinical trials and market authorisation is based on Article 114 TFEU, which provides for the adoption of harmonising legislation for the establishment and functioning of the internal market. Article 114(3) requires the Commission to take 'as a base a high level of protection' of, inter alia, health, 'taking account in particular of any new development based on scientific facts'.

[58] Ibid.

[59] Ibid.

[60] Ibid.

[61] Directive 2001/20/EC on the approximation of the laws, regulations and administrative provisions of the Member States relating to the implementation of good clinical practice in the conduct of clinical trials on medicinal products for human use [2001] OJ L121/34. This requires the Commission to establish principles relating to good clinical practice and detailed rules in line with those principles. This Directive is now replaced by Regulation (EU) 536/2014 on clinical trials on medicinal products for human use, and repealing Directive 2001/20/EC [2014] OJ L158/1, but it does not become applicable until at least 28 May 2016. The Regulation is planned to apply from 2019 (see the Preface).

[62] Discussed further in ch 7.

In the EU there are several types of procedure for market authorisation.[63] The centralised procedure is compulsory for products derived from biotechnology, orphan medicinal products, and products for human use containing an active substance authorised and intended for the treatment of HIV/AIDS, cancer, neurodegenerative disorders or diabetes.[64] Products that represent a significant scientific, therapeutic or technical innovation or that benefit public health can also make use of this route to the market. Mutual recognition applies to most conventional products and means that a manufacturer can obtain market authorisation in one Member State after which it is recognised in all others—adding competition between Member State regulators to that between the EU and the US. Finally, there is the less well used decentralised procedure, which allows for simultaneous approval in several Member States.

Each of these requires compliance with the Directive on the Community code relating to medicinal products for human use (Community code), which mentions clinical trials data as the basis for the market authorisation of pharmaceutical treatments on the grounds of their quality, safety and efficacy,[65] rather than 'comparative therapeutic efficacy' and genuine need. Clinical trials are subject to specific regulation through the CTD's (and from 2019 the new CTR's) aforementioned requirements of good practice, in particular that Member States set standards for the planning, performance, reporting, and archiving of research. Member States are also required to establish systems of monitoring and inspection in relation to good clinical practice (GCP), many of which are concretised further in subsequent legislation.[66]

Clinical trials, pharmaceuticals and market authorisation must be placed within the context of the overarching architecture of EU governance and its programmatic priorities and concerns.[67] The latter steers, underpins, shapes and directs EU law's central role in the market authorisation of pharmaceuticals. It is against the normative background of the overarching architecture that the EU regulates pharmaceuticals and their marketing. Facilitating speedier approvals is in the interests of getting drugs to market, making it easier for producers to profit more quickly from their investment in research and development, which, in turn, grows a more profitable pharmaceutical sector that can invest in the pharmaceutical development pipeline or 'cycle of innovation'. The latter begins with an idea that drives basic research, leading (where successful) to non-clinical, pre-clinical, and clinical research, and from there (where successful) to marketing and subsequent surveillance (or pharmacovigilence) within the market. Given the stages in the development

[63] For an overview see: 'Authorisation Procedures for Medicinal Products' ec.europa.eu/health/authorisation-procedures_en.htm.

[64] Regulation 726/2004/EC laying down Community procedures for the authorisation and supervision of medicinal products for human and veterinary use and establishing the European Medicines Agency [2004] OJ L136/1.

[65] Directive 2001/83/EC on the Community code relating to medicinal products for human use [2001] OJ L311/67.

[66] Directive 2005/28/EC laying down principles and detailed guidelines for good clinical practice as regards investigational medicinal products for human use, as well as the requirements for authorisation of the manufacturing or importation of such products [2005] OJ L91/13.

[67] See ch 2.

of pharmaceuticals and their obvious importance to the treatment of cancer, it is unsurprising that the EU's governance extends back from market authorisation and into the conditions for research, including the Innovative Medicine Initiative (IMI) and the European Strategy Forum on Research Infrastructures (ESFRI).

Looking first at IMI, it is described as 'a pan-European public and private sector collaboration endeavouring to support the discovery and development of better medicines, including cancer therapies'.[68] Coming from its founding regulation, the following is even more elaborate and revealing in that it recognises the importance of its citizens' health, but then moves to (re)frame the focus, orientation and rationale towards economic optimisation through enhanced competitiveness:

> The Joint Technology Initiative on Innovative Medicines should be a public private partnership aiming at increasing investments in the biopharmaceutical sector in Europe in the Members States and countries associated within the Seventh Framework Programme. *It should provide socioeconomic benefits for European citizens*, contribute to the health of European citizens, *increase the competitiveness of Europe and help to establish Europe as the most attractive place for biopharmaceutical research and development.*[69] (Emphasis added)

IMI is established under its founding regulation as a Joint Undertaking. Under Article 187 TFEU Joint Undertakings may be established to support the 'efficient execution of Union research, technological development and demonstration programmes'. According to Article 179 TFEU these serve the 'objective of strengthening … [the EU's] scientific and technological bases by achieving a European research area in which researchers, scientific knowledge and technology circulate freely, and encouraging it to become more competitive, including in its industry'.[70]

IMI is one of several Joint Technology Initiatives which:

> [R]esult from the work of European Technology Platforms, already set up under the Sixth Framework Programme, and cover selected aspects of research in their field … [combining] *private sector investment and European public funding*, including funding from the Seventh Framework Programme.[71] (Emphasis added)

Interestingly, because it is so indicative of the insinuation of market rationality into publicly funded research and its governance, it was the European Federation of Pharmaceutical Industries and Associations (EFPIA) (which represents the European pharmaceutical industry) that:

> *[T]ook the lead in establishing the European Technology Platform on Innovative Medicines* under the Sixth Framework Programme. *It developed a Strategic Research Agenda*, based on an extensive consultation with public and private stakeholders. The Strategic Research Agenda *described the research bottlenecks in the drug development process and recommends the scientific direction for a Joint Technology Initiative on Innovative Medicines.*[72] (Emphasis added)

[68] European Commission, *Action Against Cancer*, n 4 above, 6. See further: www.imi.europa.eu/.

[69] Recital 9 Regulation (EC) 73/2008 setting up the Joint Undertaking for the implementation of the Joint Technology Initiative on Innovative Medicines [2008] OJ L30/38.

[70] Art 179 TFEU.

[71] Recital 1 Regulation (EC) 73/2008, n 69 above.

[72] Ibid, Recital 6.

In other words, industry plays a central—if not 'the' central—role by providing its perspective on the reasons for delays in the pharmaceutical pipeline. In this way the industry is able to steer the IMI towards its partial and limited agenda of continued and enhanced corporate profitability.[73] This is of course reflective of the overarching architecture of EU governance and its operationalisation in the public health domain, in that it is part of the broader link between health and the economy through a focus on the pharmaceutical industry, the privatisation of biomedical research, and, therefore, pharmaceuticals and research into their development as a key driver of economic growth.[74]

The infiltration of market interests into and the consequent alignment of governance to them is thrown into sharper relief in the mention that:

> The objective of the Joint Technology Initiative on Innovative Medicines should be to foster collaboration between all stakeholders such as industry, public authorities (including regulators), organisations of patients, academia and clinical centres. The Joint Technology Initiative on Innovative Medicines *should define a commonly agreed research agenda* (hereinafter referred to as Research Agenda) *closely following the recommendations of the Strategic Research Agenda developed by the European Technology Platform on Innovative Medicines which identified efficacy, safety, knowledge management and training as important areas.*[75] (Emphasis added)

The focus on efficacy and safety is to be expected given their centrality to market authorisation.[76] As such bottlenecks in producing and demonstrating efficacy and safety need to be cleared. However, the focus on these criteria ensures that research governance is framed by and directed at dealing with risk instantiated as product safety in order to ensure market authorisation and produce economic optimisation through the development and marketing of innovative treatments. Consequently questions about the normative orientation, direction and use of scientific innovation, such as about ensuring improvements over and above existing treatments, are side-lined. I return to and elaborate on this in the second part of the book.[77]

Another important support for cancer research comes from ESFRI. With a focus on 'enabling science'[78] research infrastructures are important for the advancement

[73] A point taken up again in ch 7 with reflection on the discussion of the overarching architecture of EU governance in ch 2.

[74] Eg: European Commission, *A Stronger European-based Pharmaceutical Industry for the Benefit of the Patient—A Call for Action*, COM (2003) 383 final; European Commission, *Life Sciences and Biotechnology—A Strategy for Europe*, COM(2002) 27 final. See further: A Gambardella, L Orsenigo and F Pammolli, *Global Competitiveness in Pharmaceuticals. A European Perspective, Report Prepared for the Enterprise Directorate-General of the European Commission* (Brussels, European Commission, 2000).

[75] Recital 10 Regulation (EC) 73/2008, n 69 above.

[76] Regulation (EC) 726/2004 laying down Community procedures for the authorisation and supervision of medicinal products for human and veterinary use and establishing the European Medicines Agency [2004] OJ L136/1.

[77] See ch 7.

[78] European Commission, *Enabling Science. EU Support to Research Infrastructures in the Life Sciences* (Luxembourg, European Union, 2013).

of knowledge and technology. In relation to cancer the ESFRI Roadmap is particularly important in that it 'includes projects to support the establishment of clinical trials facilities and bio-banking to pave the way for a more harmonised European framework'.[79] However, ESFRI is aligned to the broader objectives of the EU's overarching architecture—'Research Infrastructures contribute to the implementation of the Europe 2020 strategy and its Innovation Union Flagship Initiative and enable the building up of the European Research Area'[80]—and is, therefore, directed at producing economic optimisation by and through cancer research.

Overall, the IMI and ESFRI highlight the link between the EU and industry, that is, between the public and private sectors—and how the link between them facilitates the insinuation of market rationality into governance and its (re)alignment in accordance with industrial or private interests. The objective 'to develop a coordinated approach to cancer research across the EU, aiming to achieve coordination of one third of research from all funding sources by 2013'[81] is therefore, at part at least, an attempt to promote economic optimisation through biomedical innovation as the foundation for innovative treatments and the regulation of cancer as a danger or threat to public health through them. The suggested actions for EPAAC seek to augment IMI and ESFRI by engaging in 'a collective effort to address obstacles in European cancer research' and to (re)constitute and (re)frame cancer research and further develop the gathering and production of knowledge as a key concern of the EU's identity and legitimacy. There is also a focus on optimising research through the 'Identification of gaps in research and methodology, enhancement of research cooperation to avoid duplication of efforts and strengthening research on prevention and translational research'. Although another objective is 'Strengthening … public access to information on cancer research and clinical trials in particular', this is arguably partly an effort in communicating governance efforts in order to shape public perceptions. Finally, given previous discussion, the objective to 'further improve the regulatory environment on clinical research in the EU', including by regards to the CTD, can be read as being about further serving the interests of the pharmaceutical industry.[82]

In summary, coordination and cooperation in relation to research helps to further delimit the EU's responsibility and accountability as a support for the Member States. By and through its central role in fostering coordination and cooperation the EU is made important to research and as such it is able to further constitute

[79] European Commission, *Action Against Cancer*, n 4 above, 6.

[80] B Vierkorn-Rudolph, ESFRI Chair, 'Foreword' in European Commission, *European Strategy Forum on Research Infrastructures, Strategy Report on Research Infrastructures. Roadmap 2010* (Luxembourg, European Union, 2010).

[81] European Commission, *Action Against Cancer*, n 4 above, 7.

[82] Ibid.

its role and identity as a public health actor. Yet, given the alignment of research to economic optimisation, the focus is less on health as a value in itself, and more on the contribution health makes to economic optimisation. Industrial and private interests are served by the structuring of governance by market rationality and its extension into the formally non-market domain of public health through the gathering, production, use and instrumentalisation of knowledge.

iv. Facilitating Technologies of Agency and Performance: The Benchmarking Process

The normative orientation, direction and wider importance of the areas and actions for EPAAC's work is likewise reflected in the benchmarking process. Touched on in the previous chapter, benchmarking is also given specific attention in and is important for the monitoring, measuring and ranking of Member States discussed above. Indeed, benchmarking is part of wider technologies of agency and performance that seek to govern Member States at a distance through *their* responsibilisation and prompts to increase their performance through ranking in relation to other Member States on the basis of the benchmark. In cancer governance this occurs by and through the monitoring and measuring made possible by commonly agreed indicators, especially the ECHI. The production of indicators is facilitated by the EU Health Programmes[83] and builds on the work of Eurostat and other international organisations such as the European Cancer Observatory, which was developed by the (WHO's) International Agency on Research on Cancer (IARC).[84] This data is collected at minimal cost by Member State and regional population based registries[85] in accordance with data protection legislation.[86] Gathering and producing data for the construction of indicators and the establishment of benchmarks is necessarily a subject of governance. For example, there are continuing efforts to remove obstacles to data collection, such as by ensuring the accuracy and comparability of 'data on cancer incidence, prevalence, morbidity, cure, survival and mortality',[87] and to reach agreement on the core indicators (for integration in the ECHI). There are also efforts to facilitate these foundational features of knowledge governance through cooperation and coordination between the national cancer registries generating the data for each Member State.[88]

[83] Such as EUROCHIP (European Cancer Health Indicator Project) which has produced and gradually refined a list of cancer health indicators (see further: www.tumori.net/eurochip/) and Fighting Against Cancer Today (FACT), which has tracked patterns in the incidence of cancer (see: M P Coleman and others (eds), *Responding to the Challenge of Cancer in Europe* (Institute of Public Health of the Republic of Slovenia, 2008).

[84] 'International Agency for Research on Cancer' www.iarc.fr/.

[85] Eg in Finland in 2007 spending on its cancer registries accounted for just 0.0037% of its total spending on cancer. See: European Commission, *Action Against Cancer*, n 4 above, 7.

[86] Directive 95/46/EC on the protection of individuals with regard to the processing of personal data and on the free movement of such data [1995] OJ L281/31. Regulation (EU) 2016/679 on the protection of natural persons with regard to the processing of personal data and on the free movement of such data, and repealing Directive 95/46/EC (General Data Protection Regulation) OJ 2016 L 119/1 entered into force on 24 May 2016, but will not apply until 25 May 2018.

[87] European Commission, *Action Against Cancer*, n 4 above, 8.

[88] Ibid, 8.

Previous 'European comparisons have ... *brought to light considerable differences in cancer survival in the EU* between countries with similar levels of wealth and health care provision' (emphasis added).[89] Benchmarks make it possible, therefore, to identify and deal with such inequalities, which are of course one of the key rationales for EU 'added value'. On the basis of such comparisons Member States are prompted to reflect on their own performance. So, for example, several Member States that reported high cancer mortality in comparison to other Member States in the early 1990s have revised their policies and are 'today reporting improved cancer survival'.[90] In short, 'sharing relevant information for statistical purposes is essential for developing effective public health interventions and the European benchmarking process'—and the latter provides 'the comparable information necessary for policy and action',[91] in short, EU governance.

As such benchmarking underscores the tightening and co-productive relations between and alignment of knowledge and power, the opening up of national knowledge domains to EU norms, values and rationalities, and the (re)framing of cancer governance as (in part at least) an EU matter. Benchmarking therefore facilitates the extension of EU power beyond the apparently limited formal boundaries of responsibility found in Article 168 TFEU. The deployment of knowledge through benchmarking is a way of further delineating the EU's responsibility and accountability. More particularly the EU governs the Member States at a distance through their agency, that is, through their responsibilisation and accountability for failures to improve performance in line with the benchmark they help to construct. The centrality and valorisation of scientific and technical knowledge and expertise through the benchmarking process—the creation of the benchmark and its use and deployment—also underlines the enrolment of knowledge in supporting and configuring governance in relation to the governed across the territory of the EU. In these ways neoliberalism becomes more apparent as that which undergirds governance and the achievement of the EU's programmatic priorities, especially the production and legitimation of its identity and socio-political order based on augmenting biomedical knowledge for the marketing of innovative treatments. These latter in turn facilitate the development of a competitive industry, healthy population and optimised economy, and through them the perpetuation of the project of European integration.

C. The Partnership Approach as Steering

i. Broad Overview

These areas and actions—the most cost effective response, the identification and dissemination of good practice, cooperation and coordination in cancer

[89] Ibid, 7.
[90] Ibid.
[91] Ibid.

governance, and the benchmarking process—although presented as suggestions in *Action Against Cancer*, in fact provide a strong guide for and help to set the parameters of EPAAC's work. So although *Action Against Cancer* 'broadly defines the objectives for European action against cancer' the aim of EPAAC 'is to determine specific key activities and actions to prevent and control cancer *through the … approach*' (emphasis added).[92] The areas and actions set out, and which together mark the partnership approach of governing cancer at a distance, have at their heart the gathering, production and instrumentalisation of knowledge by and through governance, and as I have explained, this structuring theme emerges as foundational to others, especially the (re)configurations between power and responsibility, the extension of EU governance over the territory of the Member States, and governance and the governed. The continuity between *Action Against Cancer* and EPAAC is reinforced given, as noted further below, the Commission has a central role as the former's author as well as in the organisation of the latter. Moreover, the Commission's central role is to 'ensure the *cooperative and action-oriented* approach of the Partnership' and to 'make certain that the proposed actions and activities are appropriate for action at EU level' (emphasis added).[93] Funding of EPAAC under the EU Health Programme, noted above, provides further scope for Commission control, since in accordance with the procedures and conditions that apply to joint actions under the EU Health Programmes, the secretariat submits interim and final implementation reports to the Executive Agency for Health and Consumers (EAHC), thereby providing an additional level of control from a distance.

EPAAC's establishment was preceded by an initial brainstorming workshop in October 2008, which was followed by consultations involving Member States, experts and stakeholders in 2009.[94] EPAAC was formally launched by the Commission on 29 September 2009 and has been followed by meetings of the steering committee (denoted the 'steering group' in *Action Against Cancer*,[95] and which comprises Member State representatives (plus Norway and Iceland), the WHO and its IARC, European Local and Regional Health Authorities (or EUREGHA), European Observatory on Health Systems and Policies (or EOHSP), Commission, representatives of patients, representatives of industry, and individual invited experts) and the working group on NCPs (which comprises Member State representatives (and Norway and Iceland), European Commission, WHO, EUREGHA and EOHSP).[96] The steering committee reviews the work done by the working group, which itself reviews the work undertaken by multi-stakeholder working

[92] Ibid, 9.

[93] Ibid.

[94] Involving a call: 'Open call for interested stakeholders to apply for participation in the preparatory meeting for the European Partnership for Action Against Cancer' ec.europa.eu/health/major_chronic_diseases/diseases/cancer/epaac/index_en.htm.

[95] European Commission, *Action Against Cancer*, n 4 above, 8–9.

[96] 'The initial meetings of the Steering Committee and of the Working Group on national cancer plans' ec.europa.eu/health/major_chronic_diseases/events/ev_20101208_en.htm.

groups. Further, the steering committee submits annual reports to the EPAAC secretariat and the open forum. The latter:

> [A]ims to provide a platform for the members of the Partnership and other stakeholders at EU level to deepen their understanding of the challenge of cancer for European society, and *to identify where common action can bring added value to national efforts in combating the burden of cancer*.[97] (Emphasis added)

That is, the forum provides an additional space in and through which knowledge can be exchanged, which helps to augment the (re)framing of public health as (at least in part) an EU matter that warrants, justifies and legitimates its current and future governance.

ii. Work Packages

The work undertaken and reviewed by the working group and then the steering committee is organised across 10 work packages (WPs) reflecting the areas and actions set out in *Action Against Cancer*: coordination and management (WP 1); dissemination and virtual partnership (WP 2); evaluation (WP 3); secretariat and open forum (WP 4); health promotion and prevention (WP 5); screening and early diagnosis (WP 6); healthcare (WP 7); research (WP 8); information and data (WP 9); and NCPs (WP 10). The first four are so-called horizontal WPs in that they cut across EPAAC's activities and are principally dealt with by the secretariat and steering committee. The remainder are so-called core WPs in that they more directly concern the substantive work of EPAAC. These WPs are dealt with by multi-stakeholder working groups focused on the four areas and actions outlined in the previous section organised around the following themes: prevention, dealing with WPs 5 and 6 and focused on cost effectiveness responses to cancer; health care, dealing with WP 7; research into cancer, dealing with WP 8; and information and data, dealing with WP 9 and facilitating monitoring, measuring and ranking. The collective efforts contribute to WP 10 on NCPs.

The multi-stakeholder working groups are supported by the Commission, which provides technical expertise as well as administrative and scientific support. Progress on the WPs is itself measured and propelled through the use of non-statistical indicators that identify a particular task, the measure of progress and the outcome. Indicators are, therefore, the basis for review, first by the working group and then the steering committee. These indicators provide for 'regular monitoring and evaluation of the work undertaken by the initiative'.[98] In addition, 'the activities of the stakeholder working groups … [are] coordinated by a steering group, which will report to the Partnership secretariat and the open forum … held once a year'.[99]

[97] European Commission, *Action Against Cancer*, n 4 above, 9.
[98] Ibid.
[99] Ibid, 8.

WP 5 on health promotion and prevention provides a useful example of how the most cost effective response as an area and action for EPAAC is facilitated. WP 5 focuses on campaigns to raise awareness about cancer promotion and prevention through the dissemination of the ECAC (noted above), particularly among those at highest risk and with the help of partner organisations. ECAC is a key primary prevention tool that focuses on tackling the major health determinants for cancer, including smoking as well as unhealthy diet and physical inactivity. ECAC is based on scientific evidence and works by conveying two essential messages that it seeks to have taken up by individuals: it is possible to avoid certain cancers and health can be improved through the adoption of a healthy lifestyle; the earlier cancer is detected the better the prospect of cure.

These two main messages are made through a series of 11 commands (the website is revealing in that it draws on the religious imagery of Moses and the Ten Commandments in order to make the point!).[100] In relation to the first message, there are seven commands on lifestyle and the environment, the first of which states 'Do not smoke; if you smoke, stop doing so. If you fail to stop, do not smoke in the presence of non-smokers' and the fourth 'Increase your daily intake and variety of vegetables and fruits: eat at least five servings daily. Limit your intake of foods containing fats from animal sources'. A further four commands comprise the second message by reference to EU guidelines discussed above. The first of this group (or eighth overall) points out that 'Women from 25 years of age should participate in cervical screening. This should be within programmes with quality control procedures in compliance with European Guidelines for Quality Assurance in Cervical Screening'. The second of this group (or ninth overall) makes a similar point: 'Women from 50 years of age should participate in breast screening. This should be within programmes with quality control procedures in compliance with European Union Guidelines for Quality Assurance in Mammography Screening'.[101] The latter is followed by a command on screening for colorectal cancer and the final command on vaccination against hepatitis B. In short, ECAC is ethical in the sense that it seeks to foster self-governance and in doing so it responsibilises those to whom its messages are directed, that is, (principally) EU citizens. As such the regulation of the threat or danger of cancer occurs not only at a population level signifying the governmentalisation of security, but also at the individual level. Further, the focus on the individual also highlights the securitisation of public health by and through the responsibilisation of the individual for his or her own health.

In order to more effectively communicate ECAC and its efforts at responsibilisation the European Week Against Cancer (EWAC) has been relaunched. EWAC ran between 1989 and 2005 as part of EPAAC's predecessor, the Europe Against

[100] 'European Code Against Cancer (third version)' www.cancercode.eu.
[101] Ibid.

Cancer. The previous EWAC had been coordinated by the Association of European Cancer Leagues (ECL), with ECL member leagues playing a role in planning and implementation from the beginning. Under WP 5 EWAC actions are based around ECAC promotion and prevention messages, which have hitherto 'been under-utilised and under-communicated'. More than that, 'much expertise and research [that] went into the development of the Code ... has now been lost and forgotten' with literature on ECAC no longer being available. Against this background and in an effort to ensure 'added value' EPAAC '*will not duplicate or reinvent* but gather how Member States are communicating promotion messages in an effective manner and use proven methods and strategies to communicate promotion and prevention messages related to ECAC' (emphasis added).[102] EWAC is supported with the help of the ECL and its network, which includes engagement with Members of the European Parliament Against Cancer II (usually referred to as MAC II, and the follow-up to the original pre-EPAAC MAC). The relaunched EWAC (including a conference) takes place in the last week of May so as to coincide with World No Tobacco Day on 31 May, but is now aligned more closely to ECAC so that its messages are relayed more effectively. One key element of the conference is to 'showcase and share best practices and tools for *raising cancer prevention awareness for European populations*'[103]—and (re)frame cancer as a European problem and legitimate part of the EU's growing global role in the regulation of cancer.

The use and deployment of ECAC denotes a more explicitly (bio)ethical turn in governance—and as such it is a key way through which the EU produces and exercises power and extends its involvement in cancer governance. In a specific comment on codes it was observed that 'the very process of deliberating about codes' helps to 'build shared agendas' and enable 'future co-ordinated initiatives'.[104] Codes also help to legitimate governance and build public trust.[105] The responsibilisation of EU citizens through ECAC also helps to mediate and delimit the EU's own responsibility and accountability. That is, the EU's responsibility is limited to creating public health campaigns and messages. The EU is able to claim the credit for resulting successes and shift blame in the event of failure towards those it works with in order to project prevention and promotion messages and ultimately the failure of individuals to take up the messages in their actions.

A similar delimitation of responsibility and accountability is apparent in relation to secondary prevention through screening and early diagnosis, which is the subject of WP 6. As a foundation for its work this WP develops links with the European Science Advisory Network for Health, European Network for Health

[102] EPAAC, *Health Promotion and Prevention*, available at: www.epaac.eu/health-promotion-and-prevention.

[103] Ibid.

[104] B Rappert, 'Pacing Science and Technology with Codes of Conduct: Rethinking What Works' in GE Marchant, BR Allenby and JR Herkert (eds), *The Growing Gap between Emerging Technologies and Legal-Ethical Oversight: The Pacing Problem* (Dordrecht, Springer, 2011) 110.

[105] *Cf* B Salter and C Salter, 'Bioethics and the Global Moral Economy: The Cultural Politics of Human Embryonic Stem Cell Science' (2007) 32(5) *Science, Technology & Human Values* 554.

Technology Assessment, and with the European Network on Cancer Screening and Prevention Programmes.[106] Improving the implementation of the Council Recommendation on cancer screening (noted above) is central to this WP, and it is to be achieved through the 'added value' engendered by the alleviation of key barriers to screening and early diagnosis in order to ensure they are of the correct quality and '*accessible to all citizens* who may benefit' (emphasis added).[107] In this regard a key focus is the identification of inequalities in participation and compliance in screening programmes takes place through a survey of national screening managers and the sorts of interventions that have helped to reduce them, which in turn provides the basis for information that can be 'exchanged between regions to improve implementation of population-based breast, colorectal and cervical screening programmes'. Another focus is on the development of quality criteria for health checks, for which there tends to be a weak or absent evidence base. The EU plays a role here in disseminating experience from one Member State (the Netherlands) with other Member States in order to develop an 'initial consensus on pan-European quality criteria'.[108] This presumably lays the foundations for further work and perhaps additional guidelines that reinforce the EU's extant efforts.

As elsewhere, barriers to public health infrastructures are constituted as a European problem, which in turn helps to justify and legitimate EU governance. Additional value is to be added by 'promoting synergy between cancer screening and other areas of early detection'. As part of this the network of European Schools of Screening Management was established. In a move that again signifies the governmentalisation of the regulation of the danger or threat of cancer, the network focuses on building the capacity for 'implementation and improvement of *population-based* cancer screening programmes. The *innovation* is that comparable courses do not exist in Europe' (emphasis added).[109] The network is small (for 'at least 15 competitively selected participants'), but designed so that those participating 'will constructively work on implementation or improvement of cancer screening programmes in the next few years. This, along with networking in order to develop certification, will promote *sustainability of the results*' (emphasis added)[110]—and further 'added value'.

A final example is WP 9 on cancer information and data, which facilitates monitoring, measuring and ranking as a key area and activity for EPAAC by seeking to identify the 'priority information needed to support policy action on cancer control' and make this available at the EU level through a 'comprehensive cancer information system for the European Union'. In order to achieve this EU level system there are four objectives: mapping the main sources of cancer data in the EU and identifying the priority topics to be supported by EPAAC; unifying cancer

[106] EPAAC, *Screening and Early Diagnosis*, available at: www.epaac.eu/screening-and-early-diagnosis.
[107] Ibid.
[108] Ibid.
[109] Ibid.
[110] Ibid.

burden indicators for incidence, mortality, survival and prevalence from existing EU and wider European activities 'under a common platform'; a task force on 'population-based cancer cost investigation' in the EU; and finally, to 'develop an inventory of statistical methods to analyse population based cancer data'.[111] So as to underpin and facilitate these objectives the WP brings together, and seeks to facilitate action and legitimacy, from Member State governments, authorities and cancer registries, European (that is, not solely EU) networks, as well as patient associations, the media and representatives of citizens, meeting in the open forum.

To detail these objectives a little further, the first seeks to build on projects funded principally under the EU Health Programme. The European Cancer Health Indicator Project (EUROCHIP) is one main example that seeks to tackle inequalities in the identification and treatment of cancer through improved information about the disease. Another main example is a project for the optimisation of the use of registries for scientific excellence in research (EUROCOURSE) since cancer registries are the most important population based source of data. As such a key effort is seeking to further monitor and improve the quality and coverage of that data in order to integrate it with data on health care systems and populations provided by statistical institutes, administrative sources, and cancer institutes. Mapping the available information and its quality is a core function of WP 9. As such this effort, supported by projects like EUROCOURSE provides the foundations—that is the disparate sources of data—that can then be used, rationalised and refined for the application of the indicators created by EUROCHIP and ECHI. All of this is in order to build a '*European map* of cancer information' that identifies 'areas of data availability and data needs'. This then provides the basis for future-oriented action: a meeting of those involved in EPAAC in order to 'provide proposals and recommendation for the *next programme*' (emphasis added).[112]

Bringing together the activities of '*all* the existing European partners working on cancer burden *indicators*' (emphasis added)[113] is central to the second objective. This includes the cancer incidence rates provided by cancer registries working through the European Network of Cancer Registries (ENCR) and consolidated and published by IARC, the prevalence data provided by a project measuring cancer prevalence (EUROPREVAL), the survival rates provided by the European Cancer Registries' Study on Cancer Patients' Survival and Care (or EUROCARE) network as well as the Cancer Registry-Based Project on Haematologic Malignancies (or HAEMACARE) and Surveillance of Rare Cancers in Europe (or RARECARE) (surveillance is discussed further in the subsequent two chapters),[114] and the mortality data provided by official death certificates and collected and disseminated by IARC. The purpose of assembling these related activities is to '*coordinate the analysis and provision* of [data on] incidence, mortality, survival and prevalence'

[111] EPAAC, *Cancer Data and Information*, available at: www.epaac.eu/cancer-data-and-information.
[112] Ibid.
[113] Ibid.
[114] Chs 4 and 5, in relation to which surveillance is a central concern for EU governance.

(emphasis added)[115] and as such create the common EU platform. This creation, definition and dissemination of indicators on the basis of coordination allows the EU to create 'added value'.

The task force on population-based cancer cost investigation, which is the third objective, seeks to bring together cancer experts, epidemiologists, health planners, economist and stakeholders in order to map and evaluate the 'comparability of available data across Europe' on the cost of cancer, including on the health and life of cancer survivors. This assessment creates the opportunity to discuss the '*best methodology* to be applied in order to collect *comparable data on cancer costs at population level across Europe*' (emphasis added),[116] and in doing so it constitutes population as being that of the EU and again demonstrates the governmentalisation of security, here through the need to track and compare costs as part of the threat or danger posed by cancer. This in turn lays the foundations for more intrusive and expansive EU involvement in the regulation of cancer through the potential production of standardised data that can be harnessed and used by other techniques, processes and practices, such as the NCPs. The wider window of opportunity for this expansion in governance provided by the EU's continuing economic and financial crisis, as well as the pressures generated by wider societal and demographic changes,[117] is also implicit in the statement that 'Cancer incidence is increasing and fortunately prognosis is also tending to improve. Pharmaceutical, clinical and diagnostic costs are increasing faster than the available resources of most countries, *thus costs are a fundamental aspect of cancer control*' (emphasis added).[118] Creating and providing comparable data on cancer costs allows the EU to define them as an area where it can add value. And since costs are central to cancer controls, that is to the regulation of the danger and threat of cancer, the governance of costs also demonstrates the securitisation of this area of public health regulation.

The fourth and final objective of developing an inventory of statistical methods to analyse population based cancer data makes methodology even more central to the EU's contribution to cancer governance. Building on existing experiences, and led by the International Staging System (or ISS)[119] working with, inter alia, ENCR and the IARC, the focus is on developing and honing methodology—and this is figured as a future-oriented activity. Attention to methods begins with 'a European network on data analysis ... to better coordinate the efforts, to provide scientists with wide pan-European datasets, and *to start build[ing] [sic] a European capacity* for statistical analysis, projections and forecasting epidemiological cancer indicators' (emphasis added).[120] The establishment of techniques, processes and

[115] EPAAC, *Cancer Data and Information*, n 111 above.

[116] Ibid.

[117] Discussed in relation to the overarching architecture in ch 2.

[118] EPAAC, *Cancer Data and Information*, n 111 above.

[119] An international research initiative on the means for quantifying the extent of cancer in the body ie staging systems.

[120] EPAAC, *Cancer Data and Information*, n 111 above.

practices—in short, infrastructures—for the production, gathering, use and dissemination of scientific and technical knowledge is an activity for the present that lays the foundations for future refinement and use.

In sum, the creation of the comprehensive cancer information system that is the objective of WP 9 is an attempt to increase the use and efficacy of existing efforts. A central consequence of which is an enhancement in the authority of EU produced and assembled knowledge—both in relation to the EU's citizens and amongst international actors. This occurs through its (re)use and harnessing in further and sometimes higher and more widely used or useful technologies like the common platform—which in turn ensures a strengthened basis for and legitimation of the continued expansion of EU cancer governance.

iii. Extending and Deepening Governance: National Cancer Plans

WPs 1–9 feed into WP 10 on NCPs. An NCP is a:

> *[P]ublic health programme* designed to: reduce the number of cancer cases and deaths and improve quality of life of cancer patients, through the systematic and equitable implementation of evidence-based strategies for: prevention, early detection, diagnosis and treatment, rehabilitation, palliation and research to search for innovative solutions and evaluate outcomes.[121] (Emphasis added)

In particular, supported by the first four (horizontal) WPs that are to do with managing and supporting EPAAC's activities, work from the remaining (core) WPs—WP 5 on health promotion and prevention, WP 6 on screening and early diagnosis, WP 7 on healthcare, WP 8 on research and WP 9 on information and data—all help to provide the techniques, processes and practices, often linked to the gathering, production and dissemination of scientific and technical knowledge and expertise, that make possible the formulation and subsequent refinement of NCPs. Moreover, this work from across EPAAC essentially opens national frames of reference including knowledge domains for cancer governance and facilitates (re)framing and the infiltration of EU level norms, values and rationalities, which are of course ultimately oriented to market optimisation.

In sum, EPAAC provides:

> *[A] platform for analysing* the present cancer burden and trends, *national strategies* for cancer prevention and control, *insufficiencies and discrepancies, and desired objectives for future cancer action at EU level.* Through the exchange of information, expertise and best practice, the Partnership *will contribute to reducing inequalities in health by assisting underperforming Member States to more efficiently prevent and control cancer.*[122] (Emphasis added)

NCPs are essentially the culmination of EPAAC's work; they bring together, augment and steer the various risk-based techniques, processes and practices

[121] EPAAC Steering Committee Meeting, WP 10, *National Cancer Plans*, Brussels, 8 December 2010.
[122] European Commission, *Action Against Cancer*, n 4 above, 8.

and ensure they bring about action at the Member State level. Although that action is towards the achievement of the EU's target for reducing the incidence of cancer, it is also about ensuring the implementation of the wider aims and objectives of the EU's public health strategy and beyond that the programmatic priorities of the overarching architecture of governance. The EU's various forays into the governance of cancer, such as the development of indicators, benchmarks and highlighting best practice, provide the basis for more intrusive interventions into the Member State level through EPAAC and 'the basis for determining future Community action on cancer'.[123] Much of EPAAC and the NCPs is about steering actors, often through their responsibilisation by and through the gathering, production and dissemination of knowledge.

Moreover, NCPs have a key role in the communication of governance and through it the shaping of public perceptions and relations between Member States:

> [NCPs] are also an *effective tool for the communication of the decisions and the plans* identified and chosen by a Member State *and the evidence supporting and influencing them* in a transparent fashion *both to [the] public within the Member State and also with and between other members of the European Union.*[124] (Emphasis added)

This relates to the focus of WP 2 in shaping the public face of EPAAC:

> [T]he outlined objectives and outcomes of the Partnership will be presented on a separate website. This website, the so-called Virtual Partnership, will provide an extensive overview of the initiatives and work undertaken by the Partnership. The website *should be part of a wider communication strategy to ensure dissemination throughout the Community* (Emphasis added)

and this is so as to '*ensure* transparency and accountability'.[125]

A key function of these communication efforts is the further delimitation of the boundaries of EU responsibility and accountability in cancer governance, and beyond that the production and legitimation of not just that governance, but through it the EU's broader programmatic priorities found in the overarching architecture.

IV. CONCLUSION

The EU's interventions in the governance of cancer have proven an important success. EPAAC, a partnership assembling and steering a range of actors, also serves as a model for the governance of other public health problems, including but not limited to other chronic and major diseases and conditions. In examining cancer the chapter advanced the first main argument of this book, which is that through its regulation as a danger or threat to the circulation of people (effectively as economic actors) and things (to the extent that they are consumed by

[123] Ibid, 10.
[124] 'National Cancer Plans' available at: www.epaac.eu/national-cancer-plans.
[125] European Commission, *Action Against Cancer*, n 4 above, 10.

people and their consumption is undermined by illness), cancer is effectively (re) framed by and its governance is directed towards economic optimisation. In this way the EU's risk-based cancer governance demonstrates the governmentalisation of security, ie through the focus on population at the European level, and the securitisation of public health. Ethics and human rights emerged as legitimating devices for the central focus on risk directed towards the promotion of economic optimisation, which was most apparent in their roles as part of the justification for EU involvement in the regulation of cancer. Although strategies of prevention *and* control are important to the EU's approach, attention and resources are directed towards innovative treatment of cancer through new technologies (which can of course be vital and absolutely necessary), but that is motivated in large part by a concern for promoting industrial development and corporate profitability rather than health as a value in itself.

More deeply, the chapter also extended the second main argument of this book, which is that the infiltration, dissemination and operation of neoliberalism is apparent through the (re)configurations—especially between knowledge and power, power and responsibility, governance and the governed, and sovereignty and territoriality—or structuring themes undergirding EPAAC's rationale and objectives as well as its implementation through risk-based techniques, processes and practices. These technologies of governing at a distance, usually by and through the gathering and production of knowledge, are central to and constitutive of the EU's (re)framing of cancer governance and its implementation through NCPs. However, the dominance of the scientific and technical depoliticises EU governance and obscures the ways in which it is reflective of and embedded within, in turn, the public health strategy constitutive of the technology governing public health and the policy domain, and the programmatic priorities found in the broader overarching architecture of EU governance.

Most importantly the EU's involvement in cancer is oriented towards the production and legitimation of its identity as a public health actor, a socio-political order founded upon economic optimisation and the perpetuation of the project of European integration. At the same time the centrality and valorisation of scientific and technical knowledge and expertise in the EU's approach configures governance in relation to those it governs, and in doing so it implicitly limits the potential contribution of citizens to decision-making. In the next chapter I turn to examine HIV/AIDS, which as I go on to explain is a quite different public health problem, the governance of which has a significant global dimension. The next chapter therefore continues to extend the platform and basis for the diagnosis of the current institutionalisation of citizen participation in governing public health as a key problem, as I go on to set out in the second part of the book.

4

HIV/AIDS

I. INTRODUCTION

A QUICK GLANCE back to the start of the previous chapter highlights that in relation to cancer the focus of the European Union's (EU's) web-based introductory comments is on the effectiveness and success of its governance. In relation to HIV/AIDS the information introducing and framing governance is quite different in tone:

> Over 50,000 people a year are diagnosed with HIV in the EU and *neighbouring countries. Effective treatment* of human immunodeficiency virus (HIV) infections exists but there is still no cure, nor a preventive vaccine. That is why EU policy focuses on *prevention*, and *support for people living with HIV/AIDS*.[1] (Emphasis added)

This stress advances the first core argument of this book, in that it immediately highlights risk as the dominant frame for the EU's governance of HIV/AIDS. Moreover, risk is attuned towards achieving security, which is understood as being about regulating HIV/AIDS as a danger of threat to the circulation of people and things (such as blood products), within the internal market, on its periphery and, as I shall point out, beyond. The latter suggests the importance of regional and even global cross-borderness to the EU's governance as the space for its interventions, which itself marks a more explicit shift in the direction and scope of governance towards the extra-territorial as part of attempts at regulating HIV/AIDS and other emergencies that seem to pose a danger or threat to the EU, its aims and priorities. A part of this move is the further figuration of the EU's population and territory and its identity as a public health actor.

The stress on external governance provides a contrast with the EU's approach to cancer, but also helps to further illustrate the operationalisation of *Together for Health*[2] and, with that, the overarching architecture underpinning EU public health governance.[3] More specifically, the example of HIV/AIDS emphasises the

[1] 'HIV/AIDS' ec.europa.eu/health/sexual_health/hiv_aids/index_en.htm. AIDS or acquired immune deficiency syndrome is the later stage of HIV infection when the body can no longer fight life-threatening infections.

[2] European Commission, *White Paper, Together for Health: A Strategic Approach for the EU 2008–13*, COM (2007) 630 final.

[3] See ch 2.

EU's role as a *global* public health actor and exporter of normative power governing an increasingly large range of places and people. Further, the focus on the external dimension of HIV/AIDS hints towards a proactive and perhaps more security-oriented posture and identity. As I shall point out, in that regard medical and technological responses are particularly important both as treatments and as part of prevention efforts. As in EU governance of cancer, ethics and human rights shall again emerge more as legitimating devices for EU involvement in HIV/AIDS.

In the next section, I introduce the EU's governance of HIV/AIDS, trace its position as part of and importance in relation to the governance of communicable diseases, and explain how it and that wider governance is situated and embedded within and reflective of the broader overarching architecture and programmatic priorities of EU governance. Subsequently I examine a little further the main components of the central EU intervention in HIV/AIDS—outlining the key contours and the broad distribution of responsibilities, the centrality of prevention, the attention to most 'at risk' regions and groups, and finally the special focus on developing technologies for the gathering and production of knowledge—and elaborate on these introductory points.

In doing so as well as tracing the importance of risk as the central frame I advance the second core argument, which is that neoliberalism undergirds and operates through the governance of HIV/AIDS, and that is in turn linked to the EU's broader programmatic priorities—the production and legitimation of the EU's identity, socio-political order and the project of European integration—found in the overarching architecture of governance. The latter argument shall be underscored in particular by reference to the distribution and delineation of the boundaries of responsibility and accountability, seen in the EU's security-oriented approach, and the importance of creating and developing the knowledge base for governance within and outside the EU. Overall, this chapter uses the example of HIV/AIDS in order to extend the platform for the diagnosis of the current institutionalisation of citizen participation in governing public health as a control concern, and provide the basis for the prescription for its enhancement and with it the quality of governance and its regulatory interventions, both of which are set out in the second part of the book.

II. FROM THE OVERARCHING ARCHITECTURE OF GOVERNANCE TO *COMBATING HIV/AIDS WITHIN THE EU AND IN THE NEIGHBOURING COUNTRIES*—REFLECTING *TOGETHER FOR HEALTH*

As noted in the previous chapter, the introduction of highly active retroviral therapy means HIV/AIDS is considered to be a major and chronic disease. However, the absence of a cure means HIV remains infectious via exposure to infected bodily fluids of an infected person, including blood (which is subject to specific regulation),[4] semen, vaginal fluids, anal fluids and breast milk, but excluding saliva that does not contain any of these. Consequently, HIV/AIDS principally falls within the EU's governance of communicable diseases[5] and their regulation as a danger or threat to the circulation of people and things—and the EU's approach is reflective of, embedded and situated within its public health strategy and the broader overarching governance architecture. Over recent decades the success of treatment and prevention strategies in EU Member States has meant 'Rates of infectious diseases have either fallen or remained stable, and the majority of deaths in EU countries are now due to non-infectious diseases such as cancer and heart disease' ie major and chronic diseases. At the same time, and in a move that situates HIV/AIDS within a cluster of evolving regulatory targets producing a gradually heightened sense of urgency and even medical emergency 'micro-organisms *adapt themselves* and *we have to expect new and emerging infections*, as with HIV/AIDS in the 1980s, variants of Creutzfeldt-Jakob disease in the 1990s, SARS [Severe Acute Respiratory Syndrome] in 2003 and pandemic influenza' (emphasis added).[6]

Further, in the face of the range of harms with various degrees of probability and even uncertainty and increasingly non-knowing posed by these targets (and others),[7] treatment is being undermined by the growing resistance of micro-organisms to antibiotics—which thwarts a key means of regulating communicable diseases as a danger or threat to the circulation of not just people but also things, and therefore presents another challenge that has 'to be tackled'.[8] Preventative measures seek to govern the future by forestalling dangers or threats. These measures are most often deployed against those targets for which there is (now) scientific agreement as to the probability of occurrence and risk posed (such as Creutzfeldt-Jakob disease (variant or vCJD) and HIV/AIDS). Preventative measures are also used in respect of regulatory targets for which the potential harm is high (such as SARS and pandemic influenza), but for which there is little or no scientific agreement as to the likelihood of occurrence. The limits of prevention

[4] See Directive 2002/98/EC setting standards of quality and safety for the collection, testing, processing, storage and distribution of human blood and blood components and amending Directive 2001/83/EC [2002] OJ L33/30. (hereinafter referred to as the Blood Directive). See further: A-M Farrell, *The Politics of Blood: Ethics, Innovation and the Regulation of Risk* (Cambridge, Cambridge University Press, 2012).

[5] As per Art 3(b) Decision 1082/2013/EU on serious cross-border threats to health and repealing Decision 2119/98/EC [2013] OJ L293/1, 'communicable diseases' are defined as 'infectious disease caused by a contagious agent which is transmitted from person to person by direct contact with an infected individual or by indirect means such as exposure to a vector, animal, fomite, product or environment, or exchange of fluid, which is contaminated with the contagious agent'.

[6] 'Communicable diseases' ec.europa.eu/health/communicable_diseases/policy/index_en.htm.

[7] Other noteworthy examples include: anthrax, chlamydial infection-including lymphogranuloma, cholera, hepatitis, human papilloma virus, influenza, malaria, smallpox, tetanus and tuberculosis.

[8] 'Communicable diseases', n 6 above.

measures provide the scope for the use of preparedness in the organisation of governance, as I go on to discuss in the next chapter.

The EU's approach to communicable diseases is organised around surveillance, '*rapid* detection' and '*rapid* response': a three step approach for the EU's '*response to the threat* of communicable diseases' (emphasis added).[9] Those diseases are constituted as the public health problem presenting a danger or threat, and the EU's approach is to govern them at a distance consistent with Article 168 Treaty on the Functioning of the European Union (TFEU). An EU network was established in 1999 in order to facilitate epidemiological surveillance of communicable diseases, early warning and response coordination.[10] This was bolstered with the creation of the European Centre for Disease Prevention and Control (ECDC) in 2005. The latter 'assist[s] the EU by *identifying and assessing the risk of current and emerging threats to human health* posed by infectious diseases' (emphasis added),[11] the results of which are published in its annual epidemiological report. This governance infrastructure underlines the importance of the gathering and production of knowledge both as governance and as a support for wider (risk-based) governance efforts and regulatory interventions through prevention, preparedness and treatment. The creation, use and dissemination of knowledge is increasingly aligned to, supportive of, but also shaped by power, that is, knowledge and power are co-productive.

Since HIV can be transmitted via infected bodily fluids during sexual contact, HIV/AIDS also falls within the EU's governance of sexually transmitted infections (STIs). Although HIV can be transmitted through intravenous drug taking involving needles carrying infected bodily fluids, this is not given as much prominence as the role of sexual contact, which is the overwhelming means for the transmission of HIV via infected bodily fluids. In relation to STIs, and reflecting the approach taken in the EU's broader public health governance, in order to produce 'added value' the European Commission (Commission) seeks to improve the surveillance systems across its Member States through improved notification, completeness and comparability of data. The Commission also seeks to support prevention of STIs, including through strategies of increased awareness and guidance, and to assist in their control, particularly in relation to chlamydia, which is the most prevalent STI. This work is implemented through meetings between the Commission, representatives of the Member States, youth groups and researchers in the sexual health forum. Interestingly, although 'Innovative projects promoting health development can receive EU funding from the health programme, as a means of implementing the EU health strategy',[12] many of the projects focus on HIV/AIDS,[13] a fact that attests to its importance and prioritisation.

[9] Ibid.

[10] Decision 2119/98/EC on a network for the epidemiological surveillance and control of communicable diseases [1998] OJ L268/1, now replaced by Decision 1082/2013/EU, n 5 above.

[11] 'Communicable diseases', n 6 above.

[12] 'Sexually transmitted diseases' ec.europa.eu/health/sti_prevention/policy/index_en.htm.

[13] 'Projects' ec.europa.eu/health/sti_prevention/projects/index_en.htm.

The EU's approach to communicable diseases marks a more explicit use of risk regulation directed at producing security in order to frame, organise and legitimate governance and its regulatory interventions. The focus on risk is about ensuring the regulation of the dangers or threats to the free circulation of people and things within the internal market, that is economic optimisation. That focus indicates both the governmentalisation of public health (through the focus on regulating population) and the securitisation of EU governance in respect of communicable diseases (in that security entails the regulation of HIV/AIDS as a danger or threat to the circulation of people and things). In relation to HIV/AIDS these twin dynamics become apparent in *Combating HIV/AIDS in the European Union and Neighbouring Countries* (*Combating HIV/AIDS*),[14] which is the central policy document in the area of HIV/AIDS. Although *Together for Health* is not mentioned explicitly in this document, *Combating HIV/AIDS* is certainly embedded within and reflective of it, the legal foundations provided by Article 168 TFEU, and the programmatic priorities of the broader overarching architecture of EU governance.[15] Indeed, as I explain below, strengthening the EU's voice in global health and protecting citizens from health threats, respectively the last of the four core principles and the second of the three strategic objectives in *Together for Health*, are especially important to HIV/AIDS governance.

Indeed, these are operationalised through and reflected in the title, rationale and aims, broad contours and content of *Combating HIV/AIDS*. Within these a number of features are especially prominent: risk and security; the extra-territorial scope of EU regulation of HIV/AIDS; and the adoption of a proactive stance in the protection of the EU and (at least) its neighbours (if not the wider world). Given the importance of HIV/AIDS in EU regulation of communicable diseases, these features are strongly indicative of the overall orientation, pattern and shape of that wider governance—a point that shall become more apparent in the next chapter on pandemic influenza. Although so far more implicit, that regulation is concerned with generating economic optimisation and meeting the broader programmatic priorities. That is, governance of HIV/AIDS (and other communicable diseases) is also directed at producing and legitimating the EU's identity as a public health and security actor, its socio-political order based on a competitive and optimised market economy and through them the project of European integration.

In the introduction to *Combating HIV/AIDS* it is noted (echoing the online statement cited above):

> EU Member States and the European neighbouring countries face a *high number of new HIV and associated infections and the resulting medical, social and economic consequences.* 50,000 newly diagnosed HIV cases in the EU *and the neighbouring countries* alone in

[14] European Commission, *Combating HIV/AIDS in the European Union and Neighbouring Countries, 2009–13*, COM (2009) 569 final. See further: European Commission, *Action Plan on HIV/AIDS in the EU and Neighbouring Countries: 2014–2016*, SWD (2014) 106 final.

[15] See ch 2.

> 2007 and *an estimated 2 million people* living with HIV/AIDS … illustrate the *serious dimension* of the situation.[16] (Emphasis added)

This stark epidemiological situation helps to provide the rationale for EU governance. The scale of the numbers of people actually and likely to be infected are combined with medical consequences and as yet unspecified (if obvious) social and economic ones to generate the basis for EU intervention. The geographical area for governance interventions is mapped as comprising both the EU and neighbouring countries. This highlights the extra-territorial scope of the EU's approach to regulating HIV/AIDS as well as the (re)configuration between sovereignty and territoriality, in that EU governance extends over the territory of its Member States and beyond.

Further, despite past EU action,[17] the danger or threat posed by HIV/AIDS means that '*combating* … [it] remains a public health concern and a political priority for the European Union and neighbouring countries'. Indeed, although there are effective treatments such that those with access to them can live as long as those who are not infected, there is no cure for HIV/AIDS, and consequently this limit in the regulatory tools available means that '*Intensifying prevention* is therefore the *key to combat* HIV/AIDS', while 'neglecting prevention is a waste of lives and resources' (emphasis added).[18] Here prevention is figured as a central responsibility for which the EU can be held accountable in the event of failure constructed as neglects. That is the promotion and facilitation of preventative measures by the EU helps it to fulfil its responsibility and avoid accountability in the event of a growing (or stable) incidence of infection. The underlying concern is with ensuring security understood as being about regulating HIV/AIDS through preventative interventions in population, which underscores the securitisation of this area of public health governance. Importantly, *Combating HIV/AIDS* 'complements'[19] *A European Programme for Action to confront HIV/AIDS, Malaria and Tuberculosis through External Action (2007–11)*.[20] Discussed further below this is focused on external action in developing and middle-income countries, and extends the importance of the (re)configuration between sovereignty and territoriality through the development of EU governance.

The situation presented by HIV/AIDS impels an urgent and proactive preventative response. This response is formulated bearing in mind the consequences of failure, and encompassing a wide range of interventions:

> After three decades of HIV/AIDS there is still no room for complacency. The *best response* to the epidemic remains a *combination of health specific and wider social interventions.*

[16] European Commission, *Combating HIV/AIDS*, n 14 above, 2.

[17] European Commission, *Combating HIV/AIDS within the European Union and in the Neighbouring Countries 2006–09*, COM (2005) 654.

[18] European Commission, *Combating HIV/AIDS*, n 14 above, 2.

[19] Ibid.

[20] European Commission, *A European Programme for Action to Confront HIV/AIDS, Malaria and Tuberculosis through External Action (2007–11)*, COM (2005) 179.

> People will continue to suffer *unless prevention is accelerated* and universal access to treatment, care and support is ensured for all people in need.[21] (Emphasis added)

In other words, the nature of the danger or threat to the circulation of people and things that is posed by HIV/AIDS necessitates and provides the scope for faster, more forward looking or future-oriented, and more intrusive and wide-ranging action by the EU in population via prevention efforts. Yet, as I go on to explain, the operationalisation of EU governance through concrete techniques, processes and practices, aligned to, reflective of and embedded within the broader priorities of EU governance, increasingly privilege medical and technological responses. Ethics and human rights concerns are inflected here in the attention to reducing suffering, but provide a starting point and justification for EU risk-based action directed at producing security. As such ethics and human rights operate more as legitimating devices for that dominant framing and orientation.

These starting points for HIV/AIDS governance highlight the importance of neoliberalism to its organisation, normative orientation and direction. That is apparent in the (re)configuration between sovereignty and territoriality reflected in the extension of EU governance across its own territory and beyond. Another key (re)configuration is that between power and responsibility, which is seen in the extension of EU power despite the delimitation of its responsibility and accountability. The gathering and production of knowledge is particularly important in that regard; indeed, knowledge has begun to emerge as both a core component of governance and as a support and condition for wider governance and regulatory interventions. As is already starting to become apparent, the EU's governance of HIV/AIDS and especially its regulatory interventions aimed at regulating the danger or threat to the functioning of the internal market, are also important to the production and legitimation of the EU's identity as a public health and security actor, its socio-political order based upon competitive and optimised market economy, and ultimately the project of European integration.

III. TAKING ACTION: *COMBATING HIV/AIDS WITHIN THE EU AND IN THE NEIGHBOURING COUNTRIES*

A. Mapping 'HIV in Europe': Constituting a Problem for EU Governance

The grounds for EU action noted in the previous section in relation to communicable diseases including HIV/AIDS are fleshed out further through references to the epidemiological, legal and social, and political contexts of HIV/AIDS. Those references are presented and leveraged in order to constitute HIV/AIDS as a danger or threat to the circulation of people and things, a problem for EU governance, and a risk that should be subject to regulatory interventions. As regards the context provided by epidemiology it is noted that the numbers of people living with

[21] European Commission, *Combating HIV/AIDS*, n 14 above, 2.

HIV/AIDS (PLWHA) and 'new HIV diagnoses differ significantly between countries, as do the prevalence rates of HIV, in a range from 0.1% to 1.2% across Europe. Currently in Eastern Europe HIV and AIDS are increasing at an alarming rate'.[22] The ways in which HIV is transmitted depends on the geographic location. At the time of the publication of *Combating HIV/AIDS* within the EU the principal means of transmission for HIV was (and still is) through sexual contacts between heterosexuals and men who have sex with men (MSM). However, in the EU's neighbouring countries the principal means of transmission was through injecting drug use at 57 per cent. In the EU/EFTA MSM present 39 per cent of new HIV cases, which make this the highest proportion by group. Moreover, heterosexual transmissions of HIV were (and are) also increasing in several of those countries. Other particularly at risk groups include women, commercial sex workers and prisoners. A particular concern is around ignorance of HIV status. It is estimated that within the EU 30–50 per cent of HIV infected people are unaware of their status, while the figure in the EU's neighbouring countries is up to 70 per cent. Consequently 'Early diagnoses of HIV accompanied by counselling and timely treatment play a crucial role in reducing transmission of HIV, as well as the morbidity and mortality related to HIV/AIDS'.[23] Further, HIV infection commonly occurs alongside infection with tuberculosis and hepatitis.

The legal and social situation focuses on 'obstacles and particularities'.[24] This points to the role of national law in the regulation of the danger or threat posed by HIV/AIDS through different legal responses. Importantly, through these responses barriers to diagnosis and treatment are created and perpetuated, with considerable differences existing between countries within the EU and on its periphery.[25] In particular, 'Social exclusion, discrimination due to HIV status and the non-respect of basic human rights of PLWHA still persist'—and in some countries the sexual transmission of HIV can be a crime.[26] In terms of free movement in the EU's area of freedom, security and justice,[27] which is of course a central concern to the EU as it relates directly to the circulation of people, there remain restrictions on the entry, stay and residence of those with HIV. These are noted as discriminatory measures which 'do not protect public health',[28] which suggests they cannot be justified and permitted on the basis of EU free movement law.[29] This in turn emphasises EU law's role in (re)regulating the dangers and threats attendant to

[22] Ibid.

[23] Ibid.

[24] Ibid, 3.

[25] WHO/UNAIDS, *Progress on Implementing the Dublin Declaration on Partnership to Fight HIV/AIDS in Europe and Central Asia* (2008).

[26] Discussed further in ch 8.

[27] Mentioned in ch 2 and again in ch 8.

[28] See: *Statement on behalf of the European Union at the 63rd session of the General Assembly on the Implementation of the Declaration of Commitment on HIV/AIDS and the Political Declaration on HIV/AIDS*, New York, 16 June 2009. Cited in: European Commission, *Combating HIV/AIDS*, n 14 above, 3.

[29] Discussed further in ch 8.

the circulation of people and things—including the laws of EU Member States, which must be disapplied when found to be incompatible with directly effective EU law.[30]

Finally, the political context comprising a series of EU, broader European and international initiatives[31] is noted as defining:

> *[C]ommitments and targets* in the response to HIV/AIDS. They *call upon the EU, national governments, international organisations, and civil society to act and to deliver*. There are commitments to ensure universal access to HIV prevention, treatment, care and support, to invest into research for the development of novel preventive and therapeutic tools, to promote support for and solidarity with PLWHA and most at risk populations, to involve civil society and PLWHA in policy making and implementation, and to create a supportive social environment.[32] (Emphasis added)

This context helps to delimit, mediate and distribute responsibilities and accountabilities between a diverse range of actors, among them the EU, and it foregrounds the more detailed specification, to which I return in the next section. Targets are used as the basis for determining failure ie the trigger for accountability. This also reflects some central principles and values for EU public health governance (universality, solidarity), while highlighting the ongoing and central importance of prevention and treatment, the wider use of risk to focus the interventions on those most 'at risk', while at the same time ensuring this does not feed into prejudice, stigma and the consequent production of an unsupportive social environment. Finally, the involvement and harnessing of those infected with HIV/AIDS as well as wider civil society as part of a broader societal response underlines their role in the regulation of the danger or threat posed by HIV/AIDS. This harnessing is also part of attempts to distribute and define the boundaries of responsibility; the responsibilisation of individuals and groups is part of the attempt to delimit EU responsibility and accountability, while extending its power through attempts at governing at a distance.

Perhaps the most important international commitment is the 2004 Dublin Declaration on Partnership to Fight HIV/AIDS in Europe and Central Asia.[33] This is one of a number of key international documents referenced in EU documents,[34] all of which highlight the alignment of the EU level of the multi-level system of

[30] The free movement of goods, services and persons was noted in ch 2. The relevant Treaty provisions (and applicable secondary legislation) noted in the latter are directly effective (Case 26/62 *Van Gend & Loos v Netherlands Inland Revenue Administration* [1963] ECR 1) and therefore take precedence over conflicting national laws and administrative practices (Case 11/70 *Internationale Handelsgesellschaft mbH v Einfuhr- und Vorratsstelle für Getreide und Futtermittel* [1970] ECR 1125; Case 106/77 *Amministrazione delle Finanze dello Stato v Simmenthal SpA* [1978] ECR 629).

[31] Such as the Dublin Declaration 2004 and the Millennium Development Goals 2000.

[32] European Commission, *Combating HIV/AIDS*, n 14 above, 3.

[33] Available at: www.unicef.org/ceecis/The_Dublin_Declaration.pdf (last accessed 15 May 2012).

[34] Especially those linking to development and poverty reduction, specifically, Millennium Development Goals 2000 and Paris Declaration 2005, and which are cited in European Commission, *Together for Health*, n 2 above, 6, fn 23.

governance with broader international developments. The EU's role in producing this broader global setting also indicates how its priorities and approaches are projected and mediated internationally, and how they are in turn leveraged in order to (re)legitimate the design, shape and implementation of EU governance, including its neoliberal underpinnings and orientation. Global goals are refracted and operationalised through the EU's risk-based approach to governing public health problems, and as shall become even more apparent below, the values, objectives, and programmatic priorities underpinning and found in the overarching architecture of EU governance.

Like *Combating HIV/AIDS* the Dublin Declaration begins with the context and rationale for its creation: 'the background of the *global emergency of the HIV/AIDS epidemic* with 40 million people worldwide living with HIV/AIDS, 90 per cent in developing countries and 75 per cent in Sub-Saharan Africa'. The focus on population highlights the governmentalisation of HIV/AIDS as a global public health problem; while the focus on HIV/AIDS as a global emergency emphasises its securitisation. These twin dynamics are especially apparent in the series of hortatory recitals that are, as just traced, also duplicated in the EU's approach. For instance, the:

> [R]apid escalation of the epidemic among young people in *Eastern Europe*, where HIV prevalence in the adult population is reaching *critical levels* in a number of countries and also the significant potential for the *rapid spread of HIV in South-Eastern Europe and Central Asia*.[35] (Emphasis added)

Moreover, there is 'serious concern with the *resurgence of HIV/AIDS prevalence in Western Europe*, including HIV resistant to anti-retroviral therapy, where the disease remains a potent threat to our young people'. Importantly, the wider global situation is referenced, underlining the scale of the medical emergency and helping to sketch out the broader danger or threat to the circulation of people and things: 'the most seriously affected countries, mainly in *southern Africa*, are *facing collapse* in one or more sectors of society' (emphasis added).[36]

The focus on transnational circulation of population explains the space for global intervention by the EU. There is also agreement 'that the HIV/AIDS epidemic *threatens to become a crisis of unprecedented proportions in our region*, undermining public health, development, social cohesion, *national security and the political stability* in many of our countries' (emphasis added).[37] HIV/AIDS—and by implication public health governance—are positioned as of foundational importance for socio-political order itself. In this way HIV/AIDS is not just a medical emergency; it is also of existential importance in that a failure to regulate HIV/AIDS as a danger or threat to the circulation of people (and things like blood products) could undermine the EU's wider programmatic priorities, and ultimately

[35] Recital 9, Dublin Declaration 2004.

[36] Ibid, Recital 11.

[37] Ibid, Recital 11.

the project of European integration. Importantly given it indicates the broader shift away from prevention interrogated further below (especially in the final subsection), care and treatment, ie medical and technological responses, are also key: '*The goal of providing effective anti-retroviral treatment* must be conducted in a poverty-focused manner, equitable, and [directed] to those people who are at the highest risk of and most vulnerable to HIV/AIDS' (emphasis added).[38] In this way ethics and humans rights related concerns are noted and made central to ensuring the effectiveness of EU policy. However, ethics and human rights appear to be instrumentalised as legitimating supports for risk as the dominant frame of EU HIV/AIDS governance.

Further, pointing to the pharmaceuticalisation of HIV/AIDS, that is through the growing preference for medical and pharmaceutical responses, and resonating with key aspects of the EU's approach to regulating HIV/AIDS considered below, the provision of anti-retrovirals is to proceed by working with:

> [T]he national and international pharmaceutical industry in a public-private partnership including with relevant international organisations such as the World Health Organisation in helping to tackle *the epidemic along all points of the drug supply chain*—from manufacturing to pricing to distribution.[39] (Emphasis added)

Timely and sustained access to pharmaceuticals are clearly vital as part of the response to HIV/AIDS. In that regard working with the pharmaceutical industry is clearly important. Yet, in light of the discussion in the last two chapters, and as underlined below, when taken up in the EU context the focus on 'partnership' might actually facilitate the insinuation of market rationality and corporate interests into public health governance. The latter might also shape and determine the (de)selection of regulatory interventions, such that despite the apparent centrality of prevention in the socio-economic and political conditions that help to cause public health problems, there is a shift in focus, attention and resources towards medical and technological responses.

As the 'partnership' approach to providing treatment suggests, the EU is part of the assemblage of actors governing HIV/AIDS. The EU is given a central role under the Dublin Declaration in international cooperation,[40] including the funding of preventive measures, care and treatment,[41] and engagement with those living with HIV/AIDS.[42] For instance, the ECDC has a central role in the monitoring of progress on the actions mandated by the Dublin Declaration.[43] A key action is to 'Fund, improve, and harmonise surveillance systems, in line with international

[38] Ibid, Action 21.

[39] Ibid, Action 29.

[40] Ibid, Action 5.

[41] Ibid, Action 7.

[42] Ibid, Actions 32 and 33.

[43] See: 'AIDS' ecdc.europa.eu/en/healthtopics/aids/Pages/index.aspx. Moreover, the ECDC monitors HIV/AIDS and blood-borne diseases more generally: 'HIV, STI and viral Hepatitis' ecdc.europa.eu/en/publications/all_publications/HIV_STI_blood_borne_viruses/Pages/hiv_sti_blood_borne_viruses.aspx.

standards, to track and monitor the epidemic, risk behaviours and vulnerability to HIV/AIDS'.[44]

The gathering and production of knowledge is also noted as part of the context for EU governance—indeed, the focus on treatment is augmented through a stress investment in '*public research and development* for the development of affordable and easier to use therapeutics and diagnostics to support expanded treatment access and improve the quality of life of people living with HIV' (emphasis added)[45] as well as surveillance and information gathering—and this is leveraged in order to build and legitimate its regulatory interventions. In this way the gathering and production of knowledge is of fundamental importance both *as* governance and as a foundation for *other* aspects of governance, including the delineation of the wider boundaries of responsibility and accountability. As I stress below, the focus on scientific and technical knowledge and expertise, while clearly vital, also helps to configure EU governance in relation to those it governs (especially the vulnerable groups noted above).

All together these key contexts are used to justify HIV/AIDS as a problem for and to legitimate EU governance. Consistent with the wider framing of the technology governing public health, and as seen in the previous chapter in relation to major and chronic diseases and conditions, risk is the dominant frame, and it is directed at producing security through prevention and treatment as the key interventions in population that regulate the danger or threat posed by HIV/AIDS to the circulation of people (and things like blood products—which when infected become a target for the regulation noted above). Ethics and human rights concerns around dealing with differences and inequalities in the incidence of HIV/AIDS across the EU and within particular population groups provide important justifications for EU governance and help to shape the regulatory interventions chosen and their use. Nevertheless, ethics and human rights essentially support the risk-based framing of governance and its contours. In the next section I outline the distribution of responsibilities in more detail, and subsequently, the declared centrality of prevention, the focus on most 'at risk' groups and regions, before turning to examine technologies for the gathering and production of knowledge. There I highlight a key concern: the way in which knowledge technologies prefigure the distribution of attention and resources towards medical and technological responses to HIV/AIDS and away from the avowed focus on prevention.

B. Key Contours of the EU's Governance

i. Distributed Responsibilities

Against the backdrop of the epidemiological, legal and social, and political contexts of HIV/AIDS there is a far more explicit attempt in *Combating HIV/AIDS* to

[44] Action 17 Dublin Declaration 2004.
[45] Ibid, Action 24.

establish and delimit EU and especially Commission responsibility and accountability. This occurs through lists that refine Article 168 TFEU and its implementation through the public health strategy in *Together for Health*. An initial concern is with highlighting the importance of coordination and cooperation between the EU and its neighbours as well as with international organisations. These are the 'overall objectives' of *Combating HIV/AIDS*, and they have three dimensions: reducing new HIV infections 'across all European countries by 2013'—an underspecified objective by a clear target date; improving access to prevention, treatment, care and support; and seeking to improve the quality of life of not just PLWHA, but also those 'affected by or most vulnerable to HIV/AIDS in the European Union *and* neighbouring countries' (emphasis added).[46] The policy domain is set out as encompassing 'All EU Member States, candidate and potential candidate countries, European Free Trade Agreement (EFTA) countries and *countries in the European Neighbourhood Policy area* as well as the Russian Federation', all parties who 'are *invited to contribute* to the implementation of these goals' (emphasis added).[47] Although the focus is on seeking to work with other actors, cooperation is central to the EU's role, and it becomes a way of governing at a distance, by extending EU governance and power over its territory, its periphery and beyond. In this way cooperation underlines the (re)configuration between power and responsibility as a key underpinning and structuring theme of the EU's governance of HIV/AIDS, and it is strongly related to the (re)configuration between sovereignty and territoriality.

There is also a renewed stress on promoting the 'human rights of PLWHA and affected communities, embedded in the Charter of Fundamental Rights of the EU', but this overlaps with concern for ensuring the effectiveness of risk regulation. Reference to epidemiology and its mapping of current and expected future trends are deemed to be 'best addressed' by a three pronged approach underpinned by risk and directed at facilitating security understood as being about regulating the danger or threat posed by HIV/AIDS to the circulation of PLWHA and affected communities. First, there is a focus on regulatory interventions through the 'Scaling up the implementation of *prevention strategies*, which effectively target local realities and needs', which highlights the ongoing centrality of prevention in an attempt to govern and forestall the danger or threat of HIV/AIDS in the future, 'while working towards ensuring *universal access* to prevention, *treatment*, care and support' (emphasis added).[48]

Second, 'Supporting an effective response to HIV/AIDS in *priority regions*, such as the mostly affected EU Member States, the Russian Federation and the most affected neighbouring countries', helps to direct and determine the geographical focus of efforts and legitimate internal and external governance of HIV/AIDS.

[46] European Commission, *Combating HIV/AIDS*, n 14 above, 4.

[47] Ibid. On the European Neighbourhood Policy, see: N Ghazaryan, *European Neighbourhood Policy and the Democratic Values of the EU* (Oxford, Hart Publishing, 2013).

[48] Ibid.

Finally, the third prong of 'Developing means to reach and support the populations most-at-risk and most vulnerable to HIV/AIDS across Europe',[49] rounds out the use of risk by complementing the geographical focus on the space beyond the EU's borders with attention to those who literally transmit and circulate HIV/AIDS. In this way components of population are produced and specified as the target of governance and Europe is the focus of efforts, that is the EU and its periphery. Although unsurprising, this is also revealing of how the EU's external efforts are essentially self-interested; they are an attempt to ensure the EU's security.

These priorities and actions provide the broad contours of EU governance and its regulatory interventions. Overall, the EU's principal responsibility and means of legitimation is providing political leadership. Indeed, it is '*an important asset the European Union can provide in the fight against HIV/AIDS*'.[50] Further:

> HIV/AIDS remains a stigmatised condition which, within the European Union and its neighbouring countries, mainly affects marginalised groups. *Not addressing the HIV epidemic would cause considerable harm to the individual and public health, and increasing costs to societies.* An effective response to HIV requires political leadership to ensure that the *health and rights* of vulnerable and affected groups are promoted. Political leadership is important to *define and assure the implementation of priorities and actions*. Unambiguous political advocacy is indispensable to align these priorities to needs and resources.[51] (Emphasis added)

The EU's leadership role is obviously important in light of the social and cultural barriers to tackling HIV/AIDS—it is also a role that augments and extends EU governance and power despite the apparently limited formal boundaries of responsibility provided by Article 168 TFEU. Human rights and ethics related concerns again help to support and legitimate governance, which is seen here through the focus on those who are vulnerable and affected by HIV/AIDS. The difficult position of these groups can be compounded by coercive government policies that seek to control HIV/AIDS but in doing so infringe on the rights of individuals that are known or suspected to be infected, and which decrease the effectiveness of public health interventions. Consequently, protecting and promoting human rights is increasingly important as a means of protecting health at an individual and societal level.[52] Without denying the importance of this, rights support risk-based governance and the broader neoliberal power relations undergirding and structuring the EU's approach.

More specifically, the focus on political leadership centralises the Commission and augments its authority, while at the same time there is a further attempt to support and specify its responsibility. These include efforts at '(1) … decreasing HIV-related *stigma*, (2) *promoting respect* for the human rights of all PLWHA and

[49] Ibid.

[50] Ibid.

[51] Ibid.

[52] LO Gostin and Z Lazzarini, *Human Rights and Public Health in the AIDS Pandemic* (Oxford, Oxford University Press, 1997). For further discussion see ch 8.

(3) addressing all forms of HIV-related *discrimination* and *support the social inclusion* of PLWHA' (emphasis added).[53] Further, echoing Article 168(1) TFEU there is a focus on promoting 'the mainstreaming of HIV/AIDS-related issues across EU policies, legislation and agreements'. International initiatives are leveraged to support and legitimate the EU's engagement—and arguably finer grained control through 'monitoring the implementation of international commitments at country and European level, and [in this way these activities support] international organisations such as UNAIDS in their work to mobilise political leadership in Eastern Europe'. Augmenting this strengthening of the gathering and production of knowledge as the foundation for governance is the work of the ECDC, which is called 'upon … to continue monitoring the progress in meeting commitments of the Dublin, Vilnius and Bremen Declarations'.[54]

The central role of civil society, especially those representing PLWHA and affected communities in combating HIV/AIDS is noted and even lauded (they 'were instrumental in developing practical and political solutions to address HIV/AIDS' (emphasis added)).[55] The EU seeks to responsibilise, shape and govern civil society at a distance or indirectly through the HIV/AIDS Civil Society Forum, which becomes a technology of governing through agency. More specifically, it is for the Commission to 'maintain the HIV/AIDS Civil Society Forum as the principal interface to advise … [it] and the HIV/AIDS Think Tank'.[56] The former comprises a group of major European networks and non-governmental organisations which advise on policy formulation and implementation.[57] The think tank comprises representatives of EU Member States and neighbouring countries, which exchange information and seek to strengthen cooperation.[58] Together these are tasked with helping to implement policy and strengthen cooperation among countries, civil society and international organisations. Involving civil society in this way is also a means of gathering and producing important knowledge and expertise, and opening up the public health knowledge domain and governance.

Moreover:

> The Commission wants to ensure that civil society stays involved in HIV/AIDS related policy development and implementation and remains a front line partner in a coordinated response, *sharing responsibility for meeting commitments*. Civil society should have the necessary freedom to act and to be involved at all levels in the response to HIV/AIDS across Europe and beyond.[59] (Emphasis added)

[53] European Commission, *Combating HIV/AIDS*, n 14 above, 5.

[54] Ibid, 4–5.

[55] Ibid, 5.

[56] Ibid.

[57] 'HIV/AIDS Civil Society Forum' ec.europa.eu/health/sexual_health/hiv_aids/civil_society_forum/index_en.htm.

[58] 'The HIV/AIDS Think Tank' ec.europa.eu/health/sexual_health/hiv_aids/think_tank/index_en.htm.

[59] European Commission, *Combating HIV/AIDS*, n 14 above, 5.

The focus is ultimately on leveraging civil society actors and their efforts in order to assist the EU in shoring up and legitimating its governance—the Commission 'supports the involvement of civil society organisations, including those representing PLWHA and affected communities, in planning, implementing and evaluating the response to HIV/AIDS in the European Union and neighbouring countries'[60]—and delimiting its responsibility, ensuring the credit for success while also limiting blame and accountability in the event of failure (which as noted above is already subject to efforts at defining it as being about 'neglecting' prevention).

Moving beyond the EU and civil society organisations, the wider responsibilities of society at large are noted. Human rights is deployed here to specify these and to shape and legitimate the Commission's role, through its focus on 'the need to ensure the respect for the human rights of all persons irrespective of their health status, sexual orientation, lifestyle, national and social origin', providing the basis for 'work[ing] with all relevant stakeholders and public authorities to step up awareness raising efforts and to initiate public campaigns on HIV/AIDS' and encouraging 'wider professional training on HIV, in particular in the health and social sectors as well as in law enforcement and education'.[61] In particular, the aim is to identify preventative actions that help to reduce the number of new HIV/AIDS infections as well as to help improve the quality of life for people living with HIV/AIDS. The focus of EU policies is on encouraging self-management and engagement through political support offered to national authorities and stakeholders in both EU Member States and neighbouring countries.

Underlining human rights and ethics related concerns is also part of the EU's role (especially the Commission's), responsibility and identity as a public health and security actor. Indeed, it is noteworthy that:

> Any form of HIV/AIDS related *discrimination and stigmatisation is unacceptable*. National policies *should prioritise improvements across the general population* of basic knowledge on HIV/AIDS and the prevention of HIV transmission. *Unprejudiced attitudes* remove potential barriers to gaining HIV-related information and may support risk reducing behaviour patterns.[62] (Emphasis added)

This statement also responsibilises society at large (through respect for human rights), public health education and information efforts. This also helps to demarcate and legitimate the EU's central responsibility through the Commission: 'HIV/AIDS associated stigma and discrimination create barriers to access HIV testing, treatment and care. *The Commission will further address this issue on a political level and in its equal treatment policies*' (emphasis added).[63] Cutting across these

[60] Ibid.

[61] Ibid, 6.

[62] Ibid, 5.

[63] Directives in the area of anti-discrimination are: Directive 2000/43/EC implementing the principle of equal treatment between persons irrespective of racial or ethnic origin [2000] OJ L180/22 and Directive 2000/78/EC establishing a general framework for equal treatment in employment and occupation [2000] OJ L303/16.

different groups of responsibilities is additional attention to universal access to prevention, treatment, care and support.[64]

References to human rights, ethics and non-discrimination support and extend EU governance and power; and within neoliberalism they become key tactics in the (re)configuration between power and responsibility. Human rights and non-discrimination effectively extend those who are governed by EU governance beyond PLWHA and affected communities to encompass society; it is governed at a distance through its responsibilisation. Overall, the distribution of responsibility and accountability across a range of actors and groups helps to delimit and mediate the EU's responsibility and accountability, while at the same time extending EU power in spite of the formal limits found in Article 168 TFEU.

ii. The Centrality of Prevention

As already noted, prevention is the first main prong of the EU's approach to governing HIV/AIDS and a key regulatory intervention in population and especially most affected and vulnerable groups and communities. Prevention is therefore reflected in the distribution of responsibilities and it is also important for constituting governance and configuring it in relation to those who are governed. Epidemiological knowledge is vitally important to prevention—and its production is therefore part of the EU's governance, role and responsibility, and a precondition for wider governance, prevention and treatment as the key regulatory interventions. That is, the effectiveness of prevention '*requires a solid evidence base and robust surveillance systems*, including meaningful behavioural data to ensure that the key forces behind the epidemic are adequately addressed' (emphasis added). A key aspect of prevention is the 'sexual and reproductive health and rights of PLWHA [which] are important aspects for national policy planning and programmes'. In this respect the promotion of safer sexual behaviour is key, as is the correct and consistent use of condoms. Drawing on evidence, these are 'the most effective means of HIV prevention through sexual transmission', whereas the ensuring access to sterile needles and injecting equipment and the availability of substitution treatment for addiction are 'the most effective means of HIV prevention through injecting drug use'.[65] In order to enhance this prevention is aimed at addressing the situation of children and young people as well as attempts to avoid mother-to-child transmission, improving HIV testing, and ensuring universal access to treatment, care and support.

These dimensions of prevention echo the Dublin Declaration, which highlights the continued interrelationship between the EU and the *broader* international effort:

> [H]e *prevention of HIV infection*, through the promotion of safer and responsible sexual behaviour and practices, including through condom use, *must be the mainstay of*

[64] European Commission, *Combating HIV/AIDS*, n 14 above, 6.
[65] Ibid, 7.

> *the sub-national, national, regional and international response* to the epidemic and that *prevention, care, support and treatment* for those infected and affected by HIV/AIDS *are mutually reinforcing elements* of an effective response and *must* be integrated in a comprehensive approach to combat the epidemic.[66] (Emphasis added)

However, as I have already noted and go on to discuss further below, the focus on prevention is supplemented with a concern for medical and technological responses through treatment, and this has implications for the actual rather than stated prioritisation of regulatory interventions, in that prevention might lose out. The latter shall become apparent below where I look at knowledge in greater detail by reference to the techniques, processes and practices—the technologies of—knowledge creation. Before doing so I turn to discuss the refinement of prevention through its focus on priority regions and populations that are most 'at risk'.

iii. Most 'At Risk' Regions and Groups

The focus on most 'at risk' regions and groups brings together the two other main prongs (the second and third) of the EU's approach to regulating HIV/AIDS. This prioritisation channels and directs regulatory efforts and nuances the EU's responsibility and accountability as part of its approach to regulating HIV/AIDS as a danger or threat to the circulation of people and things. The focus on most 'at risk' groups—including 'Men having Sex with Men' (subject to stigma, discrimination and homophobia), injecting drug use (accounting for around two-thirds of new cases in Eastern Europe), and mobile populations who might not have access to comprehensive prevention measures, testing and treatment[67]—intersects with most 'at risk' regions, particularly in Eastern Europe (including newer Member States), the eastern and southern periphery and beyond. Attention to most 'at risk' regions makes it possible to direct regulatory interventions towards and focus on most 'at risk' groups and vice versa. Importantly:

> The Commission recognises the *need to step up cooperation among EU Member States, candidate, potential candidate, and other neighbouring countries*, and to support countries to develop tailor-made strategies. There is a need to introduce effective prevention measures, in particular harm reduction measures. Public health and social policies should take into account the needs of ethnic minorities. *Social inequalities and barriers to health care should be overcome at both political and operational levels.*[68] (Emphasis added)

There are three main areas of activity in relation to most 'at risk' regions and groups: those concerning the EU's immediate periphery or neighbours, those in the wider region, and those beyond, principally in the global South. These zones for the EU's regulatory interventions underline the (re)configuration between

[66] Recital 14 Dublin Declaration 2004.
[67] European Commission, *Combating HIV/AIDS*, n 14 above, 8.
[68] Ibid, 7.

sovereignty and territoriality as a continuing structuring theme, in that the EU's public health governance extends beyond the territories of EU Member States to intervene in specific target populations in specific target areas. Further, since the population that is integral to the governmentalisation of EU HIV/AIDS governance is not limited to the EU, the focus on most 'at risk' regions and groups also (re)configures governance and the governed. That is because the basis for governance and the territories and groups for the EU's regulatory interventions extends beyond the EU and its Member States, so too do those that are governed by and through them.

Consistent with the mainstreaming required by Article 168(1) TFEU, governing public health across these territories and groups requires action through other policy domains 'such as health, development cooperation, external action, research and trade'.[69] The external nature of many of these domains establishes a role for the 'EU in the world',[70] which is noted in *Together for Health* as its final core principle of 'strengthening the EU's *voice in global health*'. This is reflected here in the focus on producing 'sustained collective *leadership* in global health'.[71] Since public health governance is concerned with regulating the dangers or threats attendant to the circulation of people and things, the *extension* of EU public health governance also helps to promote the exportation of the EU's normative power and the securitisation of wider areas of EU activity.

The relationship between the internal and external dimensions of the EU's approach creates the broad frame for HIV/AIDS governance:

> In our globalised world it is *hard to separate national or EU-wide actions from global policy*, as global health issues have an impact on internal Community health policy and vice versa. The EC can contribute to global health by *sharing its values, experience and expertise*, as well as by taking concrete steps to improve health. Work can support efforts to ensure *coherence between its internal and external health policies in attaining global health goals*, to consider health as an important element in the *fight against poverty through health-related aspects of external development cooperation with low income countries*, to respond to health threats in third countries.[72] (Emphasis added)

The intertwinement of the internal and external dimensions of EU regulation is leveraged in order to provide the rationale for and justify EU involvement beyond its own territory as well as the approach taken within the EU. Linking back, within *Combating HIV/AIDS* the importance of politics is further specified through its role in enhancing the various components of the EU's external governance: 'Political commitments should lead to a constructive dialogue and help to overcome

[69] European Commission, *Together for Health*, n 2 above, 6–7, and at 6, fn 22: 'This follows from the Article 152 calling for cooperation with third countries and international organisations in public health and from the Commission's strategic objective of Europe as a World Partner' (see: European Commission, *Annual Policy Strategy for 2008*, COM (2007) 65).

[70] 'EU in the World' ec.europa.eu/health/eu_world/policy/index_en.htm.

[71] European Commission, *Together for Health*, n 2 above, 6.

[72] Ibid.

existing implementation barriers of existing or new strategies. Building on current cooperation, the Commission is ready to *strengthen cooperation through existing mechanisms and instruments*' (emphasis added).[73] The external dimension of EU HIV/AIDS governance, its importance for the internal dimension and the broader programmatic priorities and concerns of the overarching architecture of EU governance, can be made more apparent by reference to, first, accession policy and relations with countries on the EU's wider periphery (some of which will not be in line for accession), and subsequently relations with regions and countries beyond the periphery through development policy.

Accession policy is central to the EU's approach to facilitating cooperation between its Member States, candidates and potential candidates, and it concerns countries bordering the EU. Indeed, the:

> EU regularly exchanges information and advises candidate countries and potential candidates on its health policy, and evaluates the progress they are making in incorporating it into their domestic legislation. In the accession negotiations with candidate countries, '*public health is discussed in Chapter 28* on consumer and health protection'.[74] (Emphasis added)

In terms of broader relations regional cooperation is particularly important. Facilitating and structuring relations with these countries is a key area of activity. In order to 'familiarise the regions with EU public health policy and exchange best practices in public health, the EU Commission supports and participates in meetings with regional networks and groupings'.[75] These include the South-Eastern Europe Health Network (SEEHN),[76] the European Neighbourhood Policy (ENP),[77] the Euro-Mediterranean Partnership (EUROMED)[78] and the Northern Dimension Partnership in Public Health and Social Well-Being (NDPHS).[79]

Unsurprisingly, given the prevalence of HIV/AIDS and its transmission in the countries concerned, ENP is especially important. As such the need to enhance cooperation and effective prevention measures:

> *[A]pplies particularly* to the eastern *European Neighbourhood Policy area … countries and the Russian Federation* where the HIV epidemic is concentrated in most at risk populations, with a potential to drift into the general population as heterosexual transmission is increasing. Although measures and strategies in response to HIV/AIDS are generally in place, access to HIV prevention, treatment, care and support still needs improvement.[80] (Emphasis added)

[73] Ibid, 8.
[74] 'EU in the World', n 70 above.
[75] Ibid.
[76] 'SEEHN' ec.europa.eu/health/eu_world/policy/seehn/index_en.htm.
[77] 'European Neighbourhood Policy' ec.europa.eu/health/eu_world/policy/enp/index_en.htm.
[78] 'Euro-Mediterranean Partnership (EUROMED)' eeas.europa.eu/euromed/index_en.htm.
[79] 'Northern Dimension Partnership in Public Health and Social Well-Being' ec.europa.eu/health/eu_world/policy/northern_dimension/index_en.htm.
[80] European Commission, *Together for Health*, n 2 above, 7.

There is a strong overlap between most 'at risk' groups and regions—and ENP is particularly revealing of the self-interested and security-oriented rationale for the EU's external public health governance: 'Supporting the efforts of neighbouring countries will prevent the spread of HIV and associated infections such as tuberculosis *into the EU* and to improve the conditions of PLWHA in the region' (emphasis added).[81] ENP and by implication the EU's wider external governance are concerned with regulating the danger or threat to the circulation of people and things *into* the EU—which is a way to prevent circulation *within* the EU. Put differently, the EU's attempts to govern the groups and regions beyond its own territory is a way of forestalling dangers or threats within it. External governance is an adjunct of internal governance and it is principally about safeguarding the EU by and through the regulation of the dangers or threats attendant to the circulation of people and things.

To focus on ENP, this was developed in 2004, and has the 'objective of avoiding the emergence of new dividing lines between the enlarged EU and our neighbours and instead *strengthening the prosperity, stability and security of all*' (emphasis added).[82] Economic priorities are linked to socio-political order and security. Public health plays a key role in these and is, in an echo of the understanding of its use and importance noted above, about regulating the dangers or threats attendant to free circulation in an effort to achieve security and economic optimisation. Indeed, public health was recognised as a key area for cooperation between the EU and its ENP partners in *Strengthening the European Neighbourhood Policy*.[83] Although ENP encompasses a very wide range of issues, such as democracy, human rights, social and economic issues, environment, energy and education, all ENP action plans make reference to cooperation in public health, and the plans are supported by specific EU financing.[84] The latter seeks to facilitate the participation of third countries, especially those 'to which the European Neighbourhood Policy applies, countries that are applying for, are candidates for, or are acceding to, membership of the [EU]',[85] and non-participant third countries and 'relevant international organisations, in particular the WHO'.[86] Funding is key to and facilitative of governing at a distance, and thereby expanding the reach of EU governance and power.

Although individual countries have leeway over the precise areas of cooperation, three fields are noted as those where 'cooperation is envisaged': health sector

[81] Ibid.

[82] See: 'What is the European Neighbourhood Policy?' eeas.europa.eu/enp/about-us/index_en.htm. Also see: European Commission, *Wider Europe—Neighbourhood: A New Framework for Relations with our Eastern and Southern Neighbours*, COM (2003) 104 final; European Commission, *European Neighbourhood Policy Strategy Paper*, COM (2004) 373 final.

[83] European Commission, *Strengthening the European Neighbourhood Policy*, COM (2006) 726 final.

[84] Regulation (EC) 1638/2006 laying down general provisions establishing a European Neighbourhood and Partnership Instrument [2006] OJ L310/1.

[85] Art 11(b) Decision 1350/2007/EC establishing a second programme of Community action in the field of health (2008–13) [2007] OJ L301/3.

[86] Art 12 Decision 1350/2007/EC, ibid.

reform and health policy; health information and knowledge; and, communicable disease surveillance and health security. Cooperation in first of these is clearly intended to bolster domestic capabilities of dealing with public health problems, whereas the second and third fields are essentially concerned with the gathering and production of knowledge as part of ENP and as a way of strengthening regulatory interventions and ensuring they are better attuned to the nature of the danger or threat posed by public health problems, including HIV/AIDS. These two fields of cooperation highlight the (re)configuration between knowledge and power—in particular the extension of power through the gathering and production of knowledge—as a key structuring theme of ENP. In this way the external dimension of public health governance is again closely aligned to, and reflective and supportive of the EU's domestic policy.

Health is also part of 'achieving aims in the fields of socio-economic development, poverty reduction, the environment, food safety, research and development, road safety or the information society (e-health) will also contribute to better health'.[87] HIV/AIDS gains in prominence in ENP in relation to references that: 'Certain ENP countries face specific challenges from *communicable diseases such as HIV/AIDS* and tuberculosis (notably Eastern Europe and, in particular, Ukraine). Communicable diseases represent potential *cross-border risks to both the EU and our neighbourhood*' (emphasis added).[88] In this way cross-borderness becomes key to the EU's governance: communicable diseases are the focus of ENP since they are key dangers of threats to the free circulation of people and things across borders (consistent with Article 168 TFEU). The cross-borderness of public health problems and their regulation in order to achieve security are linked in order to provide a particular justification for EU external governance of HIV/AIDS and the extension and dissemination of its power across the territories closest to its borders. The (re)configuration of sovereignty and territoriality apparent in governance of the EU's periphery continues and extends through the EU's relations with the wider world.

In those wider relations the focus is on the EU's global role, responsibility and identity, and here development policy is particularly important. According to the title of the key policy document, the focus is on *The EU Role in Global Health*.[89] This is built on in other documents,[90] perhaps most notably *European Research and Knowledge for Global Health*.[91] Echoing *Together for Health*, the Commission states:

> Global health is a term for which no single definition exists. It is about worldwide improvement of health, reduction of disparities, and protection against global health

[87] 'European Neighbourhood Policy', n 77 above.

[88] Ibid.

[89] European Commission, *The EU Role in Global Health*, COM (2010) 128 final. Followed by a high-level conference on 10–11 June 2010: onetec.be/global_health/.

[90] European Commission, *Staff Working Document, Global Health—Responding to the Challenges of Globalisation*, SEC (2010) 380 final; European Commission, *Staff Working Document, Contributing to Universal Coverage of Health Services through Development Policy*, SEC (2010) 382 final.

[91] European Commission, *Staff Working Document, European Research and Knowledge for Global Health*, SEC (2010) 381 final.

> threats. Addressing global health requires coherence of all internal and external policies and actions based on agreed principles.

Building on references in the Treaties and the Charter of Fundamental Rights of the EU:[92]

> Increased coherence between relevant internal and external policies will reinforce the EU as a global actor. The EU's social model, its strong safety norms, and its global trade and development aid position allow it to play a major role in improving global health.[93]

In other words, just as in the wider rationale and justification for the EU's external governance and regulatory interventions in public health, a range of EU policies intersect with public health and provide the basis for the EU's role in that regard, as well as the working out of responsibility and accountability.

EuropeAid development and cooperation is arguably the key area of EU policy beyond its periphery, and it is pertinent to HIV/AIDS, which is implicated as a poverty-related disease.[94] The EU is increasingly enmeshed in the global 'AIDs industry'.[95] As such, the EU's policy response—seen in its discourses—should be read as part of a broader assemblage of components that is crucial to implementing policy. As Nguyen explains, this assemblage is:

> [M]uch more than a new social movement pre-articulated around explicit objectives … it is a complex biopolitical assemblage, cobbled together from global flows of organisms, drugs, discourses, and technologies of all kinds. Institutionally, this assemblage roughly corresponds to what others have called an AIDS industry. As AIDS emerges as the foremost issue threatening economic and political futures in many countries around the world, *this AIDS industry has become ever-more entangled with the development industry*.[96] (Emphasis added)

EU policy is found in several policy documents, beginning with a 2004 framework which was developed into a common EU approach seeking to develop stronger, more effective and more concerted efforts in *A European Programme for Action to Confront HIV/AIDS, Malaria and Tuberculosis through External Action*

[92] For an overview see ch 2.

[93] European Commission, *The EU Role in Global Health*, n 89 above, 2. The EU's Foreign Affairs Council has also approved the Commission's approach, see: Council of the European Union, *Council Conclusions on the EU Role in Global Health, 3011th Foreign Affairs Council Meeting Brussels, 10 May 2010*. The EU's role as a global public health actor, with explicit reference to security and power relations in the global order, has also been supported by a Nobel Forum Seminar '*The European Union as a Global Health Actor*' (available at: onetec.be/global_health/doc/Nobelforumglobalhealthevent_report_v11_web[1].pdf).

[94] 'Development and Cooperation—EuropeAid' ec.europa.eu/europeaid/node/22_en: E Stillwaggon, *AIDS and the Ecology of Poverty* (Oxford, Oxford University Press, 2005), who argues HIV/AIDS cannot be stopped without understanding the ecology of poverty.

[95] C Patton, *Globalising AIDS* (Minneapolis, University of Minnesota Press, 2002).

[96] V-K Nguyen, 'Antiretroviral Globalism, Biopolitics, and Therapeutic Citizenship' in A Ong and SJ Collier (eds), *Global Assemblages: Technology, Politics, and Ethics as Anthropological Problems* (Oxford, Blackwell Publishing, 2005) 125. Bretton-Woods being the name for the post-World War II international global economic and financial architecture within and through which the world economy functions.

(2007–11).[97] The EU contributes to high profile responses, in part by building on international cooperation as part of its more general approach to global health, including global health goals linking to development and poverty reduction, specifically, Millennium Development Goals (especially Goal 6 'combat HIV/AIDS, malaria and other diseases'),[98] European Consensus on Development Cooperation and the 2005 Paris Declaration,[99] and working in partnership with other global actors, such as the WHO. Perhaps foremost is the Global Fund to Fight HIV/AIDS, Tuberculosis and Malaria (Global Fund).[100] This was established in 2001, and it works as a financing mechanism and means of fostering global partnership on HIV/AIDS. Since 2001 the EU has provided over 55 per cent of the total contributions to the Global Fund.[101] Moreover, building on governing at a distance through funding, HIV/AIDS is threaded through the European Consensus on Development (ECD).[102] The ECD is attuned to mainstreaming HIV/AIDS in all development policy sectors and providing predictable and long-term financing. Also implicated in development policy, and noted in the ensuing discussion, is the attunement of EU research towards the treatment of HIV/AIDS, especially in relation to clinical trials and, further down the pharmaceutical and medicine response pipeline, ensuring access and treatment.

The EU's approach underscores the extent to which its governance is increasingly proactive and not just reactive. This proactive stance is especially apparent in the exportation of normative power through public health—the reach of which is mainstreamed and extended across various policy domains—and it is underpinned by neoliberalism. The neoliberal underpinnings are reflected in the (re)configurations or structuring themes traced above and the focus on regulating the dangers or threats attendant to free circulation in order to achieve security and generate economic optimisation. The EU's external governance of HIV/AIDS draws down on global goals, and then uses them in order to legitimate and circulate its own aims, objectives and priorities, constitute its identity, extend its power and help to produce and legitimate its broader programmatic priorities. The latter include a socio-political order based on a competitive market economy and ultimately the project of European integration. Indeed:

> Contacts between the EU and its member countries and other countries and international organisations help to … foster good health in the EU and beyond … contribute to the enlargement process … *strengthen the EU's voice on global health issues, as a step to*

[97] European Commission, *A European Programme for Action to Confront HIV/AIDS, Malaria and Tuberculosis through External Action (2007–11)*, n 20 above; European Commission, *Staff Working Document, Progress Report on the Implementation of the European Programme for Action to Confront HIV/AIDS, Malaria and Tuberculosis through External Action (2007–11)*, SEC (2009) 748 final.

[98] 'Goal 6: Combat HIV, Malaria and Other Diseases' www.un.org/millenniumgoals/aids.shtml.

[99] European Commission, *Together for Health*, n 2 above, 6 at fn 23.

[100] 'The Global Fund' www.theglobalfund.org/en/.

[101] Discussed further in ch 8.

[102] For details see: 'European consensus on development' ec.europa.eu/europeaid/policies/european-development-policy/european-consensus-development_en.

> *establishing a global public health policy ... [and to] promote EU public health principles, standards and legislation.*[103] (Emphasis added)

Elsewhere the EU's governance, and especially its efforts at developing cooperation, are even more explicitly linked to and directed towards achieving its programmatic priorities:

> Strengthened coordination on health issues with international organisations, such as WHO and other relevant United Nations agencies, World Bank, International Labour Organization, OECD and Council of Europe, as well as other strategic partners and countries, will also enhance the EU's voice in global health and increase its influence and visibility *to match its economic and political weight.*[104] (Emphasis added)

IV. TECHNOLOGIES FOR THE GATHERING AND PRODUCTION OF KNOWLEDGE

The discussion so far highlights the centrality of scientific and technical knowledge and expertise to HIV/AIDS governance (also found in relation to the governance of cancer and in the public health strategy), as well as several related key (re)configurations or structuring themes. They include those between power and the delimitation of responsibility and accountability, the configuration of governance in relation to the governed, and especially important for this section, that between power and knowledge. The final main aspect of *Combating HIV/AIDS* is about '*improving* the knowledge' (emphasis added)[105]—which is a quite specific emphasis that again underlines the gathering and production of knowledge both *as* governance as well as the *foundation* of wider governance and regulatory interventions, and an important aspect and underpinning of the other structuring themes of HIV/AIDS governance. Two areas stand out as the focus of attention through specific technologies: first, surveillance and pharmaceuticals, and second, other technological fixes for public health problems. The first area also covers monitoring and evaluation and it is part of the wider systems in place for the surveillance of communicable diseases, which I introduce here and then sketch further in the next chapter.

A. Surveillance

Earlier in this book I described surveillance as part of technologies of agency and performance.[106] Surveillance systems 'provide information for monitoring the trend of communicable diseases, early detection of outbreaks, and help to identify risk factors, and need for interventions'. This provides the information and basis

[103] 'EU in the World', n 70 above.
[104] European Commission, *Together for Health*, n 2 above, 7.
[105] European Commission, *Combating HIV/AIDS*, n 14 above, 9.
[106] See ch 2.

for 'priority setting, planning, implementation and resource allocation for preventive programmes and for evaluating preventive programmes and control measures'.[107] Within the EU the network for the epidemiological surveillance and control of communicable diseases was established in 1998,[108] and this was followed by several implementing measures as well as a list of communicable diseases (and related public health issues) and their case definitions, which can now be rapidly adopted (such as for pandemic influenza H1N1).[109] Prior to the creation of the ECDC disease surveillance was carried out by 17 Dedicated Surveillance Networks (DSNs). These included European Influenza Surveillance Network (EISS), European Network for STI Surveillance (ESSTI), European Invasive Bacterial Diseases Surveillance Network (EU-IBIS), European Tuberculosis Surveillance Network (EuroTB) and European HIV/AIDS Surveillance Network (EuroHIV). Most of the DSNs are now defunct, with their work being taken over by the ECDC.[110]

Consequently, the ECDC is now central to communicable disease surveillance, and the gathering and production of knowledge is central to EU governance, and provides the basis and support for the EU's wider governance and regulatory interventions. As provided in its founding instrument, the ECDC:

> [S]hall … identify, assess and communicate current and emerging *threats to human health from communicable diseases*. In the case of other outbreaks of illness of unknown origin which may spread within or to the Community, the Centre shall act on its own initiative *until* the source of the outbreak is known.[111] (Emphasis added)

Reflecting the legal basis in what is now Article 168 TFEU this is 'In order to *enhance the capacity* of the Community and the Member States to *protect human health* through the *prevention and control* of human disease' (emphasis added).[112] Underlining the focus of the ECDC's work and limits of its responsibility and accountability in relation to *communicable* diseases, in the event of an outbreak which 'clearly is *not* caused by a communicable disease' the ECDC 'shall act *only in cooperation* with the competent authority *upon request from that authority*' (emphasis added).[113] In other words, the 'added value' of and justification for EU action (here that of the ECDC) requires a strong cross-border dimension.

[107] 'Surveillance of communicable diseases' ec.europa.eu/health/communicable_diseases/policy/surveillance_en.htm.

[108] Decision 2119/98/EC on a network for the epidemiological surveillance and control of communicable diseases, n 10 above, now replaced by Decision 1082/2013/EU, n 5 above, and Decision 2000/96/EC on the communicable diseases to be progressively covered by the Community network under Decision 2119/98/EC [1998] OJ L28/50 (as amended).

[109] Decision 2002/253/EC laying down case definitions for reporting communicable diseases to the Community network under Decision 2119/98/EC [2002 OJ L86/44 (as amended).

[110] For a full list see: 'Evaluation and assessment of Dedicated Surveillance Networks' ecdc.europa.eu/en/activities/surveillance/european_surveillance_networks/Pages/evaluation_assessment_DSNs.aspx.

[111] Art 3(1) Regulation (EC) 851/2004 establishing a European Centre for Disease Prevention and Control [2004] OJ L142/1.

[112] Ibid, Art 3(1).

[113] Ibid.

The ECDC 'shall ... search for, collect, collate, evaluate and disseminate *relevant scientific and technical data*' (emphasis added)[114] and provide '*scientific opinions* and *scientific and technical assistance* including training' (emphasis added).[115] The gathering, production and dissemination of scientific and technical knowledge and expertise—including its provision through training others—underpin and legitimate the ECDC's role and areas of responsibility and its identity as an authority. This role takes more specific shape and is strengthened through the provision of '*timely information* to the Commission, the Member States, Community agencies and international organisations active within the field of public health' (emphasis added).[116] The constitution of the knowledge domain for public health is augmented through the coordination of the 'European networking of bodies operating in the fields within the Centre's mission' (emphasis added),[117] and the exchange of information, expertise and best practices.[118]

Surveillance is carried out by seven disease-specific networks involving Member State surveillance contact points, including: HIV, STI and blood-borne viruses (especially relevant to this chapter); influenza (relevant to the next chapter); tuberculosis; vaccine preventable diseases and invasive bacterial infections, which includes measles, mumps and rubella.[119] Data is collected from, for example, population-based data processed by clinicians (in the case of measles), laboratories (in the case of salmonellosis) and sentinel surveillance systems where only a proportion of practitioners or microbiologists report cases (for influenza). These different means of surveillance ensure Member States are able to report data on an agreed list of 52 communicable diseases that comprise the networks according to the standardised case definitions, which are periodically revised by experts. Data is submitted by epidemiologists and information technology or data managers serving as national contact points. The frequency of data reporting differs from disease to disease. For example, influenza is reported weekly, and this permits the production of the Weekly Influenza Surveillance Overview. Most other diseases are reported annually.

The data is uploaded to and collected, validated, refined, exchanged, analysed and disseminated through The European Surveillance System (TESSy). Launched in 2008, TESSy is the culmination of the network for the epidemiological surveillance and control of communicable diseases, and its 'key aim is to provide the basis for high quality data analysis and interpretation to *provide evidence for public health action*' (emphasis added).[120] In other words, the possibility of evidence-

[114] Ibid, Art 3(2)(a).

[115] Ibid, Art 3(2)(b).

[116] Ibid, Art 3(2)(c).

[117] Ibid, Art 3(2)(d).

[118] Ibid, Art 3(2)(e).

[119] The remaining networks cover anti-microbial resistance and healthcare-associated infections; emerging and vector-borne diseases; food and water-borne diseases and zoonoses. See further: 'European disease networks/ECDC disease specific surveillance' ecdc.europa.eu/en/activities/surveillance/european_surveillance_networks/Pages/european_surveillance_networks.aspx.

[120] 'The European Surveillance System (TESSy)' ecdc.europa.eu/en/activities/surveillance/tessy/pages/tessy.aspx.

based decision-making leading to public health interventions is the central rationale for surveillance. A distinct advantage of TESSy is that is replaces the DSNs and their disparate ways of gathering and reporting data, providing 'experts with a *one-stop-shop* for EU surveillance data' (emphasis added).[121] The ECDC coordinates and develops the surveillance through seven disease-specific programmes that correspond to the disease-specific networks.

The responsibilities and accountabilities of the ECDC and the Member States are set out and specified further in order to ensure the 'added value' of EU level action. Indeed, reflecting in particular the legal foundation in Article 168 TFEU 'In pursuing its mission the Centre shall take full account of the responsibilities of the Member States' (their primary responsibility in relation to (public) health and especially health services), and also 'the Commission and other Community agencies, and of the responsibilities of international organisations active within the field of public health, *in order to ensure comprehensiveness, coherence and complementarity of action*' (emphasis added).[122] The ECDC's responsibilities are given further and clearer shape and substance through its long-term surveillance strategy that contributes to '*reducing the incidence and prevalence of communicable diseases* in the EU through public health data, information and reports to decision-makers … in an effort to promote actions that will result in the timely prevention and control of communicable diseases' (emphasis added).[123] This strategy is given specificity through objectives for a strengthened surveillance of communicable diseases. The strategy includes, inter alia, monitoring of trends in communicable diseases in order to facilitate evidence-based action, evaluating and monitoring of prevention and control programmes, identifying 'at risk' population groups that are in need of targeted prevention measures, assessing the burden of communicable diseases, and directing research into the sources, means of transmission and 'at risk' groups for communicable diseases.[124]

The complementarity of EU action to that of its Member States is also underscored through mention of Member State responsibility. Member States must provide the ECDC with the scientific and technical data relevant to its mission in a timely manner,[125] ensure they communicate messages 'forwarded to the Community network via the early warning and response system'[126] to the ECDC, and finally, they are required to identify 'recognised competent bodies and public health experts who could be made available to assist in Community responses to health threats, such as field investigations'.[127] The Member States are governed through their agency and responsibilised into making the work of the ECDC

[121] Ibid.

[122] Art 3(1) Regulation (EC) 851/2004, n 111 above.

[123] 'Long-term surveillance strategy' ecdc.europa.eu/en/activities/surveillance/legal_framework_strategy/Pages/surveillance_strategy.aspx.

[124] Ibid.

[125] Art 4(a) Regulation (EC) 851/2004, n 111 above.

[126] Ibid, Art 4(b).

[127] Ibid, Art 4(c).

possible. The Member States provide the resources (knowledge and expertise) for the ECDC's work, the basis for the production of the knowledge domain for public health, and for regulatory interventions in HIV/AIDS.

As already noted HIV/AIDS surveillance falls within the disease-specific network on HIV, STI and blood-borne viruses. The ECDC works with WHO Europe in order to coordinate HIV/AIDS surveillance in Europe, covering all 53 countries in the region.[128] As such *EU* surveillance goes well beyond the territory of the EU to encompass the *whole* of Europe. This is unsurprising given how the Dublin Declaration, for instance, with its territorial focus on Europe and central Asia, provides a key justification for the EU's central role in European (and not just EU) surveillance. In this way the ECDC is embedded within regional and wider international public health governance structures and networks of actors. Data is collected and submitted annually to TESSy by national HIV/AIDS surveillance contact points. In addition the ECDC and Commission work together on other projects, such as on the implementation of the Dublin Declaration. In *Combating HIV/AIDS* there is a focus on '*strengthening* surveillance' (emphasis added).[129] To this end the Commission 'urges all Member States … to gather even more robust and comprehensive data on HIV/AIDS and STIs, including on co-infections' and 'asks the ECDC to strengthen the cooperation with neighbouring countries and other partners such as UNAIDS'.[130]

Communication of governance efforts is a central concern. In particular the ECDC is required to 'ensure that the public and any interested parties are rapidly given objective, reliable and easily accessible information with regard to the results of its work'[131] available via its website. The focus on communication also highlights the ECDC's role in analysing and interpreting data, which is accomplished through, for example, the production of statistics, including through standardised tables and charts, all of which are provided on the TESSy website. In addition, on the basis of this data the ECDC produces the epidemiological reports, such as *Annual Epidemiological Report 2011—Reporting on 2009 Surveillance Data and 2010 Epidemic Intelligence Data*,[132] and more disease-specific reports, such as that on HIV/AIDS, which is published annually on 1 December, World AIDS Day. These provide the basis for the tracking of incidence and prevalence of disease, as well as the identification of most 'at risk' groups and other sources of vulnerability, such as geographic location (resonant with the focus of regulation interventions noted above). The latter provide the means to assess whether EU and broader global objectives are met—and as with other instances of knowledge production they render HIV/AIDS legible and open to discussion at the EU level and beyond.

[128] 'ECDC—WHO Europe Joint Surveillance' ecdcwhosurveillance.org/.

[129] European Commission, *Combating HIV/AIDS*, n 14 above, 8.

[130] Ibid, 10.

[131] Art 12(1) Regulation (EC) 851/2004, n 111 above.

[132] ECDC, *Annual Epidemiological Report 2011—Reporting on 2009 Surveillance Data and 2010 Epidemic Intelligence Data* (Stockholm, ECDC, 2011).

These various techniques, processes and practices therefore constitute and augment the field for more intrusive EU direction and control of the public health interventions of EU Member States *and* those within the wider European region. Together these are enfolded by and within EU governance.

Communication is also central to reassuring the public; they become key addressees of, and through their agency actors in, the implementation of governance and its regulatory interventions. For instance, the ECDC works in 'close collaboration with the Member States and the Commission to promote the necessary coherence in the risk communication process on health threats'[133] and 'shall cooperate as appropriate with the competent bodies in the Member States and other interested parties with regard to public information campaigns'.[134] A further purpose of communication is the production of the ECDC's—and EU's—authority and legitimacy. As noted above, this is founded on scientific and technical knowledge and expertise and it is augmented and perpetuated through the relationships with other actors (especially Member State and non-Member State governments, international organisations and civil society) and through communication with the broader public who are deemed to have the levels of agency to make use of the information.

B. Pharmaceuticals and Other Medical and Technological Responses

The second main aspect of the focus on knowledge in *Combating HIV/AIDS* is on pharmaceuticals and other technological responses to public health problems. Most important is biological, medical and social science research 'as well as *knowledge translation into effective evidence-informed* policy and programming' (emphasis added)[135] that helps to produce solutions to public health problems.[136] Interestingly, although there is mention of the need to ensure 'Broad access to integrated medical services and investment in effective health care infrastructures are critical to control of the spread of these infections', technical and medical solutions or 'fixes' receive a great deal of attention. For example, the Commission '*reiterates* the need to *amplify efforts* in vaccine, including *new technologies for vaccines*, microbicides and in new therapeutics, research and development' and 'will further support investments towards the development and implementation of *innovative preventive and therapeutic interventions*' (emphasis added).[137] So although there is attention to the social conditions for the emergence of HIV/AIDS through mention of prevention, there is growing attention on medical and other technological

[133] Art 12(2) Regulation (EC) 851/2004, n 111 above.
[134] Ibid, Art 12(3).
[135] European Commission, *Combating HIV/AIDS*, n 14 above, 10.
[136] On evidence-based policy see the discussion in ch 2. See further: ch 7.
[137] European Commission, *Combating HIV/AIDS*, n 14 above, 10.

responses, and both are framed by technoscientific innovation in research and development.

Elsewhere, *European Research and Knowledge for Global Health* stresses the importance of innovative pharmaceuticals in research and knowledge.[138] It is worthwhile noting that there is mention of the need 'to make the impact of research more equitable'.[139] Equity is perhaps not unreasonably aligned to economic concerns, such as ensuring the exploitation of, and innovation in, health. Yet, the alignment reframes equity such that it is not just linked to, but actually (re)framed and (re)oriented by the dominant focus on economic optimisation. In this way equity and health are by-products of economic optimisation. The network of actors that provide resources is noted, and this is linked to the 'common vision for the European Research Area 2020'.[140] Specifically the:

> [M]andate for international cooperation in the context of the millennium development goals. Priority areas, formulated by bi-regional dialogues in non-EU countries, regions and international fora and adapted to local needs or with the aid of partnerships, include *health policy research, health systems and healthcare service research*, maternal and child health, reproductive health, *control and surveillance of neglected communicable diseases and emerging unforeseen policy needs in the regions concerned.*[141] (Emphasis added)

Knowledge production is also being directed at fighting poverty-related diseases, including HIV/AIDS.[142] Of particular note is the support of FP7 and now Horizon 2020 funding for knowledge production[143] in the context of the European and Developing Countries Clinical Trials Partnership which began in 2003 and now runs until 2024 (usually referred to simply as EDCTP and in this book as the Partnership).[144] The Partnership aims to 'finance capacity building and clinical trials in sub-Saharan Africa',[145] and importantly this is aimed at the 'further development of successful products'.[146]

The Partnership has the ostensible purpose of augmenting public science and policy in order to close the so-called 10/90 research gap in which only 10 per cent of global health research is spent on problems that affect 90 per cent of the global population, especially poverty-related diseases,[147] and widening access to essential medicines. The Partnership focuses on Phase II and Phase III clinical trials,

[138] European Commission, *Staff Working Document, European Research and Knowledge for Global Health*, SEC (2010) 381 final.

[139] Ibid, 7.

[140] Ibid, noting the Council Conclusions on a '2020 Vision for the European Research Area', 2 December 2008.

[141] Ibid, 8.

[142] European Commission, *Accelerated Action on HIV/AIDS, Malaria and Tuberculosis in the Context of Poverty Reduction*, COM (2001) 96 final.

[143] 'The Organisation' www.edctp.org/about-edctp/the-organisation/.

[144] 'European and Developing Countries Clinical Trials Partnership' www.edctp.org/. See further, ch 8.

[145] 'HIV/AIDS research under FP7' ec.europa.eu/research/health/infectious-diseases/poverty-diseases/aids_en.html.

[146] Ibid.

[147] Global Forum for Health Research, *The 10/90 Gap in Health Research* (Geneva, GFHR, 1999).

and the establishment of good clinical practice that is equivalent to those found in the Clinical Trials Directive (and the Clinical Trials Regulation—that becomes relevant going forward).[148] For instance, many of the projects financed focus on the founding and functioning of research ethics committees and the maintenance of the International Council on Harmonisation of Technical Requirements for Registration of Pharmaceuticals for Human Use (ICH)[149] for data production and use for market authorisation purposes. The Partnership has also been the subject of a European Group on Ethics in Science and New Technologies (EGE) opinion on ethical aspects of clinical research in developing countries.[150] Further validation of the Partnership comes through its operation within the broader guidance provided by the European Medicines Agency.[151]

The Partnership and other knowledge-related efforts are situated within and configured by the broader programmatic priorities and concerns found in the overarching architecture of EU governance.[152] For instance, *Strategic European Framework for International Science and Technology Cooperation*,[153] is described as aimed at contributing to 'the free circulation of knowledge—*"the EU's fifth freedom"*—at global level' (emphasis added).[154] The objective, then, is economic optimisation, which is to be achieved by ensuring 'research priorities are geared to making the biggest impact on public health'.[155] However, this apparent prioritisation is then (re)framed by the dominant impulse of market optimisation. Indeed, the objective of FP7 (mentioned in these documents and predecessor to Horizon 2020) is to:

> *[S]trengthen industrial competitiveness* and to *meet the research needs of other Community policies*, including *health*, thereby contributing to creating a *knowledge-based society*, building on a European Research Area and complementing activities at national and regional levels. It promotes excellence in scientific and technological research, development and demonstration activities.[156] (Emphasis added)

This reflects and demonstrates the continuing salience of the programmatic priorities found in the overarching level of EU governance. The operationalisation of public health is not just linked to, but is actually prefigured by the neoliberal

148 Directive 2001/20/EC on the approximation of the laws, regulations and administrative provisions of the Member States relating to the implementation of good clinical practice in the conduct of clinical trials on medicinal products for human use [2001] OJ L121/34. This requires the Commission to establish principles relating to good clinical practice and detailed rules in line with those principles. This Directive is now replaced by Regulation (EU) 536/2014 on clinical trials on medicinal products for human use, and repealing Directive 2001/20/EC [2014] OJ L158/1, but it does not become applicable until at least 28 May 2016. The Regulation is planned to apply from 2018 (see Preface).

149 'International Council on Harmonisation of Technical Requirements for Registration of Pharmaceuticals for Human Use' www.ich.org/.

150 EGE, *Opinion on the Ethical Aspects of Clinical Research in Developing Countries* (Opinion No 17).

151 See ch 7.

152 See ch 2.

153 European Commission, *Strategic European Framework for International Science and Technology Cooperation*, COM (2008) 588.

154 European Commission, *Staff Working Document, European Research and Knowledge for Global Health*, SEC (2010) 381 final, 7.

155 Ibid, 3.

156 Ibid, 6.

concern for economic optimisation as the central aim of governance, which is to be achieved by and through the optimisation of knowledge.

Overall, in light of the aims and priorities of the overarching architecture of EU governance operationalised in *Together for Health*,[157] these various efforts, although often motivated by the desire to meet important public health needs, also point to the instrumentalisation of knowledge in the public health domain for economic optimisation and corporate profitability. This points to what Wynne describes as the 'pervasive intensification of the commercial culture of scientific research and knowledge'[158] as a key historical trend or transformation, with implications for the expansion of research into the global South, sometimes for the benefit of the people living there, but often with important benefits for industry and the political priorities of formally accountable actors like the EU in the global North. As mentioned earlier in this chapter and in this part of the book, when viewed within the wider normative setting for public health governance provided by the overarching architecture in particular, mention of public and private investment partnerships raise questions about the (de)prioritisation (or (re)prioritisation) of regulatory interventions through the concrete techniques, processes and practices aimed at implementing broader governance aims. This creates the possibility for the insinuation of market rationality and corporate interests of profitability into the knowledge creation exercise.

These technologies (including surveillance) open up national knowledge domains to EU norms, values and rationalities, and facilitate the (re)framing of HIV/AIDS governance (and communicable diseases) as (in part at least) an EU matter. As governance and the foundations for wider governance and (re)framing, these technologies for the gathering and production of knowledge extend EU power, while further delimiting responsibility and accountability. The larger point is that the focus on improving knowledge in *Combating HIV/AIDS* points to the (re)configuration of the gathering and production of knowledge in relation to power and its emergence as a central structuring theme of and foundation for the EU's governance of HIV/AIDS.

V. CONCLUSION

This chapter demonstrates the prioritisation of HIV/AIDS among communicable diseases. Part of the explanation for the latter is to be found in the framing of HIV/AIDS as a risk that could undermine security, which is understood as being about regulating the dangers or threats to the circulation of people and things. Communicable diseases in general become important for the same reason, but attention to HIV/AIDs can be explained in part by the particular risk it presents in light of

[157] See ch 2.

[158] B Wynne, 'Risk as Globalising "Democratic" Discourse? Framing Subjects and Citizens' in M Leach, I Scoones and B Wynne (eds), *Science and Citizens: Globalization and the Challenge of Engagement* (London, Zed Books, 2005) 69, with trends outlined 68–69.

epidemiological, legal and social, and political contexts. HIV/AIDS poses a risk not only to the circulation of people and things and therefore to security, but also to the production and legitimation of the broader programmatic priorities and concerns found in the overarching level of EU governance. The EU's governance of HIV/AIDS as well as wider communicable diseases is aligned to, reflective of and embedded within that broader architecture. Those priorities and concerns include the EU's identity as a public health and security actor, the socio-political order founded upon a competitive, innovative and optimal market, industries and population, and ultimately European integration. The capacity to regulate—or 'combat'—HIV/AIDS in the EU, on its periphery and further afield is important to all of these.

In this framing of EU governance of HIV/AIDS by risk and its configuration to security and broader priorities, ethics and human rights are leveraged through references to inequality, suffering and discrimination. Ethics and human rights provide part of the rationale and justification for EU level action; and they help to shape and direct regulatory interventions focused on 'at risk' groups and regions. Ethics and human rights nevertheless essentially work to provide the basis and justification for the dominant focus on risk regulation. Scientific and technical knowledge and expertise are parts of governance as well as foundations for wider governance and regulatory interventions both within the EU, on its periphery and further afield. In this way knowledge is a core way of governing at a distance and joins others, including attempts to responsibilise Member States, countries on the EU's periphery and beyond, most 'at risk' groups and wider society through their agency in coordination and cooperation arrangements.

The centrality and valorisation of scientific and technical knowledge and expertise helps to (re)configure power and knowledge (apparent in their tightening and co-productive relations seen in the gathering and production of knowledge *as* governance and as a *support* for wider governance), power and responsibility, and governance in relation to the governed, both over the EU's territory, on its periphery and beyond. In these ways neoliberalism becomes more apparent as that which undergirds, orientates and directs governance and the EU's programmatic priorities. More so than in relation to cancer, the subject of the previous chapter, the case of HIV/AIDS highlights how external governance is an important and even vital adjunct to the effectiveness of internal governance. The linkages between internal and external governance help to justify and legitimate the EU's growing global role and responsibility, and underline the (re)configuration between sovereignty and territoriality. An important dimension of the latter is the exportation of EU norms, values and rationalities, in short, normative power, through involvement in efforts to combat HIV/AIDS.

Despite the avowed primacy of prevention in EU regulatory responses, the focus of much external governance is on treatment based responses and supporting their development through efforts to improve the knowledge base. There is a pressing need to develop treatment for HIV/AIDS and other communicable diseases, which are often neglected as diseases of poverty. Yet, there are questions of fairness and justice to be asked about the prioritisation of HIV/AIDS over other diseases. The discussion in this chapter also reveals the way in which efforts to combat HIV/AIDS and other diseases of poverty are part of technologies that are supported by, aligned to, reflective of and embedded within the market driven aims and priorities of the overarching architecture of EU governance (especially funding) for treatment. Those efforts might actually serve private interests of corporate profitability rather than pressing public needs; they might also facilitate the shift of attention and resources away from prevention efforts directed at tackling the socio-political and economic causes of public health problems.

5

Pandemics and Beyond

I. INTRODUCTION

ONE KEY FEATURE of the discussion so far has been the strong security orientation of the European Union's (EU's) role and responsibility in respect of public health problems, including cancer and other (usually non-communicable) major and chronic diseases and conditions, and communicable diseases, such as HIV/AIDS. The previous chapter underlined how the danger or threat posed by pandemics has necessitated governance responses encompassing a range of regulatory interventions aimed at tackling what are presented as medical emergencies and maintaining the circulation of people and things. While the cross-borderness of communicable diseases and particularly widespread ones like HIV/AIDS ensures they are an important and legitimate target (as a matter of EU law and governance), over at least the last decade there has been growing awareness of the danger or threat posed by rarer pandemics and a far wider range of factors usually typified by a high degree of scientific uncertainty or non-knowing about, inter alia, the type, scale and likelihood of risk. In this chapter I outline the EU's efforts to govern this seemingly open-ended cluster of dangers or threats to public health through preparedness planning. To a limited extent, therefore, this chapter overlaps with the previous one, but it also goes beyond it. The chapter provides an important supplement by charting the EU's efforts at governing rare and emerging public health problems, the link between preparedness planning and security, and the importance of maintaining the generation of knowledge in the face of scientific uncertainty and non-knowing, which as in relation to other public health problems, emerges both as governance and as a support for wider governance and regulatory interventions.

The next section builds on these introductory points to situate preparedness planning for pandemics and other dangers or threats within the EU's public health strategy and the overarching architecture and programmatic priorities of EU governance. A key rationale for EU preparedness planning is ensuring the consistency of proliferating Member State level plans, particularly in relation to the regulatory interventions envisaged in the face of public health crises, and as part of an effort to ensure minimal disruption to the operation of the internal market. The EU's approach focuses on governing the preparedness of 'essential infrastructures' comprising: planning and coordination; monitoring and assessment; prevention and containment; health system response; and communication.

In the subsequent discussion I outline the broad distribution of responsibility and accountability for preparedness, and in turn risk assessment, risk management and risk communication.

Given these topics for discussion it is clear how this chapter also aims to further substantiate the first core argument of this book, which is that risk is the dominant frame for the technology governing public health. Specifically, the classic strategies and components of Member State public health governance such as prevention and treatment are increasingly subject to national preparedness planning and consequently to EU efforts that aim to ensure their consistency and resilience in the face of public health emergencies. Ethics and human rights shall again appear to operate in relation to preparedness as legitimating devices rather than as free-standing frames. The pervasiveness of preparedness serves to enhance security understood as being about regulating the dangers or threats to the circulation of people and things in order to generate economic optimisation. Preparedness planning seeks to reinforce and supplement limited epidemiological knowledge and demonstrate the ability of governance and its regulatory interventions to keep up and engage with rapidly evolving regulatory targets typified by high levels of uncertainty or even non-knowing. This (re)configuration of power and knowledge helps to maintain efficacy and is central to the production and legitimation of the EU's identity, socio-political order founded upon a competitive and innovative internal market that is resilient to often novel targets, and ultimately the perpetuation of the project of European integration.

Throughout the discussion I chart some of the ways in which preparedness planning extends the reach of the EU's technology governing public health and facilitates the mainstreaming of its related policy domain over a larger range of policy domains and activities. In this way preparedness supports the ongoing (re)framing of public health as a matter of EU governance. Moreover, perhaps even more so than HIV/AIDS and other communicable diseases, the EU's approach to preparedness demonstrates the (re)configuration between power and responsibility and an even more forthright and proactive stance to governing public health. These are apparent in the greater attention towards the extra-territorial and the development of the EU's growing global role as a security and public health actor. The EU's more expansive global role and responsibility also highlights the exportation of its normative power and, therefore, the ongoing (re)configuration between sovereignty and territoriality, as well as that between governance and the governed, seen elsewhere in the discussion of the technology governing public health. As an apparently technical way of governing public health infrastructures at a distance preparedness facilitates the circulation of the EU's security and market-oriented norms, values and rationalities across wider policy domains, places and people.

A final key contribution of this chapter is its extension of another observation that has been made several times in the preceding chapters and that will become salient to the discussion in the second part of this book. That is, preparedness planning, like wider risk-based approaches, might help to promote a shift of attention and resources towards medical and technological responses to public health problems and away from interventions in the socio-political and economic conditions generating public health problems in the first place. In addition, the growing importance of preparedness might distract attention and resources away from those public health problems that produce the greatest morbidity and mortality worldwide and that would benefit from improved prevention.

II. FROM THE OVERARCHING ARCHITECTURE OF GOVERNANCE TO *PANDEMIC INFLUENZA PREPAREDNESS*—REFLECTING *TOGETHER FOR HEALTH*

Preparedness planning is central to ensuring the circulation of people and things in the internal market and that is of course reflected at the overarching level of EU governance, in references to, for instance, the resolution that the Member States are to 'facilitate the free movement of persons, while ensuring the *safety and security* of their peoples, by establishing an area of *freedom, security and justice*' (emphasis added).[1] The concern with regulating free movement in order to ensure security (that is, free circulation) is, as noted throughout this part of the book, also seen in Article 168 Treaty on the Functioning of the European Union (TFEU).[2] As noted in Decision 1082/2013/EU on serious cross-border threats to health, which I mention again below and reference in the ensuing discussion:

> Article 168 ... states, *inter alia*, that a high level of human health protection is to be ensured in the definition and implementation of all Union policies and activities. That Article further provides that *Union action is to complement national policies*, is to cover *monitoring, early warning of, and combating serious cross-border threats to health*, and that *Member States are, in liaison with the Commission, to coordinate among themselves their policies and programmes* in the areas covered by Union action in the field of public health.[3] (Emphasis added)

These various foundations and contours for preparedness planning, some of which are also (as noted in chapter two) additions to Article 152 EC Treaty (the original Treaty base in the public health field), were preceded by a series of links between (public) health and security made in policy and practice.[4] The terrorist attacks in New York on 9/11[5] and those elsewhere in the rich global West were undoubtedly 'the' key step in the tightening of the link

[1] Recital 12 Treaty on European Union (TEU). *Cf* Art 3(2) TEU. See further (including summary of legislation): 'Justice and home affairs' europa.eu/pol/justice/index_en.htm. For discussion: N Walker (ed), *Europe's Area of Freedom, Security and Justice* (Oxford, Oxford University Press, 2004).

[2] See further ch 2.

[3] Recital 1 Decision 1082/2013/EU on serious cross-border threats to health and repealing Decision 2119/98/EC [2013] OJ L293/1.

[4] The documents are available at: 'Preparedness and response' ec.europa.eu/health/preparedness_response/policy/index_en.htm. On the revision of Art 152 EC see ch 2, n 11.

[5] F Lentzos, 'Rationality, Risk and Response: A Research Agenda for Biosecurity' (2006) 1(4) *BioSocieties* 453.

between public health and security and they prompted the EU's 'all hazards' approach to biosecurity.[6] With public health security established as a priority by the EU's Health Council on 15 November 2001, there followed a *Programme of Cooperation on Preparedness and Response to Biological and Chemical Attacks [Health Security]*,[7] dealing with deliberate human release of chemical, biological, radiological and nuclear (CBRN) agents within the EU and aimed at 'bridging security and health'.[8] The plan had as a key objective the establishment of the Health Security Committee (HSC), discussed again below. The HSC meets twice yearly and is composed of representatives from Member State health ministries, the Commission, the European Centre for Disease Control (ECDC) and the European Medicines Agency.[9]

On 27 November 2001 the Commission held a conference on preparedness planning that made explicit the importance of going beyond pandemics to address other threats to health ('Preparedness Planning in the Community: Influenza and Other Health Threats') and providing the momentum for 'next steps'.[10] The danger or threat posed by pandemics came under renewed attention with severe acute respiratory syndrome (SARS) and avian influenza in 2003, both previously unknown diseases that could spread rapidly between distant locations through the free movement of people and things (like poultry). The importance of countermeasures was highlighted by the support and guidance of the World Health Organisation (WHO).[11] In the wake of this the remit of the Early Warning and

[6] *Cf European Commission, Green Paper on Bio-Preparedness*, COM (2007) 399 final. For discussion: S Brem and S Dubois, 'Different Perceptions, Similar Reactions: Biopreparedness in the European Union' in P Katona, JP Sullivan and MD Intriligator (eds), *Global Biosecurity: Threats and Responses* (London, Routledge, 2010). More generally: DP Fidler and LO Gostin, *Biosecurity in the Global Age: Biological Weapons, Public Health, and the Rule of Law* (Stanford, Stanford University Press, 2007); A Lakoff, 'Preparing for the Next Emergency' (2007) 19(2) *Public Culture* 247; S Hinchcliffe and N Bingham, 'Securing Life: The Emerging Practices of Biosecurity' (2008) 40(7) *Environment and Planning A* 1534.

[7] European Commission, *Programme of Cooperation on Preparedness and Response to Biological and Chemical Attacks [Health Security]*, G/FS D (2001) GG.

[8] See: 'Preparedness and response', n 4 above. See further: European Commission, *Cooperation in the European Union on Preparedness and Response to Biological and Chemical Agent Attacks (Health Security)* COM(2003) 320 final. Also see: European Commission, *Strengthening Chemical, Biological, Radiological and Nuclear Security in the European Union—An EU CBRN Action Plan*, COM(2009) 273 final; European Commission, *Staff Working Document on Strengthening Chemical, Biological, Radiological and Nuclear Security in the European Union—An EU CRBN Action Plan. Impact Assessment*, SEC (2009) 790; European Commission, *Staff Working Document on Strengthening Chemical, Biological, Radiological and Nuclear Security in the European Union—An EU CRBN Action Plan. Summary of Impact Assessment*, SEC(2009) 791; European Commission, *Staff Working Document Bridging Security and Health: Towards the Identification of Good Practices in the Response to CBRN Incidents and the Security of CBR Substances*, SEC (2009) 874.

[9] Especially representatives of Directorate-General for Health and Consumers: ec.europa.eu/dgs/health_consumer/index_en.htm.

[10] Preparedness Planning in the Community: Influenza and Other Health Threats, Brussels, 27 November 2001. Available at: ec.europa.eu/health/ph_threats/com/Influenza/influenza_conference_1.htm.

[11] European Commission, *Strengthening Coordination on Generic Preparedness Planning for Public Health Emergencies at EU Level*, COM (2005) 605 final, 3.

Response System (EWRS), which was established in 1999 by Decision 2119/98/EC on a network for the epidemiological surveillance and control of communicable diseases,[12] was extended to cover a wide range of communicable diseases, including H1N1.[13] The EWRS is, after the adoption of Decision 1082/2013/EU, defined as 'a rapid alert system for notifying at Union level alerts in relation to serious cross-border threats to health' and it is described as enabling 'the Commission and the competent authorities responsible at national level to be in permanent communication for the purposes of alerting, assessing public health risks and determining the measures that may be required to protect public health'[14] (consistent with the International Health Regulations[15]). Surveillance data from the EWRS is collated into a report by the ECDC.[16] This move strengthened the knowledge available to Member States and enhanced their ability to limit contagion, it is of central importance to risk assessment, and it thereby enables risk management and risk communication.

On 26 March 2004 the Commission followed up its involvement in pandemic influenza planning by establishing a Public Health Preparedness and Response Planning Group (PHPRPG) in the HSC to advise on the actions to be taken in the event of an imminent pandemic threat. On 28 November 2005 there followed the *Pandemic Influenza Preparedness and Response Planning in the European Community* (*Pandemic Influenza Preparedness*),[17] which updated planning in light of WHO recommendations and the establishment of the ECDC, also in 2005. This uses 'the principles and components of … generic preparedness planning',[18] such as in the *Strengthening Coordination on Generic Preparedness Planning for Public Health Emergencies at EU Level*[19] and the *Interim Document: Technical Guidance on Generic Preparedness Planning for Public Health Emergencies.*[20] The Commission

[12] Decision 2119/98/EC on a network for the epidemiological surveillance and control of communicable diseases, which was repealed by Decision 1082/2013/EU, n 3 above.

[13] See ch 4, nn 108 and 109.

[14] Art 8(1) Decision 1082/2013/EU, n 3 above.

[15] The International Health Regulations require WHO Member States to notify the WHO of any potential international public health emergency (International Health Regulations (23 May 2005) WHA58/2005/REC/1 (IHR)), and are rendered applicable to the EU under Art 57(1) IHR, which states the IHR and EU Treaties 'should be interpreted so as to be compatible'. The Commission 'believes the EU and its [Member States] can and should work together to optimise IHR implementation in the context of the EU policies and health related actions and initiatives' (see press release: 'International Health Regulations—Commission calls for proactive implementation, particularly on flu aspects' europa.eu/rapid/pressReleasesAction.do?reference=IP/06/1276).

[16] Eg: ECDC, *Annual Epidemiological Report 2011—Reporting on 2009 Surveillance Data and 2010 Epidemic Intelligence Data* (Stockholm, ECDC, 2011).

[17] European Commission, *Pandemic Influenza Preparedness and Response Planning in the European Community*, COM (2005) 607 final.

[18] Ibid, 7.

[19] European Commission, *Generic Preparedness*, n 11 above.

[20] European Commission, *Interim Document: Technical Guidance on Generic Preparedness Planning for Public Health Emergencies*, 2005. This and the previous document address in martial tones, '*threats and emergencies* which are affecting or are likely to affect public health in more than one Member State' (ibid, 65, emphasis added). The guidance includes checklists 'as a guide that may be used to assist in

and ECDC have also been actively engaged with the WHO, joint international workshops,[21] and global meetings to discuss planning with third countries,[22] including the Global Health Security Initiative (GHSI), an informal, international partnership that works to strengthen health preparedness and response globally.[23] Preparedness planning is, therefore, of central importance to the EU's developing global security and public health role. The HSC's mandate was extended by the February 2007 Health Council in order to include the full range of health threats noted above.[24] The same year saw the publication of *Together for Health: A Strategic Approach for the EU 2008–13* (discussed in chapter two),[25] which encompassed communicable, non-communicable and rare diseases, vaccination, and preparedness and response to health threats.[26] The latter strategy clearly sought to ensure oversight and coherence of the EU's activities, and perhaps most important to preparedness are the focus on strengthening the EU's voice in global health and protecting citizens from health threats, respectively the last of the four core principles and the second of the three strategic objectives.

Many of these policy developments essentially relate to the extension of EU activities beyond surveillance and control of communicable diseases to encompass other threats, and these have been provided with a firmer legal basis through the replacement of Decision 2119/98/EC by the aforementioned Decision 1082/2013/EU on *serious cross-border threats to health*.[27] This replacement is consistent with

the development, revision or assessment of comprehensiveness of preparedness plans' (ibid, 3) and facilitate the '*inter-operability of national plans*, mainly by the creation of *co-ordination mechanisms* and analysis and *communication* tools that *enhance co-operation* between key Member States' and Commission players' (ibid, 2, emphasis added), and lay the basis for 'reviews, validations and tests and making recommendations for improvements and fine-tuning of national plans and EU procedures to *reduce vulnerabilities and incompatibilities*' (ibid, emphasis added).

[21] 2–3 March 2005 in Luxembourg, 24–26 October 2005 in Copenhagen, 15–17 May 2006 in Uppsala, and 25–27 September 2007 in Luxembourg. See further: 'Influenza pandemic preparedness planning at EU level' ec.europa.eu/health/ph_threats/com/Influenza/influhome/influenza_level_en.htm.

[22] Eg *Vienna Senior Officials Meeting on Avian and Human Pandemic*, 6 and 7 June 2006. Available at: ec.europa.eu/health/ph_threats/com/Influenza/SOM_Vienna.pdf.

[23] See: 'Global Health Security Initiative' www.ghsi.ca/english/index.asp.

[24] In response to: European Commission, *Transitional Prolongation and Extension of the Mandate of the Health Security Committee in View of a Future General Revision of the Structures Dealing with Health Threats at EU Level*, COM (2006) 699 final.

[25] European Commission, *White Paper, Together for Health: A Strategic Approach for the EU 2008–13*, COM (2007) 630 final; European Commission, *Commission Staff Working Document Accompanying White Paper, Together for Health: A Strategic Approach for the EU 2008–13*, SEC(2007) 1376. For an overview of initiatives, see: European Commission, *Commission Staff Working Document, Report on European Governance (2003–04)*, SEC(2004) 1153. Also see: ec.europa.eu/health/strategy/policy/index_en.htm.

[26] See ch 2.

[27] These are defined by Art 3(g) Decision 1082/2013/EU, n 3 above, as 'a life-threatening or otherwise serious hazard to health of biological, chemical, environmental or unknown origin which spreads or entails a significant risk of spreading across the national borders of Member States, and which may necessitate coordination at Union level in order to ensure a high level of human health protection'.

Article 168 TFEU and is reflective of and embedded within *Together for Health*, and it more accurately reflects the reach of EU policy and practice on preparedness beyond communicable diseases to encompass a wider range of threats to health.

The rationale for Decision 1082/2013/EU also helps to spell out the significance of the various developments since 9/11 and to constitute rarer pandemics and other dangers or threats to health as problems for EU governance and regulatory interventions:

> Apart from communicable diseases, *a number of other sources of danger to health*, in particular related to other biological or chemical agents or environmental events, which include hazards related to climate change, could by reason of their scale or severity, *endanger the health of citizens in the entire Union.*

The EU's citizenry is therefore a key focus of protection efforts and justification for EU involvement. But the danger or threat posed by public health problems also extends to the '*malfunctioning* of critical sectors of society and the economy'.[28] In other words, preparedness is not just about protecting the health of citizens; it is also about maintaining a functioning economy ie the circulation of people and things within and into the internal market. As with the other risk-based responses adopted by the EU, preparedness planning represents the governmentalisation of security, while the focus on security also represents the securitisation of public health. Preparedness planning is also, therefore, about meeting broader programmatic priorities and concerns, in particular the production and legitimation of the EU's identity as a public health and security actor, its socio-political order founded upon a functioning, competitive and innovative market-based economy, and ultimately the project of European integration.

A final part of the rationale for the decision relates to the 'added value' of EU action, which is explained by the way in which public health problems 'jeopardise an individual Member State's capacity to react'. The extension of Decision 2119/98/EC '*to cover other threats* and provide for a *coordinated wider approach to health security* at Union level' (emphasis added)[29] via Decision 1082/2013/EU is justified and legitimated by what it adds to the regulatory capacities of its Member States. In the following I explain how Decision 1082/2013/EU helps to further delineate the distribution of responsibility and accountability in relation to preparedness planning and response. The discussion also points to the ways in which the EU's approach relates to the normative orientation and direction of the EU's wider technology governing public health as well as the broader programmatic priorities and concerns.

[28] Ibid, Recital 3.

[29] Ibid. On the scope of the decision see Art 1(a)–(e).

III. GOVERNING THE FUTURE THROUGH PREPAREDNESS PLANNING

A. Ensuring Preparedness through Coordination Based on Knowledge of Member States' Plans

EU preparedness distributes responsibilities for the preparedness of 'essential infrastructures' relating to risk assessment, risk management and risk communication between several key actors, including: the Commission; the ECDC; Member State authorities; private actors such as manufacturers of vaccines; the news media and the EU's citizenry via risk communication (and responsibilisation) efforts. While Decision 1082/2013/EU operationalises and specifies further the EU's role as supporting Member State responsibility for health, it does not preempt future action by the Member States. Indeed, the Member States 'retain the right to maintain or introduce additional arrangements, procedures and measures for their national systems' and they include 'arrangements provided for in existing or future bilateral or multilateral agreements or conventions, on condition that such additional arrangements, procedures and measures do not impair the application of this Decision'.[30]

The focus of EU governance is on promoting coordination between Member States and that is achieved through an assemblage of techniques, processes and practices. To that end both the Member States and the Commission '*consult each other within the HSC … with a view to coordinating their efforts* to develop, strengthen and maintain their capacities for the monitoring, early warning and assessment of, and response to, serious cross-border threats to health' (emphasis added).[31] The central role of the HSC in policy and practice is now formalised in law,[32] and it focuses on governing at a distance through efforts aimed at '*supporting the exchange of information* between the Member States and the Commission' (emphasis added),[33] liaising with the Commission (which provides the secretariat and administrative support)[34] in order to ensure coordination of preparedness and response planning,[35] and further coordination with the Commission in relation to risk management and risk communication, that is, the 'risk and crisis communication and responses of the Member States to serious cross-border threats to health'.[36] Coordination of preparedness planning and response is a technology of agency and performance: it functions by leveraging the agency of Member States and their authorities, responsibilising them, and through ongoing consultation and communication it works to determine best practices, provide the

[30] Ibid, Art 2(6).
[31] Ibid, Art 4(1).
[32] Ibid, Art 17.
[33] Ibid, Art 17(2)(a).
[34] Ibid, Art 17(4).
[35] Ibid, Art 17(2)(b).
[36] Ibid, Art 17(2)(c).

scope for a ranking of better and worse planners and responders, and an optimisation of performance through adjustments made in light of the consultation and coordination.

The role, responsibility and significance of the HSC has developed incrementally through its activities, which as suggested above were without specific legal foundation prior to Decision 1082/2013/EU:

> Over the years the Committee has established a solid base for preparedness activities, by: enabling EU governments to exchange information and evaluate health events; functioning as a discussion forum that advises health ministers; facilitating coordinated crisis response by EU governments.[37]

Consultation through the HSC requirement hinges on Member States providing the Commission with updates on their preparedness planning and response—beginning on 7 November 2014 and 'every three years thereafter'.[38] In this way the gathering and production of knowledge on Member State preparedness planning and response is central to the EU's governance of preparedness; to a great extent coordination is a technology for the gathering and production of knowledge. Moreover, the (re)configuration between power and knowledge emerges very clearly as a particularly important theme of preparedness planning, with the two working in a co-productive way such that they are mutually constitutive, with each one shaping and providing the key conditions of possibility for the other.

This is apparent in the information to be provided by Member States in their updates, which encompasses three main elements. Together these elements generate knowledge on Member State preparedness plans, constitute an EU level knowledge domain (on preparedness), and work together to facilitate more intrusive rounds of coordination, which is also a key function and justification for the knowledge created. The first element is the core capacity standards for preparedness and response planning (which relate to surveillance, reporting, notification, verification, response and collaboration activities) in accordance with the IHR.[39] The second element is the ways in which interoperability between the health sector and other sectors (such as the veterinary sector) are to be ensured when an emergency arises, in particular those relating to ensure coordination in the event of so-called cross-sectoral incidents (those that cut across policy domains but still impact on health) and emergency operational centres or crisis centres that are identified as being critical in the case of an emergency.[40] Finally, ensuring resilience through 'business continuity plans, measures or arrangements' that seek to ensure the continuing functioning of 'critical services and products'[41] is the third element.

[37] 'Risk management' ec.europa.eu/health/preparedness_response/risk_management/index_en.htm.
[38] Art 4(2), n 3 above.
[39] Ibid, Art 4(2)(a).
[40] Ibid, Art 4(2)(b).
[41] Ibid, Art 4(2)(c).

In addition, in relation to this information when '*substantially revising* national preparedness planning' the Member States must 'inform the Commission in a *timely manner* of the main aspects of the revision' (emphasis added).[42] As I go on to explain, the tightening and co-productive relations between power and knowledge are foundational to the wider distribution of responsibility and accountability in relation to risk assessment, risk management and risk communication, as well as related further (re)configurations underpinning EU level governance and providing its structuring themes.

The relative importance of risk assessment, risk management and risk communication in relation to a specific serious cross-border threat to health depends on the precise phase of the public health emergency. The phases are drawn from EU generic planning, which is explicitly based on WHO Phases 1–6. In the following I focus on the application of these phases and the modulation of activities in relation to pandemics. The inter-pandemic period is at Phases 1 and 2. At this stage no new influenza virus subtypes have been detected in humans, but they might be present in animals. The main public health goal at this stage is to '*strengthen influenza pandemic preparedness* at the global, regional, national and sub-national levels' (emphasis added)[43] and minimisation of the risk of transmission to humans, in other words, ensuring the readiness of the 'essential infrastructure' of planning and coordination, supported by and in line with the above. This requires rapid detection and reporting of any such transmission and, therefore, attention to the 'essential infrastructure' of monitoring and assessment. The Commission and the ECDC work in consultation with the HSC, and in cooperation with the WHO, to assess, review and organise 'exercises concerning national pandemic plans, with a special focus on their interoperability'.

Phases 3–5 is the pandemic alert period and at this stage risk assessment and risk management are particularly engaged and the principal focus is again monitoring and assessment as well as the 'essential infrastructures' of prevention and containment. At Phases 3 and 4 there are no human cases in the EU, but a risk of sporadic importation of isolated cases in Member States. Rapid characterisation of the new virus subtype, and early detection, notification and response to new cases is the main public health objective. At Phase 4 containing the new virus within a limited area or delaying its spread in order to implement preparedness countermeasures, such as the development of vaccine, is the main public health objective. At Phase 5 there are larger clusters of cases outside the EU, but human-to-human contagion is still limited in area. The main public health objective is to 'maximize efforts to contain or delay spread, to possibly avert a pandemic, and to gain time to implement pandemic response measures'. The ECDC sets the terms of reference for Outbreak Assistance Teams (or OATs). These participate in 'outbreak investigation inside and outside the Community ensuring coherence and

[42] Ibid, Art 4(3).
[43] European Commission, *Pandemic Influenza Preparedness*, n 17 above, 16.

synergies with the EU's external response in co-operation with the WHO'. Generally, the Commission is responsible for reviewing its own internal contingency and coordinating guidance to national authorities so that they can review and update their plans in light of evidence. More specifically, at Phase 5 Commission staff surge capacity must be ensured.

Phase 6 is the pandemic period in which there is an increased and sustained transmission of cases around the world and now within the EU's general population. At Phase 6 a centre to coordinate EU and international level actions and evaluate effectiveness must be established. The main public health objective is minimising the pandemic's impact in the EU through the implementation of surge capacity ie risk management based on ongoing risk assessment. In order to do so the EU adopts its own Alert Levels 1–4. These take into account specifics such as the absence of internal borders, and differences between Member States (southern and eastern Member States have higher susceptibility). At EU Alert Level 1 there are no human cases in the EU, but there is a very high risk of sporadic imported cases. At EU Alert Level 2 there is a single human case inside the EU. EU Alert Level 3 occurs when there is an isolated cluster in one EU Member State or sustained transmission between humans with several clusters inside the EU. EU Alert Level 4 is when there are cases in one or more Member States. At Phase 6 risk management and risk communication are the focus and they engage with the 'essential infrastructures' of prevention and containment and to a greater extent with health system response and communication.

B. Risk Assessment and Management

i. Risk Assessment and Further Technologies for the Gathering and Production of Knowledge

The overarching requirement and objective of risk assessment, which relates to preparedness of the 'essential infrastructure' of monitoring and assessment, is to ensure that 'the assessment of risks to public health at the Union level … is *consistent as well as comprehensive* from a public health perspective'. Consistency and comprehensiveness are found to rely on 'the available scientific expertise', which 'should be *mobilised in a coordinated manner*, through appropriate channels or structures depending on the type of threat concerned' (emphasis added).[44] Risk assessment is founded upon the gathering and production of knowledge. In other words the techniques, processes and practices—technologies—of knowledge creation *are* governance as well as being *supports* for risk assessment, risk management and risk communication efforts. Decision 1082/2013/EU is of central importance to risk assessment in that it 'puts in place rapid and efficient risk assessment mechanisms' and that underpins risk assessment, which 'involves

[44] Recital 17 Decision 1082/2013/EU, n 3 above.

mobilising expertise from the relevant EU and international bodies, to provide *robust scientific advice to feed into risk management decisions*' (emphasis added).[45] Those bodies include the ECDC, European Food Safety Authority (EFSA) and WHO.

The latter summary of risk assessment immediately highlights the centrality and valorisation of scientific and technical knowledge and expertise in risk assessment, which is striking given that rarer pandemics and emerging public health problems are typified by high degrees of scientific uncertainty and even non-knowing. It seems that uncertainty and non-knowing do not make scientific expertise redundant. Far from it, scientific expertise remains important precisely because the uncertainty or non-knowing relate to science, and those who are expert in science remain competent to comment on the nature, scope and limits of scientific knowledge. Uncertainty and non-knowing prompt a (re)configuration between power and scientific knowledge with knowledge and expertise on uncertainty and non-knowing continuing to underwrite, bolster and legitimate, and also necessitate decision-making due to (and not simply despite) their limits.

The continued importance of scientific and technical knowledge also configures governance to the governed, in particular by implicitly limiting the potential contribution of those who are governed to this aspect of decision-making, with their role being marginalised to risk communication and as part of implementation of regulatory interventions (to which I return below). Epidemiological surveillance and the EWRS provide different albeit related knowledges for risk assessment, and they facilitate the figuration and construction of the EU's population and territory as the central space for governance and regulatory interventions as part of risk management. At the same time the space beyond the EU's territory also becomes a zone for interventions. In these related ways EU level preparedness planning and response reflects the (re)configuration between sovereignty and territoriality seen in the wider technology governing public health and constituting the EU's policy domain—and the expansion of the people and places that are governed.

In relation to epidemiological surveillance uncertainty and non-knowing seem to reinforce the importance of gathering, producing and rapidly updating the epidemiological information available, all of which require ongoing efforts to ensure the preparedness of those capacities. Decision 1081/2013/EU provides the ECDC with responsibility for the network on epidemiological surveillance (prior to this the ECDC had progressively become responsible for the network).[46] The networks bring the Commission, ECDC, and the Member State competent authorities responsible for epidemiological surveillance into 'permanent communication'[47]—that is preparedness requires ongoing flows of surveillance data. While the ECDC acts as a central surveillance data point for the whole EU, it is

[45] 'Risk assessment' ec.europa.eu/health/preparedness_response/risk_assessment/index_en.htm.
[46] Art 6(1) Decision 1082/2013/EU, n 3 above.
[47] Ibid, Art 6(2).

Member State authorities that are responsible for gathering and producing data relating to their territories, which indicates surveillance as part of technologies of agency and for the monitoring and assessment of performance (through cycles of preparedness planning and response review and revision). The authorities are required to provide 'comparable and compatible data and information in relation to the epidemiological surveillance of communicable diseases and related special health issues',[48] information on the 'progression of epidemic situations',[49] and information on new and emerging 'epidemic phenomena or new communicable diseases of unknown origin',[50] including those in third countries.

In addition to the epidemiological surveillance network, which provides for the preparedness of the ongoing monitoring of the epidemiological situation, the EWRS (both introduced in the previous chapter) provides for more rapid health threat alert notification, which is of course of crucial importance in the face of public health emergencies and efforts to ensure preparedness and timely and correct responses. Member State authorities or the Commission are required to notify an alert through the EWRS provided the emerging or developing serious cross-border threat to health is 'unusual or unexpected for the given place and time, or it *causes or may cause* significant morbidity or mortality in humans, or it grows rapidly or may grow rapidly in scale, or it exceeds or may exceed national response capacity'[51] (emphasis added), one or more Member States may be affected,[52] and a coordinated EU level response is or may be required.[53] Alert notification relates to Phases 3–5 is the cross-border threat alert period as well as Phase 6. The focus on reporting a possibility of a serious cross-border health threat underlines the sense of urgency and potential emergency—as well as the continuing effort to leverage uncertainty and non-knowing in order to prepare the way for regulatory interventions, by bringing the future into the present through them, and expanding EU power.

There is some overlap between the EWRS and Member State obligations under the IHR, with Member State authorities being required to notify an alert through the EWRS, and communicate any available salient information on the threat.[54] Provided the threat falls within the scope of Decision 1082/2013/EU,[55] Member States are to notify a threat through the EWRS at the same time as they notify the WHO.[56] The EWRS is also relevant to risk management in that the Commission is required to

[48] Ibid, Art 6(3)(a).
[49] Ibid, Art 6(3)(b).
[50] Ibid, Art 6(3)(c).
[51] Ibid, Art 9(1)(a).
[52] Ibid, Art 9(1)(b).
[53] Ibid, Art 9(1)(c).
[54] With examples listed in Art 9(3)(a)–(j) ibid and including 'the type and origin of the agent' (a), 'the date and place of the incident or outbreak' (b), 'means of transmission or dissemination' (c), 'detection and confirmation methods' (e), and 'public health measures implemented or intended to be taken at national level' and other types of measures ((g) and (h) respectively).
[55] Art 9(2) Decision 1082/2013/EU, n 3 above.
[56] As required by Art 6 IHR.

use it in order to communicate information on response.[57] In that regard it is important to note that surveillance information is used to identify the circumstances of infection and to produce 'risk groups'. These latter might be subject to containment and control measures, discussed below in relation to risk management. At Phase 4 the 'risk groups' and countermeasures are put under enhanced surveillance, and this attention heightens at Phase 5 when there might be importation of cases, and again at Phase 6 with the circulation of the pandemic in the EU.

An important function of the EWRS is that it provides the means for the prompt communication of a risk assessment of the 'potential severity of the threat to public health, including possible public health measures'.[58] The risk assessment is 'based on principles of excellence, independence, impartiality and transparency' and it is generated by the appropriate EU agency, either the ECDC,[59] EFSA,[60] or another agency where relevant.[61] The Commission provides a risk assessment only where the particular danger or threat falls totally or partially outside the mandates of one or more of the EU's agencies.[62] Where the public health emergency is of international concern information from other organisations such as the WHO has to be taken into account.[63] The trigger for the risk assessment is notification of an alert, and the Commission acts on the request of the HSC or on its own initiative where coordination is necessary for an EU level response. The risk assessment is made available to Member State authorities 'promptly through the EWRS'[64] and prior to any public dissemination. Information that 'may be relevant for the risk assessment' is also communicated to Member State authorities through the EWRS and to the HSC.[65] Overall, it is apparent how 'the' EU (especially the Commission, agencies (especially the ECDC) and specific fora and processes providing the means to coordinate Member State authorities) has a central role in the gathering and production of knowledge (by coordinating epidemiological surveillance and the EWRS), and ultimately risk assessment. The Member States and their authorities are governed through their agency and responsibilised into supporting the rationales of EU level preparedness planning, coordination, and the technologies that make risk assessment possible, partly in order to support their responsibility for risk management.

[57] Ibid, Art 9(4).

[58] Ibid, Art 10(1).

[59] Within the ECDC's remit as defined in Art 7(1) Regulation (EC) 851/2004 establishing a European Centre for Disease Prevention and Control [2004] OJ L142/1 and in relation to threats noted in Art 2(1)(a)(i), 2(1)(a)(ii) and 2(1)(d) Decision 1082/2013/EU, as per Art 10(1)(a) Decision 1082/2013/EU, n 3 above.

[60] In relation to threats noted in Art 2 Decision 1082/2013/EU, n 3 above, where they fall within the EFSA's remit as defined in Art 23 Regulation (EC) 178/2002 laying down the general principles and requirements of food law, establishing the European Food Safety Authority and laying down procedures in matters of food safety [2002] OJ L31/1, per Art 10(1)(b) Decision 1082/2013/EU.

[61] Art 10(1)(c) Decision 1082/2013/EU, n 3 above.

[62] Ibid, Art 10(2)(1).

[63] Ibid, Art 10(2)(3).

[64] Ibid, Art 10(2)(2).

[65] Ibid, Art 10(3).

The EU's role in preparedness planning and response relies on opening up Member State knowledge domains on preparedness planning and response through coordination. The latter facilitates the (re)framing of preparedness planning and response as an EU matter and as part of the wider technology governing public health and constituting the related policy domain. Facilitating coordination and (re)framing requires and presupposes '*uniform conditions* for the implementation' of the Decision and that requires Commission powers for the standardisation of such components of preparedness planning and response as the:

> *[T]emplates* to be used when providing the information on preparedness and response planning; the establishment and update of a *list of communicable diseases and related special health issues subject to the network of epidemiological surveillance* and the procedures for the operation of such a network; the *adoption of case definitions* for those communicable diseases and special health issues covered by the epidemiological surveillance network and, where necessary, for other serious cross-border threats to health subject to ad hoc monitoring; the *procedures for the operation of the EWRS*; the *procedures for the information* exchange on and the coordination of the responses of the Member States; the recognition of situations of public health emergency at Union level and the termination of such a recognition.[66] (Emphasis added)

These components highlight the technical nature of much EU level activity, but it is far from being neutral and it is not without important effects. Indeed, these components are central to the work of EU level governance. At the same time the components help to make wider EU level preparedness planning and response possible by supporting and facilitating the construction of a transnational knowledge domain.

ii. *Risk Management—And the Importance of Medical Countermeasures and Pharmaceutical Fixes*

To some extent risk assessment also encompasses risk management in that, as noted above, it represents an attempt to shape the public health measures adopted by national competent authorities. There are additional attempts to shape regulatory interventions in public health through preparedness planning of risk management, with recent examples of response including ebola, polio and Middle East Respiratory Syndrome Coronavirus (MERS-CoV).[67] The Member States are principally responsible for risk management, which relates most directly to the 'essential infrastructures' of prevention and containment as well as health system response. Consistent with Article 168 TFEU it is the Member States that 'have a

[66] Ibid, Recital 30. Also see Art 6(5). These powers are exercised in accordance with Regulation (EU) 182/2011 laying down the rules and general principles concerning mechanisms for control by Member States of the Commission's exercise of implementing powers [2011] OJ L55/13.

[67] 'Response to serious cross-border health threats (ebola, polio, MERS)' ec.europa.eu/health/preparedness_response/risk_management/response/index_en.htm.

responsibility to *manage public health crises at national level*' (emphasis added)[68]—and that are principally accountable in the event of failure. The EU's supporting role manifests through the extension and augmentation of coordination efforts in order to ensure that Member State emergency planning and responses disrupt the internal market to minimal possible extent. That is:

> [M]easures taken by individual Member States could damage the interests of other Member States if they are *inconsistent with one another or based on diverging risk assessments.* The aim to coordinate the response at Union level should, therefore, seek to ensure, inter alia, that measures taken at national level are *proportionate and limited to public health risks* related to serious cross-border threats to health, *and do not conflict with obligations and rights laid down in the TFEU such as those related to the restriction on travel and trade.*[69] (Emphasis added)

Treaty free movement obligations,[70] especially the requirement that interference with free movement rights are proportionate to the aim of protecting public health, are supplemented by minimal references in the relevant policy documents to the legal and ethical implications of interventions such as quarantine and selective immunisation of most 'at risk' groups. In this way, ethics and human rights operate in relation to the dominant focus on risk regulation, which is a configuration that underlines their marginal role and status as legitimating devices. This is hardly surprising given that risk management focuses on ensuring minimal disruption to the internal market through prior communication of countermeasures so as to ensure interoperability.[71]

Coordination of Member State responses occurs through the HSC and in liaison with the Commission after a request has been made by the Commission or a Member State and after an alert has been issued. The consultation encompasses exchange of information in order to ensure the coordination of 'national responses ... including where a public health emergency of international concern is declared in accordance with the IHR and falls within [the scope of the Decision]' and 'risk and crisis communication ... aimed at providing consistent and coordinated information in the Union to the public and to healthcare professionals'.[72] In this way risk communication, which I detail further below, relates to risk management. The HSC is again underlined as central to the gathering and production of knowledge on Member State risk management practices, which is used in order to coordinate and ensure the consistency of Member State responses to public health emergencies.

Importantly, before adopting measures to combat a serious cross-border threat to health a Member State is required to '*inform and consult* the other Member States and the Commission on the nature, purpose and scope of the measures,

[68] Recital 21 Decision 1082/2013/EU, n 3 above.
[69] Ibid, Recital 21.
[70] Outlined in ch 2 and referenced again in ch 8.
[71] European Commission, *Interim Document*, n 20 above, 34–35 for legal implications.
[72] Art 11(1)(a) Decision 1082/2013/EU, n 3 above.

unless the need to protect public health is *so urgent* that the immediate adoption of the measures is necessary' (emphasis added).[73] In that event the Member States are required to inform the other Member States and the Commission 'immediately upon [the] adoption [of those measures]'.[74] Efforts to bolster Member State responses are provided through a facility for a Member State to request assistance from other Member States[75] through the Community Civil Protection Mechanism.[76]

Building on these foundations EU planning of response makes a further attempt to (pre-)determine the (de)selection of regulatory interventions in the event of a serious cross-border threat to health. For example, medical countermeasures such as vaccines and social distancing are central and are modulated throughout the alert levels. It is noted that 'hand-washing and social distancing will play important roles in reducing the impact of pandemic influenza',[77] vaccination is the key countermeasure, and since the production of vaccines usually takes between six and eight months,[78] anti-virals are 'the *first pillar* of medical prevention and intervention' (emphasis added).[79] While competence ensures the EU has limited involvement in health system response, the Commission and ECDC coordinate and review non-pharmaceutical measures. For instance, at Phase 5 this involves guidance on how 'to optimise use of scarce facilities (triage, modified clinical guidelines, modified hospital infection guidelines … etc.)'.[80]

Medical countermeasures and especially pharmaceutical 'fixes' like vaccines are especially important. Preparedness planning and response uses a variety of means, including support for research (as part of the impetus in *European Research and Knowledge for Global Health* for supporting the EU's growing global role noted in the previous chapter),[81] a public–private partnership between public authorities and the vaccine industry to stimulate production, an expedited market authorisation procedure,[82] and a mechanism for joint procurement,[83] all to deliver vaccine to the EU in the 'shortest possible time'.[84] Preparedness attempts to ensure equitable distribution of scarce resources and reduce vulnerability. For example, the Commission helps to promote the '"mutualisation" of stocks to fight the disease at *source*' given 'the lack of manufacturing capacity in many countries and the

73 Ibid, Art 11(2).
74 Ibid, Art 11(3).
75 Ibid, Art 11(4).
76 Decision 2007/779/EC, Euratom establishing a Community Civil Protection Mechanism [2007] OJ L314/9.
77 European Commission, *Pandemic Influenza Preparedness*, n 17 above, 12.
78 Ibid, 10.
79 Ibid.
80 Ibid, 22.
81 European Commission, *Staff Working Document, European Research and Knowledge for Global Health* SEC (2010) 381 final, 8.
82 Market authorisation is outlined in ch 3.
83 Art 5 Decision 1082/2013/EU, n 3 above.
84 European Commission, *Pandemic Influenza Preparedness*, n 17 above, 10.

perceived imbalance between rich and powerful countries that collect strains through collaboration programmes with poor and affected ones but benefit from (their) manufacturers' production only themselves'.[85]

Throughout the alert phases the Commission, ECDC and Member State authorities are required to target—and improvise as they review and retarget in light of the unfolding pandemic—limited stocks of anti-virals and vaccines to key health personnel as part of the 'essential infrastructure' of health system response and the most vulnerable as defined in 'risk groups'.[86] Medical countermeasures are clearly an important component of preparedness planning and response. However, the prominence of those countermeasures and especially pharmaceutical responses (here in terms of prevention) might also be explained by, inter alia: the focus on ameliorating consequences promoted by the framing of the governance of pandemics and other serious health threats by preparedness; the shared competence for the internal market under Article 4(2)(a) TFEU (and therefore market authorisation under the applicable secondary legislation), and the scope that provides for EU engagement as compared to its supporting competence under Article 168 TFEU for other kinds of responses; and finally the importance of promoting innovation in pharmaceutical interventions as part of the broader programmatic aim of increasing economic optimisation.

In terms of the coordination and management of other responses, the ECDC must provide 'scientific advice on *non-pharmaceutical* public health interventions' (emphasis added),[87] and it works with the Commission and affected Member States, who must report on the effectiveness of their efforts through the EWRS in order to inform national and international planning. Social distancing becomes particularly important at Phase 6, when its use to regulate the internal market is highlighted. Indeed, the Commission must work with the Member States to 'coordinate … the position on *movement of persons* and goods and cooperate with appropriate international organizations and associations and transportation companies to implement standard measures for *travellers* on board international conveyances, consistent with the alert level'.[88]

Overall, these various efforts at risk management are underpinned by a concern for, and oriented and directed towards maintaining the optimal functioning of, the internal market rather than public health as a value in itself. This central focus of risk management and wider preparedness planning and response efforts point to their significance in terms of producing and legitimating the EU's identity as a security and public health actor, its socio-political order based upon an optimised market-based economy, and ultimately the project of European integration.

[85] Ibid.
[86] Ibid.
[87] Ibid, 20.
[88] Ibid, 25.

C. Communication

Relating to and managing public expectations occurs principally through communication, which is an important 'essential infrastructure'. Communication is threaded through the discussion above. For instance, communication is mentioned in relation to risk assessment where one important function of the gathering and production of epidemiological knowledge, for example, is so that the public can be kept informed of the health threat situation. Communication is even more directly related to risk management in that timely and accurate information is crucial to shaping the public response to a public health emergency and maintaining a functioning (and optimised) internal market. The gathering and production of knowledge on Member State risk communication strategies and practices seen in relation to risk management provides the basis for more intrusive EU involvement and the extension of its power and governance in relation to Member State preparedness. In other words, the extension of EU governance is necessary in order to ensure consistency in the communication of knowledge on the danger or threat posed by public health emergencies and the appropriate and recommended countermeasures.

Other important reasons for risk communication relate directly to the general approach established in *European Governance* in which openness, transparency, and accountability are to be ensured, and governance legitimated.[89] These principles are clearly relevant to the EU's wider public health governance, but they are especially important to planning for serious cross-border threats to health. Indeed, communication is to be facilitated through, inter alia, the provision of up-to-date and easily available (principally online) information on EU law and policy-making and, in preparedness, pandemic news media 'status' updates.[90] Each alert phase has its own communication plan, reflecting the seriousness of the threat, and based on information gathered through surveillance. Throughout the alert phases it is for Member State authorities to communicate arrangements for vaccination and distribution of antiviral agents to health professionals and the public.

Further, at Phase 3 the Commission, the ECDC, and Member States must work together in order to coordinate the sharing of 'accurate messages' about, inter alia, the global epidemiological situation (including spread and effectiveness of countermeasures). At Phase 4 (and similarly at Phases 5 and 6) the Commission and ECDC must work to promote 'sharing of templates for general health education materials'[91] and the Member States must share their intended 'public

[89] European Commission, *European Governance: A White Paper*, COM (2001) 428 final.

[90] Eg: europa.eu/press_room/press_packs/influenza/index_en.htm; www.ecdc.europa.eu/en/healthtopics/influenza/Pages/index.aspx; ec.europa.eu/health/communicable_diseases/diseases/influenza/h1n1/index_en.htm [all last accessed 5 September 2011].

[91] European Commission, *Pandemic Influenza Preparedness*, n 17 above, 20.

and educational material'.[92] The ECDC is charged with providing 'the scientific appraisal of recommended measures'[93] and, as stressed at Phase 6, it has a central role in making briefings from the EU to other actors, including the public.

Fast exchange of information and:

> [P]rompt notification during the first stages of a pandemic influenza are essential in enabling [Member States], the Commission, the ECDC, WHO and other bodies to respond with common positions in *public communications*, and *alert properly their structures, so that measures can be implemented in a timely manner*.[94] (Emphasis added)

As such Member State public authorities should 'communicate effectively with the public and the media *before and in anticipation of events* that *may* lead to public health emergencies'. Consistent with the approach taken to risk management, messages are to be coordinated,[95] and this should occur early on in any major incident, so as to ensure they establish 'themselves as the leading, if not the only, source of authoritative information',[96] and so as to avoid an 'information void'[97] and subsequent speculation, rumour and confusion. Coordination is facilitated through a 'range of ready to use media briefing materials about influenza',[98] including, basic information about the disease and the response systems in place, and clear and timely flows of information facilitated by 24/7 'operational contact points in the Member States and in the Commission',[99] and encompassing 'text, voice, and video'.[100]

Another way in which risk communication is related to risk management is in terms of its importance for the management of public expectations and establishing and delimiting the boundaries of EU responsibility and blame in the public imagination. Although the EU (and especially the Commission and ECDC) have key roles in risk communication, it is the Member States that are principally responsible for risk management and, therefore, failures that arise where people are hurt and even die because of a serious cross-border threat to their health. The EU's role and identity as a security and public health actor is limited to responsibility for facilitating and supporting preparedness, despite the ways in which its governance actually extend the EU's power and authority and legitimate its wider project of European integration. Elsewhere it is noted that coordination of communication 'will help *reinforce public confidence* in the response strategy if Member States and the Commission can demonstrate that the national strategies

[92] Ibid, 21.

[93] Ibid.

[94] Ibid, 14. *Cf* European Commission, *Generic Preparedness*, n 11 above, 6.

[95] Eg the Commission's October 2005 technical guidance document on *Procedure for Communication to Member States, the Commission and the ECDC about Highly Pathogenic Avian Influenza Events in Humans*, cited in European Commission, *Pandemic Influenza Preparedness*, n 17 above, 14.

[96] European Commission, *Generic Preparedness*, n 11 above, 7.

[97] Ibid, 13.

[98] Ibid.

[99] Ibid, 7.

[100] Ibid, 6.

across the EU are *consistent* and *based on a common assessment* of the relevant science' (emphasis added).[101] Public reassurance that a serious danger of threat is being tackled and (hopefully) ameliorated is a central function of communication.

Preparedness of risk communication efforts through their coordination also further underlines how the governance of public health is focused on security understood as being about regulating the danger or threat to the circulation of people and things: the 'distribution of accurate and timely information … is critical in order to minimise unwanted and unforeseen *social disruption and economic consequences* and to maximise the *effective outcome* of the response' (emphasis added).[102] Ensuring security and regulating dangers or threats also highlights the neoliberal orientation and direction of governance. Economic optimisation is the central focus of preparedness planning and response; public health is not an end in itself, but rather it becomes important as a way of maintaining a functioning internal market. Risk communication is a central aspect of risk management and it highlights the importance of producing and legitimating the EU's broader programmatic priorities and concerns: constructing the EU's identity as a security and public health actor, and producing and legitimating a socio-political order based upon the optimised economy and ultimately the European integration project.

While the EU's institutions and agencies and Member State authorities are both responsible for risk communication, with the EU attempting to ensure the consistency and accuracy of the information relayed, the principal addressees are, as noted, the EU's citizenry and publics. Consequently, the EU's citizenry are also governed through efforts to enhort, prompt and guide their behaviour in ways that help to disrupt the circulation of pandemics and other threats to health, and reduce the harm or hazards that arise from them or other public health emergencies. This responsibilisation relies on the agency and (most often the voluntary) compliance of individuals, groups and society at large. The specific role of citizens and publics in relation to risk communication throws their apparent absence from input into risk assessment and risk management into sharp relief—and that further attests to their marginalisation, which is partly a consequence of the centrality and valorisation of scientific knowledge and expertise in relation to decision-making within risk-based governance.

IV. CONCLUSION

The EU seeks to govern preparedness planning and response at all stages, but it does so at a distance through coordination and more specific risk-based technologies of risk assessment, risk management and risk communication. Overall, these technologies leverage the agency of a range of other actors, responsibilising

[101] European Commission, *Pandemic Influenza Preparedness*, n 17 above, 14.
[102] European Commission, *Generic Preparedness*, n 11 above, 6.

them, while at the same time delimiting the EU's own responsibility and accountability. The technologies that govern pandemics and other serious cross-border threats to health also facilitate the extension of the EU's power and the circulation of its security and market-oriented norms, values and rationalities, into the formally non-market policy domain of public health. The gathering and production of knowledge as governance (seen in coordination) and as the basis for wider governance and regulatory interventions (risk assessment, risk management and risk communication), reflects the (re)configuration between power and knowledge seen elsewhere in the EU's technology governing public health. The latter (re)configuration is closely related to others—between power and responsibility, sovereignty and territoriality, and governance and the governed—and together these are the structuring themes of the domain.

Like the EU's risk-based involvement in public health more broadly, preparedness planning and response demonstrates the efficacy of EU governance and its necessity. Through its coordination of Member State planning and response the EU shapes the (de)selection of interventions across the territory and in the populations of the EU's Member States, with surge capacity and medical responses being favoured and distracting attention and resources away from prevention as well as non-communicable diseases. The exportation of the EU's normative power via wider international preparedness planning and response coordination is another key dimension of EU level coordination. The (re)framing of the governance of pandemics and other serious cross-border threats as an EU matter also helps to produce and legitimate the EU's identity as a security and public health actor, the socio-political order founded on an optimised market economy, and ultimately the project of European integration.

This chapter puts in place the final part of the platform and basis for the discussion in the next part—the second half—of the book. There I reflect first on the key contours of EU public health governance and consider the implications for the (de)selection of regulatory interventions. Subsequently I reflect on the role and configuration of citizen participation in decision-making, make a link back to the key contours of governance, and outline my prescription for enhancing participation and through it the quality of governance and its interventions in public health.

Part II

Enhancing Citizen Participation in Governing Public Health

6

Citizen Participation in Governing: Discursive Resources, Tools and Spaces

I. INTRODUCTION

THIS CHAPTER BRIDGES the discussion in the first part of the book, by summarising the findings there and explaining how they provide a platform and resources for taking the book's agenda forward throughout the rest of the second part. So far in this book I have outlined the overarching architecture for EU governance and its operationalisation through the strategy for public health and the health programmes, and subsequently the three core public health problems of cancer, HIV/AIDS and other pandemics and serious cross-border threats to health. The discussion highlighted how the techniques, processes and practices of the technology governing public health are constitutive of the policy domain and relate to the production and legitimation of the EU's identity, socio-political order and project of European integration. Overall the first part of the book exemplifies the key contours, underpinnings and orientation of the EU level of the multi-level system of governance for public health. In the next section I highlight two things, first, risk as the dominant framing for the governing technology and second, the way in which that framing is underpinned by and oriented towards market optimisation understood as being about the circulation of people and things. Subsequently I summarise the (re)configurations ongoing in governance—those between knowledge and power, sovereignty and territoriality, and power and responsibility, and finally an introduction to the (re)configuration between governance and the governed—and identify them as the structuring themes undergirding the governing technology and related public health policy domain.

This summary and reflection of the findings provides the bridge between the first part of the book and the grounds for a diagnosis of the shape and role of the current institutionalisation of citizen participation as a key concern. The third section makes the diagnosis by highlighting the centrality and valorisation of scientific and technical knowledge and expertise by and within the risk-based technology governing public health. I explain how the framing of public health governance as a matter of risk, although useful and even vital, justifies the pessimism about the current institutionalisation of citizen participation that helped to prompt this book. That is because, buttressed by several related discourses, such as the public understanding of science and bioethics, the dominance of scientific and technical knowledge configures and implicitly devalues and limits the role and shape of citizen participation. The fourth section begins by considering how the foundations of governance, its structuring themes and effects, specifically, its distortions, paradoxes, pitfalls and blind spots, open up space and create possibilities for biopolitics and citizen participation in decision-making.

Subsequently I discuss the potential of the legitimating discourses of human rights and bioethics, and the developing notion of (supra-)stewardship responsibility, as the resources and means for facilitating and powering discussion and public querying around framing, distribution and vulnerability. I explain how that discussion might generate supplementary knowledge on the distortions, paradoxes, pitfalls and blind spots of risk-based governance and its regulatory interventions. I argue that this in turn provides a 'way in' for participation impelled by the threat that, if unaddressed, these regulatory failures and 'societal risks' could produce 'institutional risks', to the EU's standing and reputation, that undermine and delegitimate its governance, identity and project of integration. This prescription for enhancing citizen participation in decision-making—and through it governance and its regulatory interventions—underpins my optimism for the future of democratic politics in apparently dry and technical policy domains. That positive outlook is reinforced in the next two chapters, where I build on the summary of the findings to elaborate on how citizen participation might help to reveal and underline the paradoxes, pitfalls and blind spots produced by and within the risk-based technology governing public health.

II. SUMMARY OF THE FINDINGS SO FAR

A. The Centrality of Risk

Throughout the first part of the book I made the initial main argument, which is that markets, risk and security, and ethics and human rights, provide the key contours for the EU's public health policy domain and they are related in particular ways. Public health is not just about the protection of populations, the EU or its Member States. Public health problems are governmentalised in that they are constituted and understood as dangers or threats attendant to the circulation of people and things, that is the internal market, and are made the subject of risk-based governance and regulatory interventions, all together the technology governing public health. Understood in this way the regulation of public health is about ensuring the security of the internal market in order to ensure its optimisation. The importance of security (as the focus of risk governance and regulatory interventions) is even more apparent in relation to communicable diseases and other serious cross-border threats to health where risk regulation is about dealing with actual or potential emergencies. Whatever the regulatory target, risk assessment and management techniques—like those of prevention and preparedness that are dominant at the EU level in the area of public health—make the problems they govern (especially the examples of cancer, HIV/AIDS and other pandemics and serious cross-border threats to health) legible and visible in an effort to manage them and keep the economy working.[1] This is clear from chapter two, which sketched the programmatic concerns of the overarching architecture of EU governance and discussed how it shapes, orientates and directs the use of the EU's formal legal competence in the field of public health. Further legal foundations for the public health policy domain are also provided by the EU's internal market competence. EU competence is worked out through the more specific strategy aimed at consolidating, orchestrating and directing the public health policy domain as a whole.

That is especially apparent in the market-oriented rationale and neoliberal underpinnings of that strategy and the way in which they shape not only the principles, objectives and normative direction, but also the concrete techniques, processes and practices—in short, the means—for its implementation (about which more is said below). In that regard, the principle of putting health in all policies is revealing in that it is about ensuring the dangers or threats to health are regulated throughout the EU's wider governance. In that way health again shores up the EU's central market integration imperative. Resort to market reasoning is also apparent in relation to two particularly important governing technologies: impact assessment as knowledge-based policy-making and monitoring, measuring and evaluating as ways of governing through agency and performance. Funding is a particular way of influencing and regulating the behaviours of national authorities, populations and individuals. The EU's role as a security actor is also increasingly prominent, but again it is not just about the protection of the EU and its population, but is, rather, about regulating the dangers or threats attendant to the circulation of people and things beyond, into and throughout the internal market (as part of the area of freedom, security and justice). Another important point is that non-state actors including private corporate interests are key addressees and components of public health governance (particularly in relation to HIV/AIDS). In light of the neoliberal orientation of governance this signals the extension and insinuation of market interests into the organisation of public health.

The various techniques, processes and practices governing specific public health problems—cancer, then HIV/AIDS and finally other pandemics, such as those that are rare or occasional like influenza, discussed in chapters three, four and five respectively—are aligned to and configured by and within the overarching architecture and its programmatic concerns via the more specific strategy for the public health policy domain. This is apparent in the use of the partnership approach to cancer, especially in the stress on steering national responses, knowledge production and governing through the agency and performance of actors, including non-state actors like private corporate interests. In relation to HIV/AIDS and other pandemics and serious cross-border threats to health the securitisation of public health understood as the regulation of the dangers or threats to the circulation of

[1] For discussion see: S Jasanoff, 'Technologies of Humility: Citizen Participation in Governing Science' (2003) 41 *Minerva* 223, 238.

people and things becomes even more apparent. Key examples include the EU's developing governance and regulatory capacities and relations with Member State and international regulators, its attention to groups and regions that are deemed most 'at risk', and in that regard the shift of emphasis away from prevention and towards preparedness and technological and medical responses. More than that, the external dimension of EU governance becomes particularly important, such as through efforts at governing the EU's periphery and beyond, particularly in relation to communicable diseases and serious cross-border threats to health.

Human rights and ethics have far less central positions and functions in the technology governing public health. Although human rights is quite prominent at the overarching level of governance, ethics is less so. The place of human rights is unsurprising given that it is important as a 'legal or quasi-legal expression of values fundamental to a particular socio-political order'.[2] More importantly, by virtue of the *recognition* of health as a right within EU law, not only is the EU able to build and mediate relations between its governance and citizens, it is also able to draw down on the idea of human rights as a meaningful expression of the membership of a particular community (in this context the EU) and the value that (EU) community places on its constituents.[3] In this view, health is not merely a medical, technical or even private problem, but is also recognised as—and thereby elevated to—a social, collective or common good and public problem to be tackled by governance.[4] Since illness and disease can 'shape the symbolic values of society',[5] how illness and disease are dealt with is symbolic of those very values, they are part of socio-political identity and of 'citizenship, our relation to others'.[6] Moreover, as Marshall asserted, no modern government can 'disclaim responsibility for the health of its people, nor would it wish to do so'.[7] In being conferred and exercising competence over public health the EU is accessing this powerful heritage, forging an identity as a public health actor, and engaging in one of the core activities of states, all of which is ultimately useful to the project of integration and its legitimation.

However, throughout the public health policy domain both ethics and human rights are then reduced in importance to a few inflections in places. For example,

[2] T Hervey, 'The "Right to Health" in European Union Law' in T Hervey and J Kenner (eds), *Economic and Social Rights Under the EU Charter of Fundamental Rights—A Legal Perspective* (Oxford, Hart Publishing, 2003) 194.

[3] Eg as in references found in Art 6(1) Treaty on European Union (TEU) gives the previously non-binding Charter of Fundamental Rights of the EU the same status as the Treaties. Further, not only is the European Convention on Human Rights (4 November 1950, entered into force 3 September 1953) ETS 5, noted as a source for the general principles of EU law in Art 6(3) TEU, but the EU's accession to the Council of Europe is required under Art 6(2) TEU. It might even be said the EU—now with its own Fundamental Rights Agency—has become 'the' human rights organisation in Europe. On this and key cases see: ML Flear and A Vakulenko, 'A Human Rights Perspective on Citizen Participation in the EU's Governance of New Technologies' (2010) 10(4) *Human Rights Law Review* 661.

[4] For discussion, see: J Coggon, *What Makes Health Public?* (Cambridge, Cambridge University Press, 2012).

[5] J Richman, *Medicine and Health* (London, Longman, 1987) 2.

[6] P Williams, *The Alchemy of Race and Rights* (Boston MA, Harvard University Press, 1991) 164.

[7] TH Marshall, *Social Policy*, 5th edn (London, Hutchinson, 1985) 133.

they appear briefly in impact assessment as part of putting health in all policies,[8] or areas that intersect with public health governance, such as HIV/AIDS and blood (particularly in terms of donation with its strong altruistic ethic).[9] Ethics is prominent through the introduction of ethics committees in the Member States by the Clinical Trials Directive[10] (important for the European and Developing Countries Clinical Trials Partnership[11] discussed in greater depth in chapter seven in the context of more detailed consideration of the Directive and related law) and the role of the European Group on Ethics in Science and New Technologies (EGE). The EGE provides the European Commission (Commission) with a comprehensive range of opinions on 'all areas of the application of science and technology',[12] which thus function as a form of normativity beyond law or 'grey governance'[13] generating various exhortatory, persuasive and binding consequences. Those consequences include support for controversial research funding[14] and the recitals of legislation that appear only briefly in the broad sweep of public health governance traced in the first part of this book.[15]

Despite these mentions and uses ethics (and human rights usually via ethics) is often reduced to a set of procedural guarantees, for instance, as part of the normative background for assessing the appropriateness of public health interventions (especially in relation to communicable diseases like HIV/AIDS but also other serious cross-border threats to health), or through the focus on the informed consent of those involved in clinical trials and biomedical knowledge creation.[16] Further, ethics is determined by Member State *governments* and experts (such as those comprising research ethics committees for clinical trials).[17] In this light the wider function of ethics is 'to *ensure that the general public is kept properly informed*' (emphasis added)[18] and to 'keep the rapidly advancing progress in science in

[8] Discussed in ch 2.

[9] Discussed in ch 4.

[10] Directive 2001/20/EC on the approximation of the laws, regulations and administrative provisions of the Member States relating to the implementation of good clinical practice in the conduct of clinical trials on medicinal products for human use [2001] OJ L121/34. This Directive is now replaced by Regulation (EU) 536/2014 on clinical trials on medicinal products for human use, and repealing Directive 2001/20/EC [2014] OJ L158/1, but it does not become applicable until at least 28 May 2016. The Regulation is planned to apply from 2019 (see Preface).

[11] Mentioned in ch 4.

[12] Decision 2005/383/EC on the renewal of the mandate of the European Group on Ethics in Science and New Technologies [2005] OJ L127/17.

[13] H Busby, T Hervey and A Mohr, 'Ethical EU law? The Influence of the European Group on Ethics in Science and New Technologies' (2008) 33 *European Law Review* 803.

[14] Eg Opinion 10—11/12/1997—Ethical aspects of the 5th Research Framework Programme; Opinion 22—13/07/2007—The Ethics Review of hESC FP7 Research Projects.

[15] Eg in areas that relate to public health: Directive 2004/23/EC on setting standards of quality and safety for the donation, procurement, testing, processing, preservation, storage and distribution of human tissues and cells [2004] OJ L102/48 and Regulation (EC) 1394/2007 on advanced therapy medicinal products and amending Directive 2001/83/EC and Regulation (EC) 726/2004 [2007] OJ L324/121.

[16] ML Flear, 'Clinical Trials Abroad: The Marketable Ethics, Weak Protections and Vulnerable Subjects of EU Law' in A Albors-Llorens, K Armstrong and MW Gehring (eds), *Cambridge Yearbook of European Legal Studies*, Vol 16 2013–14 (Oxford, Hart Publishing, 2014). See further, ch 8.

[17] M Tallacchini, 'Governing by Values. EU Ethics: Soft Tool, Hard Effects' (2009) 47 *Minerva* 281, 293–95.

[18] 'Mandate 1991–97' ec.europa.eu/bepa/european-group-ethics/archive-mandates/mandate-1991-1997/index_en.htm.

harmony with the *ethical values of all Europeans*' (emphasis added).[19] In other words, like human rights, ethics is part of efforts at producing and legitimating the project of European integration, an integral component or precursor of which is the fostering of EU citizenship by providing a democratic basis for governance: 'European integration *must mean more* than establishing a single market; progress in science and technology must be given a *human, social and ethical dimension, otherwise European citizenship cannot be established*' (emphasis added).[20] In summary, public bioethics or that which relates governance and its use of bioethics to the public is, as Ashcroft explains, 'a set of practices for *legitimating* the "social license to practise"' (emphasis added)[21] of medicine and the broader governance of life. Overall, conferred top-down[22] the chief function of ethics and human rights is as legitimating devices for the risk-based technology governing public health—an observation that will become important later in this chapter when I consider how this might be useable by citizens in efforts to demand and contest decisions.

B. Neoliberal Underpinnings as the Structuring Themes of the Policy Domain

The analysis of the relations between markets, risk and security, and ethics and human rights, advances the second argument of this book, which is that they point to the importance of neoliberalism through the underlying use, infiltration, perpetuation and extension of market-oriented ideas, values and rationalities into public health. The circulation of neoliberalism is also apparent in the key (re)configurations between knowledge and power, sovereignty and territoriality, and power and responsibility that underpin and are reflected in the EU's risk-based technology governing public health. These (re)configurations are the structuring themes of the policy domain. While another key theme is the (re)configuration between governing and the governed, which is considered later in this chapter, the themes (as well as the effects or paradoxes, pitfalls and blind spots of governance and its regulatory interventions) also create space and possibilities for citizen participation. I consider the relationship between the governance and the governed towards the end of this section and in the subsequent discussion. In the following I prepare the way for the subsequent discussion by outlining the other themes.

In terms of the (re)configuration of knowledge and power, decision-making in the EU's public health policy domain is underpinned by the gathering, deployment and instrumentalisation of scientific and technical knowledge and expertise

[19] *Taking European Knowledge Society Seriously: Report of the Expert Group on Science and Governance* (Luxembourg, European Commission, 2007) 49.

[20] Ibid, 80, citing ec.europa.eu/european_group_ethics/archive/1991_1997/bilan_en.htm.

[21] R Ashcroft, 'Could Human Rights Supersede Bioethics?' (2010) 10(4) *Human Rights Law Review* 639, 645.

[22] An analysis noted in other contexts, see eg: M Tallacchini, 'Risks and Rights in Xenotransplantation' in S Jasanoff (ed), *Reframing Rights: Bioconstitutionalism in the Genetic Age* (Cambridge MA, MIT Press, 2011).

as a crucial support for power. This is apparent in relation to the specific public health problems considered in the first part of this book, and more broadly at the overarching level of governance. In that regard the emphasis on evidence, impact assessment as a tool for factoring health into all policy areas, and other techniques, underpin and facilitate knowledge-based policy-making. Monitoring, measuring and evaluating are also central to governing public health at a distance. Epidemiology is clearly of foundational importance to the technology governing public health since it allows the production of statistics and indicators, which in turn facilitate measurement and monitoring of performance and efforts to steer Member State responses, particularly in relation to the targeting of prevention efforts and treatment.

The EU also gathers and produces knowledge on national approaches and responses. For example, in the EU's partnership approach to cancer there is a focus on bolstering technologies of knowledge-based policy through the identification and dissemination of good practice. Cooperation and coordination in cancer research is also about gathering and producing knowledge in order to shape prevention and treatment efforts. In addition, benchmarking is a knowledge-based technique that involves the tracking and monitoring of Member State performance through the production and use of indicators, which are used to steer and shape national techniques, processes and practices. Through more specific work packages the partnership approach is extended and deepened, culminating in the design of national cancer plans and the opening up of national knowledge domains to a common set of EU ideas, norms and rationalities, and with it more intrusive steering and control over national responses.

In relation to HIV/AIDS the gathering and production of knowledge is more wide-ranging in that it has not just internal dimensions, but also very important external dimensions encompassing the EU's periphery and beyond. A key focus is on improving the quantity and quality of available knowledge through surveillance. The dearth of available data on rare and emerging diseases and other serious cross-border threats to health means that epidemiology, while important, must be supplemented by other forms of knowledge in order to provide a basis for governance and regulatory interventions. Prominent in the EU's approach to other pandemics and serious threats to health are efforts at preparedness planning and response. This demonstrates how high degrees of uncertainty or non-knowing about the probability of a disease, its size and scale, or even non-knowing (to be clear, that is in a scientific sense) do not necessarily impede risk-based governance and efforts to shape regulatory interventions.

Overall, these different forms of knowledge make it possible to define, (re)constitute and stabilise public health as a 'European' problem and the risk-based approach for governance and regulatory interventions. Moreover, not just the EU's identity as a security and public health actor, but also the project of European integration are perpetuated through more intrusive involvement in what is still (legally and in actuality) a core function of Member States and marker of their sovereignty. Knowledge is not just a crucial support for power; knowledge and power are, as noted several times in the discussion thus far, co-productive of each other.[23] The gathering and production of knowledge facilitates governance and regulatory interventions in public health (as in other policy domains). In addition, the knowledge gathered and produced for use and deployment through the technology of governing is determined (at least in part) by the framing of the policy domain by risk in order to facilitate the circulation of people and things (economic optimisation), which entails the regulation of the attendant threats and dangers (public health problems).[24] More than that, in these ways public health knowledge is central to efforts at producing and legitimating the EU's identity, socio-political order and European integration project.

Power is also extended through these tightening relations with knowledge. This is apparent in the extension of the EU's power both in terms of what its governance (and regulatory interventions) covers, and the places where it applies and people enfolded into the regime and in relation to whom it has effects. As for the former, the technology governing public health encompasses knowledge and has material dimensions via regulatory interventions such as preventative measures and treatment. In terms of the latter, the EU's governing technology and its normative power extends beyond the territory of the EU through attempts at, inter alia, monitoring and governing the interventions of public health authorities on its periphery and beyond, often through international coordination. This highlights a (re)configuration between sovereignty and territoriality as another structuring theme of the public health policy domain.

A further key theme of the EU's public health policy domain is the (re)configuration between power and responsibility. The risk-based technology governing public health is part of attempts to establish and delimit the boundaries of EU responsibility and accountability in the event of failure. In attempting to define the limits of its responsibility the EU is, in part, seeking to define failure—the trigger for determining the circumstances in which it can be held accountable. The EU has limited responsibility for public health in accordance with the boundaries of formal competence outlined in chapter two. More specifically the EU's responsibility is shaped and delimited by risk as the dominant framing for public health problems. The frame is (as already highlighted) directed at ensuring security understood as being about the regulation of the dangers or threats attendant to the circulation of people and things, as seen in chapters three, four and five. That regulation is achieved through specific techniques, processes and practices. Consistent with the separation of risk assessment and risk management functions since *European Governance*,[25] the Member States retain charge of the latter (risk *management*) as well as ethical and rights implications, especially for the (de)selection of public health interventions. In short, much of the responsibility

[23] For an introduction to these ideas, see ch 1.

[24] N Krieger, 'The Making of Public Health Data: Paradigms, Politics, and Policy' (1992) 13(4) *Journal of Public Health Policy* 412.

[25] European Commission, *European Governance: A White Paper*, COM (2001) 428 final.

and accountability for risk management is located at Member State level with the EU taking increasing responsibility for risk assessment and governing events and the responses of its Member States to public health problems at a distance.

To some extent this delimitation of responsibility and accountability is understandable: Member States are closest to their citizens and they have the resources and legitimacy to act. However, the delimitation is politically useful to the EU in that it is able to derive benefits, such as claims for success, and the production and legitimation of its identity, socio-political and project of rule by and through its public health governance and regulatory interventions, which are depoliticised and naturalised. As the same time the EU is able to eschew direct responsibility for its population and those governed beyond its borders, especially in relation to the paradoxes, pitfalls and blind spots attendant to and *produced* by, at least in part, *its* discourses. The distribution of responsibilities and shaping of accountabilities helps to shield the EU from adverse public perceptions in the event of controversy and failure (illness and even death). This and the other structuring themes are salient in that they are also embedded within, reflective of and central to efforts at producing and legitimating the EU, its identity as a security and public health actor,[26] related imagined socio-political order based on a competitive and innovative internal market, and ultimately the project of European integration.[27]

The structuring themes also become important since they shape the discursive space—the openings, possibilities, limitations and constraints—for biopolitics. In the next two chapters I suggest a few specific examples that could provide the focus of attempts to demand and contest EU decision-making and enhance citizen participation. But before that I continue with tracing the preliminary matters dealt with in this chapter, turning next to consider the final major (re)configuration and structuring theme of the regulatory technology and policy domain of public health, that between governing and the governed and the implications for citizen participation in decision-making. After which I explain how the components and structuring themes of the technology governing public health and the public health policy domain do not simply constrain but also open up the possibilities for biopolitics and citizen participation in decision-making.

III. RISK, PUBLIC HEALTH AND CITIZEN PARTICIPATION

The centrality and valorisation of scientific and technical knowledge and expertise by and within the risk-based technology used to regulate public health[28] is 'the' key

[26] *Cf* J Dratwa, 'Representing Europe with the Precautionary Principle' in S Jasanoff (ed), *Reframing Rights: Bioconstitutionalism in the Genetic Age* (Cambridge MA, MIT Press, 2011).

[27] B Anderson, *Imagined Communities* (London, Verso, 1983); Y Ezrahi, *The Descent of Icarus* (Cambridge MA, Harvard University Press, 1990); JC Scott, *Seeing Like a State* (New Haven, Yale University Press, 1998).

[28] As mentioned in ch 2 this is also seen in relation the internal market legislation adopted under (the principal legal basis) Art 114 Treaty on the Functioning of the European Union (TFEU).

finding of the first part of the book. The finding reflects an expert rationality—the 'quasiguardianship' of scientific experts[29]—which although useful and even vital for the governance of public health, implicitly devalues and limits the scope and potential for and contribution of citizen participation in decision-making. In other words, the framing of risk establishes boundaries that make public health problems governable. At the same time the process of framing establishes, configures and legitimates hierarchies and relationships between scientific and technical knowledge and expertise, governance and regulation, and citizens. The centrality of scientific and technical knowledge and expertise in the public health domain is made particularly apparent in the following:

> When preparing its policy and proposals relating to consumer safety, *public health* and the environment, *the Commission relies on independent Scientific Committees to provide it with sound scientific advice and draw its attention to new and emerging problems.* The Scientific Committees can call on *additional expertise from a pool of scientific advisors and a database of experts.*[30] (Emphasis added)

There are two notable attempts to include citizens in decision-making in the EU's public health domain, but in such a way as to configure citizens in relation to scientific and technical knowledge and expertise. One key example is impact assessment (IA), noted above and discussed in chapter two, where its implications for participation were touched upon very briefly. To extend those introductory points, as a tool aimed at integrating consideration of the implications of regulation and policy for health, IA also has the potential to ensure the concerns of citizens are taken into account across EU policy domains. Indeed, IA '*takes into account input* from a wide range of *external stakeholders*, in line with the Commission's policy of transparency and openness towards other institutions and the civil society' (emphasis added).[31] IA is about 'Gathering opinions and information from interested parties [and] is an essential part of the policy-development process, *enhancing its transparency and ensuring that proposed policy is practically workable and legitimate from the point of view of stakeholders*' (emphasis added).[32]

In a similar vein, elsewhere it is noted how IA 'demonstrates the Commission's openness to input from a wide range of external stakeholders, and shows its commitment to transparency'.[33] The integration of these external inputs from stakeholders occurs via '*consultations* … making decision makers and the public aware of likely policy impacts while also serving as a tool for communication between them' (emphasis added).[34] However, consultation limits and prefigures who can participate through a focus on 'stakeholders'. This framing of participation suggests that what is 'at stake' has already been defined, as have, by implication, those with an interest in governance. The latter abets the delegation of decision-making

[29] RA Dahl, *Democracy and its Critics* (London, Yale University Press, 1989) 335.
[30] 'Scientific Committees' ec.europa.eu/health/scientific_committees/policy/index_en.htm.
[31] European Commission, *Impact Assessment Guidelines*, SEC (2009) 92, 6.
[32] European Commission, *Impact Assessment Guidelines*, SEC (2005) 791, 9.
[33] Ibid, 5.
[34] European Commission, *Communication on Impact Assessment*, COM 2002 (276), 3.

to trusted decisionmakers and the valorisation of those providing scientific and technical knowledge and expertise.[35]

Further, while this sort of tool is said to ensure that the Commission's system is both accountable and transparent,[36] as discussed in chapter two it is within a constrained range of possible (or permitted) options. Within these options it is 'political decision-makers'[37] alone who are competent to assess supposed value-neutral technical evidence, frame and select the appropriate policy response, while also reducing the scope for ex ante participation as well as ex post contestation. Indeed, the invocation of supposedly neutral expert knowledge as a support for decisions actually attempts to reduce—and arguably thwart—such involvement, which is also limited by the dearth of clearly defined avenues for feeding back into ex ante processes and future decisions beyond the IA process. Against this background communication efforts act as a supplement to the involvement of stakeholders and the definition of their 'stake' as well as what is 'at stake'.

The second example of an attempt to include citizens in decision-making is the 'dialogue and collaboration' around risk in the context of public health, which is recognised as part of the 'new challenges for risk assessment', first underlined in *European Governance*[38] (and reflected in the health sphere)[39] and noted further below. A central concern is that 'Public opinion has become more sceptical about the neutrality and effectiveness of science, and there is a growing call for more transparency'. Moreover, 'technological developments in areas like nanotechnology have exceeded the ability of research bodies to generate safety data and of risk assessors to adapt and apply appropriate tools to evaluate new risks' and consequently pose a key challenge to risk assessors. In order to address 'this increased complexity', DG SANCO has 'initiated *risk assessment dialogues*. These have made it possible to identify collaborative projects in the area of emerging risks, risk assessment methodology and terminology, exposure assessment and new issues and challenges for risk assessment'.[40]

However, at the EU level[41] dialogue and communication in relation to risk assessment focuses on relating the views of relevant individuals—usually termed

[35] Such as 'High Level Group of National Regulatory Experts' ec.europa.eu/governance/impact/high_level_group/index_en.htm.

[36] For online publication of the impact assessments, see: 'List of impact assessments—planned and final ones' ec.europa.eu/governance/impact/ia_carried_out/ia_carried_out_en.htm.

[37] 'Impact assessment' ec.europa.eu/governance/impact/index_en.htm.

[38] European Commission, *European Governance*, n 25 above.

[39] See the documents discussed in ch 2, n 47, especially: European Commission, *White Paper, Together for Health: A Strategic Approach for the EU 2008–13*, COM (2007) 630 final. For further discussion see: ML Flear, '"Together for Health"? How EU Governance Undermines Active Biological Citizenship' (2008) 26 *Wisconsin International Law Journal* 368.

[40] 'New challenges for risk assessment' ec.europa.eu/health/dialogue_collaboration/policy/index_en.htm.

[41] There is also a dialogue at the international level, see: 'International risk assessment dialogue' ec.europa.eu/health/dialogue_collaboration/international_dialogue/index_en.htm. For commentary on the global scene see: D Held and M Koenig-Archibugi (eds), *Global Governance and Public Accountability* (Malden MA, Blackwell Publishing, 2005).

'stakeholders'—to scientific and technical knowledge and expertise as the foundation for risk-based decision-making. For example:

> The EU's risk assessment system consists of various independent bodies giving scientific advice to decision makers. These bodies operate within their specific relevant EU legal frameworks. However, close co-operation is essential to ensure consistency in the way they deal with issues of common interest (e.g. evaluating the risks posed by substances or technologies used in various applications falling under the remit of more than one Agency or Scientific Committee), and for sharing experience and best practices on risk assessment.[42]

The risk assessment system consists of three (non-food related) scientific committees managed by DG Santé (formaly DG SANCO)[43] as well as, inter alia, the European Medicines Agency (EMA) and the European Centre for Disease Control and Prevention (ECDC).[44] Further, building on the importance of ensuring transparency as a way of managing public opinion and perceptions of the risk-based decision-making process and its decisions, the bodies 'have decided to work together more closely to improve the quality, communication, added value and recognition of risk assessment, and thereby help improving risk management decisions'.[45] In other words, scientific and technical knowledge and expertise are central to decision-making with participation being reduced to risk communication efforts instead of dialogue[46]—or as in public health with dialogue taking place after communication of the relevant knowledge by recognised and credentialised experts to laypeople.

This narrowing of the role, use and potential of citizen participation has been the subject of ongoing efforts, in particular through the development and sharing of best practices between risk assessors in the meetings launched by DG Santé (or DG SANCO as it was than) in 2005. Best practices include a '*common approach, containing general principles and engagement with stakeholders*', '*Clear and effective risk communication* by using a consistent and clear terminology', a '*clear description* of the scope and nature of risks, uncertainties and their implications', and a 'framework for EU and international co-operation including procedures for the exchange of data and information' (emphasis added).[47] The limited nature of dialogue—what it entails, who it involves and its timing in the decision-making process as occurring once decisions over framing have been made—is underlined in the following way:

> [DG SANCO as it was then] regularly holds *information sessions* for members and staff of the European Parliament, and *dialogue sessions* with stakeholders. The purpose of the

[42] 'New challenges for risk assessment', n 40 above.

[43] They are Scientific Committee on Consumer Safety (SCCS), Scientific Committee on Health and Environmental Risks (SCHER) and Scientific Committee on Emerging and Newly Identified Health Risk (SCENIHR).

[44] As well as the European Food Safety Authority (EFSA), the European Chemicals Agency (ECHA), the European Environment Agency (EEA) and the Scientific Committee on Occupational Exposure Limits (SCOEL), which is managed by DG Employment.

[45] 'Risk assessment and dialogue at EU-level' ec.europa.eu/health/dialogue_collaboration/system/index_en.htm.

[46] F Fischer, 'Professional Expertise in a Deliberative Democracy: Facilitating Participatory Inquiry' (2004) 13(1) *The Good Society* 21.

[47] 'New challenges for risk assessment', n 40 above.

risk assessment days is to present the three non-food Scientific Committees and *their activities and results to these audiences, and to launch a more sustained and structured dialogue with them.* Part of the programme for those days is dedicated to joint meetings of the three Scientific Committees.[48] (Emphasis added)

Again, the relation to stakeholders as lay participants implies that what is 'at stake' has already been defined and wider citizen participation in framing and other decisions is precluded. Moreover, the provision of information here is one-way rather than symmetrical: there is an assumption that citizens have little to contribute towards decision-making and policy besides legitimation through their acceptance, trust and confidence in scientific and technical knowledge and the decisions made using it. In this way dialogue can occur only once that common body of knowledge has been established.[49]

These examples are indicative of the wider proliferation of sites, venues, strategies, techniques, rhetoric and practices of citizen involvement in the governance of life (and science) at the EU level (and indeed nationally and internationally).[50] Citizen participation is proclaimed as a core value in the EU's Treaties,[51] now (post 2009 and the coming into force of the Treaty of Lisbon) including the European Citizens' Initiative, which is described as 'the first transnational instrument of participatory democracy in world history'.[52] These legal foundations have been bolstered by, for instance, the Aarhus Convention[53] and its implementation in EU law.[54] The latter instrument focuses on supporting participation to address the

[48] Ibid.

[49] See, relatedly: C Radaelli, 'The Role of Knowledge in the Policy Process' (1995) 2(2) *Journal of European Public Policy* 159. Also see: R Freeman and S Sturdy (eds), *Knowledge in Policy: Embodied, Inscribed, Enacted* (Bristol, Policy Press, 2014).

[50] For discussion, see: H Gottweis, 'Participation and the New Governance of Life' (2008) 3 *BioSocieties* 265.

[51] Eg Art 2 TEU (the EU is 'founded on the values of respect for human dignity, freedom, *democracy*, equality, the rule of law and respect for *human rights*'), Art 10(3) TEU ('Every citizen shall have the *right to participate* in the democratic life of the Union. Decisions shall be taken as openly and as closely as possible to the citizen'), and Art 11(1) TEU ('The institutions *shall*, by *appropriate* means, give *citizens and representative associations* the *opportunity* to *make known* and *publicly exchange* their views in *all areas of Union action*'). See further: Flear and Vakulenko, n 3 above.

[52] See: 'European Citizens' Initiative' www.citizens-initiative.eu/?page_id=2. Established by Art 11(4) TEU and Art 24(1) TFEU. The practical arrangements and procedures are provided by Regulation (EU) 211/2011 on the citizens' initiative [2011] OJ L65/1. Art 11(4) TEU provides 'Not less than one million citizens who are nationals of a significant number of Member States may take the initiative inviting the Commission, within the framework of its powers, to submit any appropriate proposal on matters where citizens consider that a legal act of the Union is required for the purpose of implementing the Treaties'. This could produce a legal act under Art 168 TFEU. On Art 11 TEU see: M Dougan, 'What Are We to Make of the Citizens' Initiative' (2011) 48 *Common Market Law Review* 1807; J Mendes, 'Participation and the Role of Law after Lisbon: A Legal View on Article 11 TEU' (2011) 48 *Common Market Law Review* 1849.

[53] UN Economic Commission for Europe, Aarhus Convention on Access to Information, Public Participation in Decision-Making and Access to Justice in Environmental Matters (adopted 25 June 1998, entered into force 30 October 2001) 2161 UNTS 447.

[54] The European Community became a party through Decision 2005/370/EC on the conclusion, on behalf of the European Community, of the Convention on access to information, public participation in decision-making and access to justice in environmental matters [2005] OJ L124/1 The Convention

environmental impacts of new technologies, but it and its implementing instruments are therefore rather limited in relation to public health as they do not deal with the wider sources of disease and infirmity.[55]

Participation is constructed more through (legally) non-binding policy statements that focus on configuring it in relation to the EU's risk-based decision-making grounded on scientific and technical knowledge and expertise.[56] The most important policy statements include the aforementioned *European Governance*,[57] which in 2001 called for openness and transparency in expert work and enhanced public participation, which is to be achieved through the consultation predominantly of stakeholders[58] in the process of science-based decision-making.[59] The central objective of these moves is to reinforce accountability, engender (or restore) public trust and confidence in expertise after failures such as the crisis over BSE (bovine spongiform encephalopathy) and GMOs (genetically modified organisms), and to reinforce the legitimacy of governance and in turn the EU's project of integration.[60] This is especially oriented towards areas of risk and scientific uncertainty, including public health problems like pandemics and the more general turn to precautionary approaches to risk governance.[61] Through this there is a more express recognition of the need for societal concerns to be taken into account through the input of those who are affected by decision-making that cannot be based on science alone.[62] Yet, as the details of policy reveal, participation has a limited regulatory role.

has been implemented through several pieces of environment legislation: Directive 2003/4/EC on public access to environmental information and repealing Directive 90/313/EEC [2003] OJ L41/26; Directive 2003/35/EC providing for public participation in respect of the drawing up of certain plans and programmes relating to the environment and amending with regard to public participation and access to justice Directives 85/337/EEC and 96/61/EC [2003] OJ L156/17. In addition, several other environment Directives contain provision on participation, including Directive 2001/42/EC on the assessment of certain plans and programmes on the environment [2001] OJ L197/30 and Directive 2000/60/EC establishing a framework for Community action in the field of water policy [2000] OJ L327/1.

55 For discussion, see: J D'Silva and G van Calster, 'For Me to Know and You to Find Out? Participatory Mechanisms, The Aarhus Convention and New Technologies' (2010) 4(2) *Studies in Ethics, Law, and Technology* Art 3. See further: 'The Aarhus Convention' ec.europa.eu/environment/aarhus/index.htm.

56 For discussion, see: *Taking European Knowledge Society Seriously*, n 19 above, 52.

57 See further n 39 above.

58 European Commission, *Towards a Reinforced Culture of Consultation and Dialogue—General Principles and Minimum Standards for Consultation of Interested Parties by the Commission*, COM (2002) 704 final.

59 European Commission, *European Governance*, n 25 above, 8.

60 Mentioned in ch 1 and 2. See, relatedly: G Sundqvist, 'Recovery in the Acid Rain Story: Transparency and Credibility in Science-Based Envionmental Regulation' (2003) 5(1) *Journal of Environmental Policy and Planning* 57.

61 European Commission, *Communication on the Precautionary Principle*, COM (2000) 1 and Art 191 TFEU on the environment.

62 That is, 'the determination of a tolerable risk level generally requires the involvement of the public in one way or another' L Boisson de Chazournes, 'New Technologies, the Precautionary Principle, and Public Participation' in T Murphy (ed), *New Technologies and Human Rights* (Oxford, Oxford University Press, 2009) 179.

Another key document, *Science and Society Action Plan*,[63] contains similar themes to those apparent within *European Governance* and related documents.[64] Supported by Public Understanding of Science (PUS) techniques that actively seek to measure public opinion and knowledge,[65] such as the Eurobarometer,[66] this document works to clarify citizen/science relations in the EU and their configuration to decision-making. A related technique is questionnaires for public consultation efforts, for instance through the *Stakeholder Consultation on Strengthening European Union Preparedness on Pandemic Influenza*.[67] These kinds of techniques are used to produce statistics and reports on strengthening governance, but they also conjure citizens, their understanding of public health science, and therefore the appropriate relationship between citizens and governance. So-called 'absent presences',[68] citizens are represented and imagined by EU actors in order to provide a democratic basis for their decisions. As such, the focus is on communication efforts, especially through the promotion of scientific education and culture, public awareness and the development of responsible polices that win wider confidence in decisions. Together these construct a 'deficit model' within which participation is a means of (much needed) education for citizens who are deficient in their knowledge about science.[69]

[63] European Commission, *Science and Society Action Plan*, COM (2001) 714. See also: European Commission, *Staff Working Paper, Science, Society and the Citizen in Europe*, SEC (2000) 1973; European Commission, *Science and Technology, the Key to Europe's Future: Guidelines for Future European Union Policy to Support Research*, COM (2004) 353 final.

[64] Eg European Commission, *Life Sciences and Biotechnology: A Strategy for Europe*, COM (2002) 27 final; European Commission, *Promoting the Competitive Environment for the Industrial Activities Based on Biotechnology within the Community*, SEC (91) 629 final. See also: European Commission, *Working Together for Growth and Jobs. A New Start for the Lisbon Strategy*, COM (2005) 24 final.

[65] J Lezain and L Soneryd, 'Consulting Citizens: Technologies of Elicitation and the Mobility of Publics' (2007) 16(3) *Public Understanding of Science* 279.

[66] Eg on European attitudes to pandemic planning see: 'Influenza H1N1' ec.europa.eu/health/communicable_diseases/diseases/influenza/h1n1/docs/eurobarometer_summary_20100224.pdf. See more generally: European Commission, *Europeans, Science and Technology*, Special Eurobarometer 154, December 2001; European Commission, *Social Values, Science and Technology*, Special Eurobarometer 225, June 2005.

[67] See: 'Stakeholder Consultation on Strengthening European Union Preparedness on Pandemic Influenza' ec.europa.eu/health/preparedness_response/consultations/preparedness_cons_01_en.htm. Answers were sought to two key questions: how useful was the 2005 plan both during the pandemic preparedness phase and during the response to pandemic (H1N1) 2009 and how should it be improved? What should be done at EU level to improve EU pandemic preparedness? However, the focus of the questions is on: preparedness and coordination, surveillance, containment and mitigation (including vaccines and antivirals), health system response, international communication and communication with citizens. The final section is about multi-sectoral preparedness, which has been highlighted as an area for development. Overall, apart from the final section, the questionnaire is prefigured by what went before—and the questions asked do not seek to elicit a substantive input into preparedness besides this standalone consultation. The impression is that the 'deficit model' is being reproduced. See further: 'Stakeholder Consultation on Strengthening European Union Preparedness on Pandemic Influenza' ec.europa.eu/yourvoice/ipm/forms/dispatch?form=pandemicinfluenzan.

[68] *Taking European Knowledge Society Seriously*, n 19 above, 58.

[69] The idea of the 'deficit model' was introduced in ch 1. Some of the same points and references are repeated here. See: A Irwin and B Wynne (eds), *Misunderstanding Science? The Public Reconstruction of Science and Technology* (Cambridge, Cambridge University Press, 1996). Discussed more extensively in the EU context in, eg ML Flear, 'The EU's Biopolitical Governance of Advanced Therapy Medicinal Products' (2009) 16(1) *Maastricht Journal of European and Comparative Law* 113.

The 'deficit model' devalues the knowledge and expertise possessed by the subjects of governance and its regulatory interventions—the 'governed'—marginalising it and their role in decision-making. The model also ignores how individuals come to know things in different ways, possess different kinds of knowledge and expertise,[70] and are reflexively aware of limitations in their ability to understand, which they may actively seek to address.[71] In sum, the model reflects and installs a very particular public rationality in policy as a complement to the dominant expert rationality, and together they serve to keep citizens and science at some distance.[72] Human rights and ethics extend these complementary expert and public rationalities through their operation as legitimating devices for the risk-based technology governing public health. Ethics is particularly important as part of efforts to assuage fears and bolster public confidence and trust after the de-legitimating crises and failures of risk governance noted above, but in an attempt to tackle normative concerns. However, as summarised above, ethics is essentially an expert produced discourse and a way of communicating to the subjects of EU governance, whose own bioethical knowledge and expertise is implicitly devalued.

Overall, the focus is on the harnessing and privileging of scientific and technical knowledge and expertise for and therefore certain voices in decision-making and especially in decisions on how issues are framed. Of course, there are many hurdles and even barriers to participation that make it hard to achieve in practice at any level of governance, perhaps especially the distance between the sites of decision-making and citizenry, but also the way in which civil society is organised and being increasingly professionalised. The construction and organisation of governance, and the role, use and configuration of citizen participation in relation to it and decision-making, are part of what requires attention if participation, democracy and the quality of governance and its regulatory interventions are to be improved. Indeed, in relation to public health governance, participation occurs through the insertion of publics within restrictive techniques, processes and practices that limit opportunities for dialogue and debate, or which frame them precisely and narrowly.

Wider forms of participation are seemingly viewed with distrust or at least suspicion as irrelevant or even potentially disruptive to legal and regulatory decision-making as well as the production and legitimation of the EU's identity, socio-political order and project of European integration. As such the chief function of citizen participation is to do with building confidence and trust and

[70] A Irwin and M Michael, *Science, Social Theory, and Public Knowledge* (Maidenhead, Open University Press, 2003); M Leach, I Scoones and B Wynne (eds), *Science and Citizens: Globalisation and the Challenge of Engagement* (London, Zed Books, 2005). On the related field of the environment, see: S Jasanoff and M Long Martello (eds), *Earthly Politics: Local and Global Environmental Governance* (Cambridge MA, MIT Press, 2004).

[71] A Irwin, *Citizen Science: A Study of People, Expertise, and Sustainable Development* (London, Routledge, 1995); R Lidskog, 'Scientised Citizens and Democratised Science: Re-Assessing the Expert-Lay Divide' (2008) 11(1–2) *Journal of Risk Research* 69.

[72] A Irwin 'The Politics of Talk: Come to Terms with the "New" Scientific Governance' (2006) 36(2) *Social Studies of Science* 299.

quieting contestation and dissent. Citizen participation can, therefore, be chiefly understood as a technology of public legitimation that helps to mediate the boundaries of responsibility and accountability, in the present context, for the governance of public health and its regulation of the dangers or threats attendant to the circulation of people and things in the depoliticised economy.[73] Employing participatory technologies as a means of fabricating support for public health governance aligns regulatory strategies with the EU's goals of advancing science and technology and producing a knowledge economy built on innovation.[74] Citizen participation is, therefore, also a way through which the institutions, agencies and Member States that constitute 'the' EU produce a singular identity with aims and values and the capacity to bring them into being. As such it should come as no surprise if citizens realise their participation is elicited for instrumental reasons of public legitimation rather than in order to engender their substantive input into decisions on framing—and that that is part of the reason for their alienation instead of engagement.[75]

In sum, the EU actively shapes technologies of participation (and hence what they can do) through its use of a risk-based technology supplemented by human rights and ethics, and supported by particular configurations of science/citizen relations (including PUS). Together these might serve to simultaneously mobilise, prioritise and include certain narrow publics (typically those with a 'stake'), while marginalising and even excluding others (those implicitly without a 'stake'). This renders resort to procedural ways of fostering participation as a means of producing legitimate regulatory decisions in pluralist societies (such as the EU) even more problematic, in that the discourses shaping the conditions of possibility for participation effectively deny its potential to contribute more to decision-making than legitimation. This raises the questions: how can legitimate, inclusive and fair decisions be produced when all voices are implicitly not included, or are marginalised, and remain unheard, because they are in effect designed-out? How can the promise of citizen participation to contribute knowledge towards decision-making and enhance the quality of governance and its regulatory interventions be achieved when the capacity of citizens and their knowledge are effectively denied?

A related concern is that the framing of public health issues as matters of risk also works to depoliticise and obscure the social, political and economic origins of problems, a concern picked up in the next chapter. More importantly for the present discussion is the way in which the narrow framing of public health problems individualises responsibility and forecloses the potential of collective arrangements in tackling them, which in turn undergirds the current limited institutionalisation

[73] See ch 1, n 15, citing ML Flear and MD Pickersgill, 'Regulatory or Regulating Publics? The European Union's Regulation of Emerging Health Technologies and Citizen Participation' (2013) 21(1) *Medical Law Review* 39.

[74] Especially prominent in ch 2 and reflected throughout chs 3, 4 and 5.

[75] B Wynne, 'Creating Public Alienation: Expert Cultures of Risk and Ethics on GMOs' (2001) 10 *Science as Culture* 445.

of citizen participation.[76] Public health problems are effectively rendered as non-political and non-ideological problems requiring technical and market-oriented solutions—and that of course favours private corporate interests in formally non-market domains. The (re)organisation of formally political spaces and those that are private and self-governed is central to the EU's attempts at regulating the uncertainties and threats attendant to the flows of people and things within, into and beyond its internal market. Yet this ensures that much of the politics of public health is contained and concealed within the techniques, processes and practices—the governing technologies—of governance and effectively marked off from democratic contestation and accountability.

This is the diagnosis that substantiates the pessimism about the shape and role of the current institutionalisation of citizen participation that was a central prompt for this book and its third argument. The limited nature of citizen participation is itself a key paradox, pitfall and blind spot in that it not only undermines the democratic credentials, accountability and legitimacy of public health governance and the quality of its regulatory interventions. That is because the centrality of scientific and technical knowledge and expertise undermines and even refuses the potential of citizen participation to reveal key normative dimensions of the technical and scientific in relation to health and life, such as around the distribution of benefits and risks across society.

IV. OPENING DISCURSIVE SPACE AND POWERING TECHNOLOGIES OF PARTICIPATION

A. Openings and Possibilities for Citizen Participation

Despite the current institutionalisation of citizen participation and the narrowing of the space for democratic politics produced by the framing of public health problems as matters of risk, there remains the potential for citizens to demand and contest decisions, and to (re)fashion governance and the ways in which they are constituted by and configured in relation to it. A possibility evoked and crystallised in Foucault's term 'biopolitics',[77] this provides the encouraging basis for moving the discussion in this book from diagnosis and towards a prescription for enhancing citizen participation in governing. The starting point is the realisation that the paradoxes, pitfalls and blind spots attendant to governance, which are outlined in the next two chapters, and the effective limits on citizen participation considered above, have common foundations in—are produced by and within—

[76] A popular argument deployed to allay concerns over democratic accountability has been that the EU is (or has been) essentially a regulatory state involved in technical regulation with no or limited distributional consequences, see, eg G Majone, 'Europe's Democratic Deficit: The Question of Standards' (1998) 4(1) *European Law Journal* 5.

[77] Noted in ch 1, see in particular: M Foucault, *The Birth of Biopolitics: Lectures at the Collège de France, 1978–79* (Basingstoke, Palgrave Macmillan, 2008). Also see: T Lemke, *Biopolitics: An Advanced Introduction* (London, New York University Press, 2013).

the contours, relationships and the underpinning structuring themes of governance and regulatory design.

Reflecting on the latter in the following helps to advance the fourth argument of this book, which is that those foundations and their effects open up space and create possibilities for citizen participation in governing public health. Those openings and possibilities can be organised along two main axes.[78] The first axis is the material or substantive scope for participation, which comprises framing and (and since they are co-constitutive of each other)[79] extends into the gathering and production of knowledge, and regulatory interventions in public health. These matters have spatial or territorial scope, that is, the material and substantive openings and possibilities range along a second axis encompassing diverse territories (the EU, its periphery and beyond), and variously enfolding, implicating and impacting on a multiplicity of peoples.

The potential for bottom-up engagement by the latter—'the governed'—has been recognised in various ways. Concern around risk might be leveraged by citizens as the basis for their mobilisation and participation,[80] which might be 'uninvited' and even disruptive.[81] In a similar vein the growing cluster of terms emerging from science and technology studies (STS), sociology and anthropology—'moral pioneers',[82] 'genetic citizens',[83] 'biological citizenship'[84] and 'therapeutic citizens'[85]—highlight how people come to know and understand themselves and relate to others through knowledge of their biological and medical (risk) status. In doing so they sometimes demonstrate 'biosociality'[86] as they work together in order to (re)shape governance so that it addresses their concerns.

[78] See, relatedly: A Cornwall and V Schatten Coelho (eds), *Spaces for Change?: The Politics of Citizen Participation in New Democratic Arenas* (London, Zed Books, 2007).

[79] In light of the way in which framing, governance and regulation on the one hand and knowledge on the other are co-constitutive of each. Introduced in ch 1, threaded throughout the rest of the first part of the book, and mentioned above. See further: S Jasanoff, 'The Idiom of Co-Production' in S Jasanoff (ed), *States of Knowledge: The Co-Production of Science and the Social Order* (London, Routledge, 2004).

[80] In relation to biomedicine see: S Epstein, *Impure Science* (Berkeley CA, University of California Press, 1996). See generally: U Beck, *World at Risk* (Cambridge, Polity Press, 2008).

[81] R Doubleday and B Wynne, 'Despotism and Democracy in the United Kingdom: Experiments in Reframing Citizenship' in S Jasanoff (ed), *Reframing Rights: Bioconstitutionalism in the Genetic Age* (Cambridge MA, MIT Press, 2011).

[82] R Rapp, *Testing Women, Testing the Fetus: The Social Impact of Amniocentesis in America* (London, Routledge, 2000).

[83] D Heath, R Rapp and K-S Taussig, 'Genetic Citizenship' in D Night and J Vincent (eds), *A Companion to the Anthropology of Politics* (Oxford, Blackwell Publishing, 2004).

[84] A Petryna, *Life Exposed: Biological Citizens after Chernobyl* (Princeton NJ, Princeton University Press, 2002); N Rose and C Novas, 'Biological Citizenship' in A Ong and S Collier (eds), *Global Assemblages: Technology, Politics, and Ethics as Anthropological Problems* (Oxford, Blackwell Publishing, 2005). *Cf* J Biehl, *Will to Live: AIDS Therapies and the Politics of Survival* (Princeton NJ, Princeton University Press, 2007).

[85] V-K Nguyen, 'Antiretroviral Globalism, Biopolitics, and Therapeutic Citizenship' in A Ong and SJ Collier (eds), *Global Assemblages: Technology, Politics, and Ethics as Anthropological Problems* (Oxford, Blackwell Publishing, 2005).

[86] P Rabinow, *Essays on the Anthropology of Reason* (Princeton NJ, Princeton University Press, 1996); S Gibbon and C Novas (eds), *Biosocialities, Genetics and the Social Sciences* (London, Routledge, 2007).

As well as providing incisive critical commentary on the institutionalisation of citizen participation, STS has been particularly strident (and notable amongst cognate disciplines) for its insistence that the distortions, failures, paradoxes, pitfalls and blind spots attendant to the technical (including governance) are key normative dimensions that citizens can reveal and that they provide the basis for their participation in decision-making. Moreover, although citizens might not be able to use or understand particular technical details, since those details are produced and articulated within broader frames citizens can nevertheless participate as laypeople in relation to them.[87] In other words, not only can citizens contribute towards discussions on framing by risk,[88] they can contribute towards reflection on how those discussions should be reframed,[89] such as through discussion on the purpose of risk governance, whom it hurts, whom it benefits, and how we might know.[90]

Citizen participation around these sorts of questions paves the way for replacing PUS and the one-way communication it underpins and favours with attention to political culture and a common way of producing and gathering supplementary knowledge on framing, vulnerability, distribution and learning from throughout society.[91] Participation around these focal points is especially appealing for the project pursued in this book in that it opens up the possibility of managing and potentially correcting the paradoxes, pitfalls and blind spots attendant to the EU's public health governance. This is to be achieved by relocating science and technology based issues in politics and capitalism, pluralising the production of scientific and technical (especially biological and biomedical) knowledge and expertise, highlighting *lacunae* in knowledge, and introducing doubt and controversy into often settled assumptions, knowledges and practices.

Although the importance of law in producing political culture and as a resource for participation is implied, law and the other discourses that are integral to governance and regulating have received little attention in STS and related scholarship as avenues or platforms for citizen participation or as resources for prompting, encouraging and powering technologies of participation.[92] Much discussion in STS also misses the ways in which participation can be stymied and its contribution of valuable supplementary knowledge frustrated by the risk governance process itself. As explained by Power, within risk-based governance accountability has become linked with organisation in a single logic through which democratic ideals 'are *increasingly positioned* within ideals for good governance of the risk analysis

[87] B Wynne, 'Uncertainty and Environmental Learning: Reconceiving Science and Policy in the Preventive Paradigm' (1992) 2(2) *Global Environmental Change* 111.

[88] B Wynne, 'Risk as a Globalising "Democratic" Discourse? Framing Subjects and Citizens' in Leach, Scoones and Wynne, n 70 above.

[89] F Fischer, *Reframing Public Policy: Discursive Politics and Deliberative Practices* (Oxford, Oxford University Press, 2003).

[90] Jasanoff, n 1 above.

[91] S Jasanoff, *Designs on Nature* (Princeton NJ, Princeton University Press, 2005) ch 10 'Civic Epistemology'.

[92] In this vein see: N Fairclough, *Language and Power*, 2nd edn (Abingdon, Routledge, 2001).

process' (emphasis added).[93] Consequently, techniques for accountability such as participation become part of a broader process of rendering organisations auditable and inspectable. They 'are *increasingly framed* as an organizational *strategy to manage public expectations*' (emphasis added).[94] Indeed, to underline what was said in chapter one, public perceptions are a source of risk, and so risk management is partly an exercise in governing '*unruly perceptions*' and maintaining the '*production* of legitimacy in the face of these perceptions' (emphasis added).[95] In short, the logic of accountability and organisation helps to maintain the instrumentalisation of citizen participation and therefore its current institutionalisation.

Clearly, any proposal for enhancing citizen participation and moving beyond its current institutionalisation needs to take these kinds of pitfalls seriously while bearing in mind lessons from extant scholarship. In seeking to do so as part of the fourth argument of this book I suggest that the constraints and pitfalls should be thought of not simply as constraints, but also as part of the openings and possibilities for participation. The starting point in charting the latter is recognising that, despite its undemocratic rouses, EU governance is already sensitive to the potential for citizen participation as a generator of views (albeit so that they might then be governed and shaped) and a technique of legitimation. Indeed, the approach to citizen/science relations set out in *European Governance* is partly a response to the idea that risks are endemic to and produced by risk society, including its governance and regulatory responses.[96]

Although flawed the EU's efforts nevertheless demonstrate a willingness and effort to reflect on the integration and configuration of citizen participation in its governance and regulation. The EU's turn to risk as a way of governing and participatory techniques might also be motivated by its particular legitimacy needs. As a polity without a demos the EU is finding it harder to generate and maintain its legitimacy as compared to the nation states it seeks to integrate. Importantly for what I shall propose, the EU is seeking to legitimate not only its governance and standing as a regulator, but ultimately its project of European integration through these. Of course, citizen participation requires a range of formal and informal mechanisms, processes and fora through which to gather, produce and discipline citizen knowledge into something usable (and useful) for decision-making. I seek to encourage reflection on—and reflexive consideration of—the role, use and configuration of technologies of citizen participation in relation to decision-making.

An important part of that, and the central contribution of this book, is to focus on building and prescribing a discursive strategy that leverages the EU's sensitivity to 'institutional risk' and its legitimacy needs in combination with and so as to widen the other openings and harness the diverse possibilities for participation. In the remainder of this chapter I introduce and trace out the strategy, which is built

[93] M Power, *Organized Uncertainty* (Oxford, Oxford University Press, 2007) 20.

[94] Ibid, 20–21.

[95] Ibid, 21.

[96] Most notably: U Beck, *Risk Society: Towards a New Modernity* (London, Sage Publications, 1986).

from human rights, bioethics and the developing notion of stewardship responsibility. I argue that this strategy could prompt and empower citizen engagement and public querying that brings out the normative in the technical—and provides a 'way in' for participation in decision-making.[97] These discourses could thereby help to widen the European public and democratic sphere and support the development of the EU's institutions.[98] In the next two chapters I fill out the discussion by highlighting some more specific areas, openings and possibilities for the deployment of this strategy for citizen participation. In doing so I point to some of the ways in which the discursive strategy shows promise in existing social movements and practices and might be developed further in order to generate supplementary knowledge for decision-making, and enhance the quality of governance and its regulatory interventions.

B. Resources for Participation: Human Rights, Bioethics and (Supra-)Stewardship Responsibility

i. Human Right and Bioethics

Human rights and bioethics are central to the discursive strategy for participation advanced in this book. A key reason is their well-known contemporary cultural resonance and—therefore—capacity to pique and mobilise citizen interest. Human rights and bioethics provide different albeit related registers through which to frame and respond to injustice and unequal power relations,[99] such as in terms of the distribution of benefits and risks and vulnerability produced by particular framings of issues.[100] Bioethics is of increasing importance, as is clear from the turn to it in EU governance of public health and life, including as a way of producing engagement and deliberative practices, a use that has been the subject of growing attention in STS[101] and in law.[102] Human rights is probably the more

[97] In this sense the proposal leans towards increasing citizen participation to the widest possible extent such that citizens control the decision-making process upstream, including in framing, and throughout. See, relatedly: SR Arnstein, 'A Ladder of Citizen Participation' (1969) 35(4) *Journal of the American Institute of Planners* 216.

[98] J Habermas, *The Crisis of the European Union: A Response* (Cambridge, Polity Press, 2012). See further: J Habermas, *Legitimation Crisis* (Boston, Beacon Press, 1975).

[99] Eg AE Yamin, 'Suffering and Powerlessness: The Significance of Participation in Rights-Based Approaches to Health' (2009) 11(1) *Health and Human Rights: An International Journal* 5.

[100] Chiming with the recent turn in STS towards the idea that 'the technical is *potentially* political' and that participation makes sense only where there is injustice, see: A Moore, 'Beyond Participation: Opening Up Political Theory in STS' (2010) 40(5) *Social Studies of Science* 793. This is a review of: MB Brown, *Science in Democracy: Expertise, Institutions and Representation* (Cambridge MA, MIT Press, 2009).

[101] A Moore, 'Public Bioethics and Public Engagement: The Politics of "Proper Talk"' (2010) 19(2) *Public Understanding of Science* 197; A Moore, 'Public Bioethics and Deliberative Democracy' (2010) 58 *Political Studies* 715; MD Pickersgill, 'Research, Engagement and Public Bioethics: Promoting Socially Robust Science' (2011) 37 *Journal of Medical Ethics* 698.

[102] J Montgomery, 'Reflections on the Nature of Public Ethics' (2013) 22 *Cambridge Quarterly of Healthcare Ethics* 9. See also, the discussion on stewardship below.

successful and culturally resonant of the two discourses. More than a body of law, human rights is also a discourse, a particular form of attention to the world, with its own way of thinking, articulating and responding that encompasses the practices and projects, the 'movements or groupings of lawyers, non-governmental organisations, and others who seek to secure and defend a particular right, group of rights, or human rights in general'.[103] As noted in chapter two human rights has been very successful in demands for and contestation around issues of social justice, including in the EU.

However, in the context of the EU human rights has been underpinned by a clear internal market ideology since its inception.[104] Indeed, human rights developments in the EU were originally linked to a principle of non-discrimination in European Community (EC) law.[105] That meant a human rights consciousness in the EC (now EU) grew out of a sense that discriminating Member States should not be permitted to gain a competitive advantage over more conscientious ones. This was affirmed in case law, for instance in rulings that avoiding distortions in competition is a key objective of EC sex equality law.[106] As Stychin explained, it is 'universally acknowledged that economic factors were the motivating force behind Article 141 [which prescribed equal pay for men and women]'.[107] Moreover, the archetypal rights holder in EU law was until very recently the migrant worker who is a national of a Member State that is an economically active and mobile citizen of one of the EU Member States who relocates to work in another.[108] Human rights and bioethics can, like risk, focus on and freight individuals with responsibility and obscure the broader social and systematic roots of public health problems—as well as the true breadth of the responsibilities of formally accountable actors such as the EU for collective matters such as public health.[109] Nevertheless, human

[103] T Murphy, 'Repetition, Revolution, and Resonance' in T Murphy (ed), *New Technologies and Human Rights* (Oxford, Oxford University Press, 2009) 7.

[104] C Stychin, *Governing Sexuality: The Changing Politics of Citizenship and Law Reform* (Oxford, Hart Publishing, 2003); C Stychin, 'Same-Sex Sexualities and the Globalisation of Human Rights Discourse' (2004) 49 *McGill Law Journal* 951.

[105] Art 12 EC Treaty, now Art 18 TFEU.

[106] Case 43/75 *Defrenne v SABENA* (No 2) [1976] ECR 455.

[107] Stychin, *Governing Sexuality*, n 104 above, 79.

[108] See, eg T Hervey, *European Social Law and Policy* (London, Longman, 1998) 106 in respect to social security hierarchies. The advent of EU citizenship (Art 9 TEU and Arts 20–24 TFEU (read with Art 18 TFEU on non-discrimination)) has loosened the link and ensured that those who are not economically active have rights, but only where they are EU citizens or where their rights are parallel to (draw down on) an EU citizen. See, eg Case C-85/96 *Martínez Sala v Freistaat Bayern* [1998] ECR I-2691; Case C-413/99 *Baumbast and R v Secretary of State for the Home Department* [2002] ECR I-7091; Case C-184/99 *Grzelczyk v Centre public d'aide sociale d'Ottignies-Louvain-la-Neuve* [2001] ECR I-6193; Case C-209/03 *R (on the application of Bidar) v London Borough of Ealing and Secretary of State for Education and Skills* [2005] ECR I-2119; Case C-158/07 *Förster v Hoofddirectie van de Informatie Beheer Groep* [2008] ECR I-8507. See further: C Barnard, *The Substantive Law of the EU: The Four Freedoms*, 4th edn (Oxford, Oxford University Press, 2013) ch 12.

[109] In relation to human rights see: W Brown, *States of Injury* (Oxford, Princeton University Press, 1995); W Brown, 'Suffering Rights as Paradoxes' (2000) 7 *Constellations* 230. For discussion of the individualisation of claims and bioethics see: Ashcroft, n 21 above, 645.

rights in particular remains a powerful discourse that could power discussion and technologies of participation and highlight concerns around framing, distribution and vulnerability.

Indeed, in broad overview the discursive potential of human rights is readily apparent in public health related provisions in the EU's constitutional architecture. As mentioned in chapter two the right to health is implicated in for example Article 35 Charter of Fundamental Rights of the EU (EU Charter) on the right to health *care*, the final portion of which states: 'A *high level of human health protection* shall be ensured in the definition and implementation of *all the Union's policies and activities*' (emphasis added)—and which therefore include the internal and external dimensions of EU public health governance. After one judgment of the Court of Justice of the EU one possibility is that the final portion of Article 35 might function more as a cross-cutting requirement[110]—and that adds to its discursive potential , particularly as the final portion of Article 35 takes over from Article 168(1) TFEU.[111] Indeed, and consistent with the requirement to ensure protection of human health found in Article 9 Treaty on the Functioning of the European Union (TFEU) and reflected in Article 168(1) TFEU, both of which were also discussed in chapter two, Article 35 might be developed in light of other right to health provisions under human rights law[112] and understandings of what 'health' entails, such as that found in the World Health Organisation's (WHO's) definition that it is a state of complete physical, mental and social well-being and not merely the absence of infirmity (noted in chapter one).

In terms of other right to health provisions Articles 11 and 13 of the European Social Charter are particularly useful in that they are mentioned in the Explanatory Note for Article 35, and which provides guidance on its interpretation (as per Article 6(1) TEU). The provisions are indicative of the way in which Article 35 EU Charter might be developed in public discussion and attempts to demand and contest decision-making (if not the CJEU's jurisprudence).[113] Article 13 provides that '*anyone without adequate resources* has the right to social and medical assistance' (emphasis added). Article 11 provides that '*everyone* has the right to benefit from any measures enabling him to *enjoy the highest standard of health attainable*' and that includes 'effective exercise of the right to protection of health' by appropriate measures to 'remove as far as possible the *causes of ill-health*' and '*prevent* as far as possible epidemic, endemic and other diseases, as well as accidents' (emphasis added). In this light, and read with Article 9 TFEU and Article 168(1) TFEU, Article 35 EU Charter could be developed with them in order to, for instance: query whether public health governance and its framing

[110] Case C-544/10 *Deutsches Weintor eG v Land Rheinland-Pfalz* ECLI:EU:C:2012:526.

[111] Article 35 EU Charter was referenced in the Opinion of Advocate General Ruiz-Jarabo Colomer in Case C-444/05 *Stamatelaki v NPDD Organismos Asfaliseos Eleftheron Epangelmation* [2007] ECR I-3185, para 40, where it was stated the right to health care is 'a personal entitlement, unconnected to a person's relationship with social security' that could underpin jurisprudence on the right to receive publicly funded health care services in other EU Member States in certain circumstances. On the interpretation of Article 35 see: Explanations relating to the Charter of Fundamental Rights [2007] OJ C303/17.

[112] See ch 2, n 15.

[113] European Social Charter (Revised) (3 May 1996, entered into force 1 July 1999) ETS 163.

ensures the protection of everyone's health; reflect on whether all benefit from public health measures or if some face greater threats from public health problems or indeed the interventions developed to address them; and finally, ensure that those measures include prevention and address the preconditions and social determinants of ill health for all diseases (epidemic, endemic and others). Distortions, pitfalls, blind spots and paradoxes of public health governance could be identified and stressed by reference to these provisions, and they are of course articulated in relation to the focal points of framing, the distribution of benefits and risks, and vulnerability.[114]

Building on these provisions a link between human rights and bioethics might make them even more powerful and useful resources for articulating views, demanding and contesting decisions and therefore for enhancing participation in decision-making. The link between human rights and bioethics is apparent in several international declarations[115] and has generated much discussion on whether, as Ashcroft puts it, human rights might 'subsume or replace bioethics, at least at the level of the public governance of medicine and the life sciences'.[116] More important for the present discussion is a key implication of the developing link that is the potential of human rights in the:

> [H]ands of activists, at least to disrupt ... by *challenging the language*, the *types of problem recognised* ... and the *working methods* of the public bioethics process. This might particularly be the case where the challenge to bioethics comes from groups which have tried—and failed—to *challenge the policy consensus* by other methods.[117] (Emphasis added)

In relation to public health problems, the groups that might harness and articulate through the human rights linked to bioethics in order to demand and contest decisions include those with underlying medical conditions, limited access to education and economic resources, pregnant women, children and itinerants. Another group is non-EU citizens residing in Europe (including undocumented migrants), a large group which often has difficulty accessing health services and health insurance and tends to experience more health problems than 'regular' EU citizens. Such individuals and groups are recognised in the cluster of terms that

[114] See: JJ Amon, 'The "Right to Know" or "Know Your Rights"? Human Rights and a People-Centred Approach to Health Policy' in J Biehl and A Petryna (eds), *When People Come First: Critical Studies in Global Health* (Princeton NJ, Princeton University Press, 2013).

[115] Eg the UN Educational, Scientific and Cultural Organization (UNESCO), Universal Declaration on Bioethics and Human Rights (2005), and in the European context in, eg the Convention for the Protection of Human Rights and Dignity of the Human Being with regard to the Application of Biology and Medicine: Convention on Human Rights and Biomedicine (4 April 1997, entered into force 1 December 1999) ETS 164 (the Oviedo Convention) and its Protocols.

[116] Ashcroft, n 21 above, 640.

[117] Ibid, 645. There is clearly far more that could be said about participation and the right to health—and this chapter seeks to leverage the discursive power of the right for the book's wider project of developing technologies of participation. There is growing reflection on these issues in human rights, see: H Potts, 'Participation and the Right to the Highest Attainable Standard of Health' (Essex, University of Essex Human Rights Centre, 2009).

underscore citizen reflexivity noted above, and they might exploit human rights and bioethics in order to generate the 'politics of life itself'.[118]

Articulation of demands and contestation in terms of human rights and bioethics not only help to widen the scope of attention towards the root causes of ill health and addressing the most important public health problems, they are also discourses that can resonate with, persuade and convince others,[119] especially those formally charged with or who are influential in decision-making. Decision-makers are already familiar with and have to be cognisant of human rights and bioethical frameworks and arguments,[120] for example through impact assessment exercises.[121] Using such frameworks and arguments are particularly useful for, as Black puts it, 'putting the views of each set of participants [in governance] into a language that the others can understand'.[122] Arguments and claims framed in terms of human rights and bioethics might be particularly compelling for a related reason. Since human rights and bioethics are key legitimating discourses for the EU's technology governing public health, articulating through those discourses might transform the attendant societal failures and risks into key 'institutional risks' to the EU's standing and reputation.

This sort of argument has been advanced in relation to human rights. Murphy and Whitty explain that '*managing risk means managing the risk of rights*'. Moreover this risk is 'not limited to legal risk, that is, (potential) claims and litigation for violation of human rights obligations'. There is also what they call 'legal risk+', encompassing for example 'the potential for human rights *consciousness* (as manifested, for example, in a public campaign) to disrupt the interests and overall standing of governments and organisations' (emphasis added).[123] This is clearly of much use for citizen participation in that it creates space for the disruptive potential of human rights to enter the logic of organisation and accountability. Murphy and Whitty also point to the way in which human rights already incorporate risk within its (legal) reasoning through the requirement that regulatory interventions that impact on rights are proportionate.

The potential of human rights considerations to enter into and reframe risk-based decision-making chimes with the project pursued in this book and my proposal for enhancing citizen participation, in that, if the 'institutional risks' are left

[118] N Rose, *The Politics of Life Itself: Biomedicine, Power and Subjectivity in the 21st Century* (Oxford, Princeton University Press, 2007).

[119] F Fischer and H Gottweis (eds), *The Argumentative Turn Revisited: Public Policy as Communicative Practice* (Durham NC, Duke University Press, 2012); G Majone, *Evidence, Argument and Persuasion in the Policy Process* (Yale University Press, 1992).

[120] Human rights are especially central to the founding and organisation of national health care systems in the EU (see ch 2, n 16, for references to national constitutions and other forms of law) as well as the EU's public health governance architecture (see ch 2).

[121] Noted above and discussed in ch 2.

[122] J Black, 'Regulation as Facilitation: Negotiating the Genetic Revolution' (1998) 61(5) *Modern Law Review* 621, 623.

[123] T Murphy and N Whitty, 'Is Human Rights Prepared? Risk, Rights and Public Health Emergencies' (2009) 17 *Medical Law Review* 219, 233.

unaddressed and they manifest in disease or even loss of life, it could engender serious repercussions. Foremost among them are delegitimation of the EU's governance, identity as a security and public health actor, and ultimately the project of European integration. It is this threat that could impel the taking up of citizen demands and knowledge in decision-making. In other words, the threat of delegitimation, when combined with the articulation of knowledge through highly resonant and influential discourses, could support and produce a more equal standing for citizens as lay people vis-à-vis scientific and technical experts,[124] and counteract the way in which risk-based governance tends to transform participatory techniques into legitimating devices.

In short, in these ways human rights and bioethics can power technologies of participation and are the discourses that are most likely to succeed in (re)framing or (re)shaping governance and its regulatory interventions.[125] These are key resources for ensuring the EU is held to account and fulfils its responsibilities to its citizens, and for improving the quality and effectiveness of governance and its regulatory interventions.[126] In order to ensure these ends are met there is one further component to the discursive strategy for enhancing citizen participation: the developing discourse of (supra-)stewardship responsibility.

ii. (Supra-)Stewardship Responsibility

Further encouragement about the potential of the link between human rights and bioethics in the context of public health comes from the increasing influence of stewardship, a form of public bioethics—or a 'neat label'[127]—aimed at facilitating communication between governance and its subjects, which was mentioned in the introduction to this book.[128] Stewardship could be used to underscore points around framing, distribution and vulnerability articulated through human rights and bioethics, and in doing so add to the resources for enhancing citizen participation in public health through public querying and the contribution of supplementary knowledge to decision-making. Stewardship is likely to be particularly resonant in EU policy-making circles given the increasingly close relationship between key EU regulators such as the European Commission and the ECDC and the WHO, which is one of the key originators and proponents of the term in the context of public health.

[124] For discussion of 'societal risk' and 'institutional risk', see: H Rothstein, M Huber and G Gaskell, 'A Theory of Risk Colonisation: The Spiralling Regulatory Logics of Societal and Institutional Risk' (2006) 35 *Economy and Society* 91.

[125] M Edelman, *Political Language: Words that Succeed and Policies that Fail* (London, Academic Press, 1973).

[126] R Löfstedt, *Risk Management in Post-Trust Societies* (Basingstoke, Palgrave Macmillan, 2005); O Renn, *Risk Governance: Coping with Uncertainty in a Complex World* (London, Earthscan, 2008).

[127] J Coggon, 'What Help is a Steward? Stewardship, Political Theory, and Public Health Law and Ethics' (2011) 62(5) *Northern Ireland Legal Quarterly* 599.

[128] See ch 1.

In the WHO's version stewardship is linked and made intrinsic to governance. The *World Health Report 2000* explains how stewardship essentially involves 'setting and enforcing the rules of the game and providing strategic direction for all the different actors involved'.[129] It is 'the very essence of good government', with state governments having the 'Ultimate'[130] responsibility. More recently the Nuffield's report *Public Health: Ethical Issues*[131] sought to develop a human rights-based approach to incorporate a precautionary way of thinking into population level bioethics for public health contexts. Three of Nuffield's authors, Baldwin, Brownsword and Schmidt, note how stewardship means 'liberal states have *responsibilities to look after important needs of people* both individually and collectively. Therefore, states are stewards *both to individual people … and to the population as a whole*' (emphasis added).[132] Brownsword notes that what he calls 'super-stewardship' is 'a significant item of unfinished business'.[133] Attempts to develop the stewardship responsibility of the EU have been suggested in academic commentary as well as in the EU's own policy evaluations, which leverage the WHO's work on stewardship in order to suggest that the EU might be the 'steward of [national] stewards'.[134] I use the term '(*supra*-)stewardship' in order to emphasise the EU's *sui generis* or *supra*national nature and its responsibilities towards its citizens defined broadly to encompass 'the governed'.

A focus on the EU's stewardship responsibilities can be used to reinforce the use of human rights and bioethics in querying the framing of public health governance, the subject of much of chapter seven. For example, when informed by the WHO's version 'supra-stewardship' could promote a focus on the social determinants of health and prevention efforts through references to '*improving overall levels of population health*'[135] and 'oversight of the entire system, *avoiding myopia*, tunnel vision and the *turning of a blind eye* to a system's *failings*' (emphasis

[129] 'Message from the Director General, Gro Harlem Brundtland' in World Health Organisation, *World Health Report 2000* (Geneva, World Health Organisation, 2000) viii.

[130] Ibid. Also see: World Health Organisation, *World Health Day: International Health Security: Invest in Health, Build a Safer Future* (Geneva, World Health Organisation, 2007).

[131] Nuffield Council on Bioethics, *Public Health: Ethical Issues* (London, Nuffield Council on Bioethics, 2007).

[132] T Baldwin, R Brownsword and H Schmidt, 'Stewardship, Paternalism and Public Health: Further Thoughts' 2(1) *Public Health Ethics* (2009) 113, 115. Citing ibid, 25.

[133] R Brownsword, 'So What Does the World Need Now? Reflections on Regulating Technologies' in R Brownsword and K Yeung (eds), *Regulating Technologies: Legal Futures, Regulatory Frames and Technological Fixes* (Oxford, Hart Publishing, 2008) 47.

[134] Public Health Evaluation and Impact Assessment Consortium (PHEIAC), *Study to Measure the Implementation of EU Health Policies at National, Regional and Local Levels, Assessing the Utility of Existing Indicaors for this Task and Developing New Indicators as Necessary* (2012) 90. For additional academic commentary see: S Holm, 'From Steward to Stuart—Some Problems in Deciding for Others' (2011) 62(5) *Northern Ireland Legal Quarterly* 617 and T Hervey, 'The European Union, its Court of Justice and "Super-Stewardship" in Public Health' (2011) 62(5) *Northern Ireland Legal Quarterly* 633 (containing an extensive review of the EU's deeply contested nature), which like Coggon, n 127 above, all appeared in ML Flear (ed), 'Papers from "A Symposium with Professor Roger Brownsword: Super-Stewardship in the Context of Public Health"' (2011) 62(5) *Northern Ireland Legal Quarterly*.

[135] 'Governance': www.who.int/healthsystems/topics/stewardship/en/index.html.

added).[136] In relation to pandemic planning, for example, references in the WHO and Nuffield versions of stewardship emphasise 'essential infrastructures', but they are part of a broader attention to population and the conditions that support it. Importantly for the EU context, Nuffield uses pandemic influenza as a jumping off point for considering cross-border obligations, noting how it is 'also reasonable' to apply stewardship at a 'much higher level' (emphasis added).[137] The central example given—duplicated by the EU and discussed in chapter five—is that countries should notify others of a serious infectious disease outbreak, following WHO procedures. Yet since such cross-border obligations require an efficient surveillance system and some countries lack such capabilities, richer countries become obligated to 'seek to enhance the capacities of developing countries to conduct effective surveillance of infectious diseases'.[138] Surveillance is 'not simply a national matter'.[139] Interestingly, the ECDC is referred to here, alongside the WHO and the Centers for Disease Prevention and Control in the United States, as 'international partners',[140] which lends support to the point I made above about the persuasiveness of claims articulated through or by reference to stewardship.

Appeals to stewardship responsibility might also be used to complement human rights and ethics based concerns around the distribution of benefits and risks, as well as the vulnerabilities attendant to the EU's risk-based governance of public health, and as discussed in chapter eight this is likely to be useful in relation to public querying of regulatory interventions. Like Nuffield the WHO suggests that the objectives of stewardship 'are likely to be framed in terms of equity, coverage, access, quality, and patients'[141] rights. Baldwin et al note stewardship means taking account of 'different needs arising from factors such as age, gender, ethnic background or socio-economic status' (emphasis added).[142] Bolstering this is a focus on supporting attention to population and social determinants of ill health through mention of the '*conditions* that allow people to be healthy *focussing attention, in particular, on reducing health inequalities*' (emphasis added).[143] These points are resonant with provisions in the EU's constitutional legal order (noted above) and public health architecture, for instance in the references to universality, access to good quality care, equity and solidarity, which together comprise the first core principle of the EU's public health strategy.[144] As such arguments framed

[136] 'Message', n 129 above, ix.

[137] Nuffield Council, *Public Health,* n 131 above, 68.

[138] Ibid.

[139] Ibid, 67.

[140] Ibid, 68.

[141] 'Governance', n 135 above.

[142] T Baldwin, R Brownsword and H Schmidt, 'Stewardship, Paternalism and Public Health', n 132 above, 115–16. *Cf* Nuffield Council, *Public Health,* n 131 above, 25.

[143] Ibid.

[144] See ch 2. Social justice is also relevant to proposals for global health law in which it is noted as an 'overarching value … which requires equitable distribution of health services, particularly to benefit the world's poorest populations', see LO Gostin and AL Taylor O'Neill, 'Global Health Law: A Definition and Grand Challenges' (2008) 1(1) *Public Health Ethics* 53, 55.

by or related to stewardship (especially when articulated with human rights and ethics) are again likely to be highly resonant in EU policy-making circles.

Despite the potential of stewardship to power citizen participation, there are a few key concerns about its use. For instance, Somsen queries the wisdom of developing a precautionary approach within human rights via stewardship, arguing that it effectively provides 'governments with a blank cheque for limiting individual liberties'.[145] Stewardship models have been criticised for limiting individual autonomy through paternalistic interventions in citizens' lives. Still, given the predominance of risk, safety and security in the EU's governance and more broadly, the link with bioethics seen in and bolstered by stewardship is valuable as part of human rights' broader efforts to develop something other than a zero-sum relationship with these.[146] In any case, safeguards against excessive action and paternalism in stewardship that might be deployed to resist disempowerment are envisaged by the WHO (especially in terms of patients rights) and Nuffield (as well as being the subject of wider debate),[147] and these could be of much use in querying the regulatory interventions in public health favoured by EU governance, discussed in chapter eight, especially as they relate to particularly vulnerable groups. In Nuffield public health programmes are constrained by an intervention ladder that attempts to minimise 'significant limitations on individual freedom'.[148] For example, while compulsory vaccination can override individual consent, its use should be minimised and be conditional on the use of procedural justice arrangements (such as democratic decision-making procedures) which provide adequate mandate and justification of public health regulation. This requirement actually provides resources for enhancing participation.

iii. Towards Participation

Nevertheless, in Nuffield's version of stewardship, for example, the focus is on aligning governance with public opinion through scrutiny and expression of views rather than providing guarantees for a substantive input into decision-making.[149] Stewardship might therefore reinforce the 'deficit model' of citizens that undermines their participation. That said, stewardship has much potential to enhance participation, especially when used to underscore demands and generate

[145] H Somsen, 'Regulating Human Genetics in a Neo-Eugenic Era' in T Murphy (ed), *New Technologies and Human Rights* (Oxford, Oxford University Press, 2009) 116.

[146] Such as 'rights as risk' and 'risk within rights' in: T Murphy and N Whitty, 'Is Human Rights Prepared? Risk, Rights and Public Health Emergencies' (2009) 17 *Medical Law Review* 219.

[147] On the creation of an ethics for pandemics capable of balancing individual and collective rights, see: MJ Selgelid, 'Pandethics' (2009) 123 *Public Health* 255.

[148] Nuffield Council, *Public Health,* n 131 above, 26.

[149] Ibid, 26: stewardship '*recognises the importance of open and transparent participatory processes* as a necessary condition for public health policy making, but it is also clear that these are not sufficient by themselves. Stewardship is not exercised simply by following the public vote, especially where issues involve complex scientific evidence. Under the stewardship model, *public health policy should be compatible with the views of the public,* and the government should create conditions that allow the public to *scrutinise and judge the appropriateness of proposed polices*' (emphasis added).

contestation around framing, distribution and vulnerability articulated through human rights and bioethics.

Human rights, bioethics and (supra-)stewardship responsibility might be most useful when deployed with critical self-consciousness to demand and contest decision-making in light of ongoing public health concerns and immediate exigencies—and resist reproduction of the 'deficit model' and the other ways of limiting citizen input into governance. In this way, these are a potentially cogent discursive means to power technologies of citizen participation, which would thereby supplement the existing dominant models of risk governance, and could reveal and assist in the identification of key distortions, failures, pitfalls and paradoxes. Crucially, the power of these discourses means they might help to prompt the gathering and production of knowledge from across society and persuade or even impel those who make decisions or with influence in the decision-making processes to take it into account. That concludes my prescription for enhancing citizen participation in decision-making—and through it governance and its regulatory interventions—and explains my optimism about the democratisation of public health governance and its potential to enhance regulatory interventions.

V. CONCLUSION

I began this chapter by summarising the findings from the first part of this book, which involved setting out the main contours, relationships and underpinnings for the EU's regulation of public health. I argued that these are constitutive and representative of the broader technology governing public health and the related policy domain. I explained how this is linked to attempts to constitute the EU's identity and to define and delimit its responsibility and accountability. Crucially for the project pursued in this book, at the same time the domain also creates a space or arena in and through which citizens—'the governed'—can demand and contest EU governance and its regulatory interventions. Nevertheless, the very construction of the policy domain together with the centrality and valorisation of scientific and technical knowledge and expertise underpinning the configuration of citizen participation to decision-making constrains the possibilities for biopolitics.

These same constraints also provide key openings and possibilities for participation in decision-making: the provision of supplementary knowledge and expertise that is not necessarily fully captured by and within the dominant risk-based techniques, processes and practices of governance. Moreover, supported by insights from several key disciplines, I drew on and nominated the legitimating discourses of human rights and bioethics, and the developing notion of (supra-)stewardship responsibility, as the resources to power technologies of participation. As resources for participation these discourses clearly require far more mining, reflection and development. In this chapter I have sought to point towards the potential of the discourses as part of a discursive strategy for participation—and to prompt further discussion.

Specifically, I have argued that human rights, bioethics and (supra-)stewardship can be used to construct and orientate a discursive space in which citizens use the focal points of framing, distribution and vulnerability to stimulate and bolster their attempts at public querying. In the next two chapters I enlarge on the discussion by outlining some examples of openings and possibilities for participation. I do so by having regard to framing and then knowledge production in chapter seven, followed by consideration of regulatory interventions in chapter eight, where I bring out further concerns around distribution and vulnerability.

7

Querying Framing and Knowledge Production: Risk, Numbers, Measurement and Evaluation

I. INTRODUCTION

GIVEN THE SHIFT in the substance and focus of discussion between the first and second parts of this book I begin this chapter by briefly retracing my steps and overviewing those that follow. The previous chapter provided a pessimistic diagnosis of the shape and role of the current institutionalisation of citizen participation in the EU's governance of public health as a key concern. That assessment was based on a summary and reflection of the findings and key arguments advanced in the first part of the book, which highlighted risk as the dominant framing for the technology governing public health and explained how it is underpinned by and oriented towards market optimisation understood as being about the circulation of people and things. I explained how the centrality and valorisation of scientific and technical knowledge and expertise to the risk-based techniques, processes and practices that regulate public health produces a blind spot in that, supported by several related discourses such as the public understanding of science, the actual and potential contribution of citizen participation is implicitly devalued and limited and the space for biopolitics is constrained.

After which I summarised the neoliberal (re)configurations ongoing in governance—those between knowledge and power, sovereignty and territoriality, and power and responsibility, and finally an introduction to the (re)configuration between governance and the governed—as the structuring themes undergirding the governing technology and related public health policy domain. I emphasised how together the foundations of governance, its structuring themes and effects, specifically, its paradoxes, pitfalls and blind spots, should not be seen just as constraints, but rather, in an optimistic turn and the fourth argument of the book, they also open up space and create possibilities and opportunities for biopolitics and citizen participation in decision-making.

The previous chapter was also positive in that it made a prescription for enhancing citizen participation and with it the quality of governance and its regulatory interventions. It did so by proposing a discursive strategy built from the legitimating discourses of human rights and bioethics and the developing notion of (supra-)stewardship responsibility as the resources and means to facilitate and power technologies of participation. With those discourses as the underpinning this chapter and the next take the discussion forward by using a broad brush and therefore non-exhaustive approach in order to chart some of those openings and possibilities for participation brought out by attention to framing, distribution and vulnerability. The discussion in this chapter, which looks first at framing and subsequently the gathering and production of knowledge by reference to indicators and clinical trials, and in the next chapter, which looks at interventions, is only the starting point for and indicative of the issues and points around which citizens might intervene to generate important supplementary knowledge on the distortions, failures, paradoxes and pitfalls—key normative dimensions—attendant to the EU's risk-based governance and its regulatory interventions.

The selection of examples in this chapter and the next trace the connections between framing, knowledge and regulatory interventions and reflect the structuring themes undergirding the public health policy domain—all together, key openings and opportunities for participation that are reinforced by their links. Throughout the discussion I continue to underscore how the openings provided by the examples relate to the production and legitimation of the EU's socio-political order, identity and ultimately its project of integration. This is vital to the success of the discursive strategy for citizen participation in that the 'way in' to decision-making it provides is impelled by the threat that, if unaddressed, the regulatory failures and 'societal risks' identified and underlined through it could produce 'institutional risks' (that is to standing and reputation) that undermine and delegitimate the EU's governance, identity and project of European integration.

II. QUERYING RISK

A. Framing, Knowledge and Responses

Like any frame for governance and regulatory technologies risk has implications for both the knowledge required in order to make decisions and the solution(s) (de)selected. Generally speaking, if the frame selected is too narrow, too wide or just plain wrong, then the regulatory response will likewise be too narrow, too wide or wrong.[1] As is apparent from the discussion in the first part of the book, framing (by risk) helps to determine, mediate and distribute responsibilities. Framing also helps to determine the knowledge required for decision-making and perceptions of what constitutes relevant, effective and legitimate solutions to public health problems. Framing is therefore the starting point for attention by citizens and

[1] See references on framing in the last chapter, especially: F Fischer, *Reframing Public Policy: Discursive Politics and Deliberative Practices* (Oxford, Oxford University Press, 2003); R Lidskog, L Soneryd and Y Uggla, *Transboundary Risk Governance* (London, Earthscan, 2009); DA Schon and M Rein, *Frame/Reflection: Toward the Resolution of Intractable Policy Controversies* (New York NY, Basic Books, 1994).

around which they might provide supplementary knowledge on the distortions, failures, paradoxes, pitfalls and blind spots attendant to the EU's technology governing public health and constituting the policy domain.

Indeed, despite the centrality and valorisation of scientific and technical knowledge to risk-based governance and the objectivity, neutrality and legitimacy it bestows, there remains a degree of indeterminacy. That indeterminacy feeds into the construction of a risk profile for any given public health problem—encompassing, inter alia, the identification of when risk materialises, the degree of risk, kind of harms or hazards to which risk pertains and their ranking—and the subsequent decision-making. Although medical and epidemiological knowledge is of central importance to the construction of risk profiles, it has its limits. Those limits are glaringly apparent in attempts not just to forestall the future through prevention (an often hugely successful strategy), but more clearly through attempts at governing the future in the present through precautionary approaches and especially in the turn to preparedness as part of the wider securitisation of public health.[2] In short, since perceived risk is not only a matter of science there arises a key opening and possibility for citizen participation.[3]

That opening widens through the realisation that science does not operate within a vacuum. Rather, science is constructed within quite specific social and historic contexts and perceptions. Since science can be incomplete and is in any case only part of the basis for legal and regulatory decision-making, those social, cultural and political forces and related perceptions also help to determine and shape the approach taken to regulating the target produced and the (de)selection of interventions to deal with it. The history of disease shows that epidemics are particularly prone to differing non-biological and extra-scientific perceptions and constructions.[4] I consider knowledge in more detail below.

Crucially for the present broad brush discussion, new or emerging diseases are usually perceived as greater threats, and this seems to be because the high degree of uncertainty or even non-knowing about the risks they pose makes them scarier. Indeed, this explanation seems accurate given that morbidity and mortality are engendered, at least in the EU, less by communicable diseases (due to the success of public health interventions) and far more by non-communicable diseases.[5]

[2] Precaution was noted in ch 2 and preparedness was the subject of ch 5. The securitisation of public health was noted throughout the first part of the book.

[3] Eg 'the determination of a tolerable risk level generally requires the involvement of the public in one way or another' in L Boisson de Chazournes, 'New Technologies, the Precautionary Principle, and Public Participation' in T Murphy (ed), *New Technologies and Human Rights* (Oxford, Oxford University Press, 2009). More generally, see: G Burchell, C Gordon and P Miller, *The Foucault Effect: Studies in Governmentality* (Chicago, University of Chicago Press, 1991).

[4] Eg see: A Preda, *AIDS, Rhetoric, and Medical Knowledge* (Cambridge, Cambridge University Press, 2005). More generally, see: J Goudsblom, 'Public Health and the Civilising Process' (1986) 64 *The Milbank Quarterly* 166.

[5] SD Moeller, *Compassion Fatigue: How the Media Sell Disease, Famine, War and Death* (New York NY, Routledge, 1999).

In sum, the perceived threat posed by a disease, and interventions selected to combat it, is related far less to its incidence or lethality, and more to its novelty, symptoms (the more objectionable usually attract more attention), the speed and ease of travel across borders and between populations, and how quickly it kills.[6]

Public authorities and the media play important roles in producing and shaping the perceived risk of novel and emerging communicable diseases.[7] Both might deploy stereotypical representations of disease and promote fear in their reporting efforts. For example, anxiety of the changing roles of women in the early twentieth century became linked to fear of sexually transmitted infections in wartime and underpinned the regulatory responses used to tackle them.[8] Similarly, the approach to tuberculosis has been explained by, inter alia, the need to demonstrate the so-called germ theory of disease, deal with the tensions arising from the influx of new immigrant groups, and even in order to support wider social welfare measures.[9]

The EU is not immune to these extra-scientific, political, economic and cultural pressures. Other institutional interests that help to determine how and why perceptions are produced and shaped include augmenting budgets,[10] bolstering prestige, obtaining legal and political authority for regulatory interventions—and legitimation. These sorts of reasons are salient for the EU and, in turn, the project of European integration. As I have noted in several places,[11] the EU's legitimacy needs have driven its interest in and turn to risk-based governance, which is underpinned and directed at broader efforts to promote economic optimisation. Public health and its interventions help to constitute and project the EU's identity as authoritative and usefulness to its Member States, international actors and private actors like corporations, but perhaps especially its citizens.

The potential for action and the production of much needed 'output' legitimacy[12] provided by public health governance implies that the EU has a vested interest beyond its formal responsibilities in paying attention to dangers or threats to public health. Through its risk-based governance the EU is able to enlarge its power and delineate the boundaries of responsibility, including through the shaping of perceptions of risk, the appropriate and legitimate response to the regulatory target as well as the broader project of European integration. The indeterminacy

[6] For discussion, see: M Humphreys, 'No Safe Place: Disease and Panic in American History' (2002) 14(4) *American Literary History* 845.

[7] S Sontag, *Illness as Metaphor and AIDS and Its Metaphors* (London, Penguin, 1991) especially 175.

[8] A Brandt, *No Magic Bullet: A Social History of Venereal Disease in the United States Since 1880* (New York, Oxford University Press, 1987); M Sturma, 'Public Health and Sexual Morality: Venereal Disease in World War II Australia' (1988) 13 *Signs* 725.

[9] N Tomes, 'The Making of a Germ Panic, Then and Now' (2000) 90(2) *American Journal of Public Health* 191.

[10] S Jenkins, 'Swine Flu? A Panic Stoked in Order to Posture and Spend', *The Guardian*, 29 April 2009.

[11] Especially chs 2 and 6.

[12] F Scharpf, *Governing in Europe. Effective and Democratic?* (Oxford, Oxford University Press, 1999).

of scientific and technical knowledge and the shaping of perceptions of risk underlines the potential of opening up framing and subsequent decision-making to querying and contestation by citizens and through it prompting the (re)shaping of perceptions and even (re)framing.

B. Skewing Attention and Resources Towards Consequences

Not only is the perception of public health problems shaped by risk open to distortion, risk also has additional normative implications for distribution and vulnerability that provide further openings and possibilities for public querying and citizen participation. At the broadest level governing through risk skews attention and resources towards consequences, away from causes and social determinants of health and the need to address them through prevention, and obscures broader normative and programmatic concerns. The latter are particularly apparent in the overarching architecture of EU governance and include the orientation and use of risk for purposes of economic optimisation, the infiltration of market rationality and with it private corporate interests into governance, and the way in which all of this relates to the production and legitimation of the EU's identity, socio-political order and project of rule aimed at European integration. The focus on consequences might be exacerbated by the growing importance of security understood as being about regulating the dangers or threats to the circulation of people and things, which is especially apparent in the turn to preparedness. These points lay the foundations for the forthcoming discussion over the rest of this chapter and into the next.

In light of the latter, preparedness therefore deserves particular attention. By producing a 'synergy' to the mutual benefit of public health and security such as in relation to surveillance and interventions, preparedness might have some use in bolstering efforts and resources to deal with pandemics as a medical emergency.[13] Indeed, as Rothstein et al point out, a focus on risk to standing or reputation, or so-called 'institutional risk' (the focus of preparedness), can figure the approach taken to 'societal risks' (like pandemics).[14] This can help to sensitise governance and its regulatory interventions to rarer pandemics, produce more and coordinated research, promote the professionalisation of the problem and create a stronger basis for decision-making. So preparedness is useful, necessary and therefore an understandable response to particular kinds of public health problems.

However, preparedness and the wider focus on security are problematic for broader public health governance. Indeed, the growing importance of preparedness is described as a 'policy revolution'[15] propelling us into 'the age of

[13] See further: DP Fidler and LO Gostin, *Biosecurity in the Global Age: Biological Weapons, Public Health, and the Rule of Law* (Stanford CA, Stanford University Press, 2007) ch 5.

[14] H Rothstein, M Huber and G Gaskell, 'A Theory of Risk Colonisation: The Spiralling Regulatory Logics of Societal and Institutional Risk' (2006) 35 *Economy and Society* 91. Cited as central to the discursive strategy proposed in ch 6, n 119.

[15] Fidler and Gostin, *Biosecurity*, n 13 above, 145.

preparedness'[16]—and as apparent from the discussion in the first part of the book, EU governance is representative of and perpetuating this shift. Preparedness is focused on consequences in a different way to prevention in that, as Collier and Lakoff point out, its goal 'is *not* necessarily to *prevent* events from happening but to *mitigate their consequences*—in other words, to keep a disaster from turning into a catastrophe' (emphasis added).[17] In the EU context preparedness is noted as 'directed towards identifying and addressing the *current impact and subsequent threat potential* of the influenza outbreak in order to *limit its consequences*' (emphasis added)[18] and especially to the internal market.[19] Growing attention to reflexive governance supports and abets preparedness and the skewing of attention and resources towards addressing consequences rather than causes (through attention to social determinants) in which economic optimisation is to be achieved through the protection of vulnerable *governance* rather than vulnerable populations. In other words, in preparedness there is only indirect responsibility for population—and within wider risk governance responsibility for public health is effectively limited to regulating consequences rather than root causes.

The widespread focus on security in governance and the growing importance of preparedness might skew attention and resources towards rare events like pandemic influenza and away from the major and chronic health problems,[20] which are often endemic and the most common causes of death and illness in populations on a daily basis.[21] Similarly, abetted by a preference for disease specific interventions in public health or so-called 'vertical' responses,[22] the (re)orientation of governance towards emergencies might skew resources towards communicable diseases at the expense of non-communicable diseases and persistent public health problems[23]—which of course suggests that preventative measures to address the social, political and economic origins of public health problems becomes deprioritised overall, despite the references to prevention in policy documents.[24] Francis et al point out how while the 'apparent assumption that devoting resources to pandemic planning is just' might be explained by the openness of the 'triage choices in pandemic planning', nevertheless 'there are *serious questions of justice*

[16] T Murphy and N Whitty, 'Is Human Rights Prepared? Risk, Rights and Public Health Emergencies' (2009) 17 *Medical Law Review* 219, 230 and 232.

[17] S Collier and A Lakoff, 'Vital Systems Security' (2007) *ARC Working Paper No 2*, 3.

[18] European Commission, *Communication on Pandemic Influenza Preparedness and Response Planning in the European Community*, COM (2005) 607 final, 8.

[19] Ibid and European Commission, *'Interim Document': Technical Guidance on Generic Preparedness Planning for Public Health Emergencies*, 2005.

[20] Such as those discussed in chs 3 and 4.

[21] *Cf* Fidler and Gostin, *Biosecurity*, n 13 above, 8.

[22] See further, ch 8.

[23] CR Sunstein and R Zeckhauser, 'Overreaction to Fearsome Risks' (2008) *John F Kennedy School of Government Faculty Research Working Paper Series, No RWP08-079*, available at: web.hks.harvard.edu/publications/workingpapers/citation.aspx?PubId=6152.

[24] D Yach and others, 'Global Chronic Diseases' (2005) 307 *Science* 317.

to be asked about the allocation of extensive resources to pandemic threats' (emphasis added).[25]

Moreover, the broader distortion of priorities and responsibilities also has feedback effects for pandemics. As Murphy and Whitty explain, without attention to broader social conditions and public health concerns like sufficient staff and resources overall and reducing inequalities, 'global surveillance, surge capacity and, more generally, preventing and coping with a pandemic will be all the more difficult'.[26] Put differently, the myopic focus on these—on managing 'institutional risk'—might be detrimental to the efficient management of the 'societal risk' of public health problems overall, a result that is hardly conducive to equal protection for all in society. In short, the focus on consequences and regulating communicable diseases can be highlighted as contrary to the spirit if not the letter of the human rights and bioethics guarantees for the protection of public health, such as Article 35 Charter of Fundamental Rights of the EU (EU Charter), and reflected in Article 9 Treaty on the Functioning of the European Union (TFEU) and Article 168(1) TFEU, as well as the EU's (supra-)stewardship responsibilities. Read together these underscore the importance of protecting everyone's health, ensuring that all benefit from public health measures, and that those measures include prevention and address the preconditions and social determinants of ill health for all diseases, rather than some (that is epidemic, endemic and others).

Other concerns and openings for citizen reflection and participation relate to the (de)selection of interventions and stem not only from the widespread focus on security and the growing importance of preparedness, but also from the orientation of governance towards market optimisation. Security and preparedness favour the distribution of resources towards surveillance, surge capacity, and as emphasised in the next chapter, treatment through magic bullet and technological interventions like pharmaceuticals as the preferred triage choice in the event of a public health emergency. While the market optimising priorities, norms and values of the broader normative architecture help to undergird these distortions, they also prompt the privileging of responses that further private corporate interests.[27] Put differently, responses like pharmaceuticals are favoured twice over: through their protection as a key way of managing and limiting consequences, and in light of their centrality to the EU's programmatic priorities reflected in concrete techniques, processes and practices that seek to enhance the internal market, optimise the economy and bolster corporate profitability. Both of these are ways of producing an optimal circulation of people and things, with key public health tools being rendered as crucial to the achievement of the objective of

[25] LP Francis and others, 'Pandemic Planning and Distributive Justice in Health Care' in M Freeman (ed), *Law and Bioethics* (Oxford, Oxford University Press, 2008) 433. *Cf* consideration of social justice in pandemic planning in: 'Bellagio Statement of Principles', available at: www.unicef.org/avianflu/files/Bellagio_Statement.pdf and www.bioethicsinstitute.org/web/page/905/sectionid/377/pagelevel/3/interior.asp. For criticism of the focus on pharmaceuticals see: A Lakoff, 'Real-Time Biopolitics: The Actuary and the Sentinel in Global Public Health' (2015) 41(1) *Economy and Society* 40.

[26] Murphy and Whitty, 'Is Human Rights Prepared?' n 16 above, 243.

[27] See further, ch 8.

economic optimisation in the overarching architecture and programmatic level of governance[28] and through its operationalisation in concrete techniques, processes and practices.[29]

The (de)selection of interventions (and production of perceptions) is likely to be influenced by other imbricating forces. A first force is a more specific valence of securitisation. Security is increasingly prevalent and powerful, and calls for greater security can trump other arguments—including within public health.[30] The necessity and potential benefits of the turn to preparedness and security are, therefore, part of what de Larrinaga and Doucet call 'the wager' of the *securitisation* of public health.[31] Securitisation is of particular concern in relation to distribution and vulnerability concerns around interventions discussed in the next chapter. This is because securitisation provides the conditions for increased surveillance, treatment through magic bullet responses and technological fixes, and an easier resort to exceptional measures.[32]

Linked closely to security as a trump is a second force: the dissemination of the wider zero-sum relationship between individual protections and risk (and safety and security). Although relevant to bioethics[33] this force has been most noted in relation to human rights. Lazarus and Goold observe the power of 'the idea that certain human rights can be "turned off" when necessary'—or less radically, narrowed—has become a 'thoroughly reasonable reaction to the dangers allegedly faced by democratic societies'.[34] Abetting this is a broader tendency stressed by Hunter in which 'all aspects of health emergency policy have shifted towards the framework of *enhanced* executive authority' (emphasis added).[35] Going so far as to describe this zero-sum game as part of the 'new "rights revolution"',[36] Murphy and Whitty note 'there are no guarantees that the securitisation of public health, the right to security or human security will be good for human rights'.[37]

These points are of greater concern in terms of the EU's external relations in the field of public health, which were noted throughout the first part of the book.

28 See ch 2.

29 See chs 3, 4 and 5.

30 S Elbe, *Security and Global Health: Toward the Medicalisation of Insecurity* (Cambridge, Polity Press, 2010).

31 M de Larrinaga and MG Doucet, *Security and Global Governmentality: Globalisation, Governance and the State* (London, Routledge, 2010) 1.

32 Generally see: ibid.

33 Eg it is a key preoccupation of the stewardship models discussed in ch 6.

34 L Lazarus and BJ Goold, 'Security and Human Rights: The Search for a Language of Reconciliation' in BJ Goold and L Lazarus (eds), *Security and Human Rights* (Oxford, Hart Publishing, 2007) 4. Also see: GJ Annas, *American Bioethics: Crossing Human Rights and Health Law Boundaries* (Oxford, Oxford University Press, 2005); LO Gostin, 'When Terrorism Threatens Health: How Far are Limitations on Personal and Economic Liberties Justified?' (2003) 55 *Florida Law Review* 1105; I Loader and N Walker, *Civilising Security* (Cambridge, Cambridge University Press, 2007); B Von Tigerstrom, *Human Security and International Law: Prospects and Problems* (Oxford, Hart Publishing, 2007).

35 N Hunter, '"Public–Private" Health Law: Multiple Directions in Public Health' (2007) 10 *Journal of Health Care Law and Policy* 101, 106.

36 Murphy and Whitty, 'Is Human Rights Prepared?' n 16 above, 231. Also see: T Murphy, 'Taking Revolutions Seriously: Rights, Risk and New Technologies' (2009) 16(1) *Maastricht Journal of European and Comparative Law* 15.

37 Ibid, 232.

There are important efforts at international collaboration, especially with poorer countries, such as through enhanced surveillance,[38] improvements in clinical trials abroad and access to pharmaceuticals,[39] and the ECDC's organisation and deployment of emergency response teams (OATs) abroad.[40] Nevertheless, the EU's focus is on protecting itself (and its economy) from threats or dangers that emerge from developing countries. This raises issues of distributional justice: skewing resource allocation in countries with already poorly equipped health care systems towards public health interventions that are arguably more for the benefit of the EU (and other rich powers). This is ultimately to the detriment of the already strained public health capacities of poorer countries, who are finding it hard if not impossible to cope with preventable endemic and non-communicable diseases.[41]

All together the focus on preparedness and the growing preoccupation with public health as a matter of security—the centrality of governing emergencies—might mask and be detrimental to wider public health objectives, skew the distribution of attention and resources and with it increase societal vulnerability to public health problems, and undermine protections against intrusive public health interventions. Recognition of the implications of framing public health as matters of risk opens up space for the normative dimensions sketched above to be revealed and opened up to public debate and contestation. Since framing is the product of distinct choices about how to govern, the EU can be made responsible and accountable for the attendant distortions, paradoxes, pitfalls and failures. In the remainder of this chapter I expand on the importance of framing for the gathering and production of knowledge, while in the next chapter I turn to discuss the implications of risk as oriented and deployed in the EU's market-oriented governance for the (de)selection of responses to public health problems. Throughout what follows I continue to highlight human rights and bioethical implications relating to distribution and vulnerability—all together what can amount to supplementary knowledge. These examples will further underline openings and possibilities for citizen participation through the provision of that supplementary knowledge to decision-making.

III. QUERYING SCIENTIFIC AND TECHNICAL KNOWLEDGE PRODUCTION

A. Looking More Closely at Knowledge Production

The openings and possibilities for citizen participation apparent in framing extend into knowledge and regulatory interventions, despite the ways in which science and

38 Seen most clearly in chs 4 and 5.

39 See ch 4, the discussion below and in ch 8.

40 See ch 5.

41 MA French, 'Woven of War-Time Fabrics: The Globalisation of Public Health Surveillance', (2009) 6(2) *Surveillance and Society* 101.

policy are often presented as discrete areas of activity.[42] In the first part of the book I sketched out the scientific and technical knowledge and expertise that is the foundation for legal and regulatory decision-making, and explained that it encompasses a wide range of techniques, processes and practices, inter alia, surveillance, monitoring, measuring and evaluating; impact assessment; the identification and dissemination of good practice; often underpinned by funding. I explained that together these provide the foundations for the regulation of public health and constitute the policy domain. In this section I elaborate on the indeterminacy of scientific and technical knowledge noted above and in doing so trace out the relations with framing and prepare the way for what follows and the discussion on interventions in the next chapter.

Importantly, the techniques, processes and practices of knowledge creation do not just mirror the framing by risk. They are also co-productive of, partially contingent upon and embedded in it and in turn the broader production and legitimation of the EU's identity, socio-political order and ultimately its project of integration.[43] Framing helps to determine the knowledge required for decision-making, but the techniques, processes and practices of knowledge[44] also help to support, make possible and perpetuate the frame. In this way knowledge and policy are dynamically interdependent, with the former facilitating the latter in its carving out of a space in which public health is made legible and rendered governable,[45] the reduction of the EU's responsibility to risk, as well as perceptions of what constitutes relevant, effective and legitimate solutions to public health problems. Scientific and technical knowledge are foundational to the (de)selection of policy options and interventions; creating some possibilities for action while foreclosing others.[46] That can be made more clearly apparent in these introductory comments by reference to the examples of prevention and preparedness as the two key rationalities for the EU's risk-based governance.

Prevention relies on archival–statistical knowledge, but this renders it less useful in dealing with targets that present highly ambiguous and uncertain (low probability, high harm) risks.[47] In other words, the production of risk profiles

[42] B Latour, 'From the World of Science to the World of Research' (1998) 280(5361) *Science* 208; S Hilgartner, *Science on Stage: Expert Advice as Public Drama* (Stanford CA, Stanford University Press, 2010).

[43] Seminally: S Jasanoff, 'The Idiom of Co-Production' in S Jasanoff (ed), *States of Knowledge: The Co-Production of Science and the Social Order* (London, Routledge, 2004). This idea was introduced and discussed further in ch 1.

[44] S Jasanoff and B Wynne, 'Science and Decision-Making' in S Rayner and EL Malone (eds), *Human Choice and Climate Change, Vol 1: The Societal Framework* (Columbus OH, Battelle Press, 1998).

[45] K Asdal, 'Enacting Things through Numbers: Taking Nature into Account/ing' (2007) 39(1) *Geoforum* 123.

[46] Fischer, *Reframing Public Policy*, n 1 above; M Hajer and H Wagenaar (eds), *Deliberative Policy Analysis: Understanding Governance in the Network Society* (Cambridge, Cambridge University Press, 2003); Lidskog, Soneryd and Uggla, *Transboundary Risk Governance*, n 1 above.

[47] R Ericson and A Doyle, *Uncertain Business: Risk, Insurance and the Limits of Knowledge* (Toronto, University of Toronto Press, 2004); SJ Collier, 'Enacting Catastrophe: Preparedness, Insurance, Budgetary Rationalisation' (2008) 37(2) *Economy and Society* 224; A Lakoff, 'From Population to Vital System' in A Lakoff and S Collier (eds), *Biosecurity Interventions: Global Health and Security in Question* (New York NY, Columbia University Press, 2008); P O'Malley, *Risk, Uncertainty and Government* (London, Glasshouse Press, 2004).

is disrupted by uncertainty (and even non-knowing) and this prompts attempts to make technologies of governance—including those using and operationalising prevention—ready for rare and emergent public health threats through preparedness.[48] A different form of knowledge, so-called imaginative enactment, therefore forms the basis of preparedness and, as Collier and Lakoff explain, it entails 'demands that experts *constantly assess* the *vulnerability of vital systems* and the *readiness* to *respond to*, and *recover from*, events that threaten them' (emphasis added).[49] This form of knowledge is apparent in the EU's approach to rare pandemics[50] in which the European Commission (Commission) uses previous experience to imagine pandemic scenarios[51] and notes 'the ability to respond to an international threat to health is profoundly influenced by the extent to which the issues have been *considered in advance and plans are in place for co-ordinated action*' (emphasis added).[52] This knowledge makes it possible to govern the future through preparedness, focus attention on vulnerable governance rather than vulnerable populations, skew attention and resources towards the former and consequences instead of causes and the social determinants of ill health, and distract attention away from broad normative and programmatic concerns.

The analysis in the first part of the book and summarised in the previous chapter also showed how neoliberalism operates and as it does so it harnesses the gathering and production of knowledge. The latter extends market rationality into the formally non-market domain of public health. However, as underlined in the previous chapter and again in this one, the framing of governance by and through risk and the reliance on related techniques, processes and practices depoliticises and obscures these normative and programmatic dimensions and paves the way for the infiltration of private corporate interests into governance.[53] Leach, Scoones and Wynne make a similar point in their discussion of risk and in doing so underline the implications for knowledge production. As they point out the framing of policy problems by risk means that:

> *[Q]uestions about the setting of science and technology agendas in the first place, about processes of innovation, and about whose priorities or visions of development or the good society these are to address, are left begging.* The assumption is that public concerns are focused on risks and consequences *rather the on the unstated and unaccountable human purposes, aspirations, priorities, expectations and aims that drive innovation-oriented scientific knowledge.* This … hugely important domain of science—partly, of course, because *innovation-oriented knowledge is usually controlled by the private sector* rather than the public sector—has been simply *excused de facto from any of the questions of*

48 Interestingly, there is far less mention of precaution (which, in any case, is usually part of risk management where there might be no risk to manage).

49 Collier and Lakoff, 'Vital Systems Security', n 17 above, 3.

50 See ch 5.

51 Eg European Commission, 'Interim Document', n 19 above.

52 Ibid, 3.

53 *Cf* K Yeung and M Dixon-Woods, 'Design-based Regulation and Patient Safety: A Regulation Studies Perspective' (2010) 71(3) *Social Science & Medicine* 613, 617.

> *public accountability, public involvement and participation* that have swept those scientific fields associated with risks and consequences.[54] (Emphasis added)

Scientific and technical knowledge is a crucial condition of possibility and support for the focus on consequences as well as the broader problems attendant to the framing by risk sketched above and developed in the next chapter.

Citizen participation can help to highlight the ways in which framing—and beyond that, the broader neoliberal power relations and structuring themes of the technology governing public health and the related policy domain—impacts on the shape and use of knowledge, and how that in turn produces concerns around distribution and vulnerability, key normative dimensions of the scientific and technical, and vital supplementary knowledge for decision-making. In the following I advance that argument by reference to two specific sets of techniques, processes and practices that produce data and make use of measurement and evaluation: first by enlarging on these opening points through the example of indicators, which provides something of a stepping stone to the more extensive consideration of clinical trials in the next section. I discuss surveillance in the next chapter since it is an important example of the gathering and production of knowledge that is, at the same time, an intervention, and which raises many of the same normative concerns as the interventions discussed there and for which it provides the basis. Indicators and clinical trials are especially indicative of the tightening relations between knowledge and power, but as I explain in relation to each of them, they also point to the operation of other neoliberal (re)configurations or structuring themes of the policy domain and key effects relating to framing, distribution and vulnerability.

B. Steering Governance Through Indicators

i. Instruments of Governance

Indicators appear as ubiquitous throughout the overarching architecture of EU governance, its operationalisation at the strategic level of the public health domain and as one of the components of the governing technology throughout the regulation of specific public health problems. That presence is sometimes more implicit, coming through more in references to monitoring, measuring and evaluation: indicators help to produce standards for benchmarking, which in turn permit evaluation and governing at a distance through the responsibilisation of the actors being monitored, especially public health authorities in the Member States. Generally speaking indicators are quantitative and expressed in numbers, rates, ratios and percentages, or qualitative and converted into quantitative

[54] M Leach, I Scoones and B Wynne (eds), *Science and Citizens: Globalisation and the Challenge of Engagement* (London, Zed Books, 2005) 10.

representations. As a brief reminder, in the Commission's definition indicators[55] are deemed 'essential for designing strategies and policies to improve the health of Europeans, and monitoring their implementation'[56]—in other words, indicators are vital to the very constitution of the domain and they are exemplary of the tightening relations between knowledge and power, the shift of sovereignty away from EU Member States and upwards across the EU's territory (the (re)configuration between sovereignty and territoriality), the delineation of the boundaries of EU responsibility and action, and the relations between EU governance and those it increasingly and more closely governs. Indeed, at a fairly broad level indicators influence EU policy and decision-making and that includes the allocation of resources, interventions that seek to regulate public health, and influencing other institutions, actors and public opinion about the nature of the problem and the nature and shape of the appropriate policy response.

At the EU level of the multi-level system of governance for public health indictors are a key nexus by and through which the techniques, processes and practices of the governing technology and ultimately risk-based governance and the (de)selection of regulatory interventions rest, are made possible and brought to life. The plans to augment the range of indicators produced and deployed at the EU level, including through a stronger foundation 'on reliable, comparable data',[57] and to increase take-up and use at the national level, attest to the continued and growing importance of EU indictors. A crucial dimension of which is the effect that wider circulation and use of indicators augments their authority and, in turn, their potential use in a self-perpetuating cycle. Although this suggests that indicators are not just very important but also significant interventions in themselves,[58] in EU legal scholarship they have received little attention outside of discussion of new governance involving innovation and experimentalism.[59] At the same time attention to the EU has also been limited in other scholarship looking at the turn to and proliferation of numbers, quantification and measurement[60] exemplified in

[55] See ch 2.

[56] 'Indicators': ec.europa.eu/health/indicators/policy/index_en.htm.

[57] Ibid.

[58] KE Davis and B Kingsbury, *Indicators as Interventions: Pitfalls and Prospects in Supporting Development Initiatives* (New York NY, Rockefeller Foundation, 2011).

[59] G de Búrca, 'New Governance and Experimentalism: An Introduction' (2010) *Wisconsin Law Review* 227; G de Búrca and J Scott, 'Introduction: New Governance, Law and Constitutionalism' in G de Búrca and J Scott (eds), *Law and New Governance in the EU and US* (Oxford, Hart Publishing, 2006); J Scott and DM Trubek, 'Mind the Gap: Law and New Approaches to Governance in the European Union' (2002) 8 *European Law Journal* 1; M Dawson, *New Governance and the Transformation of European Law* (Cambridge, Cambridge University Press, 2011).

[60] I Hacking, *The Taming of Chance* (Cambridge, Cambridge University Press, 1990); TM Porter, *Trust in Numbers: The Pursuit of Objectivity in Science and Public Life* (Princeton NJ, Princeton University Press, 1995); A Desrosières, *The Politics of Large Numbers: A History of Statistical Reasoning* (Cambridge MA, Harvard University Press, 1998); WN Espeland, and ML Stevens, 'A Sociology of Quantification' (2008) 49(3) *European Journal of Sociology* 401.

indicators across ever wider areas of global governance,[61] making them a 'technology of global governance'[62] beyond the state.

As highlighted in the first part of the book, the key indicators are Healthy Life Years (HLY), European Community Health Indicators (ECHI) and socio-economic indicators. Numbers and the way in which they are represented means they do not readily reveal their foundational theoretical assumptions, including over what should be counted in the first place, how material reality is to be understood, and the role of quantification in producing knowledge about that reality.[63] Here I focus on the HLY indicator in order to advance the argument for citizen participation in the gathering and production of knowledge. The HLY indicator is especially prominent in the overarching architecture and, as argued in the first part of the book,[64] is leveraged in order to found and justify the economic strategy that is then operationalised through the public health policy domain. The position of the HLY indicator in the overarching architecture underlines its use in the governance of risk and through that its orientation towards economic optimisation. The latter points to the revaluation and instrumentalisation of health towards that end through its construction in the indicator. This normative dimension of the HLY indicator is a core underpinning and it has implications for the distribution of resources. That is, public health is to be facilitated, but so as to facilitate economic optimisation. The normative (re)valuation of public health through the HLY indicator is something that could be highlighted by citizen participation in the gathering and production of knowledge.

That the HLY indicator is said to inform policy and decision-making, mostly at the EU level of the multi-level system of governance, but also and in the longer term at the Member State level, also directs attention to other dimensions. In tracing the relationship between indicators and governance Merry explains that: 'An indicator presents clearly the *most important features relevant* to informed decision making about one issue or question' (emphasis added).[65] The EU's selection of the

[61] C Arndt and C Oman, *Uses and Abuses of Governance Indicators* (Paris, OECD Development Centre Study, 2006); C Arndt, 'The Politics of Governance Ratings' (2008) 11(3) *International Public Management Journal* 275; C Hood, R Dixon and C Beeston, 'Rating the Rankings: Assessing International Rankings of Public Service Performance' (2008) 11(3) *International Public Management Journal* 298; T Fougner, 'Neoliberal Governance of States: The Role of Competitiveness Indexing and Country Benchmarking' (2008) 37(2) *Millennium Journal of International Studies* 303; A von Bogdandy and M Goldmann, 'The Exercise of International Public Authority through National Policy Assessment: The OECD's PISA Policy as a Paradigm for a New International Standard Instrument' (2008) 5(2) *International Organisations Law Review* 241.

[62] KE Davis, B Kingsbury, SE Merry, 'Indicators as a Technology of Global Governance', *Institute of International Law and Justice Working Paper 2010/2 Rev.* Also see: KE Davis and others (eds), *Governance by Indicators: Global Power Through Quantification and Rankings* (Oxford, Oxford University Press, 2012); HK Hansen and A Muhlen-Schulte, 'The Power of Numbers in Global Governance' (2012) 15(4) *Journal of International Relations and Development* 455.

[63] M Poovey, *A History of the Modern Fact: Problems of Knowledge in the Sciences of Wealth and Society* (Chicago, University of Chicago Press, 1998).

[64] Especially in ch 2.

[65] SE Merry, 'Measuring the World: Indicators, Human Rights, and Global Governance' (2011) 52(3) *Current Anthropology* S83.

HLY indicator 'was preferred to other possible health expectancy indicators such as Disability Adjusted Life Years (DALY) or Health Adjusted Life Expectancies (HALE)';[66] that is, the selection of the HLY indicator was a choice to highlight certain features for attention. Indeed, through its design the HLY indicator is intended to track and go beyond 'physical impairment or disability in functional tasks or presence of a specific chronic disease' to encompass '*self-assessed health*, [which] being much more global and subjective in nature, can incorporate a variety of aspects of health including cognitive and emotional as well as physical status' (emphasis added).[67]

ii. Salient Features

In this way, such factors and determinants of health as context, history, place and social connectedness *might* be captured within HLY. However, through their transformation into numerical representations these wider factors and their value in terms of individual experience are aggregated into a single account of what it is to be 'healthy' that is 'distinguish[ing] between years of life free of any activity limitation and years experienced with at least one activity limitation'.[68] This naming, simplification and reification inevitably ensures that detail and meaning are stripped away, and uncertainty and ambiguity in the data derived from subjective assessments disguised by its supposed certainty and objectivity, all consequences that can be exacerbated through the increase in authority that derives from wider circulation and usage, perhaps in combination with other indicators or if eventually combined into another single composite indicator.[69] In short, the multiple factors that go into rendering 'healthy' (that is producing the understanding) are effectively lost by the very efforts to discipline and produce standardised knowledge on '*health as a productivity/economic factor*' (emphasis added).[70] In light of this, it appears the design of the HLY indicator is such as to favour and inform market-oriented and optimising policy and decisions, the dissemination of market rationality and with it the servicing of market interests, and the production of the neoliberal identity, socio-political order and project of integration. In other words, the HLY indicator and its incipient and growing efforts at standardisation[71] seeks to produce the reality that it purports to measure, one that is populated by individuals who are active market participants.

The HLY indictor implicitly favours the distribution of resources towards those public health interventions that are most conducive to promoting economic optimisation by and through an increase in quality of life. As such the indicator is

[66] 'Developments of HLY as EU structural indicator' ec.europa.eu/health/indicators/healthy_life_years/hly_en.htm#fragment4.

[67] 'HLY and allocation of resources' ec.europa.eu/health/indicators/healthy_life_years/hly_en.htm#fragment3.

[68] 'Healthy Life Years (HLY)' ec.europa.eu/health/indicators/healthy_life_years/hly_en.htm#fragment0.

[69] WN Espeland and M Sauder, 'Rankings and Reactivity: How Public Measures Recreate Social Worlds' (2007) 113(1) *American Journal of Sociology* 1.

[70] 'Healthy Life Years (HLY)', n 68 above.

[71] L Busch, *Standards: Recipes for Reality* (Cambridge MA, MIT Press, 2011).

not neutral as to the allocation of resources across society.[72] For example, in distinguishing between years of life that are free of any activity limitation and years experienced with at least one activity limitation, life-saving interventions are not treated as being conceptually different from health-improving interventions. This is of course contrary to what most people might tend to think and value. It might also be queried whether removing a minor limitation (and producing an improvement) to many is equivalent to removing a major limitation (and producing a more significant improvement) to a few.

The HLY indicator also favours those without any pre-existing limitation; in other words, those with an existing limitation are disadvantaged and discriminated against. This implies that within the market optimising calculus of the HLY indicator equal need is not necessarily to be treated equally: ensuring those who are 'healthy' to begin with are either prevented from experiencing an activity inhibiting limitation or are treated for such a limitation seems to be preferred over treating those with a pre-existing limitation. Relatedly, those whose activity limitation cannot be treated or which can only be ameliorated (given current medical and technological knowledge or constraints on funding overall) through, say, intensive social support and palliative therapies, or with little addition of 'healthy' life years, including and especially the elderly, would appear to be less favoured than those whose activity limitation can be removed, especially where they experience a longer length of 'healthy' life. That is, in seeking to support and increase the number of health life years the HLY indicator implicitly favours and distributes resources towards those who are (within its calculus) deemed good investments.

In sum, the HLY indicator might have some effect on the distribution of resources between prevention or treatment—and it does not automatically translate into equitable and just public health friendly policies and decisions. Moreover, in light of the skewing of attention towards treatment at the level of the broad orientation and framing of governance, there is no guarantee that interventions will be directed at addressing the conditions that produce public health problems in the first place through prevention. That socio-economic indicators have a rather marginal role and position in the governance architecture[73] suggests that this concern cannot be fully resolved by reference to them alone.

So, the HLY indicator 'may be a particularly important indicator of the potential demand for health services and long-term care needs of the elderly population'[74]—but that does not on its own ensure an allocation of resources

[72] For discussion see: MR Gold, D Stevenson and DG Fryback, 'HALYS and QALYS and DALYS, Oh My: Similarities and Differences in Summary Measures of Population Health' (2002) 23 *Annual Review of Public Health* 115.

[73] See ch 2.

[74] 'HLY and allocation of resources', n 67 above.

to reduce future demand or adequately tackle it when it emerges. Moreover, it is noted that it:

> [I]s important for policy-makers *to be aware of the opportunity cost* (ie the benefits forgone) of doing too little to prevent ill-health, resulting in the use of limited health resources for the diagnosis, treatment, and management of preventable illness and injuries.[75] (Emphasis added)

Yet, again, this does not in itself ensure sources of vulnerability will actually be addressed through the allocation of resources to preventative measures—especially given 'HLY has been proposed as an appropriate indicator for the *short-term* allocation of social and health resources' (emphasis added).[76] This implies that consistent attention to and investment in preventative measures that generate effects that materialise over the *long-term* might not benefit. In this light the marginal position of the socio-economic indicators within the overarching architecture of EU public health governance (as discussed in chapter two) does not seem to be a satisfactory corrective.

Instead, the apparent neutrality of the HLY indicator arguably makes it more amenable as a support for public health interventions that are focused on managing consequences, especially emergencies, and promoting market interests. And yet, of course, the indicator is actually constructed in order to furnish that support for policy and decisions. Relatedly, the distribution of responsibilities for public health and accountabilities in the event of failure seen across the discussion in the first part of the book can also be seen here. That is, the use of self-assessment of 'health' in the construction of the HLY indicator is, at least in part, an attempt to responsibilise those included—'the public'—and manufacture legitimacy for both the indicator and the policy and decisions which are based upon it.

iii. Demanding Alternatives

The HLY indicator and other indicators are, as I have just outlined, replete with paradoxes, pitfalls and failures around distribution and vulnerability. Put differently, questions can be asked about how well these governance tools help to ensure a high level of health protection, as required by Article 9 TFEU, Article 168(1) TFEU and Article 35 EU Charter. In particular, it can be queried whether all benefit and enjoy equal protection for their health in and through these tools. At the same time the indicators discussed in this chapter also help to focus attention on (public) health, its cross-borderness, the way in which that necessitates and legitimates EU and wider transnational governance and regulatory interventions, and ensure policy at multiple levels of governance is better attuned to European wide public health problems.

Indicators also therefore open a space for discussion and political contestation.[77] By querying indicators, citizens might shed light on the limits and implications

[75] 'Healthy Life Years (HLY)', n 68 above.

[76] Ibid.

[77] CA Miller, 'New Civic Epistemologies of Quantification: Making Sense of Local and Global Indicators of Sustainability' (2005) 30(3) *Science, Technology & Human Values* 403.

of public health knowledge as it is rendered in EU discourses. This would contribute supplementary knowledge—so important to the evidence-based policy-making indicators are deemed to facilitate[78]—to policy and legal and regulatory decision-making that highlights those pitfalls and failures and which, arising as they do from hidden framing assumptions, are all too easily missed or overlooked. In providing their perspective on social reality citizens have a chance to destabilise the EU's existing efforts at quantification, and in doing so inflect, (re)shape and perhaps even (re)frame and (re)direct governance and its regulatory interventions towards wider and alternative aims, values and orientations besides economic optimisation.

In doing so citizens might contest the construction of existing indicators (including the data used, methodology for selection, combination and use)[79] and demand a reconfiguration of their position and use, such as through a greater emphasis on socio-economic determinants of health in the structural indicators.[80] Alternatively, citizens might push for the redesign of the HLY indicator such that it incorporates a weighting for social equity that is reflective of individual utilities. Such a change seems essential in order to limit the adverse distributional effects of the current design and combat any straightforward face value application of statistics and their representations in policy and decision-making.[81] Similarly, citizens might seek to supplement—or even replace—the HLY indicator with a new indicator that makes different choices about what is (de)prioritised, that is, such that distributional justice and equity are centralised. As part of these sorts of efforts citizens might themselves contribute data via such innovations as crowdsourcing.[82]

These kinds of ways forward derive strength from the EU's own attempts to refine and develop its indicators[83] as well as *their* governance.[84] The latter allows

[78] N Black, 'Evidence Based Policy: Proceed with Care' (2001) 323(7307) *British Medical Journal* 275; G Mulgan, 'Government, Knowledge and the Business of Policy Making: The Potential and Limits of Evidence-Based Policy' (2005) 1(2) *Evidence & Policy* 215; E Mykhalovskiya and L Weir, 'The Problem of Evidence-Based Medicine: Directions for Social Science' (2004) 59 *Social Science & Medicine* 1059; I Sanderson, 'Evaluation, Policy Learning and Evidence-Based Policy Making' (2002) 80(1) *Public Administration* 1.

[79] T Porter, 'Making Serious Measures: Numerical Indices, Peer Review, and Transnational Actor-Networks' (2012) 15(4) *Journal of International Relations and Development* 532.

[80] See: AR Chapman, 'The Social Determinants of Health, Health Equity, and Human Rights' (2010) 12(2) *Health and Human Rights: An International Journal* 17.

[81] S Anand and K Henson, 'Disability-Adjusted Life Years: A Critical Review' (1997) 16(6) *Journal of Health Economics* 685; P Menzel and others, 'Toward a Broader View of Values in Cost-Effectiveness Analysis of Health' (1999) 29(3) *Hastings Center Report* 7.

[82] Crowdsourcing is an increasingly popular way of gathering and producing knowledge via online platforms and techniques—but it raises questions about, inter alia, who is funding the research, why and to what ends? For discussion, see: DC Brabham, *Crowdsourcing* (London, MIT Press, 2013); J Surowiecki, *The Wisdom of Crowds: Why the Many Are Smarter than the Few* (New York, Random House, 2004).

[83] G Bauer, JK Davies and J Palikan on behalf of the EUHPID Theory Working Group and the EUPHI Consortium, 'The EUHPID Health Development Model for the Classification of Public Health Indicators' (2006) 21 *Health Promotion International* 153.

[84] European Commission, *Evaluation of the Use and Impact of the European Community Health Indicators ECHI by Member States* (Brussels, European Union, 2013) 7. See further, the discussion in ch 2.

citizens to leverage continuing calls for transparency, the giving of reasons, review, accountability and participation in EU governance[85] that resonate with similar calls in global governance. In this regard traction could be gained by reference to human rights standards for openness and accountability, reinforced by the norms and values of EU administrative law and the constitutional traditions of its Member States,[86] as well as developing global administrative law.[87] Although the production of indicators is usually expert-led, and (given the discussion in the previous chapter) this might be duplicated in their governance, together such efforts demonstrate that the knowledge domain is evolving and the power relations it both reflects and constitutes remain mutable.

These openings and possibilities for citizen participation are important and useful as part of the strategy for providing supplementary knowledge to policy and decision-making on the implications of apparently value neutral scientific and technical knowledge for the distribution of resources and attention and vulnerability. The provision of that knowledge and its articulation through and resonance with human rights and bioethics, underscored by references to the potential failure to meet (supra-)stewardship responsibilities for the provision of comprehensive public health coverage that meets the needs of all individuals, could help to ensure the HLY indicator—and other indicators—are (re)affirmed as only one input into policy and decisions. Gold and others make the same sort of point in their discussion of the health adjusted life years or HALY indicator, which is a close relative of the EU's HLY indicator:

> Consideration of *distributional issues* for those with greater needs, of allocation priorities for illnesses that are rare or expensive, and of the balance between health status improvement and life saving, *need to remain part of the political and clinical decision-making process in which HALYs may be one factor, instead of entering as distortions in the HALY calculations.* Economic efficiency ... should never be the sole criterion for resource allocation. If QALYs or DALYs [and by implication HLY] were to lead policymakers to make decisions based solely on economics, they would be used inappropriately.[88] (Emphasis added)

Overall, in these ways citizen participation might help to responsibilise the EU and—crucially given the distribution of risk management responsibilities—its Member States, and hold these actors accountable for failures that arise from their framing of public health problems and the governing technologies used to

[85] Underscored in European Commission, *European Governance: A White Paper*, COM(2001) 428 final, see ch 2.

[86] For discussion on the inadequacy of the current approach before the CJEU (which focuses on rights to be heard) and in the EU's legislative processes, see: J Mendes, *Participation in EU Rule-making: A Rights-Based Approach* (Oxford, Oxford University Press, 2011).

[87] See generally: G Anthony and others (eds), *Values in Global Administrative Law* (Oxford, Hart Publishing, 2011), especially C Harlow, 'Accountability as a Value in Global Governance and for Global Administrative Law'.

[88] Gold, Stevenson and Fryback, n 72 above, 129.

facilitate a solution. In doing so citizens might articulate their positions by reference to the HLY indicator in combination with ECHI and socio-economic indicators. The latter are particularly important in that references to them might help to (re)prioritise and distribute resources towards prevention and its benefits for tackling vulnerability as a multi-faceted phenomena at its various sources. This might help to resist the tendency for market-oriented indicators such as the HLY indicator to dominate policy and the thinking of decisionmakers and through their use to become normative.[89]

In making these suggestions it is important to highlight a couple of the main pitfalls of participation around the production and use of indicators. One pitfall is that participation might (re)legitimate and bolster the continued and wider use of indicators and, beyond that, quantification, and the problems attendant to them. Perhaps the major concern from the perspective of this book and its main biopolitical project is that participation around indicators could paradoxically assist depoliticisation and further obscure the normative in the technical, while also abetting the ongoing dissemination of market rationality into the organisation of the public health policy domain. Nevertheless, depoliticisation should be countered by the discursive strategy put forward as a way of enhancing citizen participation in that it is explicitly geared towards bringing out the normative dimensions of the technical. The growing importance of quantification as a way of representing and regulating social reality and underpinning and shaping political action begs for enhanced citizen engagement—and the discussion thus far points to engagement as a real possibility, which I turn now to consider in greater depth in relation to clinical trials.

IV. CLINICAL TRIALS

A. Producing Data in Support of Magic Bullet Responses and Pharmaceutical Fixes

Whereas indicators are integrated into the overarching architecture as well as in relation to specific public health problems, and are important in the ways discussed in the last section, clinical trials are a different albeit related form of knowledge creation. In essence clinical trials are integral to the operationalisation of policy through the growing resort to pharmaceuticals as a key medical and technological response to public health problems. Of course treatment is important, and efforts to facilitate it through the regulation of clinical trials are vital, but as detailed above the concerns attendant to the framing of governance by risk point to the growing preference for pharmaceuticals in dealing with emergencies, which is potentially to the detriment of broader public health objectives. These concerns

[89] CJL Murray and AD Lopez, *The Global Burden of Disease: A Comprehensive Assessment of Mortality and Disability from Diseases, Injuries, and Risk Factors in 1990 and Project to 2020* (Cambridge MA, Harvard School of Public Health, WHO and World Bank, 1996).

are traced out further in the next chapter where pharmaceuticals are discussed as part of the shift of attention and distribution of resources towards magic bullet responses to and technological fixes for public health problems. The discussion of the openings and possibilities for citizen participation around clinical trials in this section works with and complements the ensuing discussion of pharmaceuticals.

In what follows I build on the few mentions of clinical trials and market authorisation made in the first part of the book,[90] to focus on the increasing shift towards carrying out clinical trials abroad, that is outside the EU and the global North and principally in the global South.[91] Through a series of related and to some extent overlapping points—informed consent, the use of data from trials carried out abroad, designing trial protocols and more specifically the role of placebos—I explain how trials are embedded within and reflective of the overarching architecture of EU governance, and related to the global regulatory environment. I point to some of the ways in which the trend towards performing clinical trials abroad is prompted and facilitated, at least in part, by the orientation and normative direction of governance towards economic optimisation through the market authorisation of safe pharmaceutical products. Discussion of clinical trials abroad, the people enrolled in them, and the related human rights but (as shall become apparent) especially ethical protections, will underline several points. Perhaps foremost among them is the ongoing importance of risk (instantiated as safety) to the regulation of public health interventions at the level of the knowledge that supports them. The marginal and (because of that) instrumental use of human rights and (and to a greater extent) ethics will also become even more apparent.

More broadly, as I go on to explain, clinical trials abroad highlight additional ways in which knowledge underpins and makes risk-based regulation possible, the tightening relations between knowledge and power and the extension of EU governance and power beyond its territory, key themes of the first part of the book, but noted here for the ways in which they generate key normative implications for distribution and vulnerability. As I shall explain, these aspects of clinical trials abroad point to the importance of human rights and ethics to the production and legitimation of the EU's identity, socio-political order and project of European integration. Highlighting concerns around distribution and vulnerability by reference to human rights and especially the requirement to ensure a high level of health protection for all under Article 9 TFEU, Article 168(1) TFEU and Article 35 EU Charter, as well as ethical protections, and reinforced by reference to (supra-)stewardship responsibility, can help to prompt citizen engagement and power technologies of participation. Such engagement might impel the (re)shaping and (re)framing of the EU's pharmaceuticals regime in ways that are more conducive to public health. As I go on to point out, these discursive tools

[90] See chs 3, 4 and 5.

[91] A Petryna, *When Experiments Travel* (Princeton NJ, Princeton University Press, 2009). Also noted in the (business) media, eg A Jack, 'A New Lease of Life? The Ethics of Offshoring Clinical Trials' *Financial Times*, 28 January 2008; N Singer, 'Outsourcing of Drug Trials Is Faulted' *New York Times*, 18 February 2009.

can be and to some extent are already being deployed by those enrolled in and governed by the clinical trials and pharmaceuticals regime, and they therefore provide hope for developing biopolitics and participation in legal and regulatory decision-making.

B. Situating Clinical Trials in EU Governance

Clinical trials reflect the orientation and direction of the overarching architecture of EU governance.[92] A particular concern is that the EU is not as important as the US as a site of innovation.[93] Consequently, facilitating market authorisation is a central objective.[94] There is evidence that the EU is not just matching but perhaps even overtaking the US regulator, the Food and Drug Administration in this regard.[95] Global regulatory competition is a key driver for the alignment of clinical trials to market authorisation (the former being required by the latter),[96] and highlights how their configuration within the overarching architecture of EU governance is undergirded, shaped and directed towards the EU's efforts at producing and legitimating its imagined socio-political order and project of rule by and through the (hoped for) consequent economic optimisation.

The alignment of clinical trials to market authorisation and with it the concern with risk instantiated as product safety is central to their definition.[97] The Directive on the Community code relating to medicinal products for human use (Community code) defines clinical trials as:

> [A]ny systematic study of medicinal products in human subjects whether in patients or non-patient volunteers in order to discover or verify the effects of and/or identify any adverse reaction to investigational products, and/or study their absorption, distribution, metabolism and excretion *in order to ascertain the efficacy and safety of the products*.[98] (Emphasis added)

[92] See ch 2.

[93] European Commission, *A Stronger European-Based Pharmaceutical Industry for the Benefit of the Patient—A Call for Action*, COM (2003) 383 final; European Commission, *Putting Knowledge into Practice: A Broad-based Innovation Strategy for the EU*, COM (2006) 502 final.

[94] And approval figures are important for communicating success and performance: 'EMA Recommends 81 Medicines for Marketing Authorisation in 2013' www.ema.europa.eu/ema/index.jsp?curl=pages/news_and_events/news/2014/01/news_detail_002006.jsp&mid=WC0b01ac058004d5c1.

[95] Comparisons between the EU and FDA include: 'EMA Bests FDA in 2013 New Drug Approval Numbers', available at: www.raps.org/focus-online/news/news-article-view/article/4519/ema-bests-fda-in-2013-new-drug-approval-numbers.aspx; LJ Howie and others, 'A Comparison of FDA and EMA Drug Approval: Implications for Drug Development and Cost of Care' (2013) *Oncology*, available at: www.cancernetwork.com/oncology-journal/comparison-fda-and-ema-drug-approval-implications-drug-development-and-cost-care#sthash.SO6MTTLW.dpuf.

[96] As outlined in ch 3.

[97] For an overview of the EU approach see: 'Clinical trials' ec.europa.eu/health/human-use/clinical-trials/index_en.htm.

[98] Annex I, Pt 4, Directive 2001/83/EC on the Community code relating to medicinal products for human use [2001] OJ L311/67.

There are four phases of clinical trials. Phase I trials use between 20–80 healthy volunteers in order to determine the tolerable dose range of a new drug. Phase II trials use between 100–300 subjects who have the disease or condition to be treated in order to evaluate efficacy and safety of the drug. Phase III trials tend to be multi-centred and might involve up to 10,000 people located in between 10–20 countries. This phase generates more safety and efficacy data and the research participants included in the protocol for this type of trial tend to be those suffering from the condition the new drug is intended to treat. Phase IV trials are used to generate post-marketing data on safety and efficacy. This phase can involve millions of people.

Double-blind randomised controlled trials (RCTs) are considered the 'gold standard' for Phase II and III clinical trials. RCTs involve random allocation to the control or the active arm of the study. Participants allocated to the control group are provided with either the best standard treatment for their condition or a placebo (an inert substance). Where the former is the control the objective might be to demonstrate superiority of the trial drug or even just non-inferiority to the standard treatments that is that it falls within a pre-selected margin of effectiveness. Yet, this design provides scope for the marketing of pharmaceuticals that are, as Jackson puts it, 'not *too* inferior' or perhaps even 'just a little bit worse'.[99] The use of placebo can produce a more striking difference between those in the control group and those given the new trial drug. Placebo is therefore particularly useful where the objective of the trial is not to demonstrate superiority.

The European Medicines Agency (EMA) explains the justification for non-inferiority in its 'soft law' guidance (which should be followed in order to obtain a market authorisation):

> [I]t is *not necessary for the benefit-risk profile of an experimental medicine to [be] at least as favourable as the benefit-risk profile of any or all established medicines in order to receive marketing authorisation.* This is appropriate as frequently more than one treatment is required per indication (some medicines suit some people better than others) and clinical trials do not definitively capture all information on benefits and risks; *knowledge accumulates during a product's lifecycle.*[100] (Emphasis added)

Having multiple equally effective medicines available can be useful in order to deal with resistance to medication or so as to produce a cancer treatment that has fewer

[99] E Jackson, *Law and the Regulation of Medicines* (Oxford, Hart Publishing, 2012) 29. The subsequent use of the 'little bit worse' drug as the comparator in further trials can produce steadily decreasing effectiveness over time. More generally, see: N Cartwright, 'What is this Thing Called "Efficacy"?' in C Mantzavinos, *Philosophy of the Social Sciences: Philosophical Theory and Scientific Practice* (Cambridge, Cambridge University Press, 2009).

[100] EMA, *Reflection Paper on the Need for Active Control in Therapeutic Areas Where Use of Placebo is Deemed Ethical and One or More Established Medicines are Available*, EMA/759784/2010, 3–4.

adverse side effects. In these circumstances a non-inferiority trial using a placebo control can be useful. Importantly:

> *[T]he purpose of regulatory approval is not to determine clinical practice* (over and above the act of issuing a particular license for a medicine) and *there is no limit to the number of medicines that can be licensed for any given therapeutic indication providing the benefit risk of each is favourable.*[101] (Emphasis added)

Clinical trials need only demonstrate that pharmaceuticals are as good as or at least no worse than existing products, albeit with some sort of benefit for patients.

Under the EU's Community code data produced *outside* the EEA by the clinical trials industry can be submitted as part of an application for market authorisation of pharmaceuticals *within* the EU's internal market. In this way EU law extends beyond the territory of the EU itself through the enrolment of trials subjects abroad. That is provided principles *equivalent* to those found in the Clinical Trials Directive (CTD) and the replacement Clinical Trials Regulation (which necessarily includes good clinical practice (GCP)), and which are found in Article 8 and Annex 1, are followed.[102] Most important is the (repeated) stress on 'the freely given *informed consent* of each trial subject' (emphasis added)[103] in accordance with the Helsinki Declaration and ensuring that 'All phases of clinical investigation … shall be designed, implemented and reported in accordance with *good clinical practice*' (emphasis added).[104] The EMA seeks to verify compliance with these protections and standards.[105] For example the EMA works to ensure 'verification, at the time of the evaluation of the marketing authorization application, that trials carried out in third countries have been conducted in accordance with the required GCP and ethical standards', through 'increased GCP inspection including *further extension of the GCP policy* on increasing numbers of routine inspections as part of the need for greater supervision of the *conduct and ethical standards of clinical trials performed outside the EEA*' (emphasis added).[106]

Clinical trials literally service the EU's risk-based regulation of pharmaceuticals and, beyond that, the wider overarching normative architecture aimed at economic optimisation, and this instrumentalisation and use of knowledge creation is especially apparent in relation to trials performed abroad. Much hinges on successful trials and the crucial data on product safety they provide: market authorisation

[101] Ibid, 4.

[102] Directive 2001/83/EC, n 98 above, Art 8(3)(i) mentions the results of clinical trials, submitted in accordance with Annex I, as particulars and documents that 'shall' accompany an application for market authorisation. The Clinical Trials Regulation (noted infra n 103) duplicates the CTD's requirement—see Art 25(5).

[103] Annex 1, Pt 4, B, 1.2, ibid. Also see: Art 2(j) Directive 2001/20/EC on the approximation of the laws, regulations and administrative provisions of the Member States relating to the implementation of good clinical practice in the conduct of clinical trials on medicinal products for human use [2001] OJ L121/34. This Directive is now replaced by Regulation (EU) 536/2014 on clinical trials on medicinal products for human use, and repealing Directive 2001/20/EC [2014] OJ L158/1, but it does not become applicable until at least 28 May 2016. The Regulation is planned to apply from 2019 (see Preface). The stress on informed consent is maintained at Art 2(2)(21).

[104] Annex 1, Pt 4, B, 1.1, ibid. Also see: Art 8 Directive 2001/20/EC, ibid. To be replaced by Art 47 Regulation (EU) 536/2014, ibid.

[105] EMA, *EMEA Strategy Paper: Acceptance of Clinical Trials Conducted in Third Countries, for Evaluation in Marketing Authorisation Applications*, EMEA/228067/2008.

[106] Ibid, 1.

and production, sales and hoped for economic optimisation. The orientation of this regime towards economic optimisation is especially clear in the Community code, which states that the 'essential aim of *any rules* governing the production, distribution and use of medicinal products must be to safeguard public health' (emphasis added),[107] but that 'this objective must be attained by means which will *not hinder the development of the pharmaceutical industry or trade* in medicinal products within the Community' (emphasis added).[108] Although the Community code is based on Article 114 TFEU, which consistent with Article 9 TFEU requires a high level of health protection to be factored into legislation,[109] public health is understood in relation to and effectively subordinated to the market. Further, reflecting the narrow criteria for market authorisation and the purpose of clinical trials, the public health implications of pharmaceuticals are confined to their safety.

This specific instantiation of risk flows from and is consistent with the broader framing underpinning the governing technology and constitutive of the public health policy domain. As such the focus on safety, like the broader frame of risk, distracts attention away from the way in which market rationality is increasingly underpinning and orienting clinical trials as an example of the production of scientific and technical knowledge. This is especially clear in relation to clinical trials abroad, which demonstrate the key structuring theme of the (re)configuration between sovereignty and territoriality. That is, the EU's normative power extends beyond the territory where it is constituted (the EU—and for that matter the EEA) to govern practices of biomedical knowledge production (clinical trials) abroad, but in order to produce what is usable (data) for its domestic purposes (authorisation of pharmaceuticals for circulation and consumption in the internal market). Those purposes are in turn tied to, underpinned by and directed at meeting broader aims found within the overarching architecture of EU governance, through, inter alia, the improved competitiveness of EU industry, consequent economic growth and an optimised internal market through innovative pharmaceuticals, and the positioning of the EU as a key global regulator.

The focus on producing data that indicates product safety also paves the way for the insinuation of private corporate interests into knowledge creation (including in terms of *who* is producing the data—see below). Indeed, carrying out clinical trials abroad offers key advantages—lower costs and populations whose epidemiology makes them especially useful in order to demonstrate the quality, safety and efficacy of new drugs—to an industry dominated by 'big pharma'[110] and that enjoyed a boom period in the 1990s, but which is now finding it harder to produce sufficient numbers of so-called 'blockbuster drugs'. The focus on risk as product safety obscures knowledge creation and the alignment of regulatory processes with commercial interests in increasing profitability, but without significant innovation or the need to meet public health needs. Public accountability around key questions such as what is being done, why and how, who benefits and who is

[107] Recital 2 Directive 2001/83/EC, n 98 above.
[108] Recital 3, ibid.
[109] Art 114(3) TFEU.
[110] B Goldacre, *Big Pharma* (London, Harper Perennial, 2009).

hurt,[111] is therefore undermined. However, as I argued above, attention to framing is a starting point for citizen participation that raises these sorts of questions and, as I go on to show, others that draw attention to concerns around distribution and vulnerability.

C. Informed Consent

Protection of trial participants is especially important as a matter for citizen participation in that it raises questions about vulnerability. These relate to the undermining of human rights and ethical procedural guarantees through their (and trial subjects') instrumentalisation for the production of data that verifies the safety of and permits the marketing of pharmaceuticals. This instrumentalisation is underpinned by the importance of producing and legitimating a European socio-political order based on a more innovative, profitable and competitive pharmaceutical sector in order to foster economic growth, jobs and prosperity through the marketing of safe pharmaceuticals. Attention to individual protections also highlight the EU's role as a global regulator in international technical standard setting for pharmaceuticals, international ethical standards for research on human subjects, and in shaping the broader global regulatory environment and organisation of the global economy.

The involvement of trials subjects must be justified to research ethics committees (REC).[112] At the international level there are several human rights related but primarily ethics-based protections for research subjects,[113] which were largely prompted by the atrocities of World War II and are more specific instantiations of the values and principles found in the Nuremburg Code for the purposes of medical research.[114] Most important is the Helsinki Declaration,[115] which is produced by the World Medical Association (WMA) and has been modified many times, the last time in 2013 by the 64th WMA General Assembly. Under the Helsinki Declaration the creation, refinement and advancement of scientific knowledge—

[111] Eg on claims about justice and access to the benefits of research, see: JP Kahn and others, *Beyond Consent: Seeking Justice in Research* (Oxford, Oxford University Press, 1998).

[112] Institutional review boards in the US. See further: CL Bosk, 'Professional Ethicist Available: Logical, Secular, Friendly. Bioethics and Beyond' (1999) 128(4) *Daedalus* 47; CL Bosk and RG de Vries, 'Bureaucracies of MA Deception: Institutional Review Boards and the Ethics of Ethnographic Research' (2004) 595(1) *Annals of the American Academy of Political and Social Science* 249; J Guillemin, 'Bioethics and the Coming of the Corporation to Medicine' in R de Vries and J Subedi (eds), *Bioethics and Society* (Upper Saddle River NJ, Prentice Hall, 1998).

[113] Reflecting: Universal Declaration of Human Rights (10 December 1948) UNGA Res 217A (III), UN Doc A/810, itself highly influenced by the Nuremberg Code; International Covenant on Civil and Political Rights (16 December 1966, entered into force 23 March 1976) 999 UNTS 171; International Covenant on Economic, Social and Cultural Rights (16 December 1966, entered into force 3 January 1976) 993 UNTS 3; Convention on the Elimination of All Forms of Discrimination against Women (18 December 1979, entered into force 3 September 1981) 1249 UNTS 13; Convention on the Rights of the Child (20 November 1989, entered into force 2 September 1990) 1577 UNTS 3.

[114] GJ Annas and MA Grodin (eds), *The Nazi Doctors and the Nuremburg Code: Human Rights in Human Experimentation* (Oxford, Oxford University Press, 1992).

[115] Declaration of Helsinki: Ethical Principles for Medical Research Involving Human Subjects, available at: www.wma.net/en/30publications/10policies/b3/17c.pdf.

the scientific enterprise[116]—is central to ethics. Indeed, research involving human subjects must seek to produce generalisable knowledge and to '*improve* preventive, diagnostic and therapeutic interventions (methods, procedures and treatments)'.[117] However, the interests of trial subjects must not be subordinated to the interests of society and a calculation of risk and benefit is used to ensure the research subject is not worse off than she would have been otherwise. This narrow utilitarian calculation involves the determination of risk proportionate to anticipated benefit and necessarily entails a degree of guesswork.

This calculation provides an opening for the instrumentalisation of the scientific enterprise for *primarily* commercial ends in that provided the test drug is as good as or at least no worse than existing products it can be marketed. EU law reflects this normative background as part of justifying the enrolment of trial subjects to RECs. The CTD (duplicated in the replacement Regulation) refers to 'the protection of clinical trial subjects—and in particular the weighing of risks and inconveniences with benefits'.[118] There are references to consent throughout the CTD (and now the replacement Regulation)[119] and it is connected with the 'protection of human rights and the dignity of the human being with regard to the application of biology and medicine, as for instance reflected in the 1996 version of the Helsinki Declaration'.[120] The CTD also prohibits the carrying out of obsolete or repetitive tests within the EU or in third countries.[121]

There are also special protections for those 'who are incapable of giving legal consent to clinical trials'.[122] These protections are also apparent in the EU Clinical Trials Register. The Register brings together information on the content, commencement, and termination of clinical trials, subject to rules on confidentiality,[123] which invoke the right to privacy. Data protection legislation[124] is referred to throughout EU clinical trials legislation and guidance. As the CTD puts it, the 'clinical trial subject's protection is safeguarded through risk assessment

[116] HM Marks, *The Progress of Experiment: Science and Therapeutic Reform in the United States, 1900–90* (Cambridge, Cambridge University Press, 1997).

[117] Declaration of Helsinki, para 7.

[118] Art 3 Directive 2001/20/EC, n 103 above. Broadly duplicated in Art 3 Regulation (EU) 536/2014, n 103 above.

[119] Recitals 3, 4 and 16 and Arts 2–5 Directive 2001/20/EC, ibid. Also see Recitals 6, 29 and 30 and Arts 28–32 Regulation (EU) 536/2014, ibid.

[120] Recital 2 Directive 2001/20/EC, ibid. Also see Recital 27 Regulation (EU) 536/2014, ibid.

[121] Recital 6 Directive 2001/20/EC, ibid.

[122] Recitals 3 and 4 Directive 2001/20/EC, ibid. Eg Recital 3 reads that they should be included in clinical trials only 'when there are grounds for expecting that the administering of the medicinal product would be of direct benefit to the patient, thereby outweighing the risks'. Also see Recitals 19 and 27 Regulation (EU) 536/2014, ibid.

[123] Recital 9 and Art 11(3) Directive 2001/20/EC, ibid. Also see Recitals 66 and 67 and Arts 37 and 81 Regulation (EU) 536/2014, ibid.

[124] Directive 95/46/EC on the protection of individuals with regard to the processing of personal data and on the free movement of such data [1995] OJ L281/31. Regulation (EU) 2016/679 on the protection of natural persons with regard to the processing of personal data and on the free movement of such data, and repealing Directive 95/46/EC (General Data Protection Regulation) OJ 2016 L 119/1, entered into force on 24 May 2016, but will not apply until 25 May 2018.

based on the results of toxicological experiments prior to any clinical trial, screening by ethics committees and Member States' competent authorities, and rules on the protection of personal data'.[125]

The CTD (and the replacement Regulation) also requires the Commission to establish principles of GCP and detailed rules in line with those principles.[126] GCP is:

> [A] set of *internationally recognised ethical and scientific quality requirements* which must be observed for designing, conducting, recording and reporting clinical trials that involve the participation of human subjects. Compliance with this good practice provides assurance that the rights, safety and well-being of trial subjects are protected, and that the results of the clinical trials are credible.[127] (Emphasis added)

These rules are in fact established by the EMA[128] in accordance with the International Council on Harmonisation of Technical Requirements for Registration of Pharmaceuticals for Human Use (ICH)[129] standards. ICH standards provide a unified standard for the EU, Japan and the US that facilitates the mutual acceptance of clinical data between their respective regulatory authorities (and beyond to those jurisdictions that have little or no regulatory capacity).[130] This helps to avoid duplicating trials of new medicines and consequent inefficiency and increased costs. Under the CTD (and the replacement Regulation) clinical trials must be designed, conducted, and reported in accordance with GCP,[131] and this is again framed in terms of risk.

Concern with risk is apparent through the additional requirements relating to the investigational medicinal product used in the clinical trial, detailed requirements of data collection and handling, and provisions on inspections mechanisms. Under GCP the rights of individual trial subjects are framed as being about their protection from risk and the first principle is that 'The rights, safety and well being of the trial subjects shall prevail over the interests of science and society'.[132] The relationship between risk and markets becomes acutely apparent here: the CTD (and indeed the replacement Regulation and the detailed guidance based upon it) refers to the marketing of safe pharmaceuticals as its underlying rationale.[133] The overall thrust is towards getting new and safe products to market in order to produce consumer confidence in their quality, safety and efficacy, and in the ethics and rights dimensions of their production.

[125] Recital 2 Directive 2001/20/EC, n 103 above.

[126] Art 1(3) and 8 Directive 2001/20/EC, ibid. Also see Recital 43 Regulation (EU) 536/2014, n 103 above.

[127] Art 1(2) Directive 2001/20/EC, ibid. Also see Art 2(2)(30) Regulation (EU) 536/2014, n 103 above.

[128] EMA, *E6: Guideline for Good Clinical Practice*, CPMP/ICH/135/95. Also see: 'Inspections procedure' www.emea.europa.eu/ema/index.jsp?curl=pages/regulation/document_listing/document_listing_000140.jsp&mid=WC0b01ac05800296c6.

[129] 'International Conference on Harmonisation of Technical Requirements for Registration of Pharmaceuticals for Human Use' www.ich.org/.

[130] World Health Organisation (WHO), *Effective Medicines Regulation: Ensuring Safety, Efficacy and Quality, WHO Policy Perspectives on Medicines* (Geneva, WHO, 2003).

[131] Also see Art 47 Regulation (EU) 536/2014, n 103 above.

[132] Art 2(1) Directive 2005/28/EC n 164 below. Art 3(a) Regulation (EU) 536/2014, ibid, provides that a clinical trial may be conducted only if 'the rights, safety, dignity and well-being of subjects are protected and *prevail over all other interests*' (emphasis added).

[133] Recital 3 Directive 2001/20/EC, ibid and Recital 11 Regulation (EU) 536/2014, ibid.

Despite the centrality of consent in protecting trial participants, its specific formulation in EU law is problematic. One concern is that consent often seems to be seen as a one-time event rather than as a continual process requiring ongoing renewal. Consent also functions to protect medical researchers from claims for compensation under the law of tort,[134] which makes it a key way of avoiding liability in the event of adverse effects or negligence.[135] The focus on consent can also stymie ongoing reflection on the wider social and ethical implications of biomedical labour too. Even as ethical discourse (on consent and GCP) continues to operate those wider considerations are effectively side-lined.[136] Consequently, the focus on informed consent seems overly narrow, not least because it misses key aspects of what makes a fully informed choice about participation. For example, the wider purpose and social, political and economic value of the knowledge produced is also important but not required. These matters are arguably no more difficult and are perhaps easier to convey to prospective participants than potential benefits and risks.[137] Yet, bringing these wider factors to the attention of prospective participants is probably insufficient. This is because in Phase II and III trials abroad (in particular) participants are usually incentivised by the possibility of gaining access to health care they would not otherwise receive. Consequently, wider systematic matters should be considered in the determination of whether a trial is ethical as well as broader reforms (discussed later).

Consideration of clinical trials abroad brings these more general problems around consent into even sharper relief, for example, because it can be harder to ensure participants understand the information provided to them.[138] The idea of randomisation is particularly hard to convey. There might also be a 'therapeutic misconception'[139]—a misunderstanding that the trial is not part of standard care.[140] And the very idea of consent, especially its withdrawal at any time, might not readily translate to societies in which individual autonomy is less important than group decisions.[141] Where the trial is effectively a substitute for health care voluntariness can also be undermined.

Overall, consent is detached from the scientific enterprise, and within the framing of risk its main function is in supporting the EU's regulation of pharmaceuticals in order to ensure their safety, rather than in meeting public health needs. Ethics

[134] Eg the standard for professional liability in English tort law is notoriously high (*Bolam v Friern Hospital Management Committee* [1957] 1 WLR 582), although it has gradually become less so (*Bolitho v City and Hackney Health Authority* [1997] 4 All ER 771). Art 3(2)(f) Directive 2001/20/EC, n 103 above, requires 'provision has been made for insurance or indemnity to cover the liability of the investigator and sponsor' before any clinical trial is undertaken.

[135] Petryna, *When Experiments Travel* n 91 above, 77.

[136] M Pickersgill, 'The Co-Production of Science, Ethics, and Emotion' (2012) 37(6) *Science, Technology & Human Values* 579.

[137] H Jonas, 'Philosophical Reflections on Human Experimentation' (1969) 98 *Daedalus* 219.

[138] C Pace and others, 'Quality of Parental Consent in a Ugandan Malaria Study' (2005) 95 *American Journal of Public Health* 1184.

[139] PS Appelbaum and others, 'The Therapeutic Misconception: Informed Consent in Psychiatric Research' (1982) 5(3–4) *International Journal of Law and Psychiatry* 319.

[140] N Lynöe and others, 'Obtaining Informed Consent in Bangladesh' (2001) 344 *New England Journal of Medicine* 460.

[141] Nuffield Council on Bioethics, *The Ethics of Research Related Healthcare in Developing Countries* (London, Nuffield Council on Bioethics, 2002) para 6.22.

and protections are reduced to legitimating devices through their support and justification of market-oriented risk regulation undergirded, shaped and directed at producing a more innovative, profitable and competitive pharmaceutical sector in order to foster economic growth, jobs and prosperity. This is of course unsurprisingly in light of the defining features of the public health domain.[142] The focus on consent and GCP also abstracts the research subject[143] from social context while also freighting it with responsibility. This in turn limits the responsibilities and accountabilities of those carrying out trials, the EU as the regulator that uses the data produced in order to authorise the marketing of products on safety grounds, and the corporations who ultimately profit.

D. Designing Clinical Trials

Another opening and possibility for citizen participation is around the design of clinical trials—and it is already a reality with activists and scientists working together in order to query the reliability and validity of existing data and fashion alternative treatment guidelines.[144] What makes trial protocol design so important is its scope for manipulation in order to meet the already market friendly criteria for market authorisation. Querying trial design helps to bring out further concerns around framing, distribution and vulnerability. These could ultimately threaten to destabilise and delegitimate the EU's imagined identity, socio-political order and project of rule—but by undermining the availability and marketability of pharmaceuticals, (potential for) their innovation and a growing reputable industry.

Manipulation of trial design also raises questions over the scientific quality of the data produced. Since that means it becomes harder to justify the trial and, therefore, the involvement of research subjects, the scientific quality of data is a key ethical issue. Despite this the focus of REC approval tends to be limited to ensuring informed consent and GCP.[145] The limited scope of REC work facilitates market aims, but threatens to undermine public health aims. The skewing of trial design is supported by the increasing importance of contract research organisations (or CROs) in the performance of clinical trials, including in 'sourcing' compliant research subjects.[146] In this way private corporate interests have further

[142] See the summary of the features in ch 6.

[143] M-A Jacob, 'Form-Made Persons: Consent Forms as Consent's Blind Spot' (2007) 30(2) *Political and Legal Anthropology Review* 249. See further: M-A Jacob and A Riles, 'The New Bureaucracies of Virtue: Introduction' (2007) 30(2) *Political and Legal Anthropology Review* 181.

[144] See: Petryna, *When Experiments Travel*, n 91 above, ch 4 on pharmaceuticals and the right to health. More widely, in relation to the AIDS epidemic, in the early days US activists proved successful in focusing on the biomedical sciences and changing drug testing conventions and licensing, which accelerated the development of ARVs. See: S Epstein, *Impure Science* (Berkeley CA, University of California Press 1996).

[145] For discussion see: Jackson n 99 above, 43–47.

[146] JA Fisher, 'Coordinating "Ethical" Clinical Trials: The Role of Research Coordinators in the Contract Research Industry' (2006) 27 *Sociology of Health & Illness* 678. On compliant research subjects see: JA Fisher, *Medical Research for Hire: The Political Economy of Pharmaceutical Clinical Trials* (New Brunswick NJ, Rutgers University Press, 2009).

scope to compromise the gathering and production of knowledge that underpins the regulation of public health.

A related problem is that the focus on consent and GCP does not attend to how subjects are found, mobilised and used in trials in ways that produce the most favourable and authorisation friendly risk profiles for new drugs.[147] The *source* of clinical trials data is therefore a central concern for citizen participation. As Nguyen explains the 'Transnational socioeconomic inequalities, and the gradients of disease and inequity in access to health care that are associated with them, may unwittingly *produce ideal conditions for the conduct of clinical research that furthers … the pharmaceutical industry*' (emphasis added).[148] Particularly important factors that make subjects usable for trials that are geared towards generating the most favourable data include the vulnerability of populations identified through biological indicators produced by epidemiology (the science of prevention) and their lack of exposure to pharmaceuticals ie because those options tend to be unavailable. However, clinical trials abroad tend to be performed using the approach to medicine taken in colonial and post-colonial settings in which medicine is a technique of social control of whole populations rather than being for the benefit of individuals and the population.[149] The focus in the authorisation of clinical trials on procedural matters implies there is a break between ethics and empirical reality,[150] and that provides the scope for the revision of ethics in light of market needs.

Further, the epidemiologically convenient groups often found in the global South are usually treatment naïve and are more likely to demonstrate benefit from treatment, which can help to mask harms or so-called 'adverse events'.[151] Those most likely to benefit from treatment can be selected for inclusion in the trial while those who are least likely to benefit can be excluded.[152] Those who are most likely to use the treatment (if market authorisation is granted and treatment is accessible) might also not be selected for the trial where, say, they are less likely to comply with the instructions and therefore undermine the demonstration of efficacy.[153] Further, any harms that arise during and post-trial (including post-market

[147] S Sismondo, 'How Pharmaceutical Industry Funding Affects Trial Outcomes: Causal Structures and Responses' (2008) 66 *Social Science & Medicine* 1909.

[148] V-K Nguyen, 'Antiretroviral Globalism, Biopolitics, and Therapeutic Citizenship' in A Ong and SJ Collier (eds), *Global Assemblages* (Oxford, Blackwell Publishing, 2005) 139.

[149] W Anderson, *The Cultivation of Whiteness: Science, Health, and Racial Destiny in Australia* (New York NY, Basic Books, 2003); D Arnold, *Colonising the Body: State Medicine and Epidemic Disease in Nineteenth-Century India* (Berkeley CA, University of California Press, 1993); J Biehl, *Vita: Life in a Zone of Social Abandonment* (Berkeley CA, University of California Press, 2003); RJ Prince and R Marsland, *Making and Unmaking Public Health in Africa: Ethnographic and Historical Perspectives* (Athens OH, Ohio University Press, 2013); M Vaughan, *Curing Their Ills: Colonial Power and African Illness* (Stanford CA, Stanford University Press, 1992).

[150] Jonas n 137 above.

[151] Petryna, *When Experiments Travel* n 91 above, 25.

[152] P Farahani and others, 'Clinical Data Gap between Phase III Clinical Trials (Pre-Marketing) and Phase IV (Post-Marketing) Studies: Evaluation of Etanercept in Rheumatoid Arthritis' (2005) 12 *Canadian Journal of Clinical Pharmacology* 254.

[153] VJ Burroughs, 'Racial and Ethnic Inclusiveness in Clinical Trials in Ethics and the Pharmaceutical Industry' in MA Santoro and TM Gorrie (eds), *Ethics and the Pharmaceutical Industry* (Cambridge, Cambridge University Press, 2005).

authorisation) can be explained away as due to environmental factors. In these sorts of ways generalisable data might not be produced and the primary aim of the clinical trial (ie the production of generalisable knowledge) is undermined.[154]

The choice of the control for a clinical trial provides another way to hide or explain away harms—and to avoid responsibility and accountability. For example, the benefits, effectiveness and safety of a trial drug can be flattered by using an ineffective treatment as the control,[155] or a placebo, too high a dose of an existing drug in order to produce adverse events, or too low a dose of an existing drug.[156] It is also possible to prevent the emergence of harms by shortening the trial length. As Petryna points out, research with trials subjects and researchers has underscored the ways in which 'protection and safety considerations are weighed against immediate health benefits or the knowledge to be gained. Ethics and method are modified to fit the local context and experimental data required'.[157]

Apart from trial design, another area for citizen participation is in demanding and contesting current practices of knowledge dissemination, which are again dominated and shaped by private corporate interests. That dominance seems to explain the non-publication of results and under-reporting of negative results.[158] Consequently there might be insufficient information provided to trial subjects on existing options and their safety, the necessity of the trial, and societal benefit that follows from dissemination of trial results, all of which can undermine informed consent. A related problem is the way in which positive results are reported more than once, a problem that is magnified where results are picked up again in meta-analyses, and all of which distort the evidence base. The current system for vetting results is also inadequate: the journals where results are published often lack adequate and robust systems of peer review that can ensure the scientific rigor of trials. There are also good reasons to think that the dependency of journals on advertising by industry undermines their detachment and ability to perform a robust review. This conflict of interest implies the scientific enterprise is effectively reduced to servicing market needs for market authorisation and beyond that the advertising and sale of pharmaceuticals.[159] To reflect on the implications for healthcare providers *within* the EU, these distortions skew funding decisions—and that implies a skewing in the distribution of scarce resources.

The inadequate evidence base for market authorisation and decisions on the funding of treatment is abetted by the absence of a worldwide clinical trials

[154] Petryna n 91 above.

[155] HK Johansen and PC Gotzsche, 'Problems in the Design and Reporting of Trials of Antifungal Agents Encountered During Meta-Analysis' (1999) 282 *Journal of the American Medical Association* 1752.

[156] J Safer, 'Design and Reporting Modifications in Industry-Sponsored Comparative Psychopharmacology Trials' (2002) 190 *Journal of Nervous and Mental Disease* 583.

[157] A Petryna, 'Clinical Trials Offshored: On Private Sector Science and Public Health' (2007) 2 *BioSocieties* 21, 24.

[158] CW Jones and others, 'Non-Publication of Large Randomised Clinical Trials: Cross Sectional Analysis' (2013) 347 *British Medical Journal* doi: dx.doi.org/10.1136/bmj.f6104.

[159] For extensive discussion see: Jackson n 99 above, 50–56.

registry (required by the Helsinki Declaration)[160] and, more importantly for this book, limitations to the EU's own registry (the registry was noted above). Under the CTD's regime the EU's registry makes it possible for users to view, in particular, the summary of results of Phase-II to Phase-IV clinical trials in adults, but only where the investigator sites are in the EU or European Economic Area (EEA) (the exception being, for example, commercially sensitive information)[161] (see the Preface for a note on the implications of the new Regulation). Overall, EU law helps to maintain and even facilitates and sanctions the production of a skewed, incomplete and ethically dubious evidence base that eases market authorisation for pharmaceuticals that are not significant innovations and for which there is no need.

E. Using Placebos in Clinical Trials Abroad

Placebos have a particularly important role to play in RCTs and, as I go on to explain, they therefore deserve specific attention through citizen participation since they are a key way of using trial design in order to produce the most favourable results for the purposes of market authorisation. When used with an active control arm a placebo control arm can improve reliability of data by showing that a new drug and the existing drug both work. The Community code states:

> In general, clinical trials shall be done as controlled clinical trials, and if possible, randomized; any other design shall be justified. *The treatment of the control groups will vary from case to case and also will depend on ethical considerations*; thus it may, in some instances, be more pertinent to compare the efficacy of a new medicinal product with that of an established medicinal product of proven therapeutic value rather than with the effect of a placebo.[162] (Emphasis added)

In light of the history of abuse, often among marginalised and vulnerable populations,[163] placebo use is subject to quite extensive regulation on GCP.[164] Commenting on offshored clinical trials the European Group on Ethics in Science and New Technologies (EGE) notes:

> The use of placebos should be regulated in developing countries *in principle by the same rules* as in European countries. *Any exception must be justified*: an obvious one is when

[160] Para 19.

[161] The replacement of Directive 2001/20/EC, n 103 above, by Regulation (EU) 536/2014, n 103 above, is designed to increase transparency. The EMA currently only provides access to summaries of clinical trials data once the decision-making process on market authorisation has been completed, see further: 'Release of data from clinical trials' www.ema.europa.eu/ema/index.jsp?curl=pages/special_topics/general/general_content_000555.jsp.

[162] Annex 1, Pt 4, F, 1, Directive 2001/83/EC, n 98 above.

[163] FD Gray, *The Tuskegee Syphilis Study* (Montgomery AL, New South Press, 2013).

[164] Directive 2001/20/EC, n 103 above; Directive 2005/28/EC laying down principles and detailed guidelines for good clinical practice as regards investigational medicinal products for human use, as well as the requirements for authorisation of the manufacturing or importation of such products [2005] OJ L91/13.

> the primary goal of the clinical trial is to try to simplify or to decrease the costs of treatment for countries where the standard treatment is not available for logistic reasons or inaccessible because of the cost. It *may thus be justified to derogate from the rule of best proven treatment. The justification of using a placebo must be clearly demonstrated in the research protocol* submitted to the ethical committees and especially approved by the local committee.[165] (Emphasis added)

In other words, the default position is to use the best proven treatment as the control *unless* there is a reason for using a placebo. It would likely be unethical to treat a person who is newly diagnosed as HIV positive with a placebo instead of a new anti-retroviral drug or the best proven treatment. However, randomly allocating such a person to either a new anti-retroviral drug or the best proven treatment (the active or the control arm of a study) would not leave her worse off than if she had not been enrolled and been given the standard treatment.

The EGE's opinion supports the EMA's soft law guidance on the use of placebo control in clinical trials abroad, which refers to the International Ethical Guidelines for Biomedical Research Involving Human Subjects (CIOMS Guidelines for short) produced by the WHO and the Council for International Organisations of Medical Sciences[166] (aimed at applying the Helsinki Declaration in developing countries)[167] as well as ICH guidance outlined below. However, the EGE also explains that a 'clinical trial cannot be justified ethically *unless it is capable of producing scientifically reliable results*' and that placebo can be acceptable provided 'the rights, safety and wellbeing of the trials subjects are the most important considerations and should prevail over the interests of science and society' (emphasis added).[168] Further, 'EU Regulatory Authorities *should neither require nor accept study designs*, involving placebo or other comparator, which would not be ethically acceptable *in* the [European Economic Area or] EEA' (emphasis added).[169] Throughout the stress is on justifying placebo use regardless of where the trial is carried out in order to prevent abuse.

Nevertheless, given that placebo use is more prevalent in industry-sponsored trials these ethical requirements do not appear particularly onerous.[170] Indeed, placebo use seems useful for the commercial imperative of producing data for market authorisation. It is noted that, 'Regardless of the location of the trial, all

[165] EGE, *Opinion on the Ethical Aspects of Clinical Research in Developing Countries* (Opinion No 17), para 2.10.

[166] CIOMS Guidelines 8 and 11.

[167] That is, 'given their socioeconomic circumstances, laws and regulations, and executive and administrative arrangements'. The Council's name gives the Guidelines their abbreviated name of CIOMS. The Guidelines have been updated twice, the last time being in 2002. See further: www.cioms.ch/publications/guidelines/guidelines_nov_2002_blurb.htm.

[168] EMA, *Reflection Paper on Ethical and GCP Aspects of Clinical Trials of Medicinal Products for Human Use Conducted Outside of the EU/EEA and Submitted in Marketing Authorisation Applications to the EU Regulatory Authorities*, EMA/121340/2011, 26.

[169] Ibid.

[170] B Djulbegovic and others, 'The Uncertainty Principle and Industry-Sponsored Research' (2000) 356 *The Lancet* 635.

patients participating in these trials should receive *the same or a similar standard of care and comparable treatment options* as trial participants within the EEA' (emphasis added).[171] The focus on similarity or comparability provides scope for placebo-controlled trials in countries that do not have access to the best EEA (or indeed global) standard of care or treatment, but where local equivalents can be said to provide 'similarity' or 'comparability'. This creates the opportunity for a double standard that is the best treatment in the EEA and placebo elsewhere. The double standard might be justifiable where it leads to locally affordable options.[172] Yet, as the two members of the EGE mentioned above have observed,[173] this is unlikely given patent protection of pharmaceuticals under the Agreement on Trade-Related Aspects of Intellectual Property Rights (TRIPS),[174] which is a central part of the EU's trade policy and aligned to the programmatic priorities and aims found in the overarching architecture of EU governance. That said, the permissibility of such trials adds further reductions in costs to the other attractions attendant to carrying out clinical trials abroad (such as their populations), making them even more attractive.[175]

These examples also point to how international ethical standards are (re)aligned to the EU's regulatory processes and aims. Those standards are (de)selected and occasionally reworked so as to ensure their continued alignment and relevance to market authorisation. But this subordinates and undermines the protections for research subjects and ensures their vulnerability is made usable for market authorisation purposes. The EU has been notable in (de)selecting international ethical standards in preference to the international technical standards it co-creates. In response to the 2000 version of the Helsinki Declaration the EMA[176] noted its position that upon a 'strict interpretation … [it] appears to rule out clinical trials

[171] EMA n 168 above, 27.

[172] RK Lie and others, 'The Standard of Care Debate: The Declaration of Helsinki Versus the International Consensus Option' (2004) *Journal of Medical Ethics* 190.

[173] EGE n 165 above, para 2.10.

[174] Marrakesh Agreement Establishing the World Trade Organisation, opened for signature 15 April 1994, 1867 UNTS 3, Annex 1C (Agreement on Trade-Related Aspects of Intellectual Property Rights) (entered into force 1 January 1995) (TRIPS). This agreement is enforceable via the WTO's Understanding on Dispute Settlement. Least developed countries do not have to implement TRIPS until 2016. The EU and its Member States are all members as required by their membership of the World Trade Organisation. WTO Member States agree to recognise one single global patent that lasts 20 years and to forbid generic equivalents of the patented drug from entering the marketplace during that period. Under TRIPS it is for Member States to determine what deserves to be patented, and as such countries in the industrialised global North, ie where the biggest producers of pharmaceuticals have their homes, are effectively able to export their patent protections.

[175] M Landes, 'Can Context Justify an Ethical Double Standard for Clinical Research in Developing Countries?' (2005) 1 *Globalisation and Health* 11; U Schüklenk, 'The Standard of Care Debate: Against the Myth of an "International Consensus Opinion"' (2004) 30 *Journal of Medical Ethics* 194. One study found that 'only 16% of the trials conducted in resource-poor settings provided therapy that could be considered consistent with the best current standard of care, even when the Declaration of Helsinki required that standard'. See: D Kent and others, 'Clinical Trials in Sub-Saharan Africa and Established Standards of Care: A Systematic Review of HIV, Tuberculosis, and Malaria Trials' (2004) 292(2) *Journal of the American Medical Association* 237, 241.

[176] As the European Medicines Evaluation Agency—it lost mention of 'evaluation' in 2009.

that use a placebo control arm whenever authorised therapeutic methods already exist, preferring active controls'.[177]

While legally-speaking non-binding the value of the Helsinki Declaration is noted—'it remains *a vital expression* of medical ethics whose *aims* deserve unanimous support' (emphasis added)[178]—but strict compliance was no longer possible since its content frustrated the use of placebo, which in turn threatened to undermine market authorisations. The content of Helsinki lost its regulatory relevance even as support for its aims remained useful for the legitimation of the EU's governance. This position was reinforced by the stress on the ICH E10 guideline (which permits placebo use), but the EU's manoeuvring has tended to be missed in most extant analyses.[179] The approach of the EU and US is the same in this respect: the US has actually broken with the advisory guidance offered by the Helsinki Declaration,[180] and, like the EU, preferred that of the ICH itself.

The ICH standard supports the EU's view that placebo use can be ethical: 'the efficacy of some new medicinal products can be satisfactorily demonstrated without the use of a placebo, [but] for others the judicious use of placebo remains essential to demonstrate their value'. Specifically, 'trials that seek to prove that a new agent and an active control have *similar efficacy* are inherently less reliable than trials that seek to prove the superiority of the new agent to a comparator, whether inactive or active' (emphasis added).[181] Increasing the size of a trial does not reduce this problem and so without a placebo the only alternative is superiority trials—and these require the demonstration of increased efficacy over a currently authorised treatment. But of course this is *not* required for market authorisation. Moreover, the EMA notes that a need for increased efficacy 'may be *too* restrictive' (emphasis added)[182] and 'contrary to public health interest as there is a need for both new products and alternatives to existing medicinal products'.[183]

There can of course be a need for alternative treatments, but this focus obscures how *genuine* need is not important for market authorisation purposes: new drugs can be as good as or at least not substantially worse than existing products. This framing abets the (de)selection of international ethical standards with the effective replacement of the Helsinki Declaration in preference to the international technical standards co-authored by the EU and its partners. This prompted the (re)shaping of the former in an effort to maintain regulatory relevance.[184] Nevertheless, the (de)selection of ethics points to their

[177] EMEA, *EMEA/CPMP Position Statement on the Use of Placebo in Clinical Trials with Regard to the Revised Declaration of Helsinki*, EMEA/17424/01, 1.

[178] Ibid, 1.

[179] See further: 'Good clinical practice compliance' www.ema.europa.eu/ema/index.jsp?curl=pages/regulation/general/general_content_000072.jsp.

[180] US Food and Drug Administration, 'Human Subject Protection; Foreign Clinical Studies Not Conducted under an Investigational New Drug Application—Notice of Final Rule', see: www.regulations.gov/#!documentDetail;D=FDA-2004-N-0061-0002;oldLink=false.

[181] EMEA n 177 above, 1.

[182] Ibid, 1–2.

[183] Ibid, 2.

[184] In 2008 the Helsinki Declaration was revised such that para 33 now clarifies and provides increased scope for placebo use and, for present purposes, EU law is arguably in-line with it.

importance as a focus for citizen participation in decision-making, in that while negotiable, they play an important role in legitimating the EU's market-oriented regulatory processes, wider socio-political order and project of rule. In short, highlighting the double standard in the application of ethics, the (de)selection of standards in order to suit regulatory preferences, and finally the link with the EU's broader market oriented trade agenda (via TRIPS), work together in widening the opening for participation through the possibility that the concerns raised constitute supplementary knowledge that might delegitimate the EU's identity and project of integration—and impel the (re)shaping and perhaps (re)framing as a matter of bioethics rather than risk and market optimisation.

F. Clinical Trials Abroad and the European and Developing Countries Clinical Trials Partnership

Widening the space for citizen participation in decision-making requires emphasis on the wider significance of clinical trials for the EU's market driven agenda. The European and Developing Countries Clinical Trials Partnership (Partnership),[185] which was mentioned earlier in the book,[186] seeks to facilitate clinical trials abroad and on the surface it does not appear to be related to economic optimisation in the same way as the regime traced above. Instead, the Partnership is ostensibly geared towards addressing the 10/90 research gap, which describes how only 10 per cent of global health research is spent on problems that affect 90 per cent of the global population.[187] But further reflection reveals some concerns for the distribution of attention and resources in research funding and the vulnerability of those enrolled. For example, the available material on the Partnership does not contain explicit mention of protections in addition to those in the CTD and the replacement Regulation (such as the otherwise largely marginalised (within EU law) CIOMS guidelines), and given the foregoing discussion those seem necessary in order to protect research subjects in developing countries. The Partnership is supported by EU research funding and as such it should be viewed in light of the normative orientation and direction of the EU's overarching architecture and programmatic concerns, especially moves to prompt innovation and its facilitation by Europe 2020's so-called Horizon 2020 funding programme.[188] As discussed earlier in this book, the general thrust is towards producing economic value from research that promotes innovation in Europe.[189]

[185] 'European and Developing Countries Clinical Trials Partnership' www.edctp.org/. Introduced in ch 4.

[186] See ch 4.

[187] Global Forum for Health Research, *The 10/90 Gap in Health Research* (Geneva, GFHR, 1999).

[188] European Commission, *Towards a European Research Area*, COM (2000) 6 final; European Commission, *Putting Knowledge into Practice: A Broad-based Innovation Strategy for the EU*, COM (2006) 502 final. For discussion, see: G Bache, ML Flear and TK Hervey, 'The Defining Features of the European Union's Approach to Regulating New Health Technologies' in ML Flear and others (eds), *European Law and New Health Technologies* (Oxford, Oxford University Press, 2013).

[189] See ch 2 with further discussion and reflection on the Partnership in ch 4.

Against this background an important function of the Partnership seems to be exporting and installing clinical trials infrastructures abroad, especially through the training of research personnel outside the EU. Of course, these are and should prove of benefit to the wider community,[190] particularly where the trial drug is needed (a calculation that can take away from the individual's capacity to decide whether to participate). Nevertheless, the Partnership and its benefits also help to perpetuate the use of the data produced for market authorisation, drives towards innovation *within* the EU's internal market, and it supports private objectives of augmenting corporate profitability. Despite the local benefits that might follow from the Partnership and wider humanitarian and philanthropic efforts aimed at widening access,[191] TRIPS ensures that *global* access to essential pharmaceuticals is undermined by the unequal global trade system that produces the vulnerability that the Partnership seeks to address. As the aforementioned two members of the EGE have pointed out, clinical trials in developing countries might 'contribute to developing new treatments which can be patented in rich countries and are then *unaffordable for poor countries*, and on the other hand *the non-availability of treatment in the poorest countries is due partly to the patent costs*' (emphasis added).[192]

In other words, the increasing use of clinical trials data produced using research subjects in the global South for the patenting, production and marketing of medicines in the global North is even more problematic in light of the EU's trade policy and the unequal and unjust global regulatory environment it perpetuates and represents.[193] The global trade system is produced and sustained in part by the EU's trade policy, which undercuts the flexibilities on access to patent protected medicines under TRIPS. Here the discussion moves into pharmaceuticals and I shall discuss these, TRIPS and its relations with clinical trials, as well as the broader overarching architecture of EU governance and its programmatic concerns, in the next and final substantive chapter.

[190] EJ Emanuel, 'Addressing Exploitation: Reasonable Availability Versus Fair Benefits' in JS Hawkins and EJ Emanuel (eds), *Exploitation and Developing Countries: The Ethics of Clinical Research* (Princeton NJ, Princeton University Press, 2008).

[191] Such as the WHO's essential drugs list, the Global Fund, and the Gate Foundation's support of the latter and other initiatives. For discussion see: JA Greene, 'Making Medicines Essential: The Emergent Centrality of Pharmaceuticals in Global Health' (2011) 6 *BioSocieties* 10; T Yamada, 'Global Health and the Bill and Melinda Gates Foundation' (2009) 373 *The Lancet* 2195.

[192] EGE n 165 above, para 2.10.

[193] For discussion see: SR Benatar, 'Distributive Justice and Clinical Trials in the Third World' (2001) 22(3) *Theoretical Medicine and Bioethics* 169; SR Benatar and PA Singer, 'A New Look at International Research Ethics' (2000) 321 *British Medical Journal* 824; P Farmer, 'Can Transnational Research Be Ethical in the Developing World?' (2002) 360 *Lancet* 1301; DJ Rothman, 'The Shame of Medical Research' (2000) 47 *New York Review of Books* 60; U Schuklenk and R Ashcroft, 'International Research Ethics' (2000) 14(2) *Bioethics* 158.

G. Contesting Regulatory Design and Demanding Redesign

Much of the discussion over the course of this section has drawn attention to the way in which a number of related points—informed consent, the use of data from trials carried out abroad, designing trial protocols and more specifically the role of placebos—highlight concerns around distribution and vulnerability. Through the unequal protections the vulnerability of those enrolled in trials (now governed and subjects of EU law, whether they are within the EU or abroad) is marginalised and effectively erased, but rendered usable for market authorisation and private commercial purposes. The market-friendly ethics sketched above provide weak(er) protections for subjects enrolled in trials abroad. These ethics work to authorise the continued and growing use of the data produced through those trials for market authorisation and corporate profitability in the EU, while access for those where the data was produced remains stymied by global patent rules (under TRIPS). At the same time the EU's responsibilities and accountabilities are limited to safety matters (such as adverse reactions to medicines), to the exclusion of others (such as distortions in public health governance attendant to risk and the wider limits on accessing pharmaceuticals).

Crucially, the concerns outlined are attendant to risk as the framing that underpins the EU's regulatory technology governing public health and that constitutes the policy domain. EU law and its pharmaceuticals regime are part of that broader neoliberal technology: they function to optimise the circulation of people and things (pharmaceuticals and clinical trials data as the basis for their marketing) and tackle the attendant dangers through risk regulation (with clinical trials data being central to the safety of pharmaceuticals). The concerns discussed in this section are, therefore, products of governance and regulatory design, and they are often explicitly related to ethics. Citizen participation that draws attention to these concerns by reference to and articulation through bioethics especially when linked to human rights, and underscored by reference to the failure to meet (supra-)stewardship responsibilities for the provision of health care for all and especially the individuals enfolded in the EU's regime (via access to the result of research), could generate key 'institutional risks' to the EU's standing and reputation.

Citizen participation entails demanding and contesting several aspects of the current design of governance (and not simply decision-making within the governance structures), which I summarise from the above discussion in order to make a few proposals for redesign. Perhaps foremost among them is the criteria for market authorisation, which should be revised by the Commission and the EU legislature (on top of the Clinical Trials Regulation), so that it is more consistent with the high level of health protection required by Article 114(3) TFEU and Article 9 TFEU—and for that matter Article 35 EU Charter and Article 168(1) TFEU. Revision of the market authorisation criteria could entail the drafting of criteria that require the demonstration of 'comparative therapeutic efficacy' and genuine need for the new pharmaceutical—in place of the current focus on safety and efficacy. The reliance on CROs for the performance of clinical trials and the insinuation of market logic into *their* design indicates that there should be a new independent regulator with distance from the pharmaceutical industry.

The justification for clinical trials could also be tightened up: where improved 'therapeutic efficacy' and genuine need for the new pharmaceutical are not the objective then the trial should not be justified by a REC, which means that data would not be produced and market authorisation would not follow. Informed consent to participation in trials could also be bolstered so as to enhance the protections for often vulnerable research subjects by requiring there is a genuine need and hoped for 'comparative therapeutic efficacy' for the pharmaceutical being trialed. Participants should also be told whether post-trial access for themselves and their wider communities will be undermined in the event of successful auhorisation (patents make this very likely).

Citizen participation around the EMA's soft law guidance on the design of trials could also emphasise the need for tightening up so that it is less open to contingent and exploitative behaviours by the private commercial actors (usually CROs) that locate research subjects and perform the trials (at home or abroad). Since the design of trials and the scientific quality of the data likely to be produced are key ethical issues, citizen participation could pressure for them to become central to the work of RECs, particularly if the issue becomes whether the trial data demonstrates *comparative* efficacy, quality and safety. Citizens could also leverage the EU's existing efforts to increase the transparency in the results of clinical trials by demanding the obligation should apply to those trials performed *outside* the EU and not just those carried out *within* the EU. Finally, citizen participation around clinical trials needs to extend towards the systematic links with the EU's broader trade agenda and its role and position in terms of the overarching architecture of governance. As noted above the trade agenda is a matter for the next chapter, and I return to this final point there.

V. CONCLUSION

This chapter looked first at framing and subsequently the gathering and production of knowledge by reference to indicators and clinical trials. Through these two examples (the former as something of a stepping stone for the more extensive discussion of the latter) I pointed to the co-productive relations between framing and knowledge and traced related key normative issues around framing, distribution and vulnerability. The discussion underscores the extent to which the structuring themes of the public health policy domain—between knowledge and power, sovereignty and territoriality, and power and responsibility, and finally an introduction to the (re)configuration between governance and the governed—underpin and support the extension and dissemination of market rationality and with it commercial interests into knowledge creation, dissemination and use. Knowledge not only supports risk as the central framing of EU public health governance, it is also central to attempts at delineating and mediating responsibilities through risk. Knowledge reflects and supports the attention to a focus on regulating the dangers or threats attendant to the circulation of people and things. Knowledge is, therefore, a crucial battleground for citizen demands and contestation.

These normative dimensions are usually latent within scientific and technical discourses supporting and reflected in the concrete techniques, processes and practices of governance and its regulatory interventions. But I have also advanced the idea and the fourth main argument of this book that the issues and dimensions are also resources for participation in that they provide openings and possibilities for citizens to demand and contest the gathering, production and use of knowledge. The legitimating discourses of human rights and bioethics and the developing notion of (supra-)stewardship responsibility can be developed and used by citizens (those subject to governance) in order to articulate concerns, bring out the normative dimensions of scientific and technical knowledge creation and dissemination, and facilitate and power technologies of participation. In particular the two examples discussed in this chapter underline the potential of the discursive strategy in querying: whether public health governance and its framing ensures the protection of everyone's health; whether all those who are subject to the EU's regime benefit or if some face greater threats from public health problems than others; and whether the framing of governance and its knowledge foundations skew attention and resources away from prevention as a way of addressing the preconditions and social determinants of ill health for all diseases (epidemic, endemic and others).

The concerns raised in this chapter also point to knowledge creation as providing a 'way in' for participation impelled by the threat that, if unaddressed, the regulatory failures and 'societal risks' identified and underlined through it (supplementary knowledge) could produce—and indeed *are* producing—'institutional risks' ie risks to the EU's standing and reputation, that undermine and delegitimate the EU's governance, identity and project of integration. Moreover, this chapter further substantiates the core or overall argument of this book: that is, citizen participation is vital because it can help to reveal the paradoxes, pitfalls and failures attendant to, and thereby improve the quality of, governance and its regulatory interventions. In the next chapter I extend the discussion from framing and knowledge to the regulatory interventions they underpin, shape and help to direct, and in doing so I chart several more key openings and possibilities for citizen participation in governing public health by stressing matters relating to the distribution of benefits and risks as well as vulnerability.

8

Querying Interventions: Magic Bullet Responses and Technological Fixes

I. INTRODUCTION

IN THE PREVIOUS chapter I directed attention towards framing and its connection to the gathering and production of knowledge in order to chart some openings and possibilities for citizen participation in governing public health. As explained in that chapter, the framing of the technology governing public health and the policy domain by risk shifts attention towards consequences, both in order to bolster security understood as regulating the dangers or threats attendant to the circulation of people and things, and in order to produce economic optimisation. That framing might generate a shift of attention and distribution of resources towards governing emergencies and tackling communicable diseases—but away from addressing endemic and non-communicable diseases, root causes and wider public health objectives. These distortions, paradoxes and pitfalls of risk-based public health governance imply the favouring of regulatory interventions such as surveillance, surge capacity, and interventions like pharmaceuticals as the means to address consequences more than root causes.

This chapter discusses those interventions and as such it extends the broad discussion on distribution of resources and vulnerability by reference to framing and knowledge undertaken in the previous chapter. Specifically, the chapter continues to advance the fourth argument of this book by explaining how the favouring of magic bullet responses and technological fixes produces additional openings and possibilities for citizen participation, especially around vulnerability. In other words, in this chapter I outline some, but by no means all, key matters relating to those who might be hurt by and through the favouring of these sorts of interventions. I point out the European Union's (EU's) responsibility in that regard—and more particularly, the way in which the EU is (or could be) failing to ensure a high level of health protection as required by Article 9 Treaty on the Functioning of the European Union (TFEU), Article 168(1) TFEU and Article 35 Charter of Fundamental Rights of the European Union (EU Charter). In particular the discussion underlines how the magic bullet responses and technological fixes privileged by EU public health governance are at best stop gap measures and at worst are often deployed with little concern for addressing root causes—and either way they mask those deeper causes and fail to properly tackle wider public health problems.

Throughout the discussion I continue to highlight how the (de)selection of interventions relates to the production and legitimation of the EU's socio-political order, identity and ultimately its project of integration. I go on to show in a broad brush way how concerns around vulnerability might be highlighted by reference to the discursive strategy built from the legitimating discourses of human rights and bioethics and the developing notion of (supra-)stewardship, and including reflection in light of the provisions noted above. As I explained in the last two chapters, these discourses provide the resources and means—and the prescription—to facilitate and power technologies of participation. When deployed as part of a participatory strategy the discourses provide an opening into decision-making and resources for (re)shaping and perhaps even (re)framing governance through the provision of supplementary knowledge. Taking this knowledge into account in decision-making is impelled by the threat that, if unaddressed, the regulatory failures and societal risks identified and underlined through the discourses could produce risks to standing and reputation or 'institutional risks' that undermine and delegitimate the EU's governance, identity and project of integration.

The chapter begins with a brief discussion of surveillance and then more notable interventions (particularly those that impact on human rights and ethical protections), before turning to introduce how pharmaceuticals relate to vulnerability. That is followed by a more extensive discussion of the role of pharmaceuticals in the EU's external governance of public health. Pharmaceuticals are especially prominent simply because hitherto the other interventions, while certainly raising important normative concerns around vulnerability that could provide instances where citizens might demand and contest decisions, are simply less central to the EU's regulatory interventions in public health. This is partly because the division of competence for public health between the EU and its Member States under Article 168 TFEU ensures that it is the latter rather than the former which have primary responsibility for surveillance and non-pharmaceutical interventions. By contrast the EU shares responsibility with its Member States for the internal market and one consequence of this is EU legislation on pharmaceuticals necessitated by their status as an important component of the internal market. That, plus the importance of pharmaceuticals to meeting the EU's market optimising priorities, ensures they are probably 'the' key public health intervention, and are crucial to advancing its market oriented project of integration.

The particular attention to the role of pharmaceuticals abroad (rather than within the EU) also brings concerns around vulnerability into sharper relief. These examples are especially indicative of the material outputs (in this case drugs) that are made possible by and flow from the tightening relations between knowledge and power traced in the first part of the book and underlined in the previous chapter. As I explain in relation to each, the examples also point to the continued operation of the other neoliberal (re)configurations of sovereignty and territoriality, power and responsibility, and governance and the governed (especially those abroad) as the structuring themes of the policy domain and the basis for citizen participation. Overall, the chapter rounds out the discussion of the openings and possibilities for citizen participation and highlights the utility and efficacy of the discursive strategy proposed in chapter six as a prescription to enhance public health governance and the quality of its regulatory interventions.

II. INTERVENTIONS

A. General Reflections on Vulnerability

i. A Brief Note on Surveillance

I touched on surveillance in the previous chapter as part of the discussion on the importance of numbers and statistics to the knowledge base for decision-making. I consider surveillance here since it is also an intervention in its own right. Indeed, as discussed in the first part of the book, a core concern of the EU's public health governance is coordinating and facilitating pan-European surveillance, which indicates a tightening of the relations between knowledge and power and the extension of EU governance both within and beyond its territory. Improving surveillance is a particular focus of EU involvement in and growing responsibility for communicable diseases, for which accurate and up-to-date data on the spread of disease is vital for determining responses within the EU's territory, on its periphery and further afield.

One useful example from earlier in the book is the approach to rare pandemics. Throughout the alert phases the European Centre for Disease Control works with the European Commission, other EU agencies and Member State authorities to coordinate epidemiological surveillance.[1] This is in common with and against the background of international obligations on states (including EU Member States) to enhance epidemiological surveillance,[2] especially the International Health Regulations (IHR), and is consistent with the EU's (supra-)stewardship responsibilities. The IHR define surveillance as 'the systematic ongoing collection, collation and analysis of data for public health purposes and the timely dissemination of public health information for assessment and public health response as necessary'[3]—a definition that is mirrored in EU law.[4] Surveillance information is used to identify the circumstances of infection and to produce 'risk groups'. These latter might be subject to containment and control measures, which I return to below.

[1] European Commission, *Pandemic Influenza Preparedness and Response Planning in the European Community*, COM(2005) 607 final, 9. See ch 5.

[2] Arts 12 and 16, Committee on Economic, Social and Cultural Rights, 'General Comment No 14: The Right to the Highest Attainable Standard of Physical and Mental Health (Art 12)' (11 August 2000) UN Doc E/C.12/2000/49.

[3] Art 1 International Health Regulations (23 May 2005) WHA58/2005/REC/1.

[4] Eg in Art 3(d) Decision 1082/2013/EU on serious cross-border threats to health and repealing Decision 2119/98/EC [2013] OJ L293/1 'epidemiological surveillance' is defined as 'means the systematic collection, recording, analysis, interpretation and dissemination of data and analysis on communicable diseases and related special health issues'.

Surveillance itself raises more specific concerns around vulnerability that might provide areas for attention by citizens in attempts to contribute supplementary knowledge to the EU's risk-based governance of public health. Historically one area of debate has been over the circumstances in which individual consent and non-discrimination can be overridden via mandatory testing, screening and reporting.[5] This has been highlighted most acutely in national government medical responses to HIV/AIDS, which quite often involved the involuntarily testing of vulnerable groups, inter alia, prisoners, travellers and sex workers, and prompted much debate.[6] As highlighted in the first part of the book,[7] the EU's efforts are focused on linking and augmenting pan-European surveillance through coordination and cooperation, and in doing so this more problematic type of surveillance, as well as name-based reporting, has been eschewed in favour of non-discriminatory access to health care systems, voluntary participation and anonymity in reporting of the incidence of disease.[8] The principal reason is that such a failure to respect individual rights can prevent people from coming forward for testing and participation in public health programmes, thereby undermining their efficacy and individual and group human rights, including the right to health.[9]

Although the problems attendant to such problematic types of surveillance are largely absent in respect of the EU level of multi-level system of governance for public health,[10] this background nevertheless raises awareness of the potential concerns for vulnerability, particularly as they raise human rights risks for liberty, privacy and equality.[11] For instance, mandatory reporting of cases of public health problems, even when used for the compilation of data that is anonymised in an

[5] See, relatedly: M Fox and M Thomson, 'The New Politics of Male Circumcision: HIV/AIDS, Health Law and Social Justice' (2012) 32 *Legal Studies* 255.

[6] For a history and discussion see: UNAIDS, 'The Role of Name-Based Notification in Public Health and HIV Surveillance', UNAIDS/00.28E (2000), available at: www.who.int/hiv/strategic/surveillance/en/unaids_00_28e.pdf); WHO and UNAIDS, 'UNAIDS/WHO Policy Statement on HIV Testing', WHO (June 2004), available at: www.who.int/ethics/topics/en/hivtestingpolicy_who_unaids_en_2004.pdf); WHO and UNAIDS, 'Guidance on Provider Initiated HIV Testing and Counselling in Health Facilities', (May 2007), available at: whqlibdoc.who.int/publications/2007/9789241595568_eng.pdf); UNAIDS Reference Group on HIV and Human Rights, 'Statement and Recommendations on Scaling Up HIV Testing and Counselling' (2007), available at: data.unaids.org/pub/BaseDocument/2007/070216_HHR_1_PITC.pdf).

[7] Especially in chs 5 and 6.

[8] For discussion, see: J Harrington, 'The Instrumental Uses of Autonomy: A Review of AIDS Law and Policy in Europe' (2002) 55(8) *Social Science & Medicine* 1425.

[9] For a particularly interesting discussion see: J Blake Scott, *Risky Rhetoric: AIDS and the Cultural Practices of HIV Testing*, updated edn (Carbondale, IL, Southern Illinois University Press, 2014).

[10] Deployed in, eg parts of Africa (S Rennie and B Mupenda, 'Ethics of Mandatory Premarital HIV Testing in Africa: The Case of Goma, Democratic Republic of Congo' (2008) 8(2) *Developing World Bioethics* 125), Cuba (SC Smallman, *The AIDS Pandemic in Latin America* (Chapel Hill NC, North Carolina Press, 2007)) and the United States (C Weinstein and J Greenspan, 'Mandatory HIV Testing In Prisons' (2003) 93(10) *American Journal of Public Health* 1617).

[11] MA Stoto, 'Public Health Surveillance in the Twenty-First Century: Achieving Population Health Goals While Protecting Individuals' Privacy and Confidentiality' (2008) 96 *Georgetown Law Journal* 703; P Baldwin, *Disease and Democracy: The Industrialised World Faces AIDS* (Berkeley CA, University of California Press, 2005).

effort to respect confidentiality and respect privacy,[12] can still help to construct notions of normality and create ideas about appropriate behaviours against which others might be said to deviate.[13] Relatedly, surveillance data can reinforce stigma and discrimination against vulnerable groups.[14] The history of HIV/AIDS is again illustrative in that it provides perhaps the most notable recent example of the use of data in linking disease to already marginalised and stigmatised groups. Indeed, the initial prevalence of the disease amongst men who have sex with men gave rise to the syndrome's initial name (Gay-Related Immune Deficiency or GRID) and while the name changed and the link has faded, it has proven hard to dissolve, even as it increasingly attaches to immigrants from sub-Saharan Africa, another marginalised group.

Even as the EU seeks to ensure compliance with human rights and ethical protections, and seems particularly sensitive towards the dangers attendant to surveillance, there remains much scope for misuse and misinterpretation of data, and that provides a key opening for citizen participation and oversight that underlines such problems and seeks to address them. In that regard, the requirement to ensure a high level of health protection found in Article 9 TFEU, Article 168(1) TFEU and Article 35 EU Charter might be useful, particularly when read with (supra-)stewardship responsibility. Indeed, these can be used to reflect on whether all benefit from public health measures or if some face greater threats from public health problems—or the interventions developed to address them.

ii. Wider Interventions and the Hierarchy of Public Health Problems

Turning to other interventions, as I have already explained (and discussed in chapter seven), the importance of risk and security ensures there is a focus on dealing with consequences and that privileges the (de)selection of interventions, with attention to social determinants of ill health losing out in favour of social distancing and medical and technological responses, especially strategies of immunisation and treatment to deal with infectious or communicable diseases.[15] EU free movement law regulates public health interventions, but only where the two intersect. EU free movement of persons distinguishes between circulation within the EU's territory and entry into it from the outside, which concerns the area of freedom, security and justice and is particularly relevant to those who are not nationals of an EU Member State, so-called third country nationals.

Public health is an objective public interest that can be used to justify a restriction on the free movement of persons, including those who are not EU citizens moving into the EU's territory, and it has to been specified further in secondary

[12] As required by Art 45 IHR and discussed in chs 4 and 5 in particular.

[13] D Lupton, *The Imperative of Health: Public Health of the Regulated Body* (London, Sage Publications, 1995).

[14] S Burris, 'Surveillance, Social Risk, and Symbolism: Framing the Analysis for Research and Policy' (2000) 25 *Journal of Acquired Immunodeficiency Syndromes* S120.

[15] J Chalmers, *Legal Responses to HIV and AIDS* (Oxford, Hart Publishing, 2008).

legislation. In relation to third country nationals that legislation includes Directive 2003/96/EC, which was aimed at uniting third country nationals who are legally resident in the territory of a Member State with their family members, and provides that public health can be grounds for refusing entry and residence of family members, subject to a proportionality assessment including regard to family circumstances.[16] In respect of movement within the EU by EU citizens and their family members Article 4 of Directive 64/221/EEC, the predecessor to Directive 2004/38/EC, provided that the 'only diseases or disabilities justifying refusal of entry into a territory or refusal to issue a first residence permit *shall be those listed in the Annex*'.[17] The Annex mentions diseases that are subject to quarantine listed in International Health Regulation No 2 of the World Health Organisation of 25 May 1951; tuberculosis that is either active or showing signs of developing, syphilis; and 'Other infectious diseases or contagious parasitic diseases if they are the subject of provisions for the protection of nationals of the host country'.[18] Although the Directive was silent on HIV/AIDS (and the diseases covered by the Annex did not include HIV/AIDS), and the approach taken by the EU institutions towards its own employees or job applicants favoured equal treatment,[19] those who were HIV positive or who suffered with AIDS nevertheless found themselves subject to attempts to deny them admission to Member States.[20] This was part of the Commission's reason for concluding Directive 64/221/EEC was in need of an update

[16] Directive 2003/96/EC on the right to family reunification [2003] OJ L251/12. Art 6(1) states that the 'Member States may reject an application for entry and residence of family members on grounds of public policy, public security or public health' and Art 6(2) provides 'Member States may withdraw or refuse to renew a family member's residence permit on grounds of public policy or public security or public health'. Art 6(2) second paragraph states: 'When taking the relevant decision, the Member State shall consider, besides Article 17, the severity or type of offence against public policy or public security committed by the family member, or the dangers that are emanating from such person'. Art 17 deals with family circumstances and requires that 'Member States … take due account of the nature and solidity of the person's family relationships and the duration of his residence in the Member State and of the existence of family, cultural and social ties with his/her country of origin where they reject an application, withdraw or refuse to renew a residence permit or decide to order the removal of the sponsor or members of his family'. For discussion, see: S Peers, 'Family Reunion and Community Law' in N Walker (ed), *Europe's Area of Freedom, Security and Justice* (Oxford, Oxford University Press, 2004). Also see Art 6 Directive 2003/109/EC concerning the status of third-country nationals who are long-term residents [2003] OJ L16/44, which follows the same approach. On EU citizenship see: ch 1, n 135.

[17] Art 4(1) Directive 64/221/EEC on the co-ordination of special measures concerning the movement and residence of foreign nationals which are justified on grounds of public policy, public security or public health [1964] OJ 56/850.

[18] Ibid, Annex.

[19] It has been held that employees who are HIV positive and do not show signs of AIDS should be treated as normal employees: Case T-10/93 *A v Commission* [1994] ECR II-179.

[20] W Van Overbeek, 'AIDS/HIV Infection and the Free Movement of Persons within the Community' (1990) 27 *Common Market Law Review* 791. Also see: J Carlier, *The Free Movement of Persons Living with HIV/AIDS* (Luxembourg, Office of Official Publications of the European Community, 1999); E Guild, 'Security of Residence and Expulsion of Foreigners: European Community Law' in E Guild and P Minderhoud (eds), *Security of Residence and Expulsion: Protection of Aliens in Europe* (The Hague, Kluwer, 2000).

and rejecting measures that could produce 'social exclusion, discrimination or stigmatisation of persons with HIV/AIDS'.[21]

The update came in Directive 2004/38/EC, Article 29(1) and put an emphasis on diseases with epidemic potential and non-discrimination by limiting the application of interventions to situations where nationals of the host Member State are also subject to protective measures:

> The only diseases justifying measures restricting freedom of movement shall be the *diseases with epidemic potential* as defined by the relevant instruments of the World Health Organisation and other infectious diseases or contagious parasitic diseases if they are the *subject of protection provisions applying to nationals of the host Member State*. (Emphasis added)

The public health objective justification is only available to justify the initial refusal of entry to the Member State territory or the first residence certificate or card.[22] However, where there are 'serious indications that it is necessary' the host Member State is permitted to require those entitled to the right of residence to undergo a medical examination within the first three months of arrival.[23] It seems the same principles apply to those moving within and entering the EU under Directive 2003/96/EC.

For each the focus on equal treatment subject to proportionate limits reflects the general principle of non-discrimination, which is now concretised in (and post-Lisbon now legally binding within the scope of application of EU law) Article 21 EU Charter. The latter is broadly drafted and underlines the importance of non-discrimination in the overarching architecture of governance:

> Any discrimination based on any ground such as sex, race, colour, ethnic or social origin, genetic features, language, religion or belief, political or any other opinion, membership of a national minority, property, birth, disability, age or sexual orientation shall be prohibited.

This is subject to, inter alia, Article 52(1) EU Charter:

> Any limitation on the exercise of the rights and freedoms recognised by this Charter must be provided for by law and respect the essence of those rights and freedoms. Subject to the principle of proportionality, limitations may be made only if they are necessary and genuinely meet objectives of general interest recognised by the Union or the need to protect the rights and freedoms of others. (Emphasis added)

[21] European Commission, *Special Measures Concerning the Movement and Residence of EU Citizens which are Justified on Grounds of Public Policy, Public Security or Public Health*, COM(99) 372, 12.

[22] Diseases that occur after three months from the date of arrival cannot provide the grounds for expulsion from the national territory, per Art 29(2) Directive 2004/38/EC on the right of citizens of the Union and their family members to move and reside freely within the territory of the Member States amending Regulation (EEC) 1612/68 and repealing Directives 64/221/EEC, 68/360/EEC, 72/194/EEC, 73/148/EEC, 75/34/EEC, 75/35/EEC, 90/364/EEC, 90/365/EEC and 93/96/EEC [2004] OJ L158/77. This limitation on the use of public health as a means of justifying restrictions on free movement contrasts with the use of public policy and public security, which can be invoked upon initial entry or at any time prior to the first five years of the migrants stay.

[23] Art 29(3) Directive 2004/38/EC, ibid.

Given the focus on epidemic potential, non-discrimination and proportionality it is unlikely that the entry into the EU or free movement within the internal market by either EU citizens or others could be limited in relation to individuals with HIV/AIDS or other diseases where the risk of transmission is very slight. The same cannot be said for individuals with other communicable diseases that have epidemic potential. Where there is scientific uncertainty as to the risk posed by a public health problem the margin of discretion available to Member State authorities is likely to be wider. In those circumstances it is more likely that a measure will be found suitable, necessary and reasonable, ie proportionate to the end of protecting public health.[24]

Although EU *law* is highly relevant to public health interventions where the two intersect, EU public health *policy* is probably even more important, and that is especially apparent by reference to the example of preparedness. The Commission must work with the Member States to 'coordinate ... the position on *movement of persons* and goods and cooperate with appropriate international organisations and associations and transportation companies to implement standard measures for *travellers* on board international conveyances, consistent with the alert level' (emphasis added).[25] There are only background references to the legal and ethical implications of interventions in policy documents on preparedness relating to risk management.[26] In the *Interim Document*[27] the focus is more on ensuring minimal

[24] There is limited case law on public health as a limitation on the free movement of persons (see: C Barnard, *The Substantive Law of the EU: The Four Freedoms*, 4th edn (Oxford, Oxford University Press, 2013), ch 13), but there are analogous cases relating to the movement of goods. Eg in Case C-322/01 *Deutscher Apothekerverband eV v 0800 DocMorris NV and Jacques Waterval* [2003] ECR I-14887, where the Court of Justice of the EU (CJEU) stated '*the health and life of humans* rank foremost among the assets or interests protected by [the derogation on the free movement of goods set out in Article 36 TFEU]' and 'it is for the Member States, within the limits imposed by the Treaty, to decide what degree of protection they wish to assure' (para 103). As for the objective public interest justifications the CJEU has, eg identified the 'effectiveness of fiscal supervision, *protection of public health*, fairness of commercial transactions, [and] defence of the consumer' (emphasis added) as starting points for the non-exhaustive range of mandatory requirements (Case 120/78 *Rewe-Zentral AG v Bundesmonopolverwaltung für Branntwein* ECR [1979] 649, para 8. Also see: Case 178/84 *Commission* v *Germany (Beer Purity)* [1987] ECR 1227; Case C-315/92 *Verband Sozialer Wettbewerb eV v Clinique Laboratoires SNC and Estée Lauder Cosmetics GmbH* [1994] ECR I-317; Case C-470/93 *Verein gegen Unwesen in Handel und Gewerbe Köln eV v Mars GmbH* [1995] ECR I-1923). Similar to the position under the free movement of persons Directives considered above, the limitations on the prohibition of restrictions on the free movement of goods are subject to the principle of proportionality. Eg 'national rules or practices likely to have a restrictive effect, or having such an effect ... are compatible with the Treaty *only to the extent that they are necessary for the effective protection of health and life of humans*. A national rule or practice cannot benefit from the derogation provided for in Article [36 TFEU, the mandatory requirement or indeed other CJEU created justifications] if the health and life of humans may be protected just as effectively by measures which are less restrictive of intra-Community trade' (emphasis added) (Case C-322/01 *DocMorris* [2003] ECR I-14887, para 104).

[25] European Commission, *Pandemic Influenza Preparedness*, n 1 above, 25.

[26] See ch 5 for more extensive discussion of preparedness planning and ch 7 for discussion of the implications of the focus on risk and preparedness.

[27] Eg 'full respect for ethical standards, human rights, national and local laws and cultural sensitivities and traditions' in interventions is noted (European Commission, *'Interim Document': Technical Guidance on Generic Preparedness Planning for Public Health Emergencies* (2005) Annex 8,

disruption to the internal market through techniques, processes and practices such as assessment exercises and prior communication of countermeasures so as to ensure interoperability.[28] For example, 'Ethical issues are closely related to the legal issues ... and are *part* of the normative framework needed to *assess the cultural acceptability* of measures like *quarantine or selective immunisation of pre-defined risk groups*' (emphasis added).[29]

In other words, reading EU free movement law and policy together, the focus is on ensuring the functioning of the internal market. Proportionality and non-discrimination do not in themselves prohibit particular interventions, but instead guide their (de)selection and application in accordance with the risk posed by a particular public health problem. Moreover, these principles do not counteract the focus on governing the EU's periphery and beyond. It is possible that this focus on the external dimension might help to distract attention away from and naturalise the types and degree of interventions deployed on entry to and within the EU, particularly where this is combined with efforts to protect external borders. The distinction between the internal and external dimensions of governance also alludes to a hierarchy of attention with implications for not just the distribution of resources but also the (de)selection of interventions.

Threats or dangers from 'abroad' are given top priority as emergencies, those that circulate within the EU are next in importance, and those with little cross-border dimension (ie non-communicable diseases) but which nevertheless produce the greatest morbidities and mortalities are least important. In other words, public health problems that sit towards the top of this hierarchy (ie highly infectious and potentially high impact communicable diseases) are not just likely to be given most attention and resources; their prioritisation is also likely to affect the (de)selection of interventions chosen to deal with them. I have already explained how this generates concerns for wider public health priorities, which might lose attention, resources and be undermined—it also generates concerns about the treatment of those who are targeted by public health interventions. Reference to human rights and bioethics, perhaps especially the requirement to ensure a high level of health protection under Article 9 TFEU, Article 168(1) TFEU and Article 35 EU Charter, and supplemented by the developing discourse on EU (supra-)stewardship responsibility, could underline the way in which certain kinds of disease are prioritised, certain categories of person are likely to be subject to

78). It is supposedly a question of checking that 'National plans include a leading ethical framework for responses to public health crisis and national plans include verification processes to assure that the ethical aspects of policy decisions to be used during the response to an outbreak balance individual and population rights' (ibid, 35). The identity of the 'leading' framework remains unclear.

[28] As required for compliance with EU free movement law, noted above.

[29] European Commission, n 27 above, 35 (and 34–35 for legal implications). For definitions see: Annex 3, 64–66. Available at: ec.europa.eu/health/ph_threats/Bioterrorisme/keydo_bio_01_en.pdf. On EU support for ethics in national plans see: the workshop, 'Ethical Issues in European National Preparedness for Pandemic Influenza', available at: www.eu2008.fr/webdav/site/PFUE/shared/import/1120_pandemie_de_grippe/Pandemie_grippe_Pandemic_influenza_Programme_FR_EN.pdf.

specific public health measures, and prevention efforts are effectively deprioritised. In short, in these ways public health protection (overall) might be undermined.

Indeed, a particular concern is that interventions are highly susceptible to abuse and are of special concern for already vulnerable individuals and groups, but perhaps especially those that are constituted as and which are regulated as 'risk groups'. As Jasanoff explains, generally the production of 'risk groups' is an 'effort to produce policy-relevant assessments'[30] of those thought to be differently and most affected by the threat in question and to attune governance to them and their needs. This might work to protect the vulnerable and interrupt the spread of disease, which is of course acutely important in the case of a pandemic.[31] However, those deemed 'at risk' of infection are also 'at risk' of human rights and ethical infringements in the name of protecting the wider community. The criminalisation of disease transmission is of particular concern, not least because it has a long and problematic history, and risk-based governance that is increasingly underpinned by and oriented towards security provides the ideal conditions in which a preference for criminal sanctions can operate.

Criminalisation tends to figure disease carriers as active agents, aggressors and even 'evil criminals' who must take responsibility for their condition and endangerment of others.[32] Hence concern about the appropriateness of resort to criminal law.[33] English law, for instance, provides the prosecution services with some flexibility as to the messages about personal responsibility and culpability[34] that are communicated to the public.[35] Moreover, consistency in the application of

[30] S Jasanoff, 'Technologies of Humility: Citizen Participation in Governing Science' (2003) 41 *Minerva* 223, 241.

[31] *Cf* J Upperman, 'Vulnerable Populations in Disaster Planning: Children are Different' in P Katona, J P Sullivan and MD Intriligator (eds), *Global Biosecurity: Threats and Responses* (London, Routledge 2010). Also see: C Kaposy and N Bandrauk, 'Prioritising Vaccine Access for Vulnerable but Stigmatised Groups' (2012) 5(3) *Public Health Ethics* 283.

[32] J Montgomery, 'Medicalizing Crime—Criminalising Health? The Role of Law' in CA Erin and S Ost (eds), *The Criminal Justice System and Health Care* (Oxford, Oxford University Press, 2007). *Cf* N Reis, 'The 2003 SARS Outbreak in Canada: Legal and Ethical Lessons about the Use of Quarantine' in J Balint and others (eds), *Ethics and Epidemics* (Amsterdam, Elsevier Press, 2006).

[33] S Mathiesson, 'Should the Law Deal with Reckless HIV Infection as a Criminal Offence or a Matter of Public Health?' (2010) 21(1) *King's Law Journal* 123.

[34] M Brazier, 'Do No Harm: Do Patients Have Responsibilities Too?' (2006) 65(2) *Cambridge Law Review* 397; M Weait, *Intimacy and Responsibility: The Criminalisation of HIV Transmission* (Abingdon, Routledge-Cavendish, 2007).

[35] The essential issue is where to draw the line between intention and recklessness in disease transmission and that is a matter that the prosecuting authorities play a large part in deciding in the framing of cases. Transmission has been prosecuted as grievous bodily harm under s 20 of the Offences Against the Person Act 1861 (OAPA). The leading authority of *R v Clarence* (1889) 22 QBD 23 (which also involved s 47 on actual bodily harm) involved a husband who infected his wife with gonorrhoea and who did so knowing he had the condition and that his wife did not. Although there was a guilty verdict at first instance, on appeal the conviction was overturned on the grounds that successful prosecution required intent to wound the body of the victim and not just recklessness and that consent of the wife could be assumed. In *R v Dica* [2004] 3 WLR 213, it was clarified that s 20 OAPA could apply to infection with disease that occurs without physical violence. Further, although consent to such an assault with intention to harm was irrelevant to criminal law (following *Clarence* at para 2.21 and *R v Brown* [1994] 1 AC 212; the assumption of consent to intramarital sexual intercourse was overturned in

the general criminal law and the dangers of tailoring offences in order to criminalise specific behaviours and practices that lead to disease transmission are therefore a concern, particularly given how diseases and their modes of transmission can all too easily become associated with and compound negative social effects for already stigmatised and marginalised individuals or groups. In short, those within 'risk groups' are also made 'at risk' of comparatively more intrusive governance interventions favoured by securitisation and the increasingly important medical emergency model, especially those oriented towards security and crime, that is executive authority.[36] Again the history of disease is instructive in that it reveals that far from being neutral and objective official discourses often reflect, reinforce and deploy extant societal tensions and anxieties.[37]

Applying these experiences and lessons to the EU, it is noteworthy that in respect of preparedness, prior to Phase 6 the EU is deemed free of pandemic infection, and in respect of other communicable diseases like HIV/AIDS there is a great deal of focus on managing the EU's periphery and beyond. This amounts to an externalisation of these sorts of public health problems and a naturalisation of those that are usually endemic to the EU itself, but which are caused by failures of law, policy and medical practice in the EU. These are then naturalised as part of the order of things for which no one is to blame. Despite efforts at international cooperation, especially in relation to communicable diseases, there remains a bias towards EU needs and the idea that, rather than being endemic to the operation of the EU's privileging of free movement, the 'threat' comes from 'out there'. More than that, this implies that those coming from that zone are likely to be perceived differently and subject to particularly intrusive and even repressive interventions.

History and indeed the current practice of some countries indicate that particularly vulnerable groups include immigrants.[38] In light of this, it seems that the construction of the threat to be governed by risk and regulated as such distracts

R v R [1992] 1 AC 599), in cases of recklessness consent could provide a complete defence in relation to running the risk of infection rather than sexual intercourse (*R v Konzani* [2005] 2 Cr App R 14 confirmed that informed consent is required). See further: LG Francis and JG Francis, 'Criminalising Health-Related Behaviours Dangerous to Others? Disease Transmission, Disease Facilitation and the Importance of Trust' (2012) 6 *Criminal Law and Philosophy* 47; S Ryan, 'Reckless Transmission of HIV: Knowledge and Culpability' (2006) *Criminal Law Review* 981; M Weait, 'Criminal Law and the Sexual Transmission of HIV: R v Dica' (2005) 68 *Modern Law Review* 121.

36 *Cf* T Murphy and N Whitty, 'Is Human Rights Prepared? Risk, Rights and Public Health Emergencies' (2009) 17 *Medical Law Review* 219, 237.

37 R Bivens, '"The English Disease" or "Asian Rickets"? Medical Responses to Postcolonial Immigration' (2007) 81(3) *Bulletin of the History of Medicine* 533; Lupton, n 13 above; H Markel and AM Stern, 'The Foreignness of Germs: The Persistent Association of Immigrants and Disease in American Society' (2002) 80(4) *Millbank Quarterly* 757. Particular individuals can even become irreversibly linked to particular diseases and differently subject to interventions: JW Leavitt, *Typhoid Mary: Captive to the Public's Health* (Boston MA, Beacon Press, 1996).

38 Eg cases concerning refusal of residency permit in violation of Art 8 ECHR (privacy and family life) and Art 14 ECHR (non-discrimination) (*Kiyutin v Russia* App No 2700/10, [2011] ECHR 439) and inadequate medical assistance to detainees (*AB v Russia*, App No 1439/06; *Logvinenko v Ukraine* App No 13448/07).

attention away from endemic public health problems as well as how the EU's internal conditions, such as the free movement privileged by its internal market, and public health infrastructures, facilitate the problem. Typically itinerant and already marginalised groups within the EU, such as the Roma or travelling communities, might also be subject to different and especially adverse treatment.[39]

Overall, such interventions, directed as they are at identifiable 'risk groups' can produce or work with pre-existing classifications of those who are different, often especially the poor or other vulnerable groups,[40] in order to render them (morally) responsible and absolve or abrogate the wider public and public health actors of responsibility. Medicine, law and governance, including the deployment of stereotypical representations, work with metaphors of disease carriers to produce them as different from 'normal' members of society and hazards to it.[41] This production can work to provide the rationale for interventions and help to legitimate discrimination against individuals and groups and their stigmatisation as being identifiable with the disease.[42]

Yet, similar to concerns around surveillance, the efficacy of such social distancing and public health regulation might also be undermined where individuals seek to avoid diagnosis and treatment where quarantine seems a realistic possibility. In addition, such techniques, processes and practices directly infringe personal liberty and privacy rights, and could lead to healthy individuals being put at serious risk of infection should they be mistakenly quarantined. Nevertheless, since only certain 'risk groups' are targeted for specific interventions, and risk individualises and responsibilises, there is an absence of burdens on all, and these actions could be further depoliticised and left largely uncontested. As such citizen participation could usefully query these effects and distortions of attention and application of interventions.

Given these sorts of concerns the absence of greater detail on the EU's approach to human rights and ethical protections becomes a key concern for those who are subject to interventions as well as for broader citizen engagement in public health. To be clear, I am not suggesting the EU does not already try to combat the problems associated with the production and circulation of surveillance data and other regulatory interventions. In addition to what I have already noted from the discussion in the first part of the book, there are, for example, also important attempts to modulate public health communication efforts in relation to particular diseases, especially in order to allay public fears about the nature of the threat posed by pandemic influenza. Nevertheless, the framing, normative underpinnings and direction of the technology governing public health and the policy

[39] S Žižek, 'Liberal Multiculturalism Masks an Old Barbarism with a Human Face', *The Guardian*, 3 October 2010.

[40] DF Musto, 'Quarantine and the Problem of AIDS' (1986) 64 *Milbank Quarterly* 97.

[41] S Sontag, *Illness as Metaphor and AIDS and Its Metaphors* (London, Penguin, 1991) 171.

[42] L Eichelberger, 'SARS and New York's Chinatown: The Politics of Risk and Blame During an Epidemic of Fear' (2007) 65(6) *Social Science & Medicine* 1284.

domain is open to distortion by social forces and perceptions (as explained in chapter seven). The focus on risk and security and the role of social forces and perceptions in shaping public health governance produces a bias towards the use of the more problematic interventions and their attendant problems for vulnerability. Consequently more needs to be done in order to ensure the protection of individuals and 'risk groups' from abuse—and citizen participation could usefully underline that key responsibility.

In short, the dangers or threats attendant to public health interventions provide another key opening for citizen participation. Articulating and underlining the sorts of concerns traced out above obviously entails using human rights, ethics and (supra-)stewardship, all of which were outlined in chapter six. Concerns articulated through these discourses are likely to prove influential to decisionmakers, even in circumstances of emergency, since they present 'institutional risks' (risks to standing and reputation) to the EU, its identity and ultimately the production and legitimation of the project of European integration.

iii. Framing, Responsibility and Accountability

Citizen participation around wider interventions could therefore provide important supplementary knowledge to decision-making on the problems attendant to regulating public health. As the few examples discussed above make clear, articulation of concerns through the discursive strategy for participation could help to reveal the normative in the technical and tackle the depoliticisation and naturalisation of EU governance and its role in the (de)selection of regulatory interventions. The strategy could help to underline the EU's responsibilities at the level of framing for the (de)selection of options and their cultural acceptability, which is produced in part by EU discourses and involvement in public health governance.

More specifically, the EU is not just responsible for ensuring communication and compliance with free movement law; it is also responsible for minimising the potential for abuse and highlighting instances where individuals and 'risk groups' are subject to particularly intrusive interventions. This responsibility can be underlined by references to human rights and bioethics, including the requirement to ensure a high level of health protection found in Article 9 TFEU, Article 168(1) TFEU and Article 35 EU Charter, as well as the notion of (supra-)stewardship. Yet the EU's responsibility remains underdeveloped and the focus remains on the adverse effects of interventions on the circulation of people and things in the internal market. The discussion underscores how the formal boundaries of EU responsibility for public health in Article 168 TFEU tell only part of the story. Indeed, responsibilities are worked out and power extended through the risk-based framing of public health and its operationalisation through concrete techniques, processes and practices. Citizen participation around the examples traced above could, therefore, play an important role in responsibilising the EU, (re)shaping and perhaps even (re)framing policy such that human rights and ethics become more salient to governance and discussion around its regulation of public health.

B. Pharmaceuticalisation and Vulnerability

As is apparent throughout the discussion in the first part of the book, pharmaceuticals are perhaps the EU's key regulatory intervention in public health. In the previous chapter I noted the implications for the distribution of resources. In this sub-section I lay the groundwork for the subsequent discussion, where I examine a few instances of how the preference for pharmaceuticals produces key implications for vulnerability by reference to experience outside the EU, a place where EU governance nevertheless produces important effects. It is abroad that concerns around vulnerability become particularly apparent and underline the problematic nature of EU public health governance and its regulatory interventions. The turn to pharmaceuticals as a public health intervention has been denoted 'pharmaceuticalisation'. The term also signifies the centrality of pharmaceuticals to the shaping of what we regard as public health problems.[43] For instance, pharmaceuticals work with medical diagnoses of disease so as not merely to render it treatable, but also to create, stabilise and perpetuate a disease as a phenomenon that requires an intervention, usually through pharmaceutical treatment.[44]

Pharmaceuticalisation is also one manifestation of the increasing shift of attention and distribution of scarce public resources towards treatment (medicalisation), and away from risk-based strategies of prevention and health promotion traced in the first part of the book.[45] As such there is privileging of treatment through pharmaceuticals rather than through the interventions that would be privileged by an understanding of public health issues as more complex social, economic and political problems that necessitate prevention measures.[46] Given the hierarchy of public health problems noted in the previous section, pharmaceuticalisation is perhaps most apparent in contexts of rare but potentially high impact medical emergencies like global pandemics. In those contexts vaccines and medicines are the focus of protection efforts and are often distributed by triage. The global West including the EU has tended to develop and stockpile these magic bullet and technological solutions produced using epidemiological knowledge gathered from abroad.[47]

[43] J Abraham, 'Evolving Sociological Analyses of "Pharmaceuticalisation": A Response to Williams, Martin and Gabe' (2011) 33 *Sociology of Health & Illness* 726; SJ Williams, J Gabe and P Davis, 'The Sociology of Pharmaceuticals: Progress and Prospects' (2008) 30(6) *Sociology of Health & Illness* 813; SJ Williams, P Martin and J Gabe, 'Evolving Sociological Analyses of "Pharmaceuticalisation": A Reply to Abraham' (2011) 33 *Sociology of Health & Illness* 729; SJ Williams, P Martin and J Gabe, 'The Pharmaceuticalisation of Society? A Framework for Analysis' (2011) 33 *Sociology of Health & Illness* 710.

[44] M Pickersgill, 'Sociotechnical Innovation in Mental Health: Articulating Complexity' in ML Flear and others, *European Law and New Health Technologies* (Oxford, Oxford University Press, 2013).

[45] As summarised in ch 6.

[46] SE Bell and AE Figert, 'Medicalisation and Pharmaceuticalisation at the Intersections: Looking Backward, Sideways and Forward' (2012) 75(5) *Social Science & Medicine* 775.

[47] There has been some suggestion that this can be explained by 'big pharma' companies who profit from government orders for vaccines and antivirals. See: D Cohen and P Carter, 'WHO and the Pandemic Flu "Conspiracies"' (2010) 340 *British Medical Journal* c2912. Also see: A Lakoff, 'Real-Time Biopolitics: The Actuary and the Sentinel in Global Public Health' (2015) 41(1) *Economy and Society* 40.

Although it is for Member States to determine what they fund via their health care systems,[48] the EU plays a key role in producing and supporting the preference for pharmaceutical responses. Perhaps the most marked example of this is how the EU shapes the conditions for the production of medicines through its system of market authorisation, which focuses on their quality, safety and efficacy and increasingly relies on offshored clinical trials data.[49] It is the latter—and, therefore, the EU—which in turn ensures the instrumentalisation of knowledge creation for economic optimisation by creating the possibilities for purchase and consumption of pharmaceuticals, whether in the context of publicly funded treatments or by individuals in the marketplace. Moreover, innovation in pharmaceuticals is central to the broader instrumentalisation of (public) health seen in the overarching architecture and reflected in its operationalisation across the examples set out in the first part of the book. In short, pharmaceuticals also represent the alignment of regulatory means—building on the alignment of regulatory purposes and ends at the level of knowledge creation—to economic optimisation and the infiltration of market rationality into the formally non-market domain of public health.[50]

Much discussion of pharmaceuticalisation is to be found in science and technology studies (STS), sociology and anthropology. The dearth of attention to this trend in law and regulation studies reflects the scant consideration paid by them to the normative dimensions of knowledge creation.[51] My analysis combines insights from across those former disciplines in order to encourage the growing discourse between them and law seen in other areas.[52] In this way I seek to meet one of this book's central objectives in particular—and to prompt further engagement by law and regulation studies. Specifically, building on the discussion of clinical trials in the previous chapter, I seek to complement the current attention given to the role of national regulatory regimes, especially that of the United States (US), and global patent law and technical standards on pharmaceuticals, with discussion of some of the key normative dimensions of the EU's risk-based technology of pharmaceutical regulation and its imbrication with these.

I stress and elaborate on the similarities with clinical trials, in particular how the reliance on and valorisation of the scientific and technical in public health governance is both embedded within and reflective of the EU's broader normative architecture—and how that in turn is also related to the global regulatory environment. Overall these support corporate profitability, while limiting the EU's responsibilities and accountabilities to safety matters, and eschewing the wider problems attendant to its pursuit of market optimisation. In order to highlight

[48] Respecting Art 168 TFEU. See further: ch 2.

[49] Outlined in chs 3 and 4, mentioned in ch 5, and see ch 7 for an extensive discussion on clinical trials.

[50] See ch 2. For a similar argument see: C Davis and J Abraham, *Unhealthy Pharmaceutical Regulation: Innovation, Politics and Promissory Science* (Basingstoke, Palgrave Macmillan, 2013).

[51] With some notable exceptions, such as: E Jackson, *Law and the Regulation of Medicines* (Oxford, Hart Publishing, 2012).

[52] See the references in ch 1, n 11.

normative dimensions pertaining to vulnerability around the preference for pharmaceuticals as 'the' key magic bullet and technological fix, I focus on how the EU governs access to pharmaceuticals abroad, since it is by attention to the most vulnerable places and people that the distortions, paradoxes and pitfalls attendant to the preference for pharmaceuticals can be most clearly revealed and underlined. Indeed, focusing on pharmaceuticals abroad continues to highlight the ways in which the EU's instrumentalisation of knowledge for market optimisation (in this case the data from clinical trials) has material consequences through the (non-) availability of drugs beyond its territory.

In the remainder of this chapter I turn first to tracing the barriers that undermine access to essential medicines in the global South and the EU's role in maintaining them, before outlining how pharmaceuticalisation works within inequitable conditions to augment and often produce vulnerability, some of the main biopolitical stakes around vulnerability for the subjects of EU governance. Consistent with the broad notion of 'the governed' adopted throughout this book, subjects include not just those in possession of formal citizenship, but, more specifically, those whose lives and health are literally enfolded into the regulatory regime. Those governed by and subject to the regime may not be EU citizens, and this includes those who usually reside well beyond the EU's borders.[53] Rather than perpetuating the production and distribution of pharmaceuticals, and despite its notable efforts to improve access, the EU should do more to attend to the root causes of global inequality and public health problems. These concerns will be teased out by reference to human rights, bioethics and (supra-)stewardship. That is instead of the current resort to pharmaceuticals as 'the' magic bullet and technological fix, which can be explained in large part due to their role in supporting the EU's interest in market optimisation and increasing the global competitiveness and profitability of its pharmaceutical industry. This links (as I have argued) to the wider objective of producing and legitimating the EU's identity as a trade and public health actor and beyond that the project of European integration.

III. PHARMACEUTICALS ABROAD: ACCESS, PRIORITISATION AND TRIAGE

A. Access

i. Combating Barriers and the Importance of EU Trade Policy

Unlike most of the other examples cited in this part of the book access to treatment has been an important focus for biopolitical campaigns and it remains a central area for citizen participation around vulnerability.[54] In the global North research and funding priorities have long been subject to contestation. Perhaps the

[53] Initially set out in ch 1.

[54] J Biehl and A Petryna (eds), *When People Come First: Critical Studies in Global Health* (Princeton NJ, Princeton University Press, 2013), especially the chapters in Pt II on interventions.

most marked example of the latter is in relation to HIV/AIDS, where perceptions of vulnerable groups stymied research and the development of anti-retrovirals (ARVs).[55] Access is an even more pressing issue in the global South where HIV/AIDS has also been a central site for contestation of the global regime that determines access to treatment.[56] Although the World Health Organisation proclaims 'the enjoyment of the highest attainable standard of health is one of the fundamental rights of every human being',[57] and this is indeed reflected in international human rights instruments and the EU's legal architecture,[58] access to medicines by low and middle income countries remains a hugely important public health problem. Part of the reason is to be found in the failure of the governments of those countries to tackle the endemic social, economic and political causes of ill health. Nevertheless, it would be inaccurate and wrong to place all responsibility for these failures on those countries. Indeed, one area of concern is there is a lot less research into diseases that mainly affect the poor, who usually live in low and middle income countries. But limited investment in research is only part of the explanation for lack of access.

Another notable barrier is adverse and discriminatory cultural assumptions about the efficacy of treatment in poor settings. Research has helped to confront and overcome these assumptions, for example, by demonstrating that contrary to widely held perceptions poor people can and do adhere to complex drug regimes.[59] Indeed, a model of community-based treatment is shown to disrupt the idea that comprehensive care in poor settings is not possible.[60] In short, treatment is possible and it saves lives. Campaigns have also secured access as a human right, for instance, in South Africa and Brazil,[61] and used litigation as a way to leverage and

[55] The US-based NGO Act-UP challenged and helped to change conventions on drug testing and licensing, assisting in the acceleration of antiretroviral development: S Epstein, *Impure Science* (Berkeley CA, University of California Press, 1996).

[56] J Biehl, 'Pharmaceuticalisation: AIDS Treatment and Global Health Politics' (2007) 80(4) *Anthropological Quarterly* 1083.

[57] World Health Organisation, *Constitution of the World Health Organisation* (Geneva, World Health Organisation, 1948) 14 UNTS 185, Principle 2.

[58] See chs 1, 2, 6 (summary of findings) and 7 (especially in relation to the discussion on clinical trials).

[59] P Farmer, *Infection and Inequalities: The Modern Plagues* (Berkeley CA, University of California Press, 1999). On factors affecting adherence see: R Garcia, R Schooley and R Badaro, 'An Adherence Trilogy is Essential for Long-Term HAART Success' (2003) 7(5) *The Brazilian Journal of Infectious Diseases* 307; M Malta and others, 'Case management of Human Immunodeficiency Virus-Infected Injection Drug Users: A Case Study in Rio de Janeiro, Brazil' (2003) 37 *Clinical Infectious Diseases* S386.

[60] P Farmer, 'Introducing ARVs in Resource-Poor Settings: Expected and Unexpected Challenges and Consequences', available at: quod.lib.umich.edu/c/cohenaids/5571095.0177.033?rgn=main;view=fulltext; DA Walton and others, 'Integrated HIV Prevention and Care Strengthens Primary Health Care: Lessons from Rural Haiti' (2004) 25(2) *Journal of Public Health Policy* 137.

[61] WE Forbath with others, 'Cultural Transformation, Deep Institutional Reform, and ESR Practice: South Africa's Treatment Action Campaign' in LE White and J Perelman (eds), *Stones of Hope: How African Activists Reclaim Human Rights to Challenge Global Poverty* (Stanford CA, Stanford University Press, 2011); A Petryna, *When Experiments Travel* (Princeton NJ, Princeton University Press, 2009).

broaden out access, and 'not simply as a vehicle for individualised relief for those who can afford to access the courts'.[62]

Law's role in creating or supporting barriers to access has therefore made it a central site for access to treatment campaigns. The Agreement on Trade-Related Aspects of Intellectual Property (TRIPS),[63] outlined further shortly, provides for the global patenting of pharmaceuticals, and these are therefore particularly important to the campaigns. Indeed, TRIPS has prompted and made possible a global dimension to treatment access campaigns that help to tackle the overlapping global and national barriers to access and demand alternative ways of governing pharmaceuticals. The intimate relationship between the global, national and local in mediating and governing access means that the vulnerability related implications of any single component cannot be considered in isolation. Importantly for this book, which focuses on the EU and its public health governance, the global rules on patents are supported and propagated by the EU in combination with other global actors.

Patents increase the cost of pharmaceuticals that can be used to treat non-communicable diseases and communicable diseases alike. Low and middle income countries bear by far the greatest burden of non-communicable disease, at nearly 80 per cent of the global total,[64] a figure that has prompted drives to deal with the disparity and its effects.[65] Nevertheless, these worthwhile attempts tended to focus on communicable diseases and HIV/AIDS in particular. Patents can mean that those in the most vulnerable circumstances are unable to share in treatments that are widely available in richer countries principally within the global North as well as the benefits of scientific progress in innovative treatments to which they or those in their communities play an important role (via participation in clinical trials).[66]

However, much extant scholarly attention has been on the barriers and the broader attempts to widen access, such as through addressing philanthropic and humanitarian efforts, rather than the EU as a particular site and its roles in providing the imperatives and underpinnings that produce, support and perpetuate

[62] T Murphy, *Health and Human Rights* (Oxford, Hart Publishing, 2013) 101. See further: J Biehl, 'Drugs for All: The Future of Global AIDS Treatment' (2008) 27(2) *Medical Anthropology* 1.

[63] Marrakesh Agreement Establishing the World Trade Organization, opened for signature 15 April 1994, 1867 UNTS 3, Annex 1C (Agreement on Trade-Related Aspects of Intellectual Property Rights) (entered into force 1 January 1995) (TRIPS). This agreement is enforceable via the WTO's Understanding on Dispute Settlement. Least developed countries do not have to implement TRIPS until 2016.

[64] World Health Organisation, *Global Status Report on Noncommunicable Diseases 2010: Description of the Global Burden of NCDs, their Risk Factors and Determinants* (Geneva, World Health Organisation, 2011).

[65] World Health Organisation, *Global Strategy for the Prevention and Control of Noncommunicable Diseases: Report by the Director-General* (Geneva, World Health Organisation, 1999). See further: JP Wild, 'The Role of Cancer Research in Noncommunicable Disease Control' (2012) 104(14) *Journal of the National Cancer Institute* 1051.

[66] Eg under Art 27 Universal Declaration of Human Rights (10 December 1948) UNGA Res 217A (III), UN Doc A/810.

them and their attendant problems. More specifically, there has been a lot less focus on the objectives and normative direction of the EU level of the multi-level system of governance of public health and its imbrication with other sites and actors, both national and transnational. In the following I bring the EU's roles in respect of access to treatment to the fore and suggest that the current focus on TRIPS obscures the EU's responsibility and accountability in respect of global public health. In particular, despite the EU's involvement in attempts to widen access to treatment its trade policy continues to dominate the approach to global public health. While this remains the case the EU is failing to ensure a high level of health protection in its policies—as required by Article 9 TFEU, Article 168(1) TFEU and Article 35 EU Charter, and underlined by the developing notion of (supra-)stewardship responsibility.

ii. Patents as Barriers to Access

The EU and its Member States are all members of TRIPS, an international agreement required by membership of the World Trade Organisation (WTO). TRIPS came into force on 1 January 1995 and in signing up to it Member States agree to recognise one single global patent that lasts 20 years and to forbid generic equivalents of the patented drug from entering the marketplace during that period. Under TRIPS it is for Member States to determine what deserves to be patented, and as such countries in the industrialised global North, the region where the biggest producers of pharmaceuticals have their homes, are effectively able to export their patent protections. The latter is not without deleterious effects for access to treatment, especially in the global South, places with radically different social and economic conditions where the foundational assumptions for patents do not necessarily apply.

Patents are often justified on the basis that without them there would be a lot less financial incentive for research and development into new pharmaceuticals. To some extent this reason holds up: technological innovation is often resource intensive and the losses are high because many new pharmaceuticals simply fail to satisfy the regulatory requirements for safety and efficacy. Since most such research and development is carried out by corporate actors, who not unsurprisingly or unreasonably seek profit, they can require protection for their investments. However, although it is the global North that provides the vast majority of profits for the pharmaceutical industry, it is generally from selling pharmaceuticals that are not meant to tackle diseases of the poor in the global South. Moreover, the 10/90 research gap mentioned in the last chapter indicates that 'patents are not a relevant factor or effective in stimulating R&D and bringing new products to market'[67] in respect of low and middle income markets.

[67] WHO Commission on Intellectual Property Rights, *Innovation and Public Health, Public Health Innovation and Intellectual Property Rights* (Geneva, World Health Organisation, 2006).

Further, this 'one size fits all' approach means that producers of generics such as Brazil, India (long the preferred supplier to poorer countries),[68] China and South Africa,[69] are required to wait for branded drugs to come off patent, which delays access to the latest and most innovative treatments in the countries that have little or no manufacturing capacity.[70] Moreover, TRIPS has effectively cut away lifelines. Prior to its implementation some Member States, such as India, were able to reverse engineer pharmaceuticals patented in other countries in order to produce a generic version, which could be exported to countries with little or no alternative means of access. In short, with the entry into force of TRIPS protections that are designed to protect the profitability of corporate actors based in the global North operate to limit access to treatment in low and middle income countries.

In recognition of these effects public health flexibilities were built into TRIPS. For instance, access to within patent drugs can be provided through compulsory licensing.[71] Nevertheless, the usefulness of this flexibility is undermined by the lengthy[72] and resource intensive process for obtaining a licence,[73] and the reluctance of poorer Member Sates to participate in licensing for fear of being penalised by richer Member Sates through trade agreements, which I return to below. In recognition of these sorts of difficulties the WTO produced the Doha Declaration,[74] which underlined the link between pricing and patents in inhibiting access to treatment, and reconfigured trade and human rights through its affirmation that TRIPS permits Member Sates to freely use patented pharmaceuticals where there is a 'national emergency or other circumstances of extreme urgency'.[75] This means essential medicines can be used without liability for licensing fees when necessary for the protection of public health. In other words, Member Sates have

[68] Oxfam India, *Oxfam Urges India to Remain 'Pharmacy of the Developing World'* (New Delhi, Oxfam, 2010). Also see: S Ecks, 'Global Pharmaceutical Markets and Corporate Citizenship: The Case of Novartis' Anti-cancer Drug Glivec' (2008) 3 *BioSocieties* 165.

[69] JP Ruger and NY Ng, 'Emerging and Transitioning Countries' Role in Global Health' (2010) 3 *Saint Louis University Journal of Health Law & Policy* 253.

[70] A Pollock, 'Transforming the Critique of Big Pharma' (2011) 6 *BioSocieties* 106.

[71] An alternative route is through so-called 'parallel importation', which occurs when a state imports a patented medicine from another state where it is available at a lower price, but without patent owner approval.

[72] Eg Apotex spent three years struggling to obtain a licence for the use of three drugs in a combined treatment for HIV/AIDS, but eventually it was made available in Rwanda. See: SE Davies, *Global Politics of Health* (Cambridge, Cambridge, Polity Press, 2010) 169. Also see: M Rimmer, 'Race against Time: The Export of Essential Medicines to Rwanda' (2008) 1 *Public Health Ethics* 89.

[73] E Cloatre, *Pills for the Poorest* (Basingstoke, Palgrave Macmillan, 2013).

[74] Declaration on the TRIPS Agreement and Public Health (adopted 14 November 2001) WTO Doc WT/MIN(01)/DEC/2. An interpretation supported by the World Trade Organisation (WTO), 'Declaration on the TRIPs Agreement and Public Health' (9–14 November 2001), Ministerial Conference Fourth Session (WT/MIN(01)/DEC/W/2) ('Doha Declaration') para 5(c).

[75] Art 31(b). See: M Cassier and M Correa, 'Patents Innovation and Public Health: Brazilian Public-Sector Laboratories' Experience in Copying AIDS Drugs' in J-P Moatti and others (eds), *Economics of AIDS and Access to HIV/AIDS Care in Developing Countries: Issues and Challenges* (Paris, ANRS, 2003).

what Dreyfuss terms 'wiggle room'[76] to get around patents for pharmaceuticals in circumstances of public health emergency, like HIV/AIDS,[77] and to negotiate lower prices.[78] Since this was of no benefit to countries with little or no manufacturing capacity further flexibility was added in 2003 allowing such Member Sates to import medicines from a foreign producer of generics.[79]

The EU's role in all of this tends to be marginalised—if it is mentioned at all. The EU's role is obscured, at least in part, by the focus on the barriers themselves as well as other sites of formally accountable power, particularly the United States as the hegemonic state actor. Still, an ongoing example of how access to treatments under the flexibility of this framework is being undermined, and patent protection reinforced,[80] underlines the centrality of the EU amongst other international actors. The example is bi-lateral trade agreements. These build on the minimum standards in TRIPS—and are thus so-called 'TRIPS plus' agreements—to impose harsher provisions on developing countries, but in order to protect pharmaceutical industry interests.[81] Importantly, the EU has made notable use of these agreements,[82] underlined by the title of one Oxfam report: *Trading Away Access to Medicines*, explaining *How the European Union's Trade Agenda Has Taken a Wrong Turn*.[83] Low and middle income countries, including those in Central America, Brazil and China, are under intense pressure to sign these agreements, and their room for manoeuvre is limited by their inclusion in larger free trade agreements.[84]

76 RC Dreyfuss, 'TRIPS and Essential Medicines: Must One Size Fit All? Making the WTO Responsive to the Global Health Crisis' in T Pogge, M Rimmer, K Rubenstein (eds), *Incentives for Global Public Health: Patent Law and Access to Essential Medicines* (Cambridge, Cambridge University Press, 2010) 55. Also see: S Sterckx, 'Patents and Access to Drugs in Developing Countries: An Ethical Analysis' (2004) 4(1) *Developing World Bioethics* 58.

77 JC Cohen and P Illingworth, 'The Dilemma of Intellectual Property Rights for Pharmaceuticals: The Tension Between Ensuring Access of the Poor to Medicines and Committing to International Agreements' (2003) 3(1) *Developing World Bioethics* 27; SK Sell, *Private Power, Public Law: The Globalisation of Intellectual Property Rights* (Cambridge, Cambridge University Press, 2003); M Westerhaus and A Castro, 'How Do Intellectual Property Law and International Trade Agreements Affect Access to Antiretroviral Therapy?' (2006) 3(8) *PLOS Medicine* 1.

78 VB Kerry and K Lee, 'TRIPS, the Doha Declaration and Paragraph 6 Decision: What are the Remaining Steps for Protecting Access to Medicines?' (2007) 3 *Global Health* 3.

79 Implementation of Paragraph 6 of the Doha Declaration on the TRIPS Agreement and Public Health: Decision of 30 August 2003, WTO Doc WT/L/540; Amendment of the TRIPS Agreement: Decision of 6 December 2005, WTO Doc WT/L/641.

80 See further: GB Dinwoodie and RC Dreyfuss, *A Neofederalist Vision of TRIPS: The Resilience of the International Intellectual Property Regime* (Oxford, Oxford University Press, 2012).

81 A Mitchell and T Voon, 'Patents and Public Health in the WTO, FTAs and Beyond: Tension and Conflict in International Law' (2009) 43 *Journal of World Trade* 571.

82 As has the US: Médicins sans Frontières, *Access to Medicines at Risk Across the Globe: What to Watch Out For in Free Trade Agreements with the United States* (New York NY, Médicins sans Frontières, 2004).

83 Such as the EU–India Bilateral Agreement, see further: Oxfam International and Health Action International, *Trading Away Access to Medicines: How the European Union's Trade Agenda Has Taken a Wrong Turn* (Amsterdam, Oxfam International and Health Action International, 2009).

84 Oxfam India, *Oxfam Urges India to Remain 'Pharmacy of the Developing World'* (New Delhi, Oxfam, 2010). Also see: Ecks, n 70 above; Pollock, n 72 above; Ruger and Ng, n 69 above.

'TRIPS plus' agreements underscore how legal barriers not only constrain or even preclude the use of medicines—they are also central to a key aspect of pharmaceuticalisation, that is, the role of the industry in using intellectual property law to protect its profits. The EU's use of these agreements attests to the infiltration of market rationality into its governance through the subordination of the external dimension of public health to trade policy. Moreover, this points to the configuration by and alignment of those domains to the overarching architecture and the production of the EU's socio-political order and project of rule.[85] All that is even starker given the rationale for patents in low and middle income markets and their strict application via 'TRIPS plus' agreements is undermined (as mentioned above).[86] As I pointed out in the last chapter, this engenders concerns over the equity and justice of the increasing use of clinical trials data produced in the global South for the patenting, production and marketing of medicines that are unavailable there.

Contestation around TRIPS has not only highlighted its flaws, but it has also helped to produce moves towards accountability, including the constitutionalisation of the WTO itself,[87] and contestation has also helped to shift understandings of patents and their consequences, resulting in their partial reframing as being about public health. This is seen in, inter alia, more concerted interest in TRIPS flexibilities, an incipient development agenda,[88] an increased interest in demanding and contesting the creation and direction of knowledge,[89] and discussion on alternative arrangements,[90] particularly within human rights.[91] Nevertheless, the relations between TRIPS and the EU's trade policy require far more attention as an area for citizen participation in governing public health. Specifically participation could focus on the way in which TRIPS and trade policy operate to undermine global public health and therefore generate concerns that can be highlighted by reference to human rights, bioethics and (supra-)stewardship responsibility. Widening access to treatment is a key way of protecting public health and reducing threats on the EU's periphery and further afield. But it needs to be complemented with more sustained efforts to improve prevention.

[85] *Cf* G de Búrca and J Scott, *EU and the WTO: Legal and Constitutional Issues* (Oxford, Hart Publishing, 2001).

[86] WHO Commission on Intellectual Property Rights, n 67 above.

[87] DZ Cass, *The Constitutionalisation of the World Trade Organisation* (Oxford, Oxford University Press, 2005).

[88] Eg at the World Intellectual Property Organisation, see: www.wipo.int.

[89] A Kapczynski, 'The Access to Knowledge Mobilisation and the New Politics of Intellectual Property' (2008) 117 *Yale Law Journal* 804.

[90] A Lang, *World Trade Law after Neoliberalism: Reimagining the Global Economic Order* (Oxford, Oxford University Press, 2011).

[91] P Farmer, *Pathologies of Power: Health, Human Rights, and the New War on the Poor* (Berkeley CA, University of California Press, 2003); D Kinley, *Civilising Globalisation: Human Rights and the Global Economy* (Cambridge, Cambridge University Press, 2009); TW Pogge, 'Human Rights and Global Health: A Research Program' (2005) 36(1/2) *Metaphilosophy* 182. For overview and discussion see: Murphy, n 62 above, especially ch 3 'The Cost of Human Rights'.

iii. Alternative Mechanisms

Against the background of the global trade system and the EU's role in supporting and perpetuating it, there are a range of alternative mechanisms in place to facilitate access to pharmaceuticals in poor and middle income countries. But as I go on to explain, these further underscore how important it is to address root causes for public health problems—especially legal barriers. One mechanism is research funding and technical assistance, of which the EU has been a notable supporter and provider.[92] Incentives are a different kind of alternative and they work by distorting market conditions in favour of the production of pharmaceuticals for neglected diseases. For instance, patents pools are aimed at tackling the high price of pharmaceuticals and work by facilitating the sharing of patents through licences that help to make the pharmaceutical available in resource poor settings while ensuring a return for the patent holder.[93] The Health Impact Fund[94] is a novel idea that also seeks to reduce costs while also promoting research and development into new pharmaceuticals.[95]

Incentives are also being offered by public/private partnerships. A key example is the Global Alliance for Vaccines and Immunisation (GAVI). Founded in 2000, GAVI brings together a range of private and public actors, such as the Bill and Melinda Gates Foundation, national governments, corporations and the EU. Importantly, the EU has been a donor since 2003 through direct contributions, typically through its Development Cooperation Instrument and the part of the European Development Fund directed at African, Caribbean and Pacific (the so-called ACP) countries. Between 2003 and 2010 the EU contributed US$58 million.[96] GAVI has sought to incentivise research and development through the Advanced Market Commitment, an initiative which safeguards patent rights and provides companies with a predetermined—that is, guaranteed—donor subsidised price for successful vaccines.[97]

The Global Fund to Fight AIDS, Tuberculosis and Malaria (Global Fund) is similar to GAVI in that it is also a public/private partnership involving some of the same actors (the Bill and Melinda Gates Foundation, national governments, corporations) and the EU.[98] The Global Fund seeks to fight the three pandemics through a range of interventions, such as antiretroviral therapy for people living

[92] See generally the discussion in the first part of this book, especially in ch 2.

[93] Such as the Medicines Patent Pool Foundation, see: www.medicinespatentpool.org, originally established by the International Drug Purchase Facility (UNITAID).

[94] A Hollis and T Pogge, *The Health Impact Fund: Making New Medicines Accessible for All* (Yale CT, Incentives for Global Health, 2008).

[95] See further: T Pogge, M Rimmer, K Rubenstein (eds), *Incentives for Global Public Health: Patent Law and Access to Essential Medicines* (Cambridge, Cambridge University Press, 2010).

[96] See further: 'European Union' www.gavialliance.org/funding/donor-profiles/ec/.

[97] For discussion, see: L Clarke, *Public-Private Partnerships and Responsibility under International Law: A Global Health Perspective* (London, Routledge, 2014).

[98] 'The Global Fund' www.theglobalfund.org/en/partners/governments/.

with HIV, the treatment of tuberculosis, and the distribution of insecticide treated nets to prevent the transmission of malaria. The EU has supported the Global Fund since its foundation in 2002 and with funding of US$1.5 billion up until the end of 2012 coming from the common EU budget and the EDF. The EU is the sixth largest donor to the Global Fund and together with its Member Sates the collective EU contribution is around 50 per cent of the total.

These alternative mechanisms, among others, and together with the wider attention and contestation around patent law, have helped to narrow the 10/90 funding gap, reduce costs, widen access and save lives.[99] Importantly for this book and its project of enhancing citizen participation and through it the quality of governance and its regulatory interventions, although the EU is a key partner its role tends to receive little attention. Nevertheless, the EU shares in these successes, which help to legitimate its involvement in public health. Despite its importance to access to medicines, in particular in supporting TRIPS and the wider global trading system, it is a key blind spot of current activism and scholarship that the EU has hitherto been a peripheral concern of the access to treatment campaign. That needs to change. I turn now to underline some key distortions, paradoxes and pitfalls related to vulnerability and which are products of the current approach to global health. These could form important points in relation to which citizens—to be clear, in this book that means 'the governed'—could demand and contest the EU's global trade policy as part of that which produces and maintains inequality and harm on the ground in respect of public health.

B. Prioritisation and Triage

i. The View 'On the Ground'

The focus of international efforts, including (and especially for this book) those of the EU, on the choice of pharmaceuticals as 'the' magic bullet and technological fix for tackling pandemics abroad, reflects the preoccupation with risk and security, the externalisation of public health problems and a naturalisation of those that are usually endemic to the EU itself. There follows the obscuration of the responsibilities of the EU and its Member States, especially their role in producing and maintaining global inequalities that help to produce public health problems in the first place. The implicit limitation of responsibility suggests that external public health interventions are made out of a limited kind of self-interest wherein pharmaceuticals are the key to 'vertical' or disease-specific interventions through which, as Biehl, explains 'one saves lives by finding new technical tools and cost-effective means to deliver care; that is, *medicines and testing kits en masse*'

[99] R Ilavenil and MR Reich, 'Building Effective Public-Private Partnerships: Experiences and Lessons from the African Comprehensive HIV/AIDS Partnerships (ACHAP)' (2006) 63(2) *Social Science & Medicine* 397.

(emphasis added).[100] Pharmaceuticals are central to the regulation of the public health dangers or threats (security) attendant to the circulation of people and things (markets)—and the optimisation of their consumption is also an important added benefit of this use.

The resort to pharmaceuticals flows from the ongoing distortion in the distribution of attention and resources—including the penetration of the logic of emergency into research and development[101]—to combating communicable diseases rather than non-communicable diseases. This means that those who suffer from diseases that are not so favoured are effectively made vulnerable by framing and its (de)prioritisations.[102] Moreover, the latter increases vulnerability since there is an implicit devaluation of other cheaper, often more effective, and, crucially, usually non-technological, 'horizontal' or cross-cutting, preventative interventions that require time to produce results.[103] Those sorts of interventions include public sanitation, hygiene, and the distribution of public health information, as well as broader non-discriminatory public health and social interventions in the social, political and economic conditions producing public health problems in the first place. Yet, these are the sorts of things that are key to prevention *and* the success of treatment strategies in the long-term.

Incentives for corporate action also sanction the idea that pharmaceuticals and the knowledge that underpins them (and which is patented) are private rather than public goods. That effectively obscures appreciation of the normative dimensions attendant to the turn to pharmaceuticals as key *public* health interventions as well as the scope for citizen participation. Further, public/private partnerships can be used by the pharmaceutical industry to insinuate itself into law and policy. Indeed, a key benefit of public/private partnerships for industry is that they can, as Biehl points out, gain influence over 'the decision-making process at institutions of global governance, and from there to defend its interests and vision'.[104] Moreover, although 'Development agencies (such as the WHO, UNAIDS, and the World Bank) assist this process, which has crucial ramifications for the nature and scope of national and local public health interventions',[105] the EU is noticeably absent, despite, its importance.

The discourse of corporate social responsibility also helps to recognise the reputational risk arising from the pharmaceutical industry's neglect of diseases of poverty. The participation of the largest corporations in public/private partnerships such as One World Health,[106] as well as the provision of cheap or free medicines to

[100] Biehl, n 56 above.

[101] C Bastos, *Global Responses to AIDS: Science in Emergency* (Bloomington IN, Indiana University Press 1999).

[102] See V Das, 'Power, Marginality, and Illness' (2006) 33(1) *American Ethnologist* 27.

[103] J Biehl, 'When People Come First: Beyond Technical and Theoretical Quick Fixes in Global Health' in R Peet, P Robbins and M Watts (eds), *Global Political Ecology* (Abingdon, Routledge, 2010).

[104] Biehl, n 56 above, 1099.

[105] Ibid, 1100.

[106] Part of PATH since 2011: www.path.org/. This is a non-profit organisation that seeks to produce innovative ways of saving lives through public health interventions.

low income countries, is, therefore, not purely benevolent. Initiatives such as the Access to Medicines Foundation exacerbate reputational risk in that they seek to rank corporations and use their self-interest in producing and maintaining a good image as a spur to action.[107] Corporate partnerships with public actors like the EU might also have an ulterior motive: investment in diseases of poverty has increased in the absence of incentives, which suggests that public resources are supporting decisions to invest made for reasons besides altruism, ie profitability.[108] Corporate involvement also points to the instrumental use of 'biopolitics, gaining legitimacy and presence in both state institutions and individual lives through drugs',[109] often articulating through the rights discourse fashioned by activists.[110]

The sustainability of public/private partnerships is another key concern. For example, GAVI makes active use of diagrams and 'replenishment' to track donations over time and reveal shortfalls on previous years. Public/private partnerships are contingent on continued donor participation, their goodwill and preferences—and that can include public actors.[111] The actions of public actors, such as the EU, might well be determined by the support of private actors—public actors might be less inclined to stump up funding without private support given the current constraints on public finances as well as the neoliberal preference for these sorts of arrangements, which seek to responsibilise and spur civil society actors into sharing the burden. And funds can—and do—dry up, which not only frustrates access to what was being provided, but in the case of ARVs it can mean that the drug resistant viruses produced by intervention are only treatable by new and unavailable cocktails.[112]

The paradoxical effects of well-intentioned programmes further underline their limits. For instance, Nguyen explains that demands for new and more expensive and patent-protected drugs, prompted by the reduced efficacy of older treatment lines available in generic ARVs, means that public/private partnerships produce a dynamic of increased expectations and needs that can only be met within increasingly protected markets (via TRIPS) that must be constantly renegotiated. This makes access to treatment in low and middle income countries even more vulnerable to pharmaceutical corporate self-interest. Nguyen describes how claims

[107] 'Access to Medicine Index' www.accesstomedicineindex.org/.

[108] M Moran and others, *The New Landscape of Neglected Disease Drug Development* (London, Wellcome Trust, 2005).

[109] Biehl, n 56 above, 1093.

[110] J Biehl, *Will to Live: AIDS Therapies and the Politics of Survival* (Princeton NJ, Princeton University Press, 2007).

[111] Eg Nguyen explains that the UNAIDS programme provided increased access to antiretrovirals (ARVs). However, its chief aim was to demonstrate the feasibility of public/private partnerships. This produced a conflict with individual priorities, with international consultants acting as key intermediaries establishing a complex drug procurement and distribution mechanism that was hard for patients and their medical professionals to negotiate. See further: V-K Nguyen, 'Antiretroviral Globalism, Biopolitics, and Therapeutic Citizenship' in A Ong and SJ Collier (eds), *Global Assemblages: Technology, Politics, and Ethics as Anthropological Problems* (Oxford, Blackwell Publishing, 2005).

[112] Ibid, 136.

for treatment are made on the 'global order on the basis of one's biomedical condition, and responsibilities are worked out in the context of local moral economies'.[113] In short, EU responsibility for its own activities becomes diffused, masked and limited by patent law, and yet its philanthropic and humanitarian efforts are implicated in the complex relations through which they are implemented. These efforts, although necessary, worthwhile and well-intended, are therefore not without implications for vulnerability to public health problems.

Although alternative mechanisms are obviously welcome and even essential, they tend to work within the current legal regime; they seek to manage symptoms rather than providing a cure for the underlying ailment, that is the patent system.[114] Benevolence helps to mask these underlying problems and causes of public health problems—and it is these that could be the focus of increased citizen attention. The EU has played an important and occasionally instrumental role in wider attempts to broaden access to essential medicines. But these are not without their own attendant vulnerability related paradoxes and pitfalls and they are particularly apparent in light of further problems around prioritisation.

ii. Triage, Valuing and Access

Those suffering from diseases that benefit from the (de)prioritisations attendant to the framing of the risk-based technology governing public health do not necessarily have equal access to treatment. Attempts to increase access to essential medicines and other treatments abroad typically devolve responsibility for implementation onto local actors and especially non-governmental organisations. They are involved in advocacy and service delivery, such as testing and distribution programs, and can have fuller information on local needs as well as the networks of trust and provide the roots to access that are essential if people are to gain access. While local responsibility for distribution of essential medicines is important, attention to the ways in which distribution occurs in an emergency or extreme situations further underlines the ways in which the inequity and injustice attendant to the EU's global trade policy and the inadequacy of its attempts to bolster access to treatment—the operation of its power outside its territory—relate to and actually help to engender further concerns around vulnerability.

A key method of distributing pharmaceuticals is through triage—which implies that other, longer term and more sustained 'horizontal' and non-technological interventions are further marginalised. Distribution by triage requires consideration of the types of valuing that operate 'on the ground',[115] since these help to determine access to treatment in place of, or as a supplement to, situations where

[113] *Cf* ibid, 142.

[114] EB Kapstein and JW Busby, 'Making Markets for Merit Goods: The Political Economy of Antiretrovirals' (2010) 1 *Global Policy* 75.

[115] More generally see: A Ong, *Neoliberalism as Exception: Mutations in Citizenship and Sovereignty* (London, Duke University Press, 2006).

state public health infrastructure and policies aimed at removing or ameliorating sources of vulnerability, including anti-discrimination measures, are either not in place, weak, or failing to operate at all.[116] Anthropology provides rich insights here. For example, Nguyen's ethnographic research identifies and traces the operation of the logic of emergency within a 'humanitarian/development complex' around antiretrovirals,[117] which is a 'blending [of] military and biomedical intervention' and, in a way that implicates the EU and other global actors and networks, it represents 'a *specialised and highly structured crystallisation of broader, more diffuse transnational processes*' (emphasis added).[118]

Nguyen explains how access to treatment is underpinned by biomedical knowledge and determined by forms of exchange that can involve money, networks of obligation and reciprocity, and narratives by and through which individuals come to acknowledge their condition, relate to themselves and others, form biosocial groups and communicate their needs as 'interests'. These formations of individuals and groups are responding, at least in part, to the 'vertical' interventions, which carry a 'top-down' dynamic that renders certain population segments (typically those 'at risk') visible in order to make them capable of being governed through access to treatment. Partially configuring 'bottom-up' engagement, those with 'interests' engage with their home state and the wider global system, including the EU, through various means (law-making, jurisprudence, campaigns) in order to demand and contest decision-making over their means of remaining alive. Biopolitics is configured by and within many multiple and interacting levels of decision-making—and yet the EU level remains frustratingly obscured by the wider system that it supports and perpetuates.

Resonating with broader neoliberal strategies of self-management, responsibilisation and individualisation of risk—and reflected in terms like the 'therapeutic economy'[119] and 'economies of salvation'[120]—gaining access to treatment requires those in need to be active in expressing their interests despite their often acute vulnerability. As Biehl shows, pharmaceuticalisation places—perhaps even strands—such people in a highly precarious situation where their lives become central to their identities and treatment access: 'poor AIDS patients live in a state of flux, simultaneously acknowledging and disguising their condition … Through sporadic and hard-won circuits of care, their subjectivities are refigured as a *will to live*' (emphasis added).[121] Yet, increased quantities of treatment is itself insufficient without non-discrimination and related efforts to combat stigmatisation and marginalisation of both the disease and those 'at risk', without which individuals can be deterred from

[116] For discussion see: T Murphy, 'Public Health *sans frontières*: Human Rights NGOs and "Stewardship on a Global Scale"' (2011) 62(5) *Northern Ireland Legal Quarterly* 659.

[117] Nguyen, n 111 above, 126.

[118] Ibid.

[119] Ibid.

[120] Biehl, n 56 above, 1086.

[121] Ibid. See further: Biehl, n 110.

presenting themselves for treatment. Although triage is a key way of determining who gains access and is ostensibly useful for its apparent transparency and fairness, inequality and injustice abound in that treatment options are often determined by the ability to, for instance, pay or tell a 'good story' to the right person or in the right place.[122]

Non-governmental organisation activism has enhanced state functions—but it also redistributes responsibility from the state down to civil society, and might abet and augment the hollowing out of state functions such that they (ie states) are '*pharmaceutically present* (via markets) but by and large *institutionally absent*' (emphasis added).[123] Moreover, the state is fulfilling responsibilities in respect of those with 'interests' rather than 'needs', and that is abetted and promoted by EU policy. Importantly, as a corollary of the responsibilisation of those seeking treatment there is a further obscuring of the responsibilities of powerful global actors like the EU for setting and perpetuating the conditions that help to produce public health problems and local responses to them in the first place. Indeed, resort to pharmaceuticals and its attendant problems underlines the continuing effects of patents on the ground—as well as further attempts to negotiate the regime from below.

Although largely ignored by extant scholarship in law and regulation studies as well as the cognate disciplines that have focused on the resort to pharmaceuticals and its implications, the EU's role in supporting and perpetuating the global pharmaceuticals regime and its effects actually provides a key opening for citizen participation in public health governance. In particular, participation could underline the way in which the EU's particular priorities, and especially its trade policy, undercut rather than support wider public health priorities. Through the framing of the technology governing public health and the policy domain, and continued through its operationalisation via techniques, processes and practices, pharmaceuticals are privileged as 'the' magic bullet and technological response to public health problems, but under conditions where access to treatment by the poorest is actually undermined and contingent on local circumstances and possibilities. Far from protecting the EU—that is, ensuring its security through the regulation of people and things (especially abroad) so that they do not threaten the internal market—the current underpinnings and orientation of its public health governance towards market optimisation actually undermines public health and the fulfilment of EU responsibility in that regard.

IV. CONCLUSION

Just as regulating the dangers and threats to public health is essential, so too is querying the framing that underpins the (de)selection of interventions, the impact of broader social forces on that selection, and the consequent effect and potential for (mis)use. In that regard citizen reflection and participation around

[122] Nguyen, n 111 above, 133.
[123] Biehl, n 56 above, 1093.

vulnerability could provide vitally important supplementary knowledge to legal and regulatory decision-making. Citizens—those that are governed—are (probably) best placed to speak about the impact of decisions that impact on them, and the discussion in this chapter points to the ways in which references to human rights, bioethics and (supra-)stewardship could help to power and shape discussion. Although current research already implicates the EU, there is a need for much further research into the normative dimensions of its involvement in public health interventions, and further citizen participation.

Notwithstanding international and EU proclamations encompassing preventive and treatment strategies, EU public health governance is actually skewed towards certain interventions and that is perhaps most obvious in its attempts to regulate public health abroad. The framing of the technology governing public health and the policy domain is a consequence of the EU's choice about how to govern.[124] The EU, like other formally accountable actors, makes choices in the context of globalisation about how it will govern, how it relates to other international actors—and to individuals and society.[125] This chapter underscores the EU's key role in shaping the (de)selection of regulatory interventions and helping to shape the local trajectories of global public health problems, which is especially evident in the case of HIV/AIDS and other pandemics and serious cross-border threats to health.[126]

EU governance privileges pharmaceuticals as a response to communicable diseases and other serious threats (and the importance of pharmaceuticals augments the distortion of attention towards communicable diseases in particular). Pharmaceuticals are 'the' key intervention and where the EU's global role in public health is most prominent—including the sometimes questionable effects of the (de)selection of that intervention. Attention to surveillance, wider interventions and pharmaceuticals reveal key concerns around regulatory interventions in public health and vulnerability or who is hurt, and point to the importance of querying them. It seems likely that the risk-based framing of governance skews attention and resources towards magic bullet responses and technological fixes—and away from prevention as a way of addressing the preconditions and social determinants of ill health for all diseases (epidemic, endemic and others). As such in light of the requirement to produce a high level of health protection in its policies (under Article 9 TFEU, Article 168(1) TFEU and Article 35 EU Charter, and suggested by the developing notion of (supra-)stewardship

[124] *Cf* H Epstein, *The Invisible Cure: Africa, the West, and the Fight Against AIDS* (New York NY, Farrar, Strauss, and Giroux, 2007).

[125] C Greenhouse, M Elizabeth and KB Warren (eds), *Ethnography in Unstable Places: Everyday Lives in Contexts of Dramatic Political Change* (Durham, Duke University Press, 2002); C Geertz, 'What Is a State If It Is Not a Sovereign?' (2004) 45 *Current Anthropology* 577; Ong, n 115 above.

[126] J Biehl, D Coutinho and AL Outeiro, 'Technology and Affect: HIV/AIDS Testing in Brazil' (2001) 25(1) *Culture, Medicine and Psychiatry* 87; L Cohen, 'Where It Hurts: Indian Material for an Ethics of Organ Transplantation' (1999) 128(4) *Daedalus* 135; V Das, 'Public Goods, Ethics, and Everyday Life: Beyond the Boundaries of Bioethics' (1999) 128(4) *Daedalus* 99.

responsibility), it could be queried whether all those who are subject to the EU's regime benefit or if some face greater threats from public health problems *and* the regime and its priorities than others.

At the same time, however, these concerns provide openings and possibilities for citizen participation in that they are key 'institutional risks' which if left unaddressed could imperil the EU's reputation and standing as a human rights and ethics friendly global security, public health and trade actor. In this way the production and legitimation of the EU's project of integration could also be undermined. An emphasis on vulnerability underlines how human rights, ethics and the fulfilment of (supra-)stewardship responsibilities are in fact crucial to the success or failure of public health interventions—and the latter must ensure the protection of everyone's health. Without non-discrimination in their application interventions are likely to fail. Without attention to the root causes—social, economic and political determinants—of all public health problems (whether they be epidemic, endemic or of another kind), rather than their (partial) treatment through magic bullet and technological responses, public health overall is likely to be seriously undermined. Finally, while market optimisation and corporate profitability continue to trump public health in the (de)selection of interventions, the dangers or threats the EU seeks to govern, whether they are within its own territory, or on its periphery and beyond, are likely to remain persistent and multiple. These 'institutional risks' are among the key openings and possibilities for participation in the EU's regulatory interventions in public health and they add to those charted in the previous chapter in relation to framing and knowledge production.

9

Conclusion

AS I FINISH this book about governing public health I remain pessimistic about the actual configuration, scope and use of citizen participation in legal and regulatory decision-making. But I am now far more optimistic about the potential for biopolitics and participation in governing public health—and paradoxically, some of what accounts for my pessimism also provides the basis for my optimism. The purpose of this short conclusion is to explain why the mix of pessimism and optimism has changed and the nature of the paradox, by bringing together the book's main findings and, because it is not intended to be the last word, suggesting some priorities for future research.

The first part of the book offered a map of the key contours of markets, risk and security, and ethics and human rights, the underpinning rationalities, techniques, processes and practices of the overarching architecture for EU public health governance, its operationalisation through the health strategy and health programmes, and subsequently cancer, HIV/AIDS, pandemics and other serious cross-border threats to health. These three core public health problems were selected because they exemplify the EU level of the multi-level system of public health governance—that is, the technology governing public health and the related policy domain. I argued that risk is the key frame. That framing is directed at producing security, which is governmentalised and therefore understood as being about the regulation of the dangers attendant to the circulation of people and things within and into the internal market. In other words, the central relationship in EU governance is that between risk and markets. Rights and ethics operate more as legitimating devices for this central relationship, rather than as standalone frames.

The map also revealed the integration of law into and its (re)orientation within wider ways of governing public health that (re)frame public health problems as matters for EU governance, and which are aligned to, ordered and shaped by the neoliberal objective of producing economic optimisation. The latter is in turn directed at meeting the EU's broader programmatic priorities and concerns reflected in the overarching architecture of governance, especially producing and legitimating the EU, its identity as a security and public health actor, socio-political order based on a competitive and innovative market economy, and the project of European integration. In addition, several structuring themes or key neoliberal (re)configurations undergird and support the public health policy domain, those between: knowledge and power, sovereignty and territoriality, power and responsibility, and ultimately governance and the governed.

As for the first of these themes, much more than the foundation for the constitution of the policy domain and the exercise of power through the (de)selection of interventions, the gathering and production of knowledge is also increasingly being determined by the requirements of power, especially its own legitimation. The map highlighted the (re)configuration of sovereignty and territoriality in that the EU's public health policy domain has internal and external dimensions, and the attempts to govern public health beyond the EU and export normative power are particularly marked in relation to the focus on pandemics and other serious cross-border threats to health. Although the distribution of responsibility and accountability between the EU (its institutions, agencies and arrays of specific technologies) and its Member States is formalised in law, it is worked out through policy and concrete technologies of governing. Further, the framing of governance by risk obscures the market-based norms, values and rationalities that shape, orientate and direct the technology governing public health and the policy domain. These latter facilitate the insinuation of corporate interests into the organisation and priorities of public health governance.

In relation to the (re)configuration between governance and the governed, the discussion underscores how 'the governed' are not, as much current thinking would have it, necessarily or just EU citizens in a formal legal sense or even those residing or moving within the EU's borders. Instead, as a corollary of the focus on regulating the dangers or threats attendant to the circulation of people and things, the governed should be understood as encompassing individuals and groups within and beyond the EU's borders that come to know themselves and relate to others and governance by and through knowledge of their biomedical status, situation and needs. It is because I seek to support and bolster the agency of these individuals and their collective efforts that I regard it as essential to reveal the ways in which their participation in governing and especially legal and regulatory decision-making is frustrated.

Three key ideas are reflected and embedded in the current institutionalisation of participation at the EU level of governance. A first stems from the centrality and valorisation of scientific and technical knowledge and expertise, and it is the idea that the scientific and technical, and relatedly the medical, are without significant normative content and implications. This idea implies there is nothing to demand and contest—and therefore limited (and even no) space for biopolitics. Another idea is that citizens have little or no interest in or understanding of areas of high scientific and technical complexity. This idea implies—and it is usually said to follow—that citizens have little or nothing substantive to contribute to decision-making. A final idea underpinning the current institutionalisation of participation is that the contours, features and underpinnings of the public health policy domain (or any other), are neutral as to the possibility of and field for citizen participation. This idea implies a narrowing in the scope for participation, with broader normative questions about the shape and direction of governance being removed from discussion through citizen participation.

Through the discussion in the second part of this book I have sought to challenge these ideas. In my analysis the framing of the technology governing public health and related policy domain by risk, the understandable reliance on scientific and technical knowledge and expertise in order to make problems governable (although problematic in areas of high uncertainty and non-knowing), and many of the related discourses and techniques aimed at facilitating inclusion, obscure the normative and political content of governance and decision-making. Put shortly, all together these actually produce and help to account for constraints on biopolitics and the marginalisation and undermining of citizen participation in decision-making. As it is currently institutionalised—and in the public health sphere that occurs primarily through policy documents reflecting specific expert and public rationalities—participation is not about providing for substantive citizen involvement in decision-making or facilitating its potential for enhancing the quality of decisions to be realised (especially where more or less exclusive reliance on scientific and technical knowledge and expertise are undermined). Instead, the current institutionalisation of participation implies that citizen involvement, engagement and inclusion in decision-making is to be limited so that it does not disrupt the broader programmatic priorities and normative orientation of EU governance (set and reflected in the overarching architecture). In other words, the chief function of citizen participation is as a tool—or technology—for the public legitimation of the shape, orientation and direction of the risk-based governing technology and policy domain. In light of this analysis I believe my continued pessimism about the current institutionalisation of participation remains justified.

Nevertheless, the first part of this book also provides a platform and important resources and possibilities for developing and enhancing citizen participation in governing, and through it the quality of governance and regulatory interventions in public health. My prescription for enhancing citizen participation is, so far as I can see, novel, optimistic and forward looking, and it accounts for the shift in the mix of pessimism and optimism noted at the outset of this conclusion. In chapter six I recommended that citizen participation be focused on creating and contributing supplementary knowledge to decision-making. Supplementary knowledge encompasses the paradoxes, pitfalls and blind spots of governance—points that are not necessarily already produced or fully acknowledged by and incorporated within the risk-based technology governing public health. In order to make this knowledge matter to, resonate and be taken up in decision-making it is not enough to flag 'societal risks' or the dangers or threats attendant to the circulation of people and things per se, in part because governance already purports to gather and use scientific and technical knowledge in the regulation of public health problems.

Instead, the starting point for my prescription is that any participatory strategy needs to bear in mind and make use of institutional self-interest by flagging and leveraging 'societal risks' and transforming them into 'institutional risks', particularly as risks to the EU's standing and reputation, the quality of its decisions, accountability and legitimacy. To be clear, in making this recommendation I am not suggesting that citizens are in full possession of the scientific and technical details. But it should not be automatically assumed that citizens have little or nothing to contribute towards legal and regulatory decision-making. To the contrary, there is still much for citizens to contribute and for the institutions of governance to learn. I recommend harnessing key resources within the domain itself—the legitimating discourses of human rights and bioethics and developing notions of EU (supra-)stewardship responsibility—and using them as the means to power technologies of participation and develop framing, distribution and vulnerability as key focal points that open space for biopolitics, public querying and deliberation that generates supplementary knowledge and a 'way in' for citizen participation in decision-making. The paradox, then, is that the constraints on citizen participation and biopolitics also help to provide the basis for their enhancement and through it the quality of governance and regulatory interventions.

This discursive strategy is particularly useful for highlighting 'societal risks' such as instances of inequality, inequity and injustice, particularly in relation to key distortions, paradoxes, pitfalls and failures, which are produced by and within the contours, underpinnings and structuring themes of the policy domain. These are important normative dimensions of the technical and opportunities for participation: they can form the basis for attempts to demand and contest decision-making and render the EU responsible and accountable for the consequences that flow from its choice about how to frame, organise and operationalise public health governance and its regulatory interventions. Take-up of the supplementary knowledge produced by this discursive strategy for participation in decision-making is likely to be impelled by the need to tackle the often hidden problems related to governance as 'institutional risks' that threaten to delegitimate the EU's governance, identity as a public health and security actor, and ultimately the project of European integration. The examples drawn from the map in the first part of the book—reflection on the risk-based technology, knowledge production seen in the use and deployment of indicators and clinical trials data, and extending to a more general discussion on regulatory interventions with a focus on vulnerability, before narrowing to pharmaceuticals as 'the' magic bullet and technological fix—are indicative of the potential use of the prescribed discursive strategy for participation in governing at key points throughout policy formulation and implementation in order to demand and contest decision-making.

That concludes the summary of the findings and brings me to future directions for research. A number of topics appear towards the top of my 'wish list'. A key topic is further engagement with public health (as an increasingly important policy domain) and the development of alternative and more detailed maps of this important policy domain, both at different levels of governance and tracing the interaction between multiple levels. I hope this book encourages discussion of other fields too, that is, those where the scientific, technical or medical are privileged, markets and private (usually corporate) interests operate and increasingly dominate, normative questions are obscured and governance is placed beyond the reach of democratic debate.

Above all I hope for better (and not simply more) reflection on citizen participation, including around matters such as the points in decision-making at which it makes sense, how it is to be powered, and to what ends. I would be delighted if additional focal points and discursive tools and resources for participation are discussed and developed. In particular, I hope that this book shifts thinking in law and regulation studies about the roles, uses and timing of citizen participation. In that regard I would like to see a move away from thinking about citizen participation chiefly as an instrument of ex post public legitimation of decisions. Instead I would like to see citizen participation and the biopolitics of areas such as those discussed in this book taken more seriously as an essential component of ex ante processes, and especially framing, problem definition and knowledge creation. There is far more that law and its closely related discipline of regulation studies could say—as well as specific areas of law like human rights, within which health is gaining prominence, but where citizen participation remains underdeveloped. Bioethics also needs to develop its own stance on participation, whether alone or in combination with human rights. In that regard I have a related hope that the book will help to enrich the discussion within law and regulation studies, and between them and cognate disciplines such as science and technology studies, sociology and anthropology.

Those who are subject to the EU's public health governance already have a discernible capacity to demand and contest decision-making. I hope this book provides them—'the governed'—with additional tools and thoughts on how they might tease out the normative in the scientific and technical, and expand discursive space, open up (and even create) knowledge domains, and in doing so increase the EU's accountability for framing, threat definition and its attendant distortions, paradoxes, pitfalls and failures. Overall, I hope that this book helps to promote greater substantive involvement of 'the governed' *in* governing so that it is more closely aligned to meeting their needs.

Select Bibliography

Abraham J and Lawton-Smith H (eds), *Regulation of the Pharmaceutical Industry* (Basingstoke, Palgrave Macmillan, 2003)

Arnstein SR, 'A Ladder of Citizen Participation' (1969) 35 (4) *Journal of the American Institute of Planners* 216

Arnull A and Wincott D, *Accountability and Legitimacy in the European Union* (Oxford, Oxford University Press, 2002)

Aronson J, *Genetic Witness: Science, Law, and Controversy in the Making of DNA Profiling* (Piscataway, Rutgers University Press, 2007)

Ashcroft R, 'Could Human Rights Supersede Bioethics?' (2010) 10(4) *Human Rights Law Review* 639

Baldwin R, Cave M and Lodge M, *Understanding Regulation: Theory, Strategy, and Practice*, 2nd edn (Oxford, Oxford University Press, 2013)

Baldwin R, with Cave C and Lodge M, 'Regulation, the Field and the Developing Agenda' in R Baldwin, M Cave and M Lodge (eds), *The Oxford Handbook on Regulation* (Oxford, Oxford University Press, 2011)

Baldwin R, with Brownsword R and Schmidt H, 'Stewardship, Paternalism and Public Health: Further Thoughts' 2(1) *Public Health Ethics* (2009) 113

Ballantine B and Devonald B, 'Modern Regulatory Impact Analysis: The Experience of the European Union' (2006) 44 *Regulatory Toxicology and Pharmacology* 57

Barnard C, *The Substantive Law of the EU: The Four Freedoms*, 4th edn (Oxford, Oxford University Press, 2013)

Beck U, *Risk Society: Towards a New Modernity* (London, Sage Publications, 1986)

Bell D, *The Coming of Post-Industrial Society: A Venture in Social Forecasting* (Harmondsworth, Basic Books, 1976)

Bell SE and Figert AE, 'Medicalisation and Pharmaceuticalisation at the Intersections: Looking Backward, Sideways and Forward' (2012) 75(5) *Social Science & Medicine* 775

Bellamy R, Castiglione D and Shaw J (eds), *Making European Citizens* (Basingstoke, Palgrave Macmillan, 2006)

Biehl J, 'Pharmaceuticalisation: AIDS Treatment and Global Health Politics' (2007) 80(4) *Anthropological Quarterly* 1083

Black J, 'Critical Reflections on Regulation' (2002) 27 *Australian Journal of Legal Philosophy* 1

Brem S and Dubois S, 'Different Perceptions, Similar Reactions: Biopreparedness in the European Union' in P Katona, JP Sullivan and MD Intriligator (eds), *Global Biosecurity: Threats and Responses* (London, Routledge, 2010)

Brown W, *Regulating Aversion: Tolerance in the Age of Identity and Empire* (Princeton NJ, Princeton University Press, 2006)

——, *States of Injury* (Oxford, Princeton University Press, 1995)

Brownson RC, Fielding JE and Maylahn CM, 'Evidence-Based Public Health: A Fundamental Concept for Public Health Practice' (2009) 30 *Annual Review of Public Health* 175

Brownsword R, *Rights, Regulation and the Technological Revolution* (Oxford, Oxford University Press, 2008)

Burris S, 'Surveillance, Social Risk, and Symbolism: Framing the Analysis for Research and Policy' (2000) 25 *Journal of Acquired Immunodeficiency Syndromes* S120

Busby H, Hervey T and Mohr A, 'Ethical EU law? The Influence of the European Group on Ethics in Science and New Technologies' (2008) 33 *European Law Review* 803

Carlier J, *The Free Movement of Persons Living with HIV/AIDS* (Luxembourg, Office of Official Publications of the European Community, 1999)

Cartwright N and Hardie J, *Evidence-Based Policy: A Practical Guide to Doing it Better* (Oxford, Oxford University Press, 2012)

Castells M, *The Rise of the Network Society (=The Information Age, Vol. I)* (Oxford, Blackwell, 1996)

Clarence E, 'Technocracy Reinvented: The New Evidence Based Policy Movement' (2002) 17(3) *Public Policy and Administration* 1

Cloatre E and Pickersgill M (eds), *Knowledge, Technology and Law* (Abingdon, Routledge, 2014)

Coggon J, *What Makes Health Public?* (Cambridge, Cambridge University Press, 2012)

Cornwall A and Schatten Coelho V (eds), *Spaces for Change?: The Politics of Citizen Participation in New Democratic Arenas* (London, Zed Books, 2007)

Daemmrich A, *Pharmacopolitics: Drug Regulation in the United States and Germany* (Chapel Hill, University of North Carolina Press, 2006)

Davis KE and others (eds), *Governance by Indicators: Global Power Through Quantification and Rankings* (Oxford, Oxford University Press, 2012)

Dean M, *The Signature of Power: Sovereignty, Governmentality and Biopolitics* (London, Sage Publications, 2013)

——, *Governmentality: Power and Rule in Modern Society*, 2nd edn (London, Sage Publications, 2009)

Dehousse R and Joerges C (eds), *Good Governance in an Integrated Market* (Oxford, Oxford University Press, 2002)

Desrosières A, *The Politics of Large Numbers: A History of Statistical Reasoning* (Cambridge MA, Harvard University Press, 1998)

Dreyfuss RC, 'TRIPS and Essential Medicines: Must One Size Fit All? Making the WTO Responsive to the Global Health Crisis' in T Pogge, M Rimmer, K Rubenstein (eds), *Incentives for Global Public Health: Patent Law and Access to Essential Medicines* (Cambridge, Cambridge University Press, 2010)

Edelman M, *Political Language: Words That Succeed and Policies That Fail* (London, Academic Press, 1973)

Epstein H, *The Invisible Cure: Africa, the West, and the Fight Against AIDS* (New York NY, Farrar, Strauss, and Giroux, 2007)

Epstein S, *Impure Science* (Berkeley CA, University of California Press, 1996).

Espeland WN and Stevens ML, 'A Sociology of Quantification' (2008) 49(3) *European Journal of Sociology* 401

Everson M and Vos E, 'The Scientification of Politics and the Politicisation of Science' in M Everson and E Vos (eds), *Uncertain Risks Regulated* (Abingdon, Routledge-Cavendish, 2009)

Farmer P, *Infection and Inequalities: The Modern Plagues* (Berkeley CA, University of California Press, 1999)

Fidler DP and Gostin LO, *Biosecurity in the Global Age: Biological Weapons, Public Health, and the Rule of Law* (Stanford, Stanford University Press, 2007)

Fischer F, 'Professional Expertise in a Deliberative Democracy: Facilitating Participatory Inquiry' (2004) 13 (1) *The Good Society* 21

——, *Reframing Public Policy: Discursive Politics and Deliberative Practices* (Oxford, Oxford University Press, 2003)

Flear ML (ed), 'Papers from "A Symposium with Professor Roger Brownsword: Super-Stewardship in the Context of Public Health"' (2011) 62(5) *Northern Ireland Legal Quarterly*

—— and others (eds), *European Law and New Health Technologies* (Oxford, Oxford University Press, 2013)

—— and Pickersgill MD, 'Regulatory or Regulating Publics? The European Union's Regulation of Emerging Health Technologies and Citizen Participation' (2013) 21(1) *Medical Law Review* 39

—— and Vakulenko A, 'A Human Rights Perspective on Citizen Participation in the EU's Governance of New Technologies' (2010) 10(4) *Human Rights Law Review* 661

Foucault M, *The Birth of Biopolitics: Lectures at the Collège de France, 1978-1979* (Basingstoke, Palgrave Macmillan, 2008)

——, *Security, Territory, Population: Lectures at the Collège de France, 1977–1978* (Basingstoke, Palgrave Macmillan, 2007)

——, *The History of Sexuality: Volume One, The Will to Knowledge* (London, Penguin, 1998)

——, *The Birth of the Clinic* (London, Tavistock, 1976)

Ghazaryan N, *European Neighbourhood Policy and the Democratic Values of the EU* (Oxford, Hart Publishing, 2013)

Gibbon S and Novas C (eds), *Biosocialities, Genetics and the Social Sciences* (London, Routledge, 2007)

Giddens A, *The Consequences of Modernity* (Polity Press, Cambridge, 1990)

Goffman E, *Frame Analysis: An Essay on the Organisation of Experience* (Cambridge MA, Harvard University Press, 1974)

Gostin LO, *Global Health Law* (Boston MA, Harvard University Press, 2014)

——, *Public Health Law*, 2nd edn (Berkeley, University of California Press, 2008)

—— and Lazzarini Z, *Human Rights and Public Health in the AIDS Pandemic* (Oxford, Oxford University Press, 1997)

Gottweis H, 'Participation and the New Governance of Life' (2008) 3 *BioSocieties* 265

Greer SL, *The Politics of European Union Health Policies* (Maidenhead, Open University Press, 2009)

—— and Kurzer P, *European Union Public Health Policy: Regional and Global Trends* (London, Routledge, 2013)

Habermas J, *The Crisis of the European Union: A Response* (Cambridge, Polity Press, 2012)

Hacking I, *The Taming of Chance* (Cambridge, Cambridge University Press, 1990)

Hajer M and Laws D, 'Ordering through Discourse' in M Moran, M Rein and RE Goodin (eds), *The Oxford Handbook of Public Policy* (Oxford, Oxford University Press, 2006)

Harlow C, *Accountability in the European Union* (Oxford, Oxford University Press, 2002)

Harrington J and Stuttaford M (eds), *Global Health and Human Rights* (Abingdon, Routledge, 2010)

Hatzopoulos V, 'Health Law and Policy: The Impact of the EU' in G de Búrca (ed), *EU Law and the Welfare State: In Search of Solidarity* (Oxford, Oxford University Press, 2005)

Hervey TK and McHale JV, *European Union Health Law* (Cambridge, Cambridge University Press, 2015)

Hinchcliffe S and Bingham N, 'Securing Life: The Emerging Practices of Biosecurity' (2008) 40(7) *Environment and Planning A* 1534

Hindmarsh R and Prainsack B (eds), *Genetic Subjects: Global Governance of Forensic DNA Profiling and Databasing* (Cambridge, Cambridge University Press, 2010)

Hooghe L and Marks G, *Multilevel Governance and European Integration* (Oxford, Rowman & Littlefield Publishers, 2001)

Irwin A, 'The Politics of Talk: Coming to Terms with the "New" Scientific Governance' (2006) 36 *Social Studies of Science* 299

——, *Citizen Science: A Study of People, Expertise, and Sustainable Development* (London, Routledge, 1995)

—— and Michael M, *Science, Social Theory and Public Knowledge* (Maidenhead, Open University Press, 2003)

Jackson E, *Medical Law: Text, Cases, and Materials*, 3rd edn (Oxford, Oxford University Press, 2013)

——, *Law and the Regulation of Medicines* (Oxford, Hart Publishing, 2012)

Jasanoff S, *Reframing Rights: Bioconstitutionalism in the Genetic Age* (Cambridge MA, MIT Press, 2011)

——, *Designs on Nature* (Princeton NJ, Princeton University Press, 2005)

——, 'The Idiom of Co-Production' in S Jasanoff (ed), *States of Knowledge: The Co-Production of Science and the Social Order* (London, Routledge, 2004)

——, 'Technologies of Humility: Citizen Participation in Governing Science' (2003) 41 *Minerva* 223

Joerges C and Vos E (eds), *EU Committees: Social Regulation, Law and Politics* (Oxford, Hart Publishing, 1999)

Jones LJ, *The Social Context of Health and Health Work* (London, Palgrave Macmillan, 1994)

Kerry VB and Lee K, 'TRIPS, the Doha Declaration and Paragraph 6 Decision: What are the Remaining Steps for Protecting Access to Medicines?' (2007) 3 *Global Health* 3

Knorr Cetina K, 'Laboratory Studies: The Cultural Approach to the Study of Science' in S Jasanoff and others (eds), *Handbook of Science and Technology Studies* (London, Sage Publications, 1995)

Kostakopoulou D, *The Future Governance of Citizenship* (Cambridge, Cambridge University Press, 2008)

——, 'Ideas, Norms and European Citizenship: Explaining Institutional Change' (2005) 6(2) *Modern Law Review* 233

Krieger N, 'The Making of Public Health Data: Paradigms, Politics, and Policy' (1992) 13(4) *Journal of Public Health Policy* 412

Kuhn T, *The Structure of Scientific Revolutions*, 2nd edn (Chicago, University of Chicago Press, 1970)

Lakoff A, 'Preparing for the Next Emergency' (2007) 19(2) *Public Culture* 247

Lascoumes P and Le Gales P, 'Introduction: Understanding Public Policy through Its Instruments. From the Nature of Instruments to the Sociology of Public Policy Instrumentation' (2007) 20 *Governance* 1

Latour B, *Science in Action. How to Follow Scientists and Engineers through Society* (Cambridge MA, Harvard University Press, 1987)

Leach M, Scoones I and Wynne B (eds), *Science and Citizens: Globalisation and the Challenge of Engagement* (London, Zed Books, 2005)

Lezain J and Soneryd L, 'Consulting Citizens: Technologies of Elicitation and the Mobility of Publics' (2007) 16(3) *Public Understanding of Science* 279

Lidskog R, Soneryd L and Uggla Y, *Transboundary Risk Governance* (London, Earthscan, 2009)
Lindseth PL, 'Democratic Legitimacy and the Administrative Character of Supranationalism: The Example of the European Community' (1999) 99 *Columbia Law Review* 628
Majone G, 'Europe's "Democratic Deficit": The Question for Standards' (1998) 4(1) *European Law Journal* 5
Mason JK and Laurie GT, *Law and Medical Ethics*, 9th edn (Oxford, Oxford University Press, 2013)
McKeown T, *The Role of Medicine* (Oxford, Basil Blackwell, 1979)
Mendes J, *Participation in EU Rule-making: A Rights-Based Approach* (Oxford, Oxford University Press, 2011)
Merry SE, 'Measuring the World: Indicators, Human Rights, and Global Governance' (2011) 52(3) *Current Anthropology* S83
Moeller SD, *Compassion Fatigue: How the Media Sell Disease, Famine, War and Death* (New York NY, Routledge, 1999)
Montgomery J, *Health Care Law*, 2nd edn (Oxford, Oxford University Press, 2003)
Moore A, 'Public Bioethics and Deliberative Democracy' (2010) 58 *Political Studies* 715
Murphy T, *Health and Human Rights* (Oxford, Hart Publishing, 2013)
Nguyen V-K, 'Antiretroviral Globalism, Biopolitics, and Therapeutic Citizenship' in A Ong and SJ Collier (eds), *Global Assemblages: Technology, Politics, and Ethics as Anthropological Problems* (Oxford, Blackwell Publishing, 2005)
Nowotny H, 'How Many Policy Rooms Are There?' (2007) 32 *Science, Technology & Human Values* 479
Nuffield Council, *Public Health: Ethical Issues* (London, Nuffield Council on Bioethics, 2007)
Ong A, *Neoliberalism as Exception: Mutations in Citizenship and Sovereignty* (London, Duke University Press, 2006)
Patton C, *Globalising AIDS* (Minneapolis, University of Minnesota Press, 2002)
Petryna A, *Life Exposed: Biological Citizens After Chernobyl* (Princeton NJ, Princeton University Press 2002)
——, *When Experiments Travel* (Princeton NJ, Princeton University Press, 2009)
Pogge T, Rimmer M and Rubenstein K (eds), *Incentives for Global Public Health: Patent Law and Access to Essential Medicines* (Cambridge, Cambridge University Press, 2010)
Poovey M, *A History of the Modern Fact: Problems of Knowledge in the Sciences of Wealth and Society* (Chicago, University of Chicago Press, 1998)
Porter TM, *Trust in Numbers: The Pursuit of Objectivity in Science and Public Life* (Princeton NJ, Princeton University Press, 1995)
Power M, *Organized Uncertainty* (Oxford, Oxford University Press, 2007)
Preda A, *AIDS, Rhetoric, and Medical Knowledge* (Cambridge, Cambridge University Press, 2005)
Rabinow P, *Essays on the Anthropology of Reason* (Princeton NJ, Princeton University Press, 1996)
Radaelli C, 'The Role of Knowledge in the Policy Process' (1995) 2 (2) *Journal of European Public Policy* 159
Rose N, *The Politics of Life Itself: Biomedicine, Power and Subjectivity in the 21st Century* (Oxford, Princeton University Press, 2007)
Rothstein H, Huber M and Gaskell G, 'A Theory of Risk Colonisation: The Spiralling Regulatory Logics of Societal and Institutional Risk' (2006) 35 *Economy and Society* 91

Scharpf F, *Governing in Europe. Effective and Democratic?* (Oxford, Oxford University Press, 1999)

Schon DA and Rein M, *Frame/Reflection: Toward the Resolution of Intractable Policy Controversies* (New York NY, Basic Books, 1994)

Scott C, 'Accountability in the Regulatory State' (2000) 27 *Journal of Law and Society* 38

Spector RE, *Cultural Diversity in Health and Illness*, 7th edn (London, Prentice Hall, 2008)

Stychin C, *Governing Sexuality: The Changing Politics of Citizenship and Law Reform* (Oxford, Hart Publishing, 2003)

Tallacchini M, 'Governing by Values. EU Ethics: Soft Tool, Hard Effects' (2009) 47 *Minerva* 281

Toebes B and others (eds), *Health and Human Rights in Europe* (Cambridge, Intersentia, 2012)

Walker N (ed), *Europe's Area of Freedom, Security and Justice* (Oxford, Oxford University Press, 2004)

Walters W and Haahr J, *Governing Europe: Discourse, Governmentality and European Integration* (Abingdon, Routledge, 2005)

Wiener A, *'European' Citizenship Practice: Building Institutions of a Non-State* (Oxford, Oxford University Press, 1998)

Williams SJ, Martin P and Gabe J, 'The Pharmaceuticalisation of Society? A Framework for Analysis' (2011) 33 *Sociology of Health & Illness* 710

Wilsdon J and Willis R, *See-Through Science: Why Public Engagement Needs to Move Upstream* (London, Demos, 2004)

World Health Organisation, *World Health Report 2000* (Geneva, World Health Organisation, 2000)

Wynne B, 'Misunderstood Misunderstandings: Social Identities and Public Uptake of Science' (1992) 1 *Public Understanding of Science* 281

——, 'Knowledges in Context' (1991) 16 *Science, Technology & Human Values* 111

Yamin AE, 'Suffering and Powerlessness: The Significance of Participation in Rights-Based Approaches to Health' (2009) 11(1) *Health and Human Rights: An International Journal* 5

Yeung K and Dixon-Woods M, 'Design-Based Regulation and Patient Safety: A Regulation studies Perspective' (2010) 71(3) *Social Science & Medicine* 613

Index

www.ingramcontent.com/pod-product-compliance
Lightning Source LLC
LaVergne TN
LVHW052248200926
848481LV00002B/312